DATE DUE

DEC 4		01	
FE 11 09			
5-31-05			

Demco No. 62-0549

Dimensions of Contemporary Japan

A Collection of Essays

Series Editor

Edward R. Beauchamp
University of Hawaii

A GARLAND SERIES

Series Contents

Education and Schooling in Japan since 1945

Edited with an introduction by

Edward R. Beauchamp
University of Hawaii

GARLAND PUBLISHING, INC.
A MEMBER OF THE TAYLOR & FRANCIS GROUP
New York & London
1998

Library of Congress Cataloging-in-Publication Data

Education and schooling in Japan since 1945 / edited with an
  introduction by Edward R. Beauchamp.
       p.   cm. — (Dimensions of contemporary Japan ; 3)
    Includes bibliographical references.
    ISBN 0-8153-2730-7 (alk. paper)
    1. Education—Japan—History—1945– 2. Education—Japan—
Philosophy. 3. Educational change—Japan. I. Beauchamp,
Edward R., 1933–   . II. Series.
LA1311.82.E377 1998
370'.952—dc21   98-51524
                                                      CIP

Printed on acid-free, 250-year-life paper
Manufactured in the United States of America

Contents

Introduction

Education has always played a crucial role in Japanese society, long before Japan leapt on the world stage as a modern nation in the late nineteenth and early twentieth centuries. An analysis of the reasons for this are beyond the scope of this volume, but suffice to say that Japan was not starting at ground zero when it began the modernization process in the Meiji Era (1868–1912).

There have been several enduring themes in the history of Japanese education, perhaps the most consistent of which has been the willingness to learn from other nations. There is strong evidence demonstrating that the Japanese borrowed from Chinese models at least as early as the fourth century, and this example was repeated in the late nineteenth through the middle of the twentieth century. The three most recent examples were the wholesale borrowing and adaptation from several Western nations in the Meiji period, the intellectuals' fascination with democratic education during the 1920s, and most recently during the 1945–1952 Occupation. The major difference among these three periods is that the Occupation reforms were imposed by a victorious military power and the Japanese had little choice but to generally cooperate. The American wartime planning for that occupation is analyzed in the article by Beauchamp (1995). Other essays on various aspects of the American-imposed reforms are by Thakur (textbooks) and Gottlieb (language reform). Other articles dealing with these topics in different contexts include contributions on the problem of textbooks (by Caiger, by Dore, and by Irie) and language policy (Gerbert). Amano's contribution is an extremely useful survey of educational reform and counterreform in postwar Japan.

A more "micro" approach is Lewis' analysis of what makes a successful school in the Japanese context. Examining some of the problems facing those schools realistically, she strikes an appropriate balance in her assesment. The problems of minorities in Japanese education, both ethnic and linguistic, are presented by Pharr and Maher. Beauchamp's (1989) analysis of Japan's version of democracy provides one plausible context for analyzing Japanese education, and Rhodes and Morimitsu present a cogent analysis of the "school to work" issue in Japanese education. Finally, three of the major problems confronting the Japanese educational enterprise — the cram school or "juku" phenmenon (Blumenthal), the pivotal role played by mothers in their children's education (Dickensheets), and the increasingly serious problem of school bullying (Nishiyama) — are analyzed. Higher education in Japan is discussed in the Hayes contribution.

Despite the problems facing Japan's educational system, it is clear that the system possesses many characteristics that one can admire. Whatever is admirable about the system can usually be traced to the cadre of excellent teachers who implement the curriculum. Shimahara's essay is probably the best single treatment of how teachers are educated in Japan, and the article goes a long way toward explaining the excellence of Japan's teachers. Finally, Hirano provides a compelling case for strengthening cultural relations, not only between the United States and Japan, but throughout all of Asia.

Those readers with the diligence to read and digest these studies will have a far better understanding of Japan's excellent, but somewhat flawed, system of public education.

* * * * *

This collection of articles on modern Japanese society contains over one hundred scholarly pieces that have been written by leading academics in the field. It is drawn from distinguished scholarly journals, as well as from other select sources not as well known. Many readers, however, may be struck by the absence of material from the *Journal of Japanese Studies*. This is due to our inability to secure the necessary permissions from that journal to use their materials.

Journal of Curriculum and Supervision
Fall 1995, Vol. 11, No. 1, 67–86

REFORMING EDUCATION IN POSTWAR JAPAN: AMERICAN PLANNING FOR A DEMOCRATIC JAPAN, 1943–1946

EDWARD R. BEAUCHAMP, *University of Hawaii*

On the morning of September 2, 1945, aboard the USS *Missouri,* Japan accepted the terms of unconditional surrender that were laid down by the Potsdam Declaration of July 26, 1945. This document insisted on terms that gave the Japanese virtually no negotiating space. Indeed, the Allied powers pledged that "we will not deviate from [these terms]. There are no alternatives. We shall brook no delay." The Allies insisted that "There must be eliminated for all time the authority and influence of those who have deceived and misled the people of Japan into embarking on world conquest," but promised that "we do not intend that the Japanese shall be enslaved as a race or destroyed as a nation, but stern justice shall be meted out to all war criminals. . . ."[1] Following the nuclear attacks on Hiroshima and Nagasaki, Emperor Hirohito saw the futility of further resistance and, on August 15, announced to his subjects the need to "endure the unendurable" and accept the Allied terms.[2]

As the dignitaries made their way to the simple desk on the *Missouri's* deck that sun-filled morning, Japan lay in ruins. Almost two million Japanese were dead and millions more were wounded. Suffering was extensive, but no single group suffered more than Japan's young people. The nation's educational system was in shambles. An American estimate of conditions on the day of surrender found 18 million students idle, over 4,000 schools destroyed and thousands more heavily damaged. Available teachers were screened

---

[1]"The Potsdam Proclamation" (26 July 1945), *Department of State Bulletin,* 29 July 1945; reprinted in Edward R. Beauchamp and James M. Vardaman, eds., *Japanese Education Since 1945: A Documentary Study* (Armonk, NY: M. E. Sharpe, 1994), p. 29.

[2]A good description of the final days of the war from a Japanese perspective is found in Saburo Ienaga, *The Pacific War* (New York: Pantheon Books, 1978), pp. 229–240.

for militaristic leanings, and most textbooks were deemed unsuitable because they were filled with militaristic propaganda considered inappropriate for creating a new, democratic Japan. Finally, more than one of every three institutions of higher education lay in ruins; thousands of teachers were homeless, hungry, and dispirited; and many of their pupils had been moved to safer areas. In essence, there was no functioning educational system.[3]

Less than two decades later, however, Japan's political system had been considerably, if imperfectly, reformed along democratic lines, a free market economy was beginning to show signs of robustness, and the educational system was contributing positively to both of these trends. What follows is one version of the story of this rapid and impressive educational development.

PREWAR EDUCATION

A brief description of Japan's prereform educational system provides a context for understanding the educational reforms sought by the occupation authorities. In traditional Japan the main avenues to success were family, social class, personal merit, and "connections." The primary aim of education was to make students virtuous by instilling in them the wisdom of the gods or sages, thus forming their character to meet the needs of society and of their particular social class.[4]

The diverse educational arrangements in place during the more than 250-year Tokugawa period (1603–1868) provided a strong base for the educational reformers of the Meiji period that followed.[5] Eager to learn the secrets of the West's success and transform the country into a modern nation-state, the Meiji government saw education as a key to achieving political integration and training the diverse person-

---

[3]"Educational Situation at End of War," National Archives of the United States, Military History Section, Record Group 718, General Headquarters, Supreme Command for Allied Powers, *Monthly Summary No. 1* (no date, probably November 1945); reprinted in Edward R. Beauchamp and James M. Vardaman, eds., *Japanese Education Since 1945: A Documentary Study* (Armonk, NY: M. E. Sharpe, 1994), p. 52.

[4]The key document undergirding this position was the 1890 "Imperial Rescript on Education," which reflected "the acceptable and highly moralistic Confucian virtues to which all Japanese were expected to adhere. . . ." The entire document can be found in Edward R. Beauchamp and James M. Vardaman, eds., *Japanese Education Since 1945: A Documentary Study* (Armonk, NY: M. E. Sharpe, 1994), pp. 37–38.

[5]Those interested in learning about this background will find the following books very helpful: Ronald Dore, *Education in Tokugawa Japan* (Berkeley: University of California Press, 1965; reprint, Ann Arbor: Center for Japanese Studies, University of Michigan, 1984), and Richard Rubinger, *Private Academies of Tokugawa Japan* (Princeton, NJ: Princeton University Press, 1982).

nel needed to reach their goal. Elementary education was made compulsory and emphasis was placed on practical and scientific learning.

Opening itself to the West after the self-imposed isolation of the Tokugawa period, Japan went on an orgy of borrowing in all fields, including education. The Charter Oath, promulgated by the Meiji emperor in April 1868, stated that "Knowledge shall be sought throughout the world and thus shall be strengthened the foundation of the imperial polity."[6] The Meiji oligarchs, to their great credit, seized on this sentiment and adapted modern ideas from wherever they could find them.

By 1880 the penchant for things Western had run its course, and a more conservative period of pedagogy ensued. A new, nationalist Imperial Rescript on Education was issued on October 30, 1890. It remained the foundation for education until the end of World War II in 1945. This rescript gave both legal form and moral force to the prewar educational system. It enjoined the people to practice "loyalty and filial piety," and "should an emergency arise, offer yourselves courageously to the State, and thus guard and maintain the prosperity of Our Imperial Throne coequal with heaven and earth. . . ."[7] The system that flowed from this document was not only designed to serve the interests of the state, but was also highly centralized. This combination made it vulnerable to military control, and during the 1930s it was made to serve militaristic ends.[8]

In the early 1940s, under the military government of Gen. Hideki Tojo, a Bureau of Thought Supervision (established in the 1930s), was charged with the elimination of harmful and improper thoughts—including individualism, liberalism, and democracy—as well as the inculcation of correct thoughts and attitudes. A Student Section had been created earlier within the Bureau of Special [i.e., "political"] Education "to supervise student thought, using reports sent in by each school."[9] By 1941 the aims of education were, in the words of the minister of education, "the repudiation of academic theories that have no connection with the people's life, the eradication of thoughts based

---

[6]A recent study by Mark E. Lincicome, *Principles, Praxis and the Politics of Educational Reform in Meiji Japan* (Honolulu: University of Hawaii Press, 1995) provides a fine account of this subject.

[7]Dorothy Robins-Mowry, "Westernizing Influences in the Early Modernization of Japanese Women's Education," in Edward R. Beauchamp and Akira Iriye, eds., *Foreign Employees in Nineteenth Century Japan* (Boulder, CO: Westview Press, 1990), p. 123.

[8]For details, see Teruhisa Horio, *Educational Thought and Ideology in Modern Japan: State Authority and Intellectual Freedom*, ed. and trans. Steven Platzer (Tokyo: University of Tokyo Press, 1988), especially ch. 2 and 3.

[9]Richard H. Mitchell, *Thought Control in Prewar Japan* (Ithaca, NY: Cornell University Press, 1976), p. 93.

on individualism and liberalism, and the firm establishment of a national moral standard with emphasis on service to the state."[10]

By 1943 education in Japan had become a means to an end. One Diet member was quoted as suggesting that "it was not in uniformity with the times to give cultural education to students. They should be mobilized chiefly for military service."[11] Technical college programs were expanded and others not directly connected with the war effort sharply reduced. Some schools were closed, terms shortened, and classes canceled. Military training was emphasized, and classes that taught filial piety, loyalty, and obedience were prized. The Ministry of Education insisted that students be taught the true meaning of faithfulness and loyalty to the imperial institution.

Despite the overwhelmingly authoritarian character of prewar Japanese education, however, a number of potentially democratic elements existed at least as early as the Meiji era (1868–1912).[12]

AMERICAN PLANNING FOR THE OCCUPATION

The occupation's approach to reforming Japanese education did not begin in August 1945. It was the result of a systematic secret planning process for the occupation of Japan that began in 1943, when an American victory was still in doubt. One of the key questions asked was, To what extent should the United States utilize education to change the prevailing political ideology in Japan? The State Department concluded that "only a democratically educated Japanese people would be able to stimulate and defend political progress and build upon a frame of mind conducive to peaceful cooperation with other nations. . . . The goal of the educational programs would be the reeducation of the entire Japanese population."[13]

The occupation authorities recognized that the educational system had played a major role in the inculcation of nationalism and militarism in prewar youth, but that these same schools could now be used to build a new democratic society. Planners, however, recognized the need "to prepare a positive and integrated program of

---

[10]Office of Strategic Services, Research and Analysis Branch, "Japanese Administration: Department of Education," National Archives of the United States, Military History Section, Records Group 226 (no date, probably 1943).

[11]I must paraphrase Erik Erikson who, in *Young Man Luther,* explained that he had inadvertently mislaid or lost the source of a quotation, but was sure that no fair-minded reader would accuse him of having invented it.

[12]For a description of this phenomenon, see Edward R. Beauchamp, "Education," in *Democracy in Japan,* ed. Takeshi Ishida and Ellis S. Krauss (Pittsburgh: Pittsburgh University Press, 1989), pp. 225–251.

[13]Quoted in Byron K. Marshall, *Learning to be Modern: Japanese Political Discourse on Education* (Boulder, CO: Westview Press, 1995), p. 143.

reeducation and reorientation" for Japan; the failure to do so was seen as "a basic cause of the present chaos in Italy and has already invited severe criticism of our military in Germany."[14] Lengthy discussions ensued between those planners who saw the Japanese educational system as virtually without merit, and others who wanted to ensure that the baby would not be thrown out with the bath water.

After intensive debate and numerous drafts, the document that eventually emerged as the most authoritative statement of the occupation's initial objectives was titled the "United States Initial Post-Surrender Policy for Japan." It identified the "ultimate objective" of American policy: "to foster conditions which will give the greatest possible assurance that Japan will not again become a menace to the peace and security of the world and will permit her eventual admission as a responsible and peaceful member of the family of nations." Accomplishing this goal necessitated ensuring "the abolition of militarism and ultra-nationalism in all their forms; . . . the strengthening of democratic tendencies and processes in governmental, economic and social institutions; and other encouragement and support of liberal political tendencies in Japan."[15]

THE FIRST MONTHS

During the first months of the occupation of Japan, the new government was charged with eliminating militaristic and ultranationalistic elements of the society. Education, which had been used for advancing national development and territorial expansion, was now to be used to achieve the goals of democratization, demilitarization, decentralization, and, thus, the creation of a peaceful and democratic society.

The first steps in achieving these goals required dismantling those elements of the Japanese educational system that were antidemocratic or militaristic and replacing them with components that would foster the desired ends. These initial steps were, of necessity, negative in tone—clearing away the old to make way for the new. They involved

---

[14]"Positive Policy for Reorientation of the Japanese," SWNCC 162/D, 19 July 1945, National Archives of the United States, Military History Section, Record Group 319, Records of the Army Staff, ABC 014 Japan (13 April 1944); reprinted in Edward R. Beauchamp and James M. Vardaman, eds., *Japanese Education Since 1945: A Documentary Study* (Armonk, NY: M. E. Sharpe, 1994), p. 45.

[15]"Basic Initial Post-Surrender Directive to Supreme Commander for Allied Powers," National Archives of the United States, Military History Section, Record Group 319, Records of the Army Staff, ABC 387, Japan, Joint Civil Affairs Committee 48 (30 August 1945); reprinted in Edward R. Beauchamp and James M. Vardaman, eds., *Japanese Education Since 1945: A Documentary Study* (Armonk, NY: M. E. Sharpe, 1994), p. 51.

efforts by the Japanese themselves, as well as the occupation reformers.

At the outset of the reform effort, the Japanese Ministry of Education abolished the old wartime education law and, on September 15, 1945, promulgated a new "Educational Policy for the Construction of a New Japan," which was directed at the elimination of militarism. It is significant that the Japanese anticipated the overall direction of American educational policy and made an early effort to accommodate themselves to it, at least in its broad outline.[16] Indeed, Arundel del Re, one of the first civilian employees of the Civil Information and Education section (CI&E) of the Supreme Commander Allied Powers (SCAP) and a man with extensive prewar experience in Japanese education, wrote on October 3, 1945, that "the Japanese have already shown themselves only too eager to throw overboard existing structures and policies hitherto pursued irrespective of any real merit that they possess."[17]

SCAP followed up on this Japanese initiative by issuing four basic directives between October 22 and December 31, 1945. These directives cleared away much of the foundation of prewar Japanese education by purging teachers with "militaristic and ultranationalistic" tendencies, abolishing state Shinto, and suspending all courses in morals, history, and geography. These actions basically completed the initial negative phase of education reform and compelled American authorities to think seriously about exactly what would replace the dismantled system.[18]

Presurrender planning for the occupation had been based on several assumptions, two of which were particularly important for the reformation of Japanese education. First, the United States did not envision the destruction of Japan's cultural heritage and the imposition of American values and institutions on the Japanese. Planners explicitly stated that there was no intention to destroy Japanese culture, but that they would "use it" as far as possible "in establishing new attitudes of mind conforming to the basic principles of democracy and fair dealing." They went on to suggest that "it will be possible to select

---

[16]"Educational Policy for the Construction of a New Japan," in *Shiryo Kyoikuho* (Tokyo: Gakuyo Shobo, 1973), pp. 299–300; reprinted in Edward R. Beauchamp and James M. Vardaman, eds., *Japanese Education Since 1945: A Documentary Study* (Armonk, NY: M. E. Sharpe, 1994), pp. 55–58.

[17]"Preliminary Report on Measures Pertaining to the Cultural Re-Education of Japan," memo from Arundel del Re and M. A. Plancienti, 3 October 1946, Trainor Papers, Box 46, Hoover Institution on War, Revolution and Peace, Stanford University.

[18]These documents are found in Edward R. Beauchamp and James M. Vardaman, eds., *Japanese Education Since 1945: A Documentary Study* (Armonk, NY: M. E. Sharpe, 1994), pp. 62–64, 68–71, 74–75.

from the Japanese cultural complex, numerous ideas and beliefs which by appropriate emphasis and development may be used for the furtherance of American objectives."[19] Second, American planners assumed that the "prospective emergence of a peaceful Japan presupposed the existence of those in the country who would be predisposed to accept the [liberal American] vision and carry out the task of reconstructing along liberal lines."[20]

Joseph Ballantine, one of a small group of Japanese specialists involved in the preliminary planning, spoke for the majority when he said that "we do not believe that Japanese militarism had its roots in the emperor, or in any other single institution. . . . We believe that it is grounded in the habit of thought and in an [ideology] which have persisted among the Japanese for many centuries, which can be eradicated only by the sufferings of defeat and by long drawn-out and gradual processes."[21] These assumptions required a policy that would not only encourage and sustain prewar liberal elements and a new educational system that would foster democracy, but also one that would not violate those aspects of Japanese culture that were harmonious with democracy.

The creation of a "new Japan," a liberal Japan, was in large measure dependent upon the effectiveness of the educational system in changing the Japanese "habit of thought." As Herbert Passin has written, "It was not sufficient just to win the war; we had to make sure that it would never happen again. Experience told us that negative control measures alone would not do the job. After World War I, Germany had been disarmed, occupied, saddled with reparations, and forbidden to rearm; nevertheless, within one generation she had become once again the menace of the civilized world . . . the only real safety could come from a true change of heart such that the Germans—or the Japanese—would never wish to go to war again."[22]

In October 1945 the occupation authorities thus found themselves having to decide on a new educational system that would transform Japan into a nation that "would never want to go to war again."

---

[19]"Japanese Policy for Reorientation of the Japanese," 19 July 1945, National Archives of the United States, Military History Section 319, Records of the Army Staff, ABC 014 Japan (13 April 1944); reprinted in Edward R. Beauchamp and James M. Vardaman, eds., *Japanese Education Since 1945: A Documentary Study* (Armonk, NY: M. E. Sharpe, 1994), pp. 45–48.

[20]Ibid.

[21]Akira Iriye, "Continuities in U.S.-Japanese Relations, 1941–1949," in *The Origins of the Cold War in Asia,* ed. Yonosuke Nagai and Akira Iriye (New York: Columbia University Press, 1977), p. 386.

[22]Herbert Passin, *The Legacy of the Occupation—Japan,* Occasional Papers of the East Asian Institute (New York: Columbia University Press, 1968), p. 4.

Pressure to achieve this goal was especially acute within the CI&E, which bore primary responsibility for the future direction of Japanese education. Gordon Bowles, the State Department liaison officer with the First U.S. Education Mission (USEM) to Japan, has suggested that the idea for an education mission came about because "responsible officers in the Occupation soon recognized that [the education personnel] lacked the necessary authoritative reassurance possessed by lifelong specialists in different aspects of the educational process: philosophical, administrative, character building and content. They lacked the professional status for achieving an effective operating relationship with the Japanese government, the recognized instrument for carrying out Occupation directives." In fact, Bowles continued, "Ex-Minister of Education Tamon Maeda later explained to me some time after his removal from office, 'it was extremely difficult and embarrassing for high government officials to accept and enforce or even interpret adequately to subordinates or Diet committees and branches or the public at large just why the government was obliged to carry out directives signed by military colonels and not infrequently even by sergeants. . . .' "[23]

CREATION OF THE FIRST USEM/JAPAN

The notion of an educational mission was formally proposed within CI&E in October 1945. On October 18, Navy Lt. Comdr. Robert King Hall (often referred to by his adversaries as "King Hall") and Army Maj. Edward H. Farr were assigned to prepare a staff study on the subject. Their first step was the submission of suggested names of mission members to their section chief, Col. Kenneth Dyke. The staff study and list of nominees went through several versions until, on November 3, Colonel Dyke approved it and Hall prepared the appropriate cables to Washington. A week later Gen. George Marshall in Washington and Gen. Douglas MacArthur in Tokyo "disapproved" the study and returned it to CI&E for revision. Both Marshall and MacArthur were concerned with the politics of selecting members of the proposed mission. They felt that the original list of nominees reflected a "duplication in individual universities" as well as an "inadequate geographical distribution" of proposed members.[24]

Their final criticism is, however, the most interesting. The staff study had suggested that the distinguished American scientist and

---

[23]Personal communication, "Memo: United States Education Mission to Japan, March 1946," Gordon Bowles to Edward R. Beauchamp, 23 August 1979.

[24]Chronological Record, Educational Mission of the United States, Joseph Trainor Papers, Box 49, Hoover Institution of War, Revolution and Peace, Stanford University.

educator James Bryant Conant, a man long associated with high government service, be named chairman of the mission. His nomination was, however, in the eyes of both Marshall and MacArthur, "politically inappropriate." On its face this seems strange, but Merle Borrowman, a former dean of the School of Education at Berkeley and a Conant associate during the latter's study of the American high school during the 1950s, provides an interesting explanation. In a letter to the author Borrowman says that Conant was "most unfriendly toward Japan" as a result of his son suffering lung damage when the submarine he served on was attacked in Tokyo Bay. In fact, Borrowman recalls Conant telling him that "he thought the wounding of his own son . . . had something to do with his [Conant's] own judgment that the [atomic] bomb should be dropped quickly to end the war."[25]

In any event, after making the required revisions the CI&E staff study was approved by December 31, 1945. The study outlined the poor state of Japanese education while emphasizing that the system "offers an effective instrument for changing the pattern of Japanese life, thought and action." It went on to point out that "37% of the total population of the nation is in the elementary school or preschool age group," and that these young people "are still in the formative stage of development and presumably may be reclaimed by re-education."[26] The study conceded that the Japanese authorities had, for the most part, attempted to undertake voluntary reform, but there were many problems they needed help with. Perhaps the single most difficult obstacle, in the authors' view, was that the Japanese educators "are technically not qualified to complete in a satisfactory manner the reforms which are directed [by SCAP] without technical assistance from foreign sources."[27] To clinch their argument, the authors concluded that the CI&E staff could also make good use of the assistance that a group of high-level American educators could provide. As the new Japanese school year began on April 1, it was essential, in the view of CI&E, that the mission complete its work before that date.

Among the educators recommended for membership on the USEM were many distinguished names, representing the best of the American educational elite. They included Frank Aydelotte (director of Princeton's Institute for Advanced Study), Guy Stanton Ford (ex-chancellor of the University of Minnesota), Alonzo B. Grace (Connecti-

---

[25]Personal communication, Merle Borrowman to Edward R. Beauchamp, 26 August 1980.

[26]Staff Study on Proposed Education Mission, 27 December 1945, Trainor Papers, Box 49, Hoover Institution on War, Revolution and Peace, Stanford University.

[27]Ibid.

cut's commissioner of education), Frank Porter Graham (president of the University of North Carolina), Howard Mumford Jones (distinguished scholar at Harvard), Robert Gordon Sproul (president of the University of California), Edward Lee Thorndike (emeritus professor of psychology at Columbia), Ralph W. Tyler (dean of the University of Chicago's School of Education), and George F. Zook (president of the American Council on Education and later chairman of the U.S. Education Mission to Germany).

Of these nominees, only four eventually were named to the mission. Gordon Bowles recalls that "it was the intent of the [State] Department to create as nationally and substantively representative a mission as possible."[28] As a result, the composition of the mission took on a significantly different character. Several women and a black male were named, and most of the high-powered university presidents and deans were replaced by school administrators and professors of education. One of the most fascinating aspects of this process was the conscious effort to secure representatives from labor organizations, educational associations, and religious groups. Thus, the composition of the First USEM to Japan was transformed from the meritocratic best of American universities, foundations, and governmental agencies to a high-level, broadly representative group of educators with a strong public school orientation. This is not intended to demean the mission or its members, but to point out the State Department's sensitivity to American political realities.

After the announcement in the press of the proposed mission, many individuals and groups scrambled to participate. Gordon Bowles recounts how "hundreds of letters, phone calls and personal inquiries were received from the public at large or from within the Federal Government, nominating specific individuals or offering their services and listing qualifications."[29]

Msgr. John Carroll, for example, contacted the War Department and extracted a promise of Roman Catholic participation in the mission. The War Department's agreement caused a potentially tricky problem when jurisdiction over the mission passed to the State Department shortly after the proposed mission was made public. State, naturally, did not want to be bound by War Department commitments, but it also did not want to offend an influential religious leader. After careful negotiations the problem was solved with the explanation that

---

[28]Personal communication, "Memo: United States Education Mission to Japan, March 1946," Gordon Bowles to Edward R. Beauchamp, 23 August 1979.
[29]Ibid.

"no commitment was made with respect to the Monsignor himself," but that Catholic representation on the mission was assured.[30]

Roy Deferrari, a staunch Catholic layman connected with the Catholic University of America, described the situation in a 1962 book. He tells of two earlier missions that had been sent to Europe with no representation of Catholic educators. These missions had been, he argues, "completely dominated by secularistic educators"; and when word arrived that Catholics were not to be represented on the Japan mission, "the complaints from Catholic sources, in particular the weekly *America,* were loud and numerous."[31]

At about the same time that Monsignor Carroll was approaching the War Department, Msgr. Frederick Hochwalt of the National Catholic Welfare Conference (NCWC) was talking to people in the State Department. Independently, Fr. Patrick O'Connor, a NCWC representative in Tokyo, approached Gen. MacArthur. As a result of the latter intervention, SCAP requested two Catholic educators, specifying the "President of Georgetown University and the President of the University of Notre Dame, or educators of equal caliber." By the time the SCAP cable reached Washington, however, both Hochwalt and Deferrari had been asked to serve on the mission. Years later Father O'Connor confirmed to Deferrari that SCAP requested the presidents of Georgetown and Notre Dame "on the basis of the high repute of their respective football teams."[32]

Gordon Bowles, however, was on everybody's list because of his long residence in prewar Japan, his teaching experience at the higher school level in Japan, and his service on the education desk in Assistant Secretary of State William Benton's office. He also saw a political motive in SCAP's recommendation of him for the mission. "Clearly," he suggests, "an effort was being made to include the State Department in this activity."[33]

Although both domestic and interagency political considerations were important factors in the selection of members of the First U.S. Education Mission to Japan, it is also important to stress that those eventually chosen were of high caliber and had achieved a great deal

---

[30]Memo, Harry Leverich to William Benton, 23 January 1946. I am indebted to Dr. George D. Stoddard (chair of the First U.S. Education Mission to Japan) and his son Philip for allowing me access to Dr. Stoddard's private papers. These papers have since been donated to the Hannah Collection at the Hoover Institution on War, Revolution and Peace at Stanford University.

[31]Roy Deferrari, *Memoirs of the Catholic University of America, 1918–1960* (Boston: St. Paul Editions, 1962), pp. 381–382.

[32]Ibid., p. 383.

[33]Personal communication, "Memo: United States Education Mission to Japan, March 1946," Gordon Bowles to Edward R. Beauchamp, 23 August 1979.

in their professional lives. In addition to meeting a political test, they also met the "general criteria" that served as "general guidelines" in the selection process, although these were never spelled out in any detail. They included such items as

demonstrated knowledge and practical experience in a given field of specialization; known ability to participate as a member of a team and to compromise constructively in joint decisions; physical fitness to travel and live under military orders without serious medical consequences to the individual or impositions on the military command.[34]

Although not on the original list, George Stoddard was named chairman of the mission. A former commissioner of education in the State of New York and president-elect of the University of Illinois, he was also a friend of Assistant Secretary Benton's as a result of serving with the U.S. delegation to London for the establishment of the United Nations Educational, Scientific, and Cultural Organization (UNESCO) in the fall of 1945. Recommendations by U.S. Commissioner of Education John W. Studebaker and Studebaker's assistant, Harold Benjamin, also undoubtedly enhanced Stoddard's chances for the chairmanship.

PREPARATION FOR THE MISSION TO JAPAN

In early February 1946, before leaving for Japan, several members of the USEM living in the New York–Washington corridor attended briefings at the State Department. There, several individuals expressed some confusion over the purposes of American policy in Japan. Hugh Borton, a key figure in the presurrender planning, told the group that planning for the occupation had been based on the assumption that "a basic reform in philosophy and educational system is going to last only so long as the Occupation lasts if it is not acceptable to the people." It is clear, he added, that "we can't stay there more than a limited time and allowing for demobilization it may be shorter than we realize." Borton then turned to what he saw as the true significance of the mission's work by saying that "one of the reasons General MacArthur feels that a group of this sort is so essential at this time is the fact that up until now a great deal has been done of the negative sort [and] your whole point is thinking in terms of positive policy you have to take from now on."[35] Thus, the work of the First U.S. Education Mission was to mark the end of the negative phase of the occupation's educational policy and the beginnings of the creation of a new system.

---

[34]Ibid.

[35]"Meeting with the Advisory Group to Japan," Department of State, 8 February 1946, Joseph Trainor Papers, Box 55, Hoover Institution on War, Revolution and Peace, Stanford University.

The Washington briefings were useful to those attending in that they helped clarify some of the basic problems the mission would face. There was consensus, in the words of Harold Benjamin, that the mission "will have to fight ourselves from attempting to do something that we won't have the time or the authorization to do."[36] The mission could best help SCAP, he argued, by providing the Japanese with intellectual resources, encouragement, and counsel so that they could make a statement of needed reform in education. Benjamin warned, "If we just make a statement for conquered peoples it won't be worth the powder it will take to blow it to hell."[37]

George Zook, of the American Council on Education and later chairman of a similar mission to Germany, took an active role in these meetings, although he did not accompany the mission to Japan. He argued that the mission needed to work with a group in Japan because "if we were to simply figure out a report and leave it behind for them to pick up, it is entirely possible they wouldn't pick it up at all, and it is possible that they wouldn't pick it up in the way they might."[38] The needed reforms, Zook concluded, would not occur overnight, so some mechanism was needed for keeping Japanese and American educators in close contact over a long period of time.

Undeniably the most informed briefing was that by Sir George Sansom, probably the leading Western expert on Japan, who had only recently returned from a trip to that country. His diary entries just before his February 8 session with the mission members speak of "the easy assurance with which the Americans are undertaking the political re-education of Japan," and CI&E's "cheery optimism. I do not think that they realize how deeply rooted and how strong is the Japanese intellectual tradition; they seem to think that Japan can be supplied with a new system of education as a tailor might furnish a new suit."[39]

If one of the purposes of these briefings was to provide a realistic context within which eventual reforms would be tested, they failed on at least one count. Sansom repeatedly stressed that Japan had always had an "economy of scarcity" and, in reply to a question from Teachers College sociologist George Counts, told his audience that it would be "some time" before the Japanese could hope to reach the level of their prewar material base. In fact, Sansom believed this would

---

[36]Ibid.
[37]Ibid.
[38]Ibid.
[39]Katharine Sansom, *Sir George Sansom: A Memoir* (Tallahassee, FL: The Diplomatic Press, 1972), p. 154.

not occur "for a generation or more."[40] This warning fell on deaf ears, and the mission was to recommend a very expensive 6-3-3 system, including nine years of compulsory schooling, in its final report.

Meanwhile, in Tokyo the CI&E staff was feverishly preparing to receive the American mission. They hastily wrote a 132-page document providing background data on Japanese education and basic information on a variety of topics, including an outline history of Japanese education, the organization and structure of the school system, educational finance, the role of Shinto, problems of Japanese teachers, physical education, women's education, adult education, and private schools. Each member of the mission received a copy, but how carefully it was read is problematic.

At the same time this document was being prepared, several officers in CI&E were assigned to prepare one-hour lectures on various topics to supplement the written materials provided for the mission. Presenters were told to emphasize and focus on the *current* situation, and each presenter was to make a "dry run," followed by a critique by other members of the education division, before the mission's arrival in Tokyo.

THE MISSION IN JAPAN

Finally, on February 26, 1946, the east coast members of the mission boarded a C-54 aircraft to begin the long journey to Japan. At Hamilton Field near San Francisco, the tired travelers met with the west coast members of the mission. The following day two military aircraft ferried the entire group to Honolulu, where they were briefed by several University of Hawaii faculty members and community leaders who had lived, studied, and taught in prewar Japan. Many of these briefings consisted of individuals drawing upon their personal experiences to advocate specific educational reforms. The Hawaii educators were prescient in their view that "the Japanese will be anxious to carry out reforms, if for no other reason than that the United States, not Japan, won the war." They suggested that the American authorities not view Japan as a "colonial dependency," and that "too great zeal in promoting [American educational practices] may backfire 10 or 15 years hence."[41]

From the briefing papers that survive we know that the Hawaii educators strongly advocated dismantling the prewar educational sys-

---

[40]"Conference with Sir George Sansom," Department of State, 20 February 1946, George Stoddard papers.

[41]Edward R. Beauchamp, "Hawaii and Postwar Japanese Education," *Japan Times,* 9 January 1994.

tem but cautioned against a wholesale dismissal. They pointed out, for example, that prewar moral education *(shushin)* "not only taught nationalism—[but] also taught citizenship and cooperation." As Laura Thompson told the mission, "It seems to me imperative that we build on what already exists . . . We cannot make Americans out of the Japanese, but we can . . . work toward making them good world citizens."[42]

After finally arriving in Tokyo and settling into their quarters at the Frank Lloyd Wright–designed Imperial Hotel across from the Imperial Palace, the mission members organized themselves into sub-committees. They met with SCAP (and especially CI&E) personnel and became acquainted with the Japanese Ministry of Education officials and members of a parallel committee of Japanese educators that had been created to work with the American advisors.

The mission faced a number of difficulties in carrying out its duties. First, there was the problem of logistics. Although the mission members, including secretarial staff, were given an assumed rank of brigadier general, it was difficult to find the accommodations and means of transportation they needed to effectively complete their task. Although the USEM was not bound by the provisions of SCAP's nonfraternization policy, it was not possible for Japanese counterparts or friends to share their transportation and billeting arrangements. Finally, material shortages and "lack of facilities or adequately trained personnel were ever present considerations for Mission members."[43]

The single most critical problem facing the mission, however, involved time. Soon after returning to the United States, mission member Willard Givens of the National Education Association (NEA) wrote a 19-page, single-spaced letter to friends in which he gave a detailed account of the mission's activities in Japan. The letter reveals that serious work did not begin until March 9, when the mission's subcommittees met for the first time, and that peripheral activities occupied significant periods of time during much of the mission's stay.

All told, the mission spent a little more than three weeks in Japan. The original expectation had been that it "would spend the entire time on tour or in conference on a scheduled basis and that a report would be prepared after return to the U.S." Chairman George Stoddard, however, insisted on reserving the last week [in Japan] for the completion of the report as a group before departure to the United States.[44]

---

[42]Ibid.

[43]Willard Givens, "Report on USEM," Pearl Wanamaker papers, Special Collections, Suzallo Library, University of Washington, Seattle. Washington.

[44]Personal communication, "Memo: United States Education Mission to Japan, March 1946," Gordon Bowles to Edward R. Beauchamp. 23 August 1979.

The mission's work day usually began at 9 A.M. and concluded at 5 P.M. Some of the subcommittees met periodically after dinner for a couple of hours, but this was not the normal procedure. Time was also set aside for "Japan's traditional red carpet treatment of visiting guests," resulting in "a rather elaborate schedule of tourist sites and events," which tended "to limit time available for work."[45] This judgment is not intended to cast aspersions on mission members (although Stoddard himself has written that only about half the members possessed "a solid work ethic") but merely to document that the time available for a close examination of Japanese educational problems was sharply limited. In addition, prior commitments forced at least three members of the mission to leave Japan early.

THE IMPACT OF THE FIRST USEM TO JAPAN

Underlying Conceptions

A broad consensus exists among scholars that the *Report of the First United States Education Mission* was, in the words of historian Kenneth Pyle, "tantamount to the wholesale adoption of the American educational system and its philosophy."[46] Willard Givens, in an interview with the *Honolulu Advertiser* (2 March 1946), described the mission's purpose as being "to teach each child to think for himself and use his own head." That position was symptomatic of deeply held views of the mission and represented a clear case of American "individualism" being prescribed for a society that has always been "group oriented."

The American educational anthropologist Theodore Brameld suggests that USEM member George Counts opposed the mission's report on the grounds that its members "were altogether too eager to superimpose American conceptions of education on a foreign culture and a defeated people." Brameld goes on to comment that Counts was "reacting as any well-informed sociologist or anthropologist ought to have reacted."[47] One wonders, however, if Counts's memory did not play tricks on him. After all, he was chairman of the subcommittee on language reform, which recommended radical changes in the Japanese language; and if Counts had any reservation about the propriety of this action, neither existing documents nor Counts's writings confirm it.

---

[45]Ibid.

[46]Kenneth B. Pyle, *The Making of Modern Japan* (Lexington, MA: D. C. Heath, 1978), p. 163.

[47]Theodore Brameld, *Japan: Culture, Education and Change in Two Communities* (New York: Holt, Rinehart and Winston, 1968), p. 258.

Another scholar, William Bagley, writing in the summer of 1946, described the mission's report as "just about what one would expect to come from a group of traditional educators making a brief tour of the country." Bagley described the report as one in which "the influence of American ideals and practices is clearly evident" and "a piece of work of which all Americans may well be proud." If it were followed, Bagley continued, it might enable the American occupation to hold "a place in history that will rival, if not surpass, the record of American idealism now written so large in the annals of the Philippines and China."[48] Even George Stoddard, in a letter to Assistant Secretary of State Benton on April 4, 1946, characterized the report as "truly a composite of group thinking"; and to a Japanese graduate student in 1970 he conceded that it was "[i]f anything . . . too American."[49]

Recommendations

The most important recommendations of the USEM were the following: (1) decentralization; (2) expansion of the curriculum and methods of education beyond the old pattern of a single textbook and teacher manual; (3) individualization of instruction according to student needs and abilities; (4) revision of moral education content and approach, with moral education being part of every course and no longer treated as a separate part of the curriculum; (5) installation of a 6-3-3 system, with nine years of compulsory schooling; (6) transformation of normal schools into four-year institutions; (7) expansion of educational opportunities for women; and (8) stress on guidance in the schools.[50] The recommendations were not good or bad in themselves, but they were unquestionably traditional American educational practices. They would, indeed, seem strange to many Europeans in 1946, and, in fact, they were not even universally practiced within the United States.

Could one have reasonably expected a significantly different set of recommendations from the USEM? With few exceptions, the mission was composed of men and women who (1) knew next to nothing about Japan, its history, its language or its educational system; (2) had very little prior experience outside the United States; (3) had begun their educational careers between 1890 and 1910; (4) had spent a hectic three and a half weeks in an alien cultural environment, where they were able to devote less than half their time to a serious,

---

[48]William C. Bagley, "The Report of the U.S. Educational [sic] Mission to Japan," *School and Society* 63 (1 June 1946), p. 388.

[49]George Stoddard papers.

[50]Edward R. Beauchamp and James M. Vardaman, eds., *Japanese Education Since 1945: A Documentary Study* (Armonk, NY: M. E. Sharpe, 1994), pp. 85–90.

systematic study of Japanese education; and (5) were intensely lobbied by CI&E personnel and counterpart Japanese educators (each group with its own interests).

One does not need to question the dedication, earnestness, and goodwill of these men and women to conclude that the report could just as easily have been written in New York, Chicago, or San Francisco without significant differences. Any group setting out to perform the task of reforming another nation's educational system must draw on its own accumulated knowledge and personal experience. If a different group of people, with different backgrounds, cross-cultural experiences, and a deeper knowledge of Japan had been chosen, perhaps a qualitatively different set of recommendations may have emerged. We shall never know.

The mission's report was, however, viewed as a blueprint for educational reform in Japan; it was a legitimating of sincere educational views held by many CI&E officers, a number of whom had been students of several mission members. Much of Herbert Passin's view of the occupation is equally applicable to the work of the First United States Education Mission to Japan:

[T]he use of some version . . . of American experience often led to serious mistakes. Many Americans, finding themselves in exotic environments, genuinely seem to forget that the United States is not all New England town meeting. [They do not realize] such quite acceptable democratic polities as England and France might do things differently. . . . [E]ducational reforms were, despite valuable details, on the whole misdirected, and they have left Japan a legacy of problems that will plague them for decades. [Indeed,] they were exacerbated by the imposition of American concepts of educational administration and by the unraveling of delicate organic structures that would have more easily found their own way to solve these problems. In effect, we opened a Pandora's box, and since we did it by inadvertence, we would have been wiser to leave it to the Japanese to open it themselves.[51]

CONCLUSION

If the American goal in the broader occupation of Japan was to transform the nation from a militaristic and authoritarian state to a democratic one, the relative success of the venture must be conceded. The prewar system described at the outset of this article has been swept away. As early as 1943 American planners recognized the need to use education as a vehicle for democratization in postwar Japan, and the first eight months of the occupation saw the First U.S. Education Mission lay out a blueprint for the occupation authorities to follow.

---

[51] Herbert Passin, *The Legacy of the Occupation—Japan*, Occasional Papers of the East Asian Institute (New York: Columbia University Press, 1968), p. 10.

It can be argued that the relative success of democratization occurred not because of the educational reforms instituted during American control, but rather because most Japanese were ready for change. Japan's initiation of changes in the system even before the occupation had formally begun illustrates this point.[52]

In any event, Japan's postwar record in democratic education is good, but by no means perfect. Like most modern democratic nations, contemporary Japan faces problems of bureaucratization and alienation in the school system, with consequent difficulties in maintaining feelings of purpose and value among teachers and students. Japan's particular problems include excessive pressures on students for examination achievement, and the tendency for education to become a political football in conflicts between left and right. Problems of discrimination against women and minorities remain. And finally, the high degree of centralization, while providing uniform nationwide standards, creates issues of academic freedom, as the recent textbook controversy illustrates.[53]

On the other hand, the successes of Japanese education are undeniable. The prewar authoritarian and ideological system has been thoroughly revamped, while retaining and expanding its relatively egalitarian access and meritocratic standards. Postwar education provides relatively easy access at most levels; it bases competition for the most elite schools not on the accident of birth but on merit; it provides experiences—academic and nonacademic—that reinforce basic democratic principles; it maintains world-class standards; and, for the most part, it strives to strengthen democratic elements, but within the context of Japanese culture, with its emphasis on achievement and "community" norms.

Clearly, Japan has democratized postwar education considerably, and in so doing has socialized the younger generation to life in a democratic polity. Arguably, this accomplishment is largely the result of military defeat and American planning that put Japan on the road to its own variant of democracy.[54] American wartime planners and

---

[52]Edward R. Beauchamp and James M. Vardaman, eds., *Japanese Education Since 1945: A Documentary Study* (Armonk, NY: M. E. Sharpe, 1994), p. 55.

[53]The Japanese government must approve textbooks for use in the schools. This arrangement has resulted in much criticism of the approved textbooks' treatment of various subjects, including the causes of World War II and Japan's prewar and wartime activities in China, Korea, Taiwan, and Southeast Asia. The "textbook authorization system" has been challenged in court by several "progressive" historians, most notably Professor Saburo Ienaga, whose case (with appeals) has wended its way through the legal system for 40 years. In essence, however, the courts have upheld the right of the Ministry of Education to control the textbooks used in the nation's schools.

[54]Edward R. Beauchamp, "Education," in *Democracy in Japan*, ed. Takeshi Ishida and Ellis S. Krauss (Pittsburgh: Pittsburgh University Press, 1989), pp. 225–251.

the members of the First Education Mission imposed American educational ideals and practices on Japan; but, as it had done in the Meiji period, Japan selectively accepted what was useful, adapted other elements to its cultural core, and rejected what was dysfunctional.

EDWARD R. BEAUCHAMP is Professor of Historical and Comparative Educational Studies, Department of Educational Foundations, Wist Hall 108, College of Education, University of Hawaii, 1776 University Avenue, Honolulu, HI 96822. Telephone: (808) 956-4246. Fax: (808) 956-9100. E-mail: bedward@uhunix.uhcc.hawaii.edu

History Textbook Reform in Allied Occupied Japan, 1945–52

Yoko H. Thakur

The history textbook reform in Allied Occupied Japan, 1945–52, was one of the major education policies designed to demilitarize and democratize pre-collegiate Japanese education. Since 1952, however, both history textbooks and the textbook system that certifies them have been extremely controversial. In the post-Occupation period Japan's Asian neighbors have criticized Japanese history textbooks for covering up Japanese wartime aggression in Asia. And in Japan textbook writers and teachers have repeatedly challenged the textbook certification system as unconstitutional. Ironically, the leading protestor was the very historian who had contributed to writing the first reformed history textbook under the guidance of the Supreme Commander for the Allied Powers (SCAP). Although the purpose of this article is to highlight and analyze the issues involved in the textbook reform, it also proposes to show how education policies became embedded in larger political and ideological concerns, how Japanese society resolved its textbook conflict, and how academic issues and educators were used and abused in the process of public school textbook writing.

Numerous articles and books dealing with the textbook reform in prewar, Occupied, and post-Occupation Japan, have been published, but it is still not clear how the history textbook reform in Occupied Japan relates to the controversy pertaining to the textbook certification system in post-Occupation Japan.[1] This article is an attempt to connect textbook policies in the prewar, Occupation, and post-Occupation periods and to

---

Yoko H. Thakur is a lecturer in the Department of Foreign Languages and Literatures at George Mason University. She wishes to express sincere gratitude to Dr. Marlene J. Mayo of the University of Maryland for her assistance in completing the author's doctoral dissertation in 1990, from which this article has evolved. Except in citations of English-language sources, Japanese names are written in Japanese form, with surname followed by given name.

[1]They include Karasawa Tomitaro, *Kyōkasho no rekishi* (*History of Textbooks*) (Tokyo, 1956); Nakamura Kikuji, *Monbushō chosaku sengo kyōkasho* (*Postwar Textbooks Written by the Ministry of Education*) (Tokyo, 1984); Ienaga Saburo, *Kyōkasho kentei* (*Textbook Certification*) (Tokyo, 1965); idem, *Kyōkasho saiban* (*Textbook Cases*) (Tokyo, 1981); and Takahashi Shiro, *Kyōkasho kentei* (Tokyo, 1988).

analyze the relationship between the development of these policies and the contents of pre-collegiate history textbooks. The emphasis here is on two aspects of the textbook reform: (1) the history of textbook policy and reform in Allied Occupied Japan; and (2) the legacy of Occupation textbook policy for post-Occupation Japan.

Initially, the Meiji government, established in 1868 as Japan's first modern imperial government, adopted a relatively nonrestrictive textbook policy. When the Meiji government issued the School System Law in August 1872, there was no textbook compilation bureau of the government. The Ministry of Education instructed schoolteachers to choose textbooks from the recommended list of books.[2] Early Meiji Japan was a period of enlightenment, when Western civilization was highly prized. In the 1870s a group of Japanese educators led by an American educator, Marion McCarrell Scott (1843–1922), began producing a series of texts and teachers' manuals.[3]

However, by the 1880s, surging nationalistic sentiment among Confucian scholars, led by Motoda Eifu (1818–91), challenged Westernization.[4] Under Mori Arinori (1847–89) as the Education Minister, state control of teaching materials was tightened, and the government adopted a certification system requiring the approval of the Ministry of Education for all textbooks used in elementary, middle, and normal schools.[5] As education historians Kaigo Tokiomi and Naka Arata point out, during this certification period nationalistic features, such as emperor-centered and mythologically inclined approaches, were introduced into the history textbooks.[6] The trend crystallized in the Imperial Rescript on Education of 1890, which emphasized three themes: Confucian values as the ethical foundation of the nation, the role of education in perfecting "moral power," and the duty of subjects to respect the national polity headed by the emperor.

Eventually in 1903, the government established the national textbook system (*kokutei kyōkasho*), following a series of scandals which involved extensive briberies of textbook officials and publishers.[7] Under this sys-

---

[2]Yamazumi Masami, *Kyōkasho* (*Textbooks*) (Tokyo, 1970), 20.

[3]Scott introduced American methods of training elementary school teachers, using imported educational equipment and texts.

[4]After the Restoration in 1868, Motoda, as a lecturer to Emperor Meiji, became an influential conservative in the government.

[5]Mori was an influential architect of Japan's prewar education system patterned after the German model. For more information, see I. P. Hall, *Mori Arinori* (Cambridge, Mass., 1973).

[6]Kaigo Tokiomi and Naka Arata, eds., *Kindai Nihon kyōkasho sōran: Kaisetsuhen* (Tokyo, 1969), 469–85.

[7]Yamazumi, *Kyōkasho*, 157; and Takahashi, *Kyōkasho kentei*, 65.

tem, which lasted until 1945, the Textbook Bureau of the Ministry of Education compiled all pre-collegiate textbooks.

History textbooks published between 1903 and 1940 were ultranationalistic in that they described the imperial family as descendents of the founding god of Japan and, thus, as sacred and inviolable; they defined Japan as a divine nation; and they stressed that it was the people's supreme duty and honor to serve the emperor with loyalty. For instance, the first four out of about fifty chapters in all of the five editions of the textbooks included such mythological figures as the Sun Goddess Amaterasu and Emperor Jimmu (God Warrior). They were drawn from two ancient accounts— *Kojiki (Record of Ancient Matters*, 712 A.D.) and *Nihon shoki (Chronicles of Japan*, 720 A.D.). According to these classics, Amaterasu was the divine ancestor of Japan's first emperor, Jimmu, who established the capital in Yamato in the western part of Japan after pacifying the rebels in the area.

The Ministry of Education issued an ultranationalistic text, *Kokutai no hongi (The Essence of National Polity* or *The Cardinal Principles of the National Entity)*, in May 1937. The text stressed the duty of the Japanese subject to create a new culture based on the divine emperor and was used in upper elementary and middle schools. Beginning with the fifth edition, published in 1940, the history text used a "Divine Message" (*shinchoku*), portraying the emperor as the descendent of god, as an epigraph.[8] The wartime textbooks published between 1941 and 1945 showed the escalation of militaristic and ultranationalistic tendencies which already were apparent in the 1930s.

On the other side of the Pacific, prior to the end of the war, U.S. officials began planning the occupation of Japan, and they felt compelled to rewrite Japanese history textbooks in order to demilitarize and democratize Japan. This planning was part of postwar U.S. global foreign policy.[9] Initially, the Division of Special Research of the State Department and the Advisory Committee on Postwar Foreign Policy established basic principles and goals. In 1943 and 1944, other departments, especially the War and Navy departments and such wartime agencies as the Office of Strategic Services (OSS), Foreign Economic Administration (FEA), and Office of War Information (OWI), played increasingly important roles in postwar planning. During the final stage of planning in early 1945, an interdepartmental coordination body, the State-War-Navy Coordinating

---

[8]*Kokutai no hongi* (Tokyo, 1937), 143–56. For more information, see Robert King Hall, *Education for a New Japan* (New Haven, Conn., 1949). *Shōgaku kokushi* (Tokyo, 1940).

[9]See Marlene J. Mayo, "American Wartime Planning for Occupied Japan: The Role of the Experts," in *Americans as Proconsuls: United States Military Government in Germany and Japan, 1944–1952*, ed. Robert Wolfe (Carbondale, Ill., 1984), 3–51; Harley A. Notter, *Postwar Foreign Policy Preparation, 1939–1945* (Washington, D.C., 1949); and Iokibe Makoto, *Beikoku no Nihon senryō seisaku* (Tokyo, 1985).

Committee (SWNCC), was formed to review recommendations and to determine the initial goals and priorities of the Occupation.

SWNCC 108, "The Post-Surrender Military Government of the Japanese Empire: Education System" of 17 April 1945, called for the preparation of a separate paper on education. Eugene Dooman, the chairman of SWNCC's Subcommittee on the Far East (SFE), forwarded the order to the State Department's Division of Cultural Communications, which in turn assigned Gordon Bowles to draft a paper on Japanese education policy. Bowles, an anthropologist trained at Harvard University, served successively in the FEA and the State Department. Bowles's draft of 30 July noted that "the educational system in Japan is a closely-knit government controlled organization highly integrated into the agrarian and industrial life of the nation." It criticized prewar and wartime Japanese education as "one of the most important instruments in molding the minds of the people to accept authoritarian controls with unquestioning obedience." Bowles continued, "It has fostered the concept of loyalty and of Japan's militaristic and materialistic destiny. Its ultimate purpose is to inculcate a spirit of willingness and desire to serve the state as an end in itself." The draft also stressed the need to reform textbooks and curricula, to establish liberal education, and to encourage a democratic form of government. After Japan's surrender, the SWNCC approved Bowles's paper with minor revisions in late September 1945.[10]

Between its surrender on 15 August and the formation of the SCAP on 2 October 1945, the Japanese government took the initiative in demilitarizing education by nullifying wartime education laws and ordering the censorship of undesirable phrases in textbooks.[11] These measures were taken on the basis of the Japanese government's understanding of the Potsdam Proclamation, even before the SCAP was formed.

On 26 August 1945 the government ordered the blackening out and deletion of militaristic phrases from school textbooks. These books were called blackened-out (*suminuri*) textbooks because problem phrases were marked out with a brush dipped in black ink (*sumi*), initially by the stu-

---

[10]The Bowles draft of 30 July 1945: PR-24 Preliminary, "SWNCC Politico-Military Problems in the Far East in the Post Surrender of the Japanese Empire: The Education System," Notter file, box 119, United States National Archives (USNA), quoted by Mayo in "American Wartime Planning," 37–51, and by Kubo Yoshizo in *Tainichi senryō seisaku to sengo kyōiku kaikaku* (*Occupation Policy for Japan and Postwar Education Reform*) (Tokyo, 1984), 44–72.

[11]For more information, see Mark Taylor Orr, "Education Reform Policy in Occupied Japan" (Ph.D. diss., University of North Carolina, 1954), 61; Karasawa Tomitaro, *Kyōkasho no rekishi* (Tokyo, 1959), 610–12; Yamazumi Masami, *Kyōkasho* (Tokyo, 1970), 73; Nakamura Kikuji, *Fukkoku kokutei rekishi kyōkasho: Kaisetsu* (Tokyo, 1987), 47; and idem, *Monbushō chosaku sengo kyōkasho* (Tokyo, 1984), 14–32.

dents themselves in their own textbooks as instructed by their teachers. On 15 September the Ministry issued an important instruction, "Outline of Education for Construction of New Japan" (*Shin Nihon kensetsu no kyōiku hōshin*), which stressed, among other things, the preservation of the national polity, the eradication of militaristic ideas, the construction of a peaceful nation, and the need to delete problem phrases in national textbooks. On 20 September, the Japanese government issued instructions for censoring textbooks in "Concerning Handling of Textbooks in Accordance with the Post War Situation" (*Shūsen ni tomonau kyōkayo tosho toriatsukaikata ni kansuru ken*). To be deleted were "all teaching materials that are not appropriate in the light of the Imperial Rescript proclaiming the end of the war," including phrases that emphasized national defense and armament, fostered fighting spirit, and thwarted international goodwill.[12]

According to Kubota Fujimaro, the former chief of the Youth Education Section of the Education Ministry's National Education Bureau (*kokumin kyōiku kyoku*), textbooks were censored beforehand to conceal militaristic phrases from the SCAP. Ishimori Nobuo (1897–1987), a textbook compilation officer of the National Education Bureau, explained that one reason for the deletions was to give a favorable impression of the Ministry to the SCAP through the Ministry's censorship of the militaristic phrases. The blackening-out as a form of censorship continued and was expanded in the fall of 1945 under the Civil Information and Education Section (CI&E) of the SCAP until the so-called "stop-gap" textbooks became available in the spring and fall of 1946. During November 1945, a small group of Nisei and native Japanese, as well as Eurasians, had been assembled to assist the CI&E with textbook analysis. Two professors of Tokyo Imperial University cooperated with the CI&E as advisors. Kaigo Tokiomi, an authority on education history, and his graduate students made card indices on militarism and ultranationalism for the CI&E. Kishimoto Hideo (1903–64), who received a doctoral degree in philosophy from Harvard University, was instrumental in matters related to philosophy and religion including Shintoism.[13]

Regarding the question of what should be deleted from the textbooks, Herbert Wunderlich, education officer, listed two main categories— ultranationalism and militarism. Ultranationalistic ideas included the

---

[12]Takahashi, *Kyōkasho kentei*, 69–70.
[13]Nakamura, *Monbushō chosaku sengo kyōkasho*, 16–17; Herbert John Wunderlich, "Reminiscences of Occupation Japan, 1945–1946" (unpublished paper, St. Maries, Idaho, 1984); its Japanese translation, "Nihon senry no omoide, 1945–46" was published in *Senryō kyōikushi kenkyū* 2 (1985): 46.

Greater East Asian Co-prosperity Sphere doctrine or any other doctrine of expansion; Japanese racial and national superiority; unquestioning loyalty and obedience to the Emperor; and the superiority of the sacred and immutable Tenno (emperor) system.[14] Militarism included the glorification of war as a heroic and acceptable way of settling disputes, the idealization of war heroes by glorifying their military achievements, and the elevation of military service as a subject's highest patriotic duty and dying with unquestioning loyalty toward the Emperor as the highest honor.

According to Wunderlich's CI&E staff study, the majority of the textbooks contained so much propaganda that deletion by the pen-and-ink method was neither practical nor advisable. Before and during the war, all textbooks in morals, Japanese history, and geography had been written by compilers commissioned by the Ministry of Education. The study also noted that language textbooks were equally pernicious.[15] On 31 December, the SCAP suspended textbooks and courses in history, geography, and morals until acceptable textbooks became available.

Subsequently, CI&E ordered the collection of wartime textbooks in these three subjects from all schools for the purpose of pulping. Some among the CI&E officers sensed the danger of inviting criticism for violating freedom of the press by destroying wartime textbooks. Wunderlich wrote, "Collection of texts for pulping and the manufacture of paper presented a cogent way out of the 'burning books' dilemma."[16]

Censorship was not limited to school textbooks. Regardless of the liberating image of the SCAP, all media, including film and radio, were censored by the Civil Censorship Detachment of the SCAP, which initially screened ultranationalism, militarism, and criticism of SCAP policy and personnel, and later guarded against the penetration of Communism. The contradictions inherent in the two functions of the SCAP—censor and liberator— have stirred up much controversy. While some Occupation experts see censorship as a logical step toward the ultimate goal of democratization, others are hesitant to approve the scope and depth of the censorship on prewar and wartime textbooks. Marilyn J. Mayo, a specialist in diplomatic and Occupation history, explains that censorship was practiced because "the victors, determined to avoid another war with a resurgent Japan, believed they must censor and guide Japan's media until their enemy could get rid of wrong ideas and acquire better ones—replace militaristic and aggressive ideas with democratic and peace-loving ones." Suzuki Eiichi, an education historian, points out that the severity of the

---

[14]"Writing of History Textbook" (undated), box 54, Trainor Papers, Stanford University, Stanford, Calif.

[15]Herbert John Wunderlich, "The Japanese Textbook Problems and Solution, 1945–46" (Ph.D. diss., Stanford University, 1952), 253.

[16]Ibid., 255.

fourth directive, which mandated not only suspension of courses but also the collection of all the textbooks and teachers' manuals in these courses, stunned education circles in Japan.[17]

Starting with the new year, the CI&E and Japanese educators began democratization by writing and editing new teaching materials for the classroom. The SCAP and the CI&E used the report of the First United States Education Mission of April 1946 as a policy guide to be implemented by the Japanese government. The Ministry of Education handled the recommendations of the missions as if they were SCAP orders.[18] The report, in general, approved the existing SCAP program of textbook deletions and the introduction of new curricula and textbooks for democratic education. "The preparation and publication of textbooks," the report stated, "should be left to open competition." It added that a committee of teachers from a given geographical area should select texts.[19]

The Ministry first started the history textbook project with Toyoda Takeshi (1920–80), then teaching at Tokyo Women's Higher Normal School (Tokyo Jokoshi, currently Ochanomizu Joshi Daigaku). In October 1945 he was appointed one of the compilers of the Textbook Bureau and was put in charge of compiling Japanese history textbooks for elementary and middle schools. Toyoda, a specialist in Japanese medieval commercial history, took the job unwillingly. He said at a roundtable discussion held in 1956, after the Occupation ended, that "there was nothing voluntary about new history textbooks." And he added, "Everything was done by MacArthur's instruction."[20]

To assist the history textbook project, the Ministry formed the Committee of Historians (*rekishika senmon iinkai*) in December 1945, staffing it with ten historians, including Watsuji Tetsuro (1889–1960), cultural historian at Tokyo Imperial University, which became Tokyo University in May 1947. The committee members agreed on several points—separating history from moral teachings, handling mythology as such and not as historical facts, decreasing militaristic and nationalistic terminologies, in line with some points that Wunderlich raised earlier.[21]

---

[17]"Civil Censorship and Media Control in Early Occupied Japan: From Minimum to Stringent Surveillance," in *Americans as Proconsuls*, ed. Wolfe, 264; *Nihon senryō to kyōiku kaikaku* (Tokyo, 1983), 175.

[18]*Nihon senryō to kyōiku kaikaku*, 175. See also Hoichi Tsuchimochi, *Beikoku kyōiku shisetsudan no kenkyū* (Tokyo, 1991).

[19]"Report of the First United States Education Mission," in Civil Information and Education Section (CI&E), Supreme Commander for the Allied Powers (SCAP), *Education in the New Japan* (Tokyo, 1948).

[20]"Zadankai: Shūsengo jūichinen o kaerimite," in *Nihon rekishi* 100 (Oct. 1956): 19.

[21]"Arimitsu Jiro memo," quoted in Kubo, *Tainichi senryō seisaku*, 208–9.

Toyoda's draft of March 1946, entitled *Zantei shotōka kokushi, jō* (*Stop-gap History Textbook for Elementary School*, vol. 1), combined prewar and new materials. In comparison with the prewar/wartime national textbooks, Toyoda's draft differed visibly in periodization, historiography, and methodology. Tyoda eliminated "the divine message" and the chronology of the emperors and empresses, including both mythological and historical ones; and he replaced the biography-based approach with periodization based on social, economic, and political development. Moreover, he introduced archaeological findings in the prehistoric period and replaced the bookish style of writing with a colloquial style. However, he defined *Kojiki* and *Nihon shoki* as the oldest existing historical accounts, not as legends, and retained their description of a god "Izanagi" and a goddess "Izanami" as the creators of the Japanese islands and the ancestors of the imperial line.

Watsuji criticized Toyoda's draft, stating that *Kojiki* and *Nihon shoki* should not be introduced as historical accounts. Tsuda Sokichi, an authority of ancient Japanese history, who had declined to become a committee member, argued that the history textbook should separate mythology from the facts.[22] This point of view was similar to that of the CI&E officers.

Joseph C. Trainor (1905–) succeeded Wunderlich as the project director. After receiving a Ph.D. from the University of Washington in 1940, Trainor had taught at Hampton Institute in Virginia. There were various methodological disagreements between Toyoda and Trainor in writing the Japanese history textbooks. The major one was how to handle the national creation mythology contained in *Kojiki* and *Nihon shoki*. Toyoda was a protégé of Kuroita Katsumi (1874–1946), professor of Tokyo Imperial University and the leading authority among a powerful group of conservative Japanese historians. His insistence on including a chapter on mythology in the history text led to a confrontation with Trainor, who reassigned Toyoda to a position unrelated to textbook compilation.[23]

On 15 May 1946 in an attempt to rescue the history textbook project, Trainor, Kishimoto, and Arimitsu Jiro (1903–), chief of the Textbook Bureau, began a special group project and confirmed that mythology should not be included in history textbooks. Regarding mythology, Train-

---

[22]Takahashi Shiro and Harry Wray, *Senryōka no kyōiku kaikaku to ken'etsu* (Tokyo, 1987), 249–310; and Toyoda's draft with Watsuji's comments, supplement 3–4, in ibid.

[23]"Zadankai: Shūsengo," 33–34; Conference report, 8 May 1946, box 55, Trainor Papers; Joseph C. Trainor, *Educational Reform in Occupied Japan: Trainor's Memoir* (Tokyo, 1983), 89.

or listed three principles in his memoir: "(1) that it would be referred to at the time the actual books, such as the famous Kojiki, were written; (2) it would be stressed that these works were rather heavily weighted with the personal opinions of their authors and were written for the specific purpose of supporting a particular group at the time; and (3) in general mythology and the so-called 'traditional beliefs' would be alluded to as little as possible."[24]

The SCAP's Education Division instructed Japan's Ministry of Education to select writers for the elementary, middle, and normal school textbooks. The division explained that each historical period should include: specific emperors; outstanding political events at both imperial and non-imperial levels; and descriptions of the economy, education, religion, art, and daily life of the people. The authors were selected by the Ministry and approved by the CI&E, based on qualifications outlined by Trainor and Kishimoto. To be qualified, the authors had to be Tokyo residents, family men with at least one child attending an elementary school, and employed at the Historiographical Institute or teaching at Tokyo University. Each textbook would be divided into four historical periods: ancient, medieval, modern, and present. For the elementary level, for instance, Ienaga Saburo (1913–), Morisue Yoshiaki, Okada Akio, and Okubo Toshiaki (1900–) were appointed to cover each period, respectively.[25]

On 21 May 1946, the authors were given about one month to complete the project. According to Ienaga, three guiding principles were enunciated: 1) to base the text on historical facts; 2) to incorporate cultural, social, and economic history; and 3) to foster students' critical thinking.[26] Editing and proofreading the manuscripts were time consuming, since Japanese drafts were translated into English for the Division officers, whose corrections were then translated back into Japanese. Nonetheless, the writers finished *Kuni no ayumi* (*Footsteps of a Nation*), a history text for elementary schools, on schedule about a month later.[27]

In general, a comparison of Toyoda's draft and Ienaga's text (the chapters dealing with the ancient period in *Kuni no ayumi*) reveals that the lat-

---

[24]For more information, see Nishimura Iwao, "Recollections: Memoirs of Monbushō Days," *Senryō kyōikushi kenkyū* 1 (July 1984): 46–52; Katakami Soji et al., "Zadankai: Sengo kokushi kyōiku no saikai o megutte," *Rekishi to chiri* 316 (Dec. 1981): 36–38; and Kubo, *Tainichi senryō seisaku*; Trainor, *Memoir*, 97.

[25]Okubo was a historian and a grandson of Okubo Toshimichi, one of the founders of the Meiji empire. The former's works include *Nihon kindai shigakushi* (Tokyo, 1940), *Mori Arinori* (Tokyo, 1944), and *Meirokusha kō* (Tokyo, 1976).

[26]Ienaga Saburo, "Kuni no ayumi, hensan shimatsu," in Karasawa, *Kyōkasho no rekishi*, 618–828.

[27]The English title was used in the SCAP documents.

ter was not a radical departure from the former but rather a revision.[28] For instance, there were numerous parallel sentences and traces of compilers trying to salvage parts of Toyoda's draft. However, in handling mythology there were distinct differences. While Toyoda spent seven pages describing mythological figures in a similar manner to the prewar texts, Ienaga struck out all the mythological stories and described strictly archaeological findings.

The authors' responses to the project were mixed. Ienaga, having a relatively favorable view, has reminisced that "although there were many restrictions in the process of writing, academic conscience did not have to suffer as much as it did under the wartime press code." Okubo complained that the project was done in haste, with the authors having to complete a given section of manuscript each week. Concerning CI&E control of the content, Okada stated that the CI&E required the omission of ultranationalistic phrases and references to historical figures who represented ultranationalism. In handling the controversial Nanking Incident, for example, the CI&E forced Okada to change the description from "advance from Shanghai to Nanking" to "looting at Nanking."[29]

Reformed Japanese history textbooks received both favorable and critical reviews. Naturally, the new history textbooks won high marks from the SCAP authorities. However, they also ignited strong criticism internationally as well as domestically. Internationally, the most strident objection came from members of the Allied Council for Japan (ACJ), who thought the reform had not gone far enough. The ACJ was established in Tokyo in February 1946 for the purpose of "consulting with and advising a supreme commander in implementing the terms of surrender, the Occupation and control of Japan."[30]

At the forty-sixth meeting of the ACJ held on 26 November 1947, the Chinese representative, General Shang Chen criticized the unfair treatment of Sino-Japanese relations in *Kuni no ayumi* by pointing out that chapter 12 omitted the notorious Twenty-one Demands presented to China by Japan in 1915. In response, William J. Sebald, the United States representative, conceded that "the textbooks now in use are not perfect" and that "there are now special textbook revision committees which are working on a revision of all history textbooks in use in the schools." Siding with General Shang, Major General A. P. Kislenko, the U.S.S.R. representative, criticized "many anti-scientific interpretations, tendentious distortions,

---

[28]*Kuni no ayumi* (Tokyo, 1946).
[29]Ienaga, "Hensan shimatsu"; Okubo Toshikane et al., "Zadankai: Sengo rekishi," 18–46; "Zadankai: Shūsengo," 19.
[30]FEC C4-005/3, p. 4, USNA.

and even unadulterated Japanese prewar and wartime propaganda" in the new textbooks.[31]

However, the strongest domestic criticism came from Japanese Marxist historians. Inoue Kiyoshi (1913–) argued that *Kuni no ayumi* was based too heavily on the imperial institution (*tennosei*) and was insensitive to the lives of commoners. An influential leftist organization of scholars, *Minshushugi kagakusha kyōkai* (Association of Democratic Scientists), praised the new textbook as potentially significant in redirecting history education but at the same time criticized it for failing to wipe out old absolutistic thinking and for distorting historical facts in order to maintain an emperor-centered historical interpretation.[32]

In contrast, most of the Japanese newspapers and academic journals responded to *Kuni no ayumi* positively. One schoolteacher commented that "It was very fresh. I was indeed moved by the fact that the textbook started with archeological facts, not with mythology, and felt that history should be something like this textbook."[33] The Ministry of Education published *Kuni no ayumi* for the elementary school level on 5 September 1946; *Nihon no rekishi* for the intermediate level on 19 October 1946; and *Nihon rekishi* for normal schools on 20 January 1947. These textbooks were used for only a very short period, with the exception of *Kuni no ayumi*. When the new school system and curriculum were introduced in the spring of 1947, "permanent textbooks"[34] were used in the classrooms and the Ministry of Education dropped the two upper-level "stop-gap" history books. *Kuni no ayumi* survived as a "permanent textbook" in the junior high schools until 1949 when the certified textbook system replaced the national textbook system. As a prototype, *Kuni no ayumi* influenced the postwar textbooks. It deleted mythological and emperor-centered interpretations, introduced archaeological and people-based approaches, and incorporated social and cultural aspects and international relations.

As for the textbook system, the SCAP tried to decentralize it by replacing the national textbook system with something more democratic. On 26 February 1947 the Education Division instructed the Ministry of Education to prepare a plan for a decentralized textbook system by May and to form a textbook committee to draft an outline of the system jointly with the CI&E.[35]

---

[31]"Corrected Verbatim Minutes of Forty-Sixth Meeting" of Allied Council for Japan, Tokyo, 26 Nov. 1947, USNA.

[32]*Rekishi kyōikuron* (Kyoto, 1947), 181–203; Karasawa, *Kyōkasho no rekishi*, 628–29; and Kaigo and Naka, *Kyōkasho sōran*, 512–14.

[33]Nakamura, *Fukkoku kokutei rekishi kyōkasho*, 53.

[34]The term "permanent textbook" is used in SCAP Documents and means textbooks which were intended for longer term usage, as opposed to its "stop-gap" or "interim textbook."

[35]Report of Conference, box 5595, RG331, SCAP records, National Record Center, Suitland, Md.

In the spring of 1948, the Textbook Committee became the Textbook Authorization Research Committee (*kyōkasho tosho chōsakai*), which handled certification of new textbooks. The CI&E granted the Ministry of Education the temporary textbook certification authority because local education committees were not yet formed and the CI&E needed to use the Ministry to censor textbooks. Many educators were critical because they thought that the textbook certification system represented a return of centralized control of the education administration to the Ministry of Education.[36] With some modifications, the certified textbook system continues in Japan today. Under this system, anyone can write a textbook, but only certified textbooks are allowed in the classroom.

The new system seemed contrary to the SCAP's initial intention to institute a decentralized and democratized textbook system. This adjustment in textbook policy may have reflected the redirection of Occupation policy because of the cold war in Asia, a shift in Washington's global policy, and the return of those who had been in power before and during the war to power within the Japanese government. This redirection of Occupation policy was initiated in late 1947 and was formulated in National Security Council papers in 1948 for implementation in both Allied Occupied Japan and Germany. The new direction called for less punishment and control over former enemies and a greater emphasis on their rehabilitation. Washington did not entirely abandon the initial goals of the Occupation—demilitarization and democratization; but they became secondary to the "containment" of the Soviet Union and Communism. The CI&E's reliance on the Ministry increased in the following years as the cold war escalated. Censorship of national textbooks was gradually transferred from the CI&E to the Ministry of Education until the summer of 1950, when the CI&E terminated its censorship function altogether.[37]

On 1 May 1951, the succeeding Commander General Matthew B. Ridgway (1895–), issued a statement further relaxing SCAP control of Japan. Prime Minister Yoshida Shigeru (1878–1959) quickly formed an Advisory

---

[36]See Ishida Saburo, "Kyōkasho mondai o megutte," *Akarui kyōiku* 9 (Apr. 1968): 4, Gordon Prange Collection, University of Maryland.

[37]"Onzonsareta kokutei kyōkasho" in *Akarui kyōiku* 13 (May 1948): 5, the Gordon Prange Collection; and vol. 3 of *Shakaika kyōiku shiryō* (Tokyo, 1974), 44–45; National Security Council Paper 68 (NSC-68), 1950. For more information, see John Lewis Gaddis, *Strategies of Containment: A Critical Appraisal of Postwar American National Security Policy* (Oxford, Eng., 1985); and William F. Nimmo, ed., *The Occupation of Japan: The Impact of the Korean War: The Proceedings of the Seventh Symposium* (Norfolk, Va., 1990); Suzuki, *Nihon senryō*; Kubo, *Tainichi senryō seisaku*; Yamazumi, *Kyōkasho*; Ota, *Nihon kyōikushi*; Trainor, *Memoir*; and Mark T. Orr, "Reformers: Japanese Education during the Allied Occupation" (paper presented for Florida/Japan Seminar, 3 May 1980, University of Florida); "Weekly Report of the Education Division," SCAP records; and "The Statement of the Chief of the Textbook Bureau," Ministry of Education, 1 Aug. 1950, on termination of CI&E censorship, vol. 1 of *Shakaika kyōikushi shiryō* , 31.

Committee on Government Laws (*seirei shimon iinkai*) on 4 May 1951 to study administration, education, anti-monopoly laws, labor relations, and the police system. The committee recommended re-establishing a centrally controlled education system and reinstituting standardized national and certified textbooks in schools. Yoshida's attempt to restore the centralized education system was opposed by reform-minded educators, including Kaigo Tokiomi and Katsuda Shuichi (1908–69), student of Watsuji Tetsuro and author of numerous social studies textbooks.[38]

During the decades that followed the Occupation, successive conservative cabinets introduced a series of laws to re-concentrate power in the Ministry of Education. The School Education Law of May 1953, for instance, made the Ministry, instead of local education committees, responsible for school textbook certification. In 1954 the Ministry further reduced the authority of the education committees. Thus, the Ministry re-established its centralized control over the textbook system and in the following years strengthened its control over textbook content.[39]

In March 1956 the government (the third Hatoyama cabinet) continued to centralize the textbook system within the Ministry by introducing a textbook bill (*kyōkasho hōan*), empowering the Ministry to pass and reject textbooks and deny the right to review. The bill provoked bitter criticisms from university presidents, Parent Teacher Associations, teachers, and textbook writers, who felt that it threatened the foundations of democratic education. The bill was rejected, but the administration was able to tighten its control by increasing the number of examiners and introducing ideological checks on the authors.[40]

To ensure their books were certified, textbook writers were often required by examiners to accommodate suggested changes. During the 1960s and through the early 1990s, liberal writers and citizens challenged the Japanese textbook certification system as unconstitutional. They argued that it violated academic freedom as guaranteed in the 1947 Constitution of Japan.

The most publicized controversy was the Ienaga Textbook Court Cases, consisting of three separate suits brought by Ienaga Saburo (1913–): *Ienaga v. the Japanese Government* (1965); *Ienaga v. the Ministry of*

---

[38]For Ridgway statement, see *Sengo nihon kyōikushi* (Tokyo, 1978), 201–3; J. W. Dower, *Empire and Aftermath: Yoshida Shigeru and the Japanese Experience, 1947–1954* (Cambridge, Mass., 1979), 415–18; idem, "Peace and Democracy in Two Systems: External Policy and Internal Conflict," in *Postwar as History* (Berkeley, Calif., 1993), 3–33; FEC C4-005/3, p. 4, USNA.

[39]Oe Shinobu, "Kyōiku ni okeru gyaku kōsu," *Nihon no rekishi*, vol. 31 of *Sengo kaikaku* (Tokyo, 1976), 349–53; Takahashi, *Kyōkasho kentei*, 77–79; Textbook regulation, 1952.

[40]Vol. 3 of *Shakaika kyōiku shiryō*, 86–87; Ota, *Nihon kyōikushi*, 258; Oteri Tamotsu, "Kyōkasho kentei no soshiki to un'ei," *Monbu jihō* 996 (June 1960): 19–24; Murao Jiro, "Shakaika kyōkasho kentei mondai," *Monbu jihō* 996 (June 1960): 32–40.

Education (1967); and *Ienaga v. the Japanese Government* (1984).[41] As previously mentioned, Ienaga was one of the authors of the first Japanese history text written in the Occupation era under the guidance of the SCAP/CI&E. After the Occupation, Ienaga and other historians who were involved in the SCAP's history textbook project continued to write Japanese history textbooks.

In 1957 and 1962 Ienaga's textbook, *Shin Nihonshi* (*New Japanese History*, 1957 revision) failed to win certification.[42] The original version of the text had been widely used since 1953. It was revised in order to accommodate the new course of study for high schools (*gakushū shidō yōryō*). In 1963 Ienaga submitted a new revision, which was certified on condition that 290 items be rewritten as recommended by the certification board.

According to the opinion of the Ministry issued in August, the problems of the Ienaga text included: 1) it erroneously suggested that the description in *Kojiki* and *Nihon shoki* were meant to legitimize imperial rule; 2) its historical interpretation was based on the point of view of workers, such as peasants in the feudal period and workers in capitalist society, and might mislead the students; 3) it did not balance its criticism of Japan's atrocities in China during World War II by mentioning Russian behavior at the end of the war; 4) it inappropriately criticized the education policy of the Yoshida cabinet in the 1950s; and 5) it presented an overly dark image of modern history and totally lacked patriotism. In 1965 Ienaga filed a suit against the government arguing that his constitutional rights of freedom of thought (Article 19), expression (Article 21), and academic freedom (Article 23), as well as the right of children to an education (Article 26), were infringed upon. In deciding the case on 16 July 1974 the Tokyo District Court upheld the constitutionality of the textbook certification system. The verdict (the Takatsu Decision) stated that at the lower level, in order to maintain standards and equality of opportunity in education, there should be standardized public education including

---

[41]For more information, see Ienaga, *Kyōkasho saiban*; idem, *Kyōkasho saiban jīmen* (1974); Robert N. Bellah, "Ienaga Saburo and the Search for Meaning," in *Modern Japanese Attitudes toward Modernization* (Princeton, N.J., 1965), 269–423; R. P. Dore, "Textbook Censorship in Japan: The Ienaga Case," *Pacific Affairs* 43 (Winter 1970–71): 549; Chongsik Lee, "History and Politics in Japan–Korean Relations: The Textbook Controversy and Beyond," *Journal of Northeast Asian Studies* 2 (Dec. 1983): 69–93; John J. Cogan and Walter Enloe, "The Japanese History Textbook Controversy Revisited," *Social Education* 51 (Oct. 1987): 450–54; and Lawrence W. Beer, "Japan's Constitutional System and Its Judicial Interpretation," in *Law and Society in Contemporary Japan: American Perspectives*, ed. John O. Hanley (Dubuque, Iowa, 1988), 7–35.

[42]Ienaga, *Kyōkasho kentei*, 64–172; Ienaga published the text, *Kentei fugōkaku nihonshi* (*Unauthorized Japanese History Textbook*) (Tokyo, 1974).

textbooks. The first decision was upheld by the Tokyo High Court in March 1986.[43]

The second case involved the 1966 revision of *Shin Nihonshi*. The text was certified on the condition that six problematic portions be withheld. Among them were comments that "the workers" were "the real contributors in history (society)" and that a series of emperors in the mythological era was "fabricated" by the imperial family to "justify its rule over Japan."[44]

In July 1970, Justice Sugimoto at the Tokyo District Court decided that although textbook certification (*kentei*) should not be considered censorship (*ken'etsu*), the Ministry's decision not to certify Ienaga's textbook because of its historical interpretations was a violation of the principle of "prohibition of censorship." The Tokyo High Court upheld this Azegami Decision in December 1975. As Benjamin C. Duke argues, there was a strong possibility in the early 1970s that the judicial branch would limit the power of the Ministry of Education to screen the textbooks. However, in April 1982 the Supreme Court rejected the Azegami Decision and sent the case back to the Tokyo High Court. In June 1989 the court reversed its position and decided in favor of the Ministry.[45] Ienaga declined to pursue this case further.

In 1984 Ienaga filed his third and most recent textbook suit. In 1980 Ienaga's text was certified on the condition that he rewrite his accounts of the Buddhist priest Shinran (1173–1262); the "Boshin war" of January–May 1868; "Japan's invasion of China in the 1930s and 1940s"; and the "Nanking Incident" of December 1937. The first two items involved criticism of the Imperial Government. The examiners argued that Ienaga's description of Shinran's protest against the Imperial Court was not accurate and that it was not clear if the volunteers of *sōmōtai* (grassroots army) during the Boshin war were betrayed and executed by the Imperial Government.

The second two items dealt with Japan–China relations during World War II. While Ienaga chose the term "invasion" (*shinryaku*) to describe Japan's mobilization in China, the government preferred "advance" (*shinshutsu*). In the end, the government decided not to restrict the use of the

---

[43]Ienaga, *Kyōkasho kentei*. See also, Takahashi, *Kyōkasho kentei*, 118–22. For more information, see *Jurisuto* 590 (Sep. 1970); and Nagai Ken'ichi, "Kyōkasho kentei to gakumon no jiyū: Kyōiku o ukeru kenri," in Ashibe, *Kyōkasho saiban*, 110–14.

[44]*Hanrei jihō* 1040 (July 1982): 3.

[45]Benjamin C. Duke, "The Textbook Controversy," *Japan Quarterly* 19 (July–Sep. 1972): 337–52. For more information, see *Hanrei jihō* 800 (Dec. 1976): 19–35, 1040 (Apr. 1982): 3–10, and 1317 (June 1989): 36–77; Special Issue on the textbook case, *Jurisuto* (Sep. 1970); Kaneko Masashi and Sato Tsukasa, eds., *Kyōiku saiban hanreishū* II (Tokyo, 1973), 10–11; and Ashibe, *Kyōkasho saiban*.

term "invasion" because of its embarrassing lesson in 1982. At that time Japan had been the object of international criticism, especially from China and Korea, which claimed that Japan was covering up its war crimes during the second Sino-Japanese war by imposing the term "advance" on history textbook writers. Finally, the government objected to Ienaga's use of the term "the Nanking Atrocity" (*Nankin daigyakusatsu*) instead of "the Nanking Incident" (*Nankin jiken*); a description of "Troop 731" (*731 butai*), a biological warfare unit in Manchuria; and an account of killings in Okinawa by Japanese soldiers at the end of World War II.[46]

In deciding the third case in October 1989, Justice Kato upheld the government's right to exercise textbook certification, judging that it was necessary and appropriate. However, the Justice warned that if the Education Minister misused his power in ignoring academic findings, implanting biased information, and suppressing certain ideologies, certification would be declared unconstitutional. As Lawrence W. Beer states, "For the indefinite future, Asian nations will remain acutely sensitive to how openly and straightforwardly textbooks and officials treat Japan's behavior during the Pacific War." And their criticism has sometimes restrained Japan's textbook policy. In 1986, when Japan's Asian neighbors criticized the certification of the first postwar nationalistic textbook, *Shinsen Nihonshi* (*Newly Compiled Japanese History*), the Ministry ordered an unprecedented postcertification correction of textbook descriptions relating to Japan's annexation of Korea, the second Sino-Japanese War, and the Nanking Incident.[47]

Notwithstanding the occasional challenges to the SCAP's policy, the Occupation reform of history textbooks left an invaluable legacy for Japanese history texts, not only in terms of content and approach but also in terms of the textbook system itself. The SCAP aimed at demilitarization, democratization, and decentralization of the textbook system. In order to demilitarize the texts, it deleted the glorification of war heroes and added criticism of militarism in prewar Japan; to democratize, it removed the national creation myth and introduced scientific approach-

---

[46]Special Issue, *Hanrei jihō* (Feb. 1990); Morikawa *Kyōkasho to saiban*, 23–68; and "Ienaga kyōkasho; daisanji sosyō; 'sensō kijutsu' kentei ihōsei nashi," *Yomiuri shimbun*, 4 Oct. 1989.

[47]Tokinoya Shigeru, *Ienaga kyōkasho saiban to nankin jiken* (Tokyo, 1989), 156–57, 189. Also see *Hanrei taimuzu* 709 (1989): 63–140, 124–28, 134–35; and Yamauchi Toshihiro, "Kyōkasho saiban ni okeru tekiyō ikenron," in Ashibe, *Kyōkasho saiban*, 181–92; Lawrence W. Beer, "Freedom of Expression: The Continuing Revolution," *Law and Contemporary Problems* 53 (Spring 1990): 66; "Mamorukaigi no rekishi kyōkasho: Gōkaku-go ni irei no shūsei," *Asahi shimbun*, 18 June 1986; "Kyōkasho mondai to chūgoku no hitotachi," *Asahi shimbun*, 5 Nov. 1986; "Kōkyō shimpen nihonshi," *Nihon keizai shimbun*, 21 July 1986.

es and critical thinking; and to decentralize, it replaced the national text-book system with a textbook certification system.

Most textbook writers have accepted the SCAP's policy to separate history from mythology. Their descriptions of the early books, *Kojiki* and *Nihon shoki*, are brief. Although there were some attempts by the government in the late 1980s to reintroduce myth into textbooks, the government instructed writers to include archaeological findings as well as myths and legends in courses of study for social studies (1989) for elementary and junior high schools.

The SCAP's policy to denounce Japan's prewar militarism, especially its aggression in Asia during World War II, remains highly controversial in Japan. In the 1980s under stiff protest from the former colonies and other neighboring nations in Asia, the Japanese government decided to allow the high school textbook writers to write about the Nanking Atrocity with some restrictions. In fact, none of the 1989 courses of study—elementary, junior high, and high school—heavily criticized militarism in prewar Japan, but instead all highlighted the democratization process following the war. After stating that "one of the biggest massacres of World War II, the Rape of Nanking, was a fabrication," a justice minister was forced to resign in spring 1994, showing the sensitive nature of the issue.[48]

Although Occupation reforms are highly visible in post-Occupation history textbooks, the extent of change depends on each author's historical perspective, the content of the course of study, and the decisions of the textbook examiners. A range of views regarding Japan's prewar militarism is especially visible. On the one hand, a group of historians sympathetic to Ienaga, including the former Japan Teacher's Union (*Nikkyōso*) and the Citizens' Conference for Textbook Certification Cases (*Kyōkasho kentei soshō o shiensuru shimin no kai*), believes that a "rigorous re-evaluation of the war is needed," deals with issues such as Japan's atrocity in Asia, and criticizes Japan's aggressions during World War II. On the other hand, another group including Sakamoto Taro (1901–87), a protégé of Kuroita Katsumi, in line with the Ministry of Education, says that "war is not desirable but there was a war fought for national survival," emphasizes the need to include mythology to promote patriotism, and criticizes textbooks attacking Japan's behavior in the war.[49]

---

[48]*Shin gakushū shidōyōryō o norikoeru* (Tokyo, 1989), 134, 148–50, 162, 163; *New York Times*, 8 May 1994.

[49]Ienaga Saburo, *The Pacific War: World War II and the Japanese, 1931–1945* (New York, 1978), preface; Takahashi, *Kyōkasho kentei* (Tokyo, 1988), 202.

The constitutionality of the textbook certification system will probably remain the focus of the dispute between pro-certification and anti-certification groups in modern Japan. While the former continues to advocate academic freedom and uncensored textbooks, the latter is determined to control the textbooks through the Ministry of Education and to restore a nationalistic tone to the contents. The opponents of certification stress the right of students to receive education based on the principle of academic freedom, including access to uncensored textbooks, whereas the government emphasizes its right to provide standardized education, including the use of nationally certified textbooks.[50]

There are numerous conflicting arguments among Japan scholars concerning textbook and other SCAP policies. But as several historians, including Takemae Eiji and Suzuki Eiichi, recognize, regardless of its shortcomings, the Occupation policy laid the foundations for wide-ranging and basic institutional reforms.[51] The SCAP's history textbook reform has changed ideas about textbook writing fundamentally and improved the content significantly. The first history textbook in Occupied Japan compiled by Japanese historians, including Ienaga, has become the prototype for history texts in postwar Japan. However, as a consequence of the "containment" policy adopted by the United States, the initial goal of the SCAP to establish the textbook system of "open competition" was compromised. The SCAP's establishment of the textbook certification system and temporary granting of certification authority to the Ministry in order to protect education from Communism left a legacy of censorship and an entering wedge for the government to regain control over school textbooks in post-Occupation Japan. As a result, the textbook issue has become highly politicized and has been caught up in the ongoing polarized debate between pro- and anti-certification groups involving teachers, historians, textbook writers, government officers, and other citizens. The Ienaga textbook cases, which have been contested for about thirty years, symbolize the complexity of the issue.

---

[50]Some of the leading organizations opposing censorship are Kyōkasho kentei soshō o shiensuru zenkoku renrakukai, Kyōkasho kentei soshō o shiensuru rekishigaku kankeisha no kai, Kyōkasho kentei soshō o shiensuru shimin no kai, and Shuppan rōren kyōkasho taisaku iinkai. Tokinoya, *Kyōkasho saiban*; Uesugi Chitoshi, *Sōkatsu: Kyōkasho mondai to kyōiku saiban* (Tokyo, 1990); Sugihara Yasuo, "Kyōkasho saiban to kokka no kyōikuken," in Ashibe, *Kyōkasho saiban*, 22–27.

[51]Takemae Eiji, *GHQ* (Tokyo, 1983), 201–11.

Modern Asian Studies, III, 1 (1969), pp. 1–17

Ienaga Saburo and the First Postwar Japanese History Textbook

By JOHN CAIGER

THE Allied victory in 1945 ensured that a greater degree of freedom was guaranteed to individual Japanese by law. Since the end of the Occupation Japanese intellectuals, alert to any moves that they considered an infringement of the postwar constitution, have acted as watchdogs for the whole community. Ienaga Saburo, historian and political ideologist, is one such intellectual.[1]

The suit that Ienaga brought against the Japanese government in the mid 1960s, charging violation of the postwar constitution, bids fair to become the most celebrated individual protest by an intellectual. He has sued the state for 1 million yen, claiming that approval by the Ministry of Education before a textbook is officially recognized constitutes censorship, and is therefore unconstitutional under the terms of Article 21 that guarantees freedom of speech and declares that no censorship shall be maintained.[2] The suit arises out of Ienaga's own experience in the writing of history for schools.

Ienaga has never been alone in defending what he has regarded as the freedom of the historian to write history for school-children on his own terms. But among those active opponents of close state control and conservative views Ienaga has the distinction of having helped to formulate the official policy on the teaching of history just after the end of the Second World War. Ienaga wrote part of the first postwar history textbook published by the Ministry of Education.

It is likely, as Ienaga's action against the state becomes more widely known, that his reputation as a political ideologist and defender of the postwar settlement will be enhanced.[3] This article draws attention to

[1] Robert N. Bellah, 'Ienaga Saburo and the Search for Meaning in Modern Japan' in *Changing Japanese Attitudes Toward Modernization*, ed. Marius B. Jansen, Princeton, 1965, pp. 369–423 is invaluable for the rounded picture of Ienaga's intellectual interests that is given. Bellah also refers to Ienaga's activities as a political ideologist.

[2] See *The Japan Times* of 7 November 1967 under the heading 'State Making Inroads into Education: Nambara'; for a lengthy exposition of his own views see Ienaga Saburo, *Kyōkasho Kentei* (Textbook Approval), Nihon Hyoronsha, 1965, 284 pages.

[3] Serious interest in the trial can be gauged by the promised appearance of three volumes entitled *Ienaga—Kyōkasho Saiban* (The Ienaga Textbook Trial). The first

Ienaga as one of the small group of historians that shaped a totally different official policy on the teaching of Japanese history in 1946. To assess the importance of the suit brought by Ienaga in the 1960s in terms of the values at stake it will need to be measured against the change in 1946. We can best describe this change by following the part played by the Japanese government, the occupation forces and Japanese historians, and especially by Ienaga himself in the writing of the first postwar Japanese history textbook.

I. Cut First and Create Later

No Japanese historian seems to have played an identifiable part in making the formal break with wartime policy on history teaching in 1945. On the Japanese side, officials in the Ministry of Education were all important—at least for a time.

For two months after the surrender on 2 September 1945, the initiative in banning materials unsuitable in the postwar situation lay with the Ministry of Education. Its officials took the first steps to bring teaching materials into line with the new situation. On 28 August 1945, two days before General MacArthur arrived in Japan, the Ministry of Education advised prefectural governors and school heads that:

> Concerning textbooks and teaching materials, in the light of the objectives of the Imperial Rescript proclaimed on 14 August, due care will be exercised in their use and appropriate measures taken to omit parts of lessons.[4]

Again, on 20 September 1945, a full month before the Supreme Commander for the Allied Powers (S.C.A.P.) and subordinate officers began to direct educational policy, Ministry officials showed how they had adjusted themselves to the changed situation by issuing detailed orders which did not ban the use of wartime textbooks but ordered their amendment along certain lines:

> Although it will be permitted until further notice to continue to use existing textbooks in Middle Schools, Youth Schools and National

volume, containing a collection of all documents tendered by both the prosecution and defence up to the start of the questioning of witnesses, was published in late 1967. The publisher is *Kyōkasho Kentei Soshō o Shien suru Zenkoku Renraku Kai* (National Liaison Association to Aid the Textbook Authorization Case).

[4] Kindai Nihon Kyoiku Seido Shiryo Hensan Kai (Editorial Committee for Materials on the Modern Japanese Educational System), *Kindai Nihon Kyōiku Seido Shiryō* (Materials on the Modern Japanese Educational System), Kodansha, 1957, XVIII, p. 488.

Schools, it is required that all teaching materials that are inappropriate in the light of the intentions of the Imperial Rescript proclaiming the end of the war be struck out in whole or in part or be handled with the utmost care, in accordance with what follows:

(1) The following are materials which ought to be used with care, amended or eliminated: (a) Materials that emphasise national defence and armaments; (b) materials fostering the fighting spirit; (c) materials that may be harmful to international goodwill; (d) materials that have become obsolete through being entirely removed from present postwar conditions and the everyday life of the students; and (e) other materials that are not appropriate in the light of the Imperial Rescript.

(2) In cases where it is necessary to make up for material omitted, select and supplement from the following subjects, keeping in mind place and circumstances: materials concerning the maintenance of the *kokutai* (national entity) and the establishment of high moral education; materials suitable for the education of the people of a civilized country; materials concerning increased agricultural production; materials fostering the scientific spirit and its practical application; materials on physical education and hygiene; materials on international peace.[5]

Following this order teachers and students all over the country deleted objectionable passages in the wartime textbooks with ink and scissors as they saw fit.

After the independent Japanese moves of August and September 1945, the initiative was taken by Americans. From late October, Occupation control over textbooks was gradually asserted, culminating in the total ban on the use of wartime textbooks for Japanese History, amongst other subjects, on the last day of 1945.

At first the United States Initial Post-Surrender Policy for Japan was interpreted as endorsing the conduct of business through informal meetings between the Minister of Education and an American officer from what later became the Education Division of the Civil Information and Education Section. The Minister during the postwar months of 1945, Maeda Tamon, has recalled how he was visited by a Mr H. on 15 September and was told that G.H.Q. was satisfied with his policy statements and 'did not intend to issue directives pertaining to education'. A month later Mr H. called again, this time in a state of high excitement, and explained that 'Washington now says that such a casual arrangement will never do'.[6] On 22 October, shortly after this meeting, the first directive on education entitled 'Administration of the Educational System of Japan' was issued to the Japanese govern-

[5] *Kindai Nihon Kyōiku*, XXV, p. 279.
[6] Maeda Tamon, 'The Direction of Postwar Education in Japan', in *Japan Quarterly* 3, October–December 1956, p. 415.

ment by General Headquarters, Supreme Commander for the Allied Powers.

As far as the course in History was concerned, the first American directive did no more than approve the negative aspects of the Japanese order of 20 September already quoted. The Americans made no positive suggestions as to what should be taught:

> Existing curricula, textbooks, teaching manuals, and instructional materials, the use of which is temporarily permitted on an emergency basis, will be examined as rapidly as possible and those portions designed to promote a militaristic or ultranationalistic ideology will be eliminated.[7]

As far as official American documents go, the matter stood thus until 15 December when it became apparent that Shinto was the critical factor in what Americans regarded as wartime propaganda. On that day the occupation forces issued the important directive 'Abolition of Governmental Sponsorship, Support, Perpetuation, Control, and Dissemination of State Shinto (Kokka Shinto, Jinja Shinto)' which forbade the future use of teachers' manuals and textbooks containing Shinto doctrine in any school supported by public funds.[8]

Then, on 31 December, the occupation forces banned the teaching of Japanese History along with *Shūshin* (Morals) and Geography:

> in accordance with the basic directive AG 000.3 (15 Dec. 45) CIE proclaiming the abolition of government sponsorship and support of State Shinto and Doctrine; and inasmuch as the Japanese Government has used education to inculcate militaristic and ultranationalistic ideologies which have been inextricably interwoven in certain textbooks imposed upon students.[9]

During the months of October, November and December only one attempt had been made by the Ministry of Education to take the initiative. On 28 November an official Japanese request was made for permission to discontinue using textbooks for Morals, Japanese History and Geography. It was refused.

In the words of H. J. Wunderlich who had taken over the job of overseeing textbook and curriculum problems just the day before, Japanese officials knew from conferences with their American counterparts that 'a formal directive was forthcoming and had written one of

---

[7] Education Division, Civil Information and Education Section, Supreme Commander for the Allied Powers, General Headquarters, *Education in the New Japan*, Tokyo, 1948, II, p. 27.

[8] *Ibid.*, p. 33. [9] *Ibid.*, p. 36.

their own'.[10] It appeared to Wunderlich that the Japanese request was based partly on the wish to please S.C.A.P. and partly to maintain their own prestige.

Wunderlich reports that the American decision to turn down the Japanese request was taken on the grounds that a study of textbook content initiated on 30 September had still not been completed.[11] During November a team of nisei, Eurasians and Japanese nationals had been assembled to check educational materials. Takahashi Noboru, a history graduate of Columbia and a Japanese national, had been employed to make a survey of history textbooks.

Any difficulties encountered in completing the report, and they were formidable as far as identifying Shintoism was concerned, were finally resolved by General Dyke, the head of the Civil Information and Education Section. On 5 December he laid down a policy of 'cut first and create later'.[12] Within two days a directive was drawn up banning the use of Morals, Japanese History and Geography textbooks in schools. Discussion arose as to whether the directive should be shown to the Minister of Education for his approval. When General Dyke heard that the head of the Education Division proposed that this should be done, he relieved him of his duties. The Ministry of Education was henceforth to be directed, not consulted.

Given this policy of firm American control, the best use was made of timing the announcement to show that the old order was at an end. The directive banning the use of the textbooks was made on the last day of the year of defeat. It is tempting to imagine that the Supreme Commander's subordinates deferred to his sense of occasion and histrionic flair by delaying the announcement until the full solemnity of the event could be highlighted.

II. The Writing of the First Postwar History Textbook

The Americans had chosen to do the 'cutting': they made no simultaneous attempt to 'create' a new history by dictating to the Japanese government what should, as distinct from what should *not*, be taught to children in history lessons.

[10] Herbert John Wunderlich, *The Japanese Textbook Problem and Solution, 1945–1946* (dissertation, Stanford, submitted July 1952), p. 236. My thanks are due to Dr. Wunderlich for permission to use his unpublished work.

[11] Wunderlich, p. 247. For a more emotional account of these events by the man who was replaced by Wunderlich, see Robert King Hall, *Education for a New Japan*, New Haven, 1949, pp. 475–6. [12] Wunderlich, p. 248.

The initiative in formulating a philosophy for a new history course was left to the Japanese themselves. American policy deliberately followed the Potsdam Declaration and the Initial Post-Surrender Policy, which presumed the existence of democratic tendencies in Japan and committed the Occupation to working through the Japanese government. Initially, the task of reviving and strengthening 'democratic tendencies' in textbooks was left to the Textbook Bureau of the Ministry, the very body that had compiled the prewar textbooks. The decision to use the existing textbook organisation within the Ministry prompted Wunderlich, who was still head of the Textbook and Curriculum Unit, to wonder whether 'by inverting the hour-glass, perhaps the concepts and principles of democracy could be poured into the Japanese mind as easily as the concepts of totalitarianism, militarism and ultranationalism'.[13] Apparently the Occupation had second thoughts about allowing the Ministry to draw up new materials, but not before the draft of a new history textbook had been started by a historian working in the Ministry of Education.[14]

Toyoda Takeshi first took up work in the Textbook Bureau in November 1945. In late December the Ministry formed a committee of scholars with whom Toyoda consulted as he wrote the draft. Four professors at Tokyo Imperial University took an interest in the work: Sakamoto Taro, Wada Kiyoshi, Imai Toshiki and Tsuchiya Takao. It was a sign of the times that Toyoda travelled all the way to Hiraizumi where Tsuda Sokichi had gone during the later stages of the war and talked with the man whose books had been banned during the war. The philosopher Watsuji Tetsuro also gave him the benefit of his positive opinions and put them firmly, for sixteen years later Toyoda could recall being scolded by him. Backed by independent scholarly opinion Toyoda must have felt confident when he received *nijūmaru* (full marks) from a responsible occupation officer to whom he showed the first section of the draft. Then, quite unexpectedly, Toyoda was instructed to stop working on the draft.

It has not proved possible to bring home responsibility for the decision to stop work on the Ministry's textbook to any person or to state the precise reason for it. The most reasonable explanation seems to be that either the United States Education Mission to Japan, which

[13] Wunderlich, p. 257.

[14] The following account is based on Toyoda Takeshi's statements during a symposium entitled 'Rekishi Kyokasho to Sono Jidai' (History Textbooks and Their Times) in Rekishi Kyoiku Kenkyujo (Institute for Research into History Teaching) ed. *Kikan Rekishi Kyōiku Kenkyū* (Quarterly for Research into History Teaching), April 1964, XIX, pp. 11–12.

submitted its report on 30 March, or its advisers in the Civil Information and Education Section, were responsible for the decision on grounds stated in the Report, namely that 'the responsibility for the compilation of history and geography texts should not rest within the Ministry of Education'.[15]

If the decision to stop work on the draft can be attributed to the United States Education Mission, the decision to start work on a new textbook certainly cannot. The Mission's report envisaged the rewriting of textbooks not just by one group but by many in open competition on the textbook market. They postulated that this would not happen before years of scholarly work established 'authentic and objective sources for the rewriting of Japanese history', and suggested seven interim measures.[16] Not one was put into effect. Instead, the Civil Information and Education Section decided to oversee the work of Japanese scholars who would produce the first postwar textbook in Japanese History which was at the same time to be the last of a series of National Texts begun in 1903 by the Ministry of Education.

Ienaga Saburo was one of four historians called to the Ministry of Education on 17 May 1946, with Morisue Yoshiaki, Okada Akio and Okubo Toshiaki. There they received instructions from an American called Trainor who laid down three conditions for the new book:

1. It will not be propagandistic.
2. It will not advocate militarism, ultranationalism and Shinto doctrine. It will not be based on the view of history expressed in *Kokutai no Hongi*.
3. The deeds of the emperors are not the whole of history. One supposes that matters connected with economics, inventions, learning and the arts, and other things which arose among the people must have flourished. However, if certain emperors in fact left important works behind them, there is nothing to prevent them from being included. Emperors should not be written about simply because they were emperors.[17]

Ienaga reports that he and his fellow scholars submitted their drafts at a series of weekly meetings held at Tokyo Imperial University. There, both Japanese and American officials amended the draft to suit their ideas about child psychology and educational practice. The problem of communication at these meetings was heightened by the

[15] *Report of the United States Education Mission to Japan, submitted to the Supreme Commander for the Allied Powers, Tokyo, 30 March 1946*, Washington, 1946, p. 16.

[16] *Report of the United States Education Mission to Japan*, pp. 15–16.

[17] Translated from Ienaga Saburo's notes quoted in Karasawa Tomitaro, *Kyōkasho no Rekishi* (A History of Textbooks), Sōbunsha, 1960, p. 619. The account that follows can be found on pp. 618–28.

fact that the American representative knew no Japanese. The Americans were assisted by a Japanese national whom Ienaga refers to simply as 'T', probably Takahashi Noboru who was mentioned in a similar context by Wunderlich. 'T' read the drafts in Japanese and made some changes, for example, in the use of honorifics. Ienaga and the other writers then corrected the drafts in the light of what had been said and submitted them to the Ministry of Education for translation into English. The American representative read the full draft in English and explained his objections at further meetings through 'T', who translated for him. There was ample opportunity for mutual recrimination about the lack of speed and the inconvenience of this process.

Despite these difficulties the new textbook appeared in October 1946, just five months after the project was started. It was published under the title *Kuni no Ayumi* (The Progress of the Country), a name chosen, strangely enough, by Maruyama Kunio who had been an official of the Textbook Bureau since 1929. Like prewar textbooks it was published in the name of the Ministry of Education not in the names of the four contributing authors, but for the first time in the history of National Textbooks the names of the authors involved became known.

III. Ienaga's Contribution to Kuni no Ayumi

Ienaga was assigned what was probably the most difficult part of the text to write, the opening section from ancient times to the end of the Heian period. To compound his difficulties, Ienaga found that he had to produce a manuscript for the printers within six weeks. His lack of experience in elementary education also made the task more difficult since he distrusted his judgment on questions of child development and the vocabulary, style and level of ideas suitable for children of eleven and twelve. Due to pressure of time and an understandable lack of confidence, Ienaga used the banned wartime textbook and the Ministry's own draft on which work had been stopped by the Occupation.

In view of suspicions about possible American dictation to the writers of the textbook, it is noteworthy that the first section of the Ministry of Education's 'Provisional Draft' written by Toyoda without close American supervision and Ienaga's part of the new textbook are remarkably similar. Generally speaking the draft is more detailed and is not written in so terse a style as the textbook, but in many places the wording is identical. As he wrote, Ienaga departed more and more

46

from the pattern of organization which Toyoda had followed in the draft, but very nearly the same material appears under slightly differently worded headings arranged in different order.

It is noteworthy that Ienaga laid greater emphasis on the life of the people; he mentions the existence and works of the Imperial line and of the aristocracy less frequently and employs fewer honorific terms than the draft. This change can be traced back to Trainor's instruction not to write about emperors simply because they existed.

Ienaga also rejected Toyoda's story-book approach to history. He omitted the well-known legends and stories that Toyoda had related about the Emperor Jimmu's conquest of the East and the stories of the Emperor Nintoku's benevolence and Sugawara no Michizane's exile in Dazaifu. In writing about the Emperor Jimmu, Toyoda had taken great care to distinguish between archaeological evidence and mythology, making it plain that the story of Jimmu as he gave it was legendary. Ienaga included an outline of Jimmu's activities using his more obscure name Kamuyamato Iwarehiko no Sumeramikoto, thereby avoiding the common 'godly' associations of the name Jimmu, stating that he unified the country after establishing his palace at Kashihara. However, Ienaga gives the impression that Jimmu by whatever name actually lived. Since any mention of mythological stories about emperors, even if they were so labelled, could be construed as putting emphasis on emperors for their own sake, it can be suggested that Ienaga altered the Provisional Draft in this respect also in order to please the Occupation.

It is possible that Ienaga made both these changes voluntarily, without American pressure, since he does not mention them specifically among the objections made by Trainor. As listed by Ienaga they were four in number:

1. Sentences explaining the tradition of the Imperial succession had to be omitted.
2. No account of matters pertaining to Shinto was permitted, with the result that it appeared that Japan's unique folk religion had never existed at all.
3. The Occupation was very sensitive about religions, not just Shinto, but Buddhism and Christianity as well, not permitting anything on the grounds that such explanation was outside the sphere of lessons in history. Consequently it became impossible to explain culture concretely in terms of religion.
4. Ienaga found that he was unable to emancipate himself from the old emotional expressions implying judgment. Subjective words had to be made more objective, impartial and scientific.

Of these objections, the third alone was not well covered by the
initial instructions that he had received, so that Ienaga had particularly good grounds for feeling that Americans had limited his freedom
to write. Moreover, this objection would probably have affected
Ienaga's approach to his work more seriously than it would that of
most other historians, considering the years of research he had spent
on the history of Buddhist thought.[18]

Yet, despite the three injunctions and the four objections, Ienaga
maintained in his notes of that time and has stated more recently that
'co-operation with the Occupation's policy for reforming the teaching
of history was an unexpected opportunity to put previously held beliefs
into practice'.[19]

The importance in ideological terms of Ienaga's work lay not simply
in his private satisfaction but in official adoption of his point of view
by the Ministry of Education bringing about a complete change in
the teaching of Japanese history.

The Ministry not only published *Kuni no Ayumi* in its own name but
endorsed the values of Ienaga and his fellow writers in a short guide
to the new aims of history teaching, entitled *Kokushi Jugyō Shidō Yōkō
ni tsuite* (Concerning Guiding Principles for Instruction in National
History).[20]

The Guiding Principles opened with a general statement that
differed in almost every way from the prewar aims of history teaching.[21]

Japanese History was no longer part of a larger group of subjects
taking a great deal of its character from the *Shūshin* (Morals) course.
When it laid down aims for the first time in 1881 the Ministry informed
teachers that, 'Above all it is important to inculcate patriotism and
a spirit of reverence for the Emperor'.[22] Even in September 1945 the
Ministry urged teachers to include materials concerning the main-

[18] See Bellah's article referred to in Footnote 1.

[19] Ienaga Saburo, 'Sengo no Rekishi Kyoiku' (Postwar History Teaching) in
Iwanami Kōza Nihon Rekishi (Iwanami Series on Japanese History), Iwanami, 1963,
Vol. XXII, Bekkan 1, p. 319.

[20] The full text of *Kuni no Ayumi* is reprinted in *Nihon Kyōkasho Taikei—Kindai Hen*
(Outline of Japanese Textbooks—The Modern Period) ed. by Kaigo Tokiomi and
Naka Arata, Kodansha, 1962, XX, pp. 386–464. The full text of the 'Guiding
Principles' can be found in *Kindai Nihon Kyōiku*, XXIII, pp. 10–16.

[21] For a more detailed exposition in English of prewar aims, see my forthcoming
article in *Monumenta Nipponica*, Special Commemorative Issue on the Meiji Restoration, 'The Aims and Content of School Courses in Japanese History, 1872–1945'.
For an illustration of prewar values see Appendix.

[22] Mombusho (Ministry of Education), *Meiji Ikō Kyōiku Seido Hattatsu Shi* (A
History of the Development of the Educational System since Meiji Times), Ryu-
ginsha, 1938, II, pp. 254–55.

tenance of the *kokutai* (national entity) and high moral education, as we have already seen. Now teachers were to encourage their students to study history 'with a scientific attitude of pursuing truth to the utmost, from an impartial point of view'.[23] The qualities of rational understanding and critical judgment, now thought to be so desirable, stood in sharp contrast to emotional commitment to the Imperial line and to the country itself which the prewar course had tried so hard to foster.

The Ministry instructed teachers 'not to stress the history of struggles for political power or trace the varied fortunes of war and peace but to throw light on the actual development of national life from the viewpoint of society, the economy and culture'.[24] Sovereigns and subjects were to give way to men who made contributions to the development of national life.

As far as Japan's historical relations with the rest of the world were concerned, the Ministry of Education stressed economic and cultural rather than political and military considerations. Teachers were expected to cite historical facts concerning 'international friendship, co-existence and co-prosperity, and exchange of culture'[25] with the aim of fostering world peace and the development of the culture of mankind. They were no longer expected to stress the uniqueness of the country; indeed, they were instructed to remove all traces of militarism, ultranationalism and Shintoism which had distinguished the teaching of history during the war in particular.[26] As an aid to the understanding of Japanese history from the viewpoint of world history the Ministry commended the use of the western calendar.[27]

In relation to ancient history the Ministry was particularly careful. Teachers were expected to maintain a calmly critical attitude on controversial matters and to keep in mind the results of scholarly research. The findings of archaeologists and sociologists, and evidence from Chinese records were to provide facts, now regarded as the basis of history teaching. Myths and legends, drawn from the ancient Japanese histories the *Kojiki* and the *Nihon Shoki*, were excluded so that they would not be confused with historical fact. On the question of the origin of the Japanese people, where the foundation of fact was thought to be inadequate, teachers were instructed to refrain from coming to definite conclusions. On the other hand, they were urged not to use too much archaeological detail when teaching about the early impact of foreign civilization. The Ministry expressed a new interest in the

---

[23] *Kindai Nihon Kyōiku*, XXIII, p. 10. [24] *Ibid.*, p. 11.
[25] *Ibid.*, p. 11.   [26] *Ibid.*, p. 10.   [27] *Ibid.*, p. 12.

process of social change in singling out for special mention the social effects of the introduction of rice-farming. Lastly it urged teachers to turn their attention away from political events in the period of Fujiwara dominance toward the cultural and social consequences of such rule.[28]

The Ministry in its Guiding Principles for teachers was making explicit the values already implicit in the textbook compiled by Ienaga and his fellow historians which had been published in the previous month.

In the opening paragraphs of *Kuni no Ayumi*, Ienaga set the tone of the book with a rational account of the beginnings of civilization in Japan based on material evidence:

> In the sea to the east of the Asiatic continent there are islands which stretch from north to south in a long thin line. These are the islands of Japan where we live. The heat and cold are not extreme; rain falls in good measure; the trees and grasses grow thick, and the scenery in each of the four seasons has a different appearance.
>
> It was in very ancient times that our ancestors settled down in this country. We do not know just when it was, but without a doubt it was at least several thousand years ago. All over the world, in times when culture was not developed, man still did not know how to use metal. He made tools of stone and used them. This period is known as the Stone Age. Occasionally when we are walking on the warm, southern side of hills we see shells scattered about, gleaming white in the fields. These are salt-water and fresh-water clams which the people of those days collected, ate and then piled up. We call these shell mounds. From shell mounds, besides shells, the bones of fish and tools ordinarily used by the people of those days are dug out. From these finds we can tell how the people of ancient times lived.[29]

Neither the Sun Goddess nor her Heavenly Grandson appeared in the first chapter of *Kuni no Ayumi*. Mythology had no place between the same covers as objective history.

Ienaga transformed the Emperor Nintoku, who was traditionally held up as a paragon of benevolence and personal economy, into the occupant of one of the largest burial mounds in the country. This is an instance, and one of many, of the general shift away from interest in virtuous or wicked behaviour towards knowledge of developments in material culture.

> When the society evolved further they made a practice of building fine tombs, piling earth up high. These are now known as *kofun*. They are

[28] *Kindai Nihon Kyōiku*, XXIII, p. 11.
[29] *Nihon Kyōkasho Taikei*, XX, p. 388. For a striking contrast see Appendix.

generally round, but there are also key-hole shaped ones such as are not seen on the continent. Among them, those of the Emperor Ojin and of the Emperor Nintoku are exceptionally large. In these tombs *haniwa* (clay figures) representing houses, people and animals have been discovered, and mirrors, jewels, swords, armour, helmets, etc., have been unearthed. When we see these articles we can well understand the way of life of the people of those days.[30]

These quotations incidentally reveal one of the characteristics of the range of facts that Ienaga used in the new history. He referred twice, in the opening passage of *Kuni no Ayumi* and in the last section on burial mounds, to 'the way of life of the people'. These are early indications that the first postwar textbook ignored the bond between emperor and subject and attempted to direct the attention of the young to the activities of ordinary people in society.

On the broader 'international' scene, the uniqueness of the national entity, so closely identified with ultranationalism and Shinto was no longer stressed. Instead Ienaga placed a new emphasis on cultural and economic contact with foreign peoples which overshadowed political and military relations. This new emphasis further extended to an interest in the social consequences of such contact, including, most significantly, the emergence of the Imperial line itself.

Changes in the Way of Living
. . . ways of ploughing fields, planting rice and making tools from metal were introduced from across the sea. At the time when our ancestors were still using stone tools, in neighbouring China they were using bronze tools made from mixing copper and lead, and finally they came to use iron tools. These were introduced into Japan and we too began to use tools of metal. Bronze swords and halberds were made and also iron tools. In pottery, also, new things came to be made.

The Beginning of Agriculture
The people's way of living took a step forward after agriculture began. When the method of planting rice in paddy fields spread, people were compelled to live together in a fixed place in order to cultivate the fields year after year. Thus, here and there, villages were built where people lived together. The people of the village combined their efforts and worked hard at planting time and harvest. They also pooled their efforts in digging ponds and ditches and channelling water, opening up virgin land and making paddy fields.

Along with the progress of society, outstanding people began to emerge who united a large number of villages and gave orders. This consolidation occurred everywhere. Powerful men appeared, particularly in North Kyushu and in the Yamato region, which had early been civilised, and

[30] *Nihon Kyōkasho Taikei*, XX, p. 390.

among them emerged men who had been to the continent and introduced Chinese culture. The Yamato court was the one which united Japan into one country.[31]

Within the first five pages of *Kuni no Ayumi* Japan's contact with Korea was dealt with, and in the same factual style. The Empress Jingu of legendary fame did not appear in this account. Rather, the textbook related how writing was introduced, along with Confucianism and Buddhism, and how immigrants brought new techniques like metal working, sewing, weaving and silk-worm raising from their continental homelands. The textbook went on to say:

> The court welcomed these people kindly and conferred important duties and high rank on able people, encouraging ability to flourish greatly. In this way, since they introduced a variety of new articles of culture, their way of living advanced from day to day and peoples' minds were gradually improved.[32]

Japan's cultural horizons were shown to have widened further as technological, artistic and religious ideas were brought from across the sea. It was not only China and Korea with whom Japan was in contact but India to the south, Bokkai in the Manchurian area to the north, and Persia and Arabia to the west. It is a significant example of the new open-world view that the Chinese, not Japanese, Buddhist priest Ganjin was used to illustrate the difficulties surmounted by the bearers of culture.

Ienaga did not ignore politics in writing *Kuni no Ayumi*, but political activities involving the Imperial line ceased to be of major interest. The loyalist heroes of the prewar books were mentioned but lost their dramatic appeal, as the treatment of Sugawara no Michizane shows. Ienaga made no mention of the imperial cause that Michizane was supposed to have upheld nor the traditional honour paid to him as a righteous and loyal man. In the account of Japanese history given in *Kuni no Ayumi*, flat, factual and devoid of heroics, the really powerful men are at the centre of interest, not virtuous 'failures' like Michizane.

Ienaga, when he had completed the history of the Heian period, had written only the first part of *Kuni no Ayumi*. Yet his contribution defined the approach followed throughout the rest of the book and later made explicit in the Guiding Principles published for teachers. Ienaga presented an 'open-world' view of Japan as part of the wider world; he emphasised change in telling the story of Japan's past; he made far greater use than prewar textbook writers in the Ministry of Education of cultural, economic and social aspects of the life of the

---

[31] *Nihon Kyōkasho Taikei*, XX, pp. 388–9.   [32] *Ibid.*, p. 391.

people; and, above all, he showed by force of example how rationality and critical judgment could be brought to bear on the study of Japanese history.

Ienaga broke with the values embodied in the official history textbooks of prewar days. He rejected the 'closed-world' view of Japanese history that emphasised the country's uniqueness; he no longer regarded it as the purpose of the textbook writer to stress enduring principles of correct behaviour; he moved away from an almost exclusive concern with political and politico-religious matters, with war and peace; and, most importantly, he turned away from an emotional and moral approach to his subject.

The great change in values that Ienaga helped to bring about in 1946 is the background against which we need to view Ienaga's action in the 1960s. His action can be interpreted as an expression of doubt about the future security and stability of the values that the Ministry of Education had espoused and continued to uphold well after the end of the Occupation.[33] Do fears for these values stem from the extraordinary circumstances in which they were adopted?

A foreign power had ordered the demolition of such pillars of prewar ideology as remained standing in 1945, including the teaching of Japanese history from wartime textbooks. The new values written into the new official textbook were adopted under strict American supervision, though not by the express direction of the occupation authorities. Yet the evidence shows that postwar values sprang not from American but Japanese sources.

In judging how securely these values were rooted in Japan we have only one explicit statement to depend on. We have Ienaga's claim that 'Co-operation with the Occupation's policy for reforming the teaching of history was an unexpected opportunity to put previously held beliefs into practice'. But we need not depend on the integrity of one man. Ienaga based his work largely on the draft of a textbook compiled without strict American surveillance by Toyoda Takeshi in consultation with scholars of strongly independent views. Moreover the approach followed in the balance of *Kuni no Ayumi* not written by Ienaga confirms the idea that the "previously held beliefs" spoken of by Ienaga were shared by other historians of repute, who were able to draw this new set of values out of their own experience. The Occupation created political conditions in which these men could formulate a new official outlook.

[33] See J. Caiger, 'A "Reverse Course" in the Teaching of History in Postwar Japan?' in *Journal of the Oriental Society of Australia*, 5, Nos. 1 and 2, 1967, pp. 4–16.

Ienaga's action against the government in the 1960s has dramatized the fear that the Ministry of Education may not continue to hold to the values that it endorsed in 1946.

APPENDIX

The opening chapter of the National Textbook *Jinjō Shōgaku Nihon Rekishi* (Japanese History for Ordinary Elementary Schools) used between 1911 and 1920 serves as an illustration of the values implicit in the prewar course in Japanese history. The contrast with postwar values is striking:

> Amaterasu Omikami* is the distant ancestor of the present Emperor. Her power and virtue in their height and vast scale are like the brilliance of the sun. The Kotai Shrine of Ise is the place where Omikami is worshipped.
>
> The Great Japanese Empire is the land which Omikami gave Prince Ninigi to govern in the beginning. When Omikami sent the Prince down to this country, she gave an instruction, saying, 'This country is the land where my descendants are to be rulers. You, my Imperial Grandson, go and rule it. The prosperity of the Imperial Throne, like Heaven and Earth, will endure for ever'. The foundations of our country, which will continue for ever and ever, was actually laid at this time.
>
> Amaterasu Omikami gave the Mirror, Sword and Jewel to the Prince. These are called the Three Sacred Treasures. At this time Omikami said, 'When you look on this Mirror, you look on me'. From this time, the Sacred Treasures have been handed down from generation to generation of Emperors as the symbols of Imperial rank.
>
> Prince Ninigi took the Three Sacred Treasures and descended to Hyuga. After this, until the time of the Emperor Jimmu, two generations later, the gods dwelt in Hyuga. The period before the Emperor Jimmu is called the Age of the Gods.

* The Sun Goddess.

NOTES AND COMMENT

Textbook Censorship in Japan: the Ienaga Case

THE TOKYO DISTRICT COURT recently handed down a judgement which is generally considered to have considerable importance for the future of primary and secondary education in Japan. It concerned the operation of the system whereby the Ministry of Education (*Mombushō*) examines all textbooks used in primary and secondary schools and permits only those which are approved to be used in schools as textbooks.

The present system began after the war, replacing the old system of uniform national textbooks published by the Ministry—a system which had continued since 1903 and was widely considered in post-war Japan to have been used partly for militaristic indoctrination. Under the new system anyone was free to write and publish textbooks, but no textbook could be used in schools unless it had been approved as suitable by the Ministry. All approved textbooks were placed on display at regular intervals and schools—or individual teachers—made their own choice.

Two changes have taken place since the present procedures began some 23 years ago. First, whereas in the early years the Ministry officials and panels of advisers concerned took a very broad view of what was "suitable," the limits of suitability have been considerably narrowed. Examples of the kind of points at issue in the 60s are given below. Secondly, the freedom of individual teachers to choose among the textbooks which are published, has been limited. Following the abolition of direct elections for local education committees and the creation of committees appointed by local mayors (and prefectural governors) and approved by local assemblies, the new education committees were given, by *Mombushō* directive, the final authority to choose textbooks in 1957.

In 1963, following a further *Mombushō* directive, local authorities established "combined textbook areas." That is to say, the education committees of neighbouring communities established joint committees (usually including teachers) to choose the same textbooks for common use throughout the area. Tokyo has 47 such areas, but in the extreme case, Aomori Prefecture has only one so that a single committee for each subject chooses the textbook which shall be used throughout the prefecture. In other prefectures where there are several textbook areas there is also a certain measure of centralisation effected by the power of the prefectural education committee (which frequently contains former *Mombushō* officials) to offer advice and guidance to local committees. The *Yomiuri* of 14 July 1970 offers as an example of such centralisation of control at the prefectural level, the fate of a Japanese language textbook, the particular feature of which was that it included many examples of school-children's own compositions and placed a great emphasis on the stimulation of creativity. Immediately before the introduction of the "textbook area" system it accounted for nearly one-third of the text-books sold for Japanese language courses in Gifu prefecture. Immediately afterwards it sold none at all and total sales fell from 1,200,000 to 700,000.

The approval procedure at present operates as follows: publishers send copies to the Ministry which are then sent out—without the names of authors or publishers attached—to several of a panel of lay examiners (346 in 1970). The latter send their comments to the 41 examining officials—full-time officials of the Ministry of Education. These officials then make their report, taking account of the comments of the lay examiners, to one of nine subject panels of the Textbook Examination Research Committee. The decisions of the Committee are personally conveyed, and interpreted, to publishers by the examining officials. Since the members of the Committee are mostly part-time members, it is generally assumed that effective control rests in fact with the 41 examining officials.

An *Asahi* article on 14 July reports publishers' complaints concerning the operation of the system. If a textbook is considered faulty but not beyond redemption, they will be told what points must be changed if the book is to be approved, and secondly what it is "advisable" to change. And if they do not take the advice, they fear for the fate of later textbooks which they may present for inspection. If the textbook is considered beyond redemption, they will be given examples of what is wrong with it, but no overall assessment. In either case the information and advice is orally given, and no obligation rests on the Committee to explain its reasons for rejecting a textbook. The article goes on to describe how publishers, as a result, have come to exercise a tight self-censorship—or rather a censorship over their authors. It adds, however, that the self-censorship works also in the opposite ideological direction. A new factor in the situation since 1965 is the regular publication by the Japan Teachers' Union (JTU) of a critique of current textbooks. Publishers are also concerned not to be condemned by the JTU as purveying a reactionary militaristic textbook, and this is why such 19th century military figures as General Nogi and Admiral Togo do not appear in modern history books.

The tightening of the approval system and the moves towards centralisation of the textbook choice procedure are generally seen as part of a general trend towards centralisation of control over the content of education. Other notable signs of this trend are, first the abolition of directly elected education committees in 1955, and secondly, the designation, in 1958, of the detailed

Ministry of Education Curriculum Outlines, as directives (until then published as suggested guidelines only). This trend towards centralisation is variously interpreted: (a) as simply a nostalgic throwback towards the pre-war period (when many senior administrators began their official career) and when Japan had one of the most highly centralised educational systems in the world; (b) as simply part of the power-struggle between the Ministry of Education and the Japan Teachers' Union. Whether, as the JTU claims, it seeks freedom and diversity in education in contra-distinction to uniformity and centralisation, or whether, as its critics claim, it seeks an equally centralised—though anti-governmental—control over the content of education, the fact remains that the power-struggle exists clearly in the perception of both parties, and it is hard for those engaged in education in Japan to be neutral. There are a large number of education committees in Japan—some would say the vast majority—where either the Ministry of Education has decisive influence and the JTU has none, or *vice versa*. Few can maintain a truly independent position vis-a-vis both sides.

On the underlying reason for this power-struggle, there are three by no means contradictory views. The first is that, whatever the original points at issue, the battle now is sustained by its own momentum as a "pure" struggle for power between two irreconcilably opposed bodies. The second is that it reflects a conflict between opposing sets of deeply held ideological beliefs—whether, for instance, the teaching of history should concentrate on the miseries of the nation's past or on its glories, whether it should emphasise the doings of the rulers or of the ruled, whether it should inculcate the values of patriotism and dedication to national progress or of resistance to authority and the establishment of individual rights. The third is that behind this ideological conflict lies a political party conflict: the JTU supports opposition parties and the type of education it favours is thought likely to inculcate critical attitudes towards the established government, whereas the Ministry of Education, like any other Ministry, is subject to the political direction of the Liberal-Democratic Party which has held power in Japan for the last fifteen years.

These issues have recently come to public attention by the lawsuit brought by Professor Saburo Ienaga of Tokyo University of Education, a well-known Japanese historian.[1] His textbook on Japanese history was rejected in 1963. In 1964 it received conditional acceptance. Professor Ienaga agreed to the conditions under pressure from the publishers and made the necessary changes. In 1965 he brought a civil suit against the Ministry of Education, claiming damages for loss of royalties (due to the non-publication of the book in the previous year) and mental distress (due to his being forced

---

[1] His intellectual development is analysed in a chapter by R. N. Bellah in M. B. Jansen (ed.), *Changing Japanese Attitudes to Modernization*, Princeton, 196.

to relinquish some of his views in order to be able to publish the rest). This suit is still pending. In 1966 he re-submitted his textbook in its original form and it was rejected. This time he brought an administrative suit against the Ministry asking for reversal of the decision on the grounds that it was illegal and unconstitutional. It was on this complaint that judgement in his favour was delivered in the Tokyo District Court on 17 July. The trial attracted great public attention and each of its 28 hearings was reported in detail in the press. Seventeen witnesses appeared for Professor Ienaga, including such notables as Professor Nambara, former president of Tokyo University, and fourteen for the Ministry of Education including such notables as Professor Morito, Chairman of the Central Council for Education. Supporters' societies were formed to rally support for each side. Professor Ienaga's house was the scene of frequent demonstrations and he had occasionally to ask for police protection. The judgement was reported in the evening papers on 17 July under some of the biggest banner headlines that had been seen for months, together with pictures of the jubilant demonstrations of Professor Ienaga's supporters. The disputed passages in the textbook were as follows:

1. Each historical period was introduced with an illustration. The examiners had objected to the choice of illustrations and to the captions. (In 1964 when the book was published the final compromise was to retain the illustrations and remove all the captions.) Each caption was headed "The people who supported history" or—the phrase is hard to translate—"The people on whose labours history was built." As an example, the illustration for the Tokugawa period showed peasants delivering rice to samurai intendants, and the caption read: "It was the productive labour of the peasants which supported feudal society. As this picture shows, the rice produced by the sweat of the peasants' brow passed into the hands of the warrior class." The objection raised was that "supported" was a difficult concept for children to understand. Moreover, the fact that four of these introductory pictures were of the same type (steel workers for the Meiji period, craftsmen for the Heian period and a stone-age mask) seemed rather one-sided; it would be better to take material representing all classes.

2. The following passage concerning Japan's earliest chronicles of the 7th century: "Both the Kojiki and the Nihongi begin with stories of the "Age of the Gods." *Not only the stories of the "Age of the Gods," but also those relating to the first several generations after the [first human] Emperor Jimmu were all invented after the Imperial Family had united the country in order to justify the Imperial Family's rule over Japan,* but they are intermingled with a variety of myths and legends told amongst the magnates and the common people, and they constitute a precious record of the ideas and the arts of ancient times." The examiners required the clause under-

lined to be removed on the grounds that it did not adequately represent the ideas and intentions of the people of the period.

3. The following passage dealing with the Russo-Japanese Non-aggression pact: "In April 1941, in order to strengthen her strategic position for a southward advance, Japan concluded a non-aggression pact with the Soviet Union." The examiners required insertion of the phrase "at the suggestion of the Soviet Union."

The following is a summary of the Court's judgement:

Article 26 of the Constitution states that every child has an equal right to receive an education adapted to his abilities as the law shall provide, and every parent has the duty to see that children receive a basic education.

This is to be interpreted as meaning that in a democratic society which respects individual dignity, every citizen has the duty, not only towards his own children, but towards the whole of the next generation, to help them to develop their own personalities, to transmit to them the cultural heritage and to develop them as individuals capable of sustaining a healthy society and a healthy world.

This fundamental notion may be called, in contrast to the concept of the state's right to educate, the concept of the people's (or of the nation's) freedom to educate.

The role of the state is primarily to assist the people to perform their duty to educate their children, and accordingly the powers entrusted to the state in this regard do not require involvement in the content of education, but only the provision of the necessary facilities.

The provision "as the law shall provide" indicates that education is not a matter for control by administrative action not specified by law. But the scope of legislation is also limited. While the provision of the external conditions for education should be legally regulated through the representative parliamentary system, this does not apply to matters of content. These are matters which do not easily consort with the principle of majority decision influenced by party politics. They are to be worked out in the personal contact between teacher and pupil: teachers, through their own study and efforts at self-improvement, should seek to embody the rational "will to educate" of the people as a whole and, owning a direct responsibility to the people as a whole, to fulfill the task which the people have entrusted to them.

Concerning the guarantee of academic freedom contained in Article 23 of the Constitution: this naturally includes the right of scholars freely to publish the results of their academic work, including their theories and opinions as scholars, and the publication of textbooks is naturally included as one form of such publication. It is a particularly appropriate form of publication in as much as (Fundamental Law of Education, Article 1) it is one of the purposes of school education to foster an eagerness for the pursuit of truth which is also the function of university research.

A further guarantee of the right to publish is contained in Article 21 of the Constitution which forbids censorship. It is accepted that the freedom to publish may in some circumstances be limited by considerations of public welfare, but the essence of the ban on censorship is that where the ideological or philosophical content of a work is at issue, it is forbidden for public authority to be used to prevent publication, even in the name of public welfare.

The requirement (School Education Law, Article 21) that all textbooks should be approved by the Ministry before they may be published as textbooks therefore constitutes censorship in so far as, and only in so far as, ideological and philosophical judgements enter into the decision to approve or not to approve.

Ideological and philosophical judgements should be understood to include not just political views, but everything relating to the life of the spirit, naturally including theories and opinions which scholars might hold as a result of their research. In the case of history textbooks this means not only a general philosophy of history or the evaluation of particular historical events, but also such matters as periodization in so far as they reflect a view of history.

In so far as it is designed to provide an education adapted to each child's stage of mental and physical development and to secure equality of educational opportunity, and in so far as it does not involve censorship in the terms above defined, the licensing system itself is not an infringement of the Constitution.

But, given also that it is the role of the State to provide the external facilities for education and in the matter of content to confine itself to guidance and advice, the only considerations involved in the examination of textbooks should be misprints and clearly recognisable objective errors; the physical make-up of the book and other technical matters, and whether the content falls within the broad outlines of the indicated curriculum.

An examination of the three points at issue and of the arguments advanced by both sides suggests that in none of these cases was any clear error of fact involved and that they were all points involving a personal perspective on history. The rejection of the textbook therefore constitutes censorship and represents an impermissible use of the licensing system.

In his *obiter dicta* the judge went on to distinguish between "educational freedom" which means the right of the individual citizen to educate, in contradistinction to the state's right to educate, and the "freedom of the teacher." The latter is basically guaranteed by Article 23 of the Constitution, concerning academic freedom. Hence, he stated, it is not permitted for the State unilaterally to require teachers to use certain textbooks, or to limit the participation of teachers in the choice of textbooks, or to give legal force to its curriculum guides and so circumscribe the teacher's activity in detail.

Newspaper editorial comments were in a guarded way mostly favourable to the judgement. Most pointed out that the Ministry was bound to appeal and that it would be many years before a final judgement was given, but that meanwhile certain changes ought to be made. A *Mainichi* columnist (18 July) gave one of the most positive expressions of support for the judgement, pointing out that most of the countries of Western Europe and America have nothing like the Japanese system of control over textbooks; by contrast Communist countries have national textbooks like pre-war Japan, and it was ironical that Japan should in this regard be more like the Communist countries than the rest of the free world.

The opposition parties welcomed the verdict, the Democratic Socialist Party a little more guardedly than the others. The Secretary-General of the Liberal Democratic Party, on the other hand, was strongly critical: "The function of educational administration necessarily includes responsibility for the content of education. In order to eliminate biased education and ensure that children are correctly taught it is essential for the Ministry of Education to correct the mistakes in textbooks" (*Yomiuri*, 17 July, evening edition). Legal scholars quoted in the newspapers were generally favourable to the verdict, some very positively so (e.g. Kaneko, *Mainichi*, evening, 17 July, Arikura, *Mainichi*, 18 July). The Association of Constitutional Legal Scholars had, in fact, during the course of the trial passed a resolution supporting the view taken by the judge, and it is said that the Ministry had had difficulty in finding an expert on constitutional law to testify on its behalf. In addition there were various comments from other scholars and educators, and symposia including members of the Ministry of Education in all the major newspapers. Some of the points made are as follows:

Professor Umene (President of Wako University and author of a rejected textbook): Japanese textbooks are thin volumes compared with American ones, and they contain only a bare outline. What they ought to do is present a variety of ideas and opinions and train the child to think things out for himself. But instead textbooks in Japan are treated as Bibles. (*Asahi*, 18 July).

Professor Nakamura (Professor of Political Science, Keio University): If the judgment is followed there will be chaos in the classroom because, unlike a country like England there is an enormous gulf between scholars of different persuasions—particularly historians. Of course there should be no censorship of academic publications, but the matter is different when it comes to textbooks with a prescribed readership. If these widely divergent opinions are brought to the classroom it utterly confuses the children. In general the judgement sees the matter too much from the point of view of authors and publishers and not enough from the point of view of the schoolchild. (*Asahi*, evening, 17 July).

Minister of Education, Mr. Sakata: . . . . It is a mistake to consider the "freedom of the teacher" and "academic freedom" as the same thing . . . Academic freedom as guaranteed in the Constitution—the freedom to do research and to publish the results—is permitted in universities, but it is a mistake to try to apply this principle from primary schools up. Professor Ienaga's contention, as a university professor, that what is permitted in universities should apply also to lower schools ignores the need to adapt education to the mental and physical development of the child. It inevitably will lead to the idea that Article 8 of the Fundamental Law of education concerning the (political) neutrality of the educational system can simply be ignored. If academic theories of a political partisan nature are allowed in the classroom it will cause great disquiet. The Fundamental Law is based on the Constitution, the School Education Law on the Fundamental Law and the Ministry's Curriculum Outlines are based on the School Education Law. Of course one ought not to circumscribe the teacher in the classroom in every little detail; there's got to be some free discretion allowed. But the judgement takes a big leap. . . . There seems to be a logical gap in the judgement in the discussion of how the people's "right to educate" is entrusted to the teacher. . . . To take Mr. Ienaga's own case. On the first draft of his textbook submitted there were over three hundred problem passages. Of these he accepted the criticism made in the case of a hundred of them. On the rest there was argument back and forth and in the end only the passages he complained of in the court case were left. By accepting the criticism in a hundred cases he was admitting the value of the licensing system. (*Mainichi*, 18 July).

Mr. Sakata (in response to a question whether teachers ought not to be more respected):

Yes, but at the same time the education they give ought to be worthy of respect. For example, it is absurd to discuss the relative merits and demerits of socialism and capitalism in primary and middle schools. In a university, when teachers propound an academic theory one assumes a certain critical faculty on the part of the student. But in the schools, whatever a teacher says the children implicitly believe. (*Asahi*, 18 July).

Director of the Bureau for Primary and Middle School Education, Ministry of Education, Mr. Miyaji: . . . The judgement is contradictory. On the one hand it says that textbooks should be treated like any other books. On the other it says that the Ministry may correct factual errors in textbooks. Then why not factual errors in ordinary books? . . . The judge says that the content of education is not to be determined as a political matter by majority decision. And yet he takes his stand on the Fundamental Law of Education which depends on majority decision. . . . Professor Ienaga says that we can leave the content of textbooks to authors, but just because a professor believes deeply in the truth of his theory, what will happen if he insists on putting it in a textbook? Do you really want to have biased textbooks coming out? There's a difference between teaching academic theories in a university and teaching them in a school. Education must be geared to children's mental and physical development. The mere thought of the disorder which would arise if the Ministry did not prescribe standards sends shivers down my spine. (*Asahi*, 18 July). . . . (If the judgement goes in favour of Professor Ienaga). It would not just be a terrible thing for the Ministry of Education, it would be a terrible thing for everyone. Anything could become a textbook—comic books, pornographic books, anything the teacher likes to choose. To put it in Ienaga style, thanks to the Ministry's licensing powers it's impossible to give detailed sex education to little girls of seven or eight. Education has got to be geared to the child's development. If you yourself were asked by your own child: "Where do babies come from?," would you tell him? It's not a matter of telling the truth under all circumstances. As the proverb says: "trim your sermon to the listener." (*Mainichi*, 15 July).

Mr. Miyaji also took part in a *Yomiuri* symposium (18 July) together with Professor Umene, President of Wako University, Mrs. Niijima, a leader of a women's Christian organisation, and Mr. Kato, an editorial writer of the *Yomiuri*:

Miyaji: When there are a variety of academic opinions, if you teach only one of them, how can you maintain and raise the level of education? What happens to the child's right to receive an equal education?

Umene: I've had the experience of having a textbook turned down, but I think one's got to look at the matter separately from two points of view—that of the author and that of the users. The author has got his own opinions. For example, there is a controversy as to whether the Horyuji [temple] was rebuilt or whether the present one is the original temple. I don't think it's a disaster if some textbooks say one and some say the other. The schools should have both. Of course it's not a good thing if the children are taught just the one view, but one can leave the teachers to handle that.

Miyaji: One can't put that much responsibility on the teachers.

Kato: Isn't that just the point?—Whether or not you trust the teachers? Educational administration should be predicated on an unlimited faith in the teachers.

Miyaji: That's what you say, but what happened during the university crisis? Then the Ministry was criticised for doing nothing.

Niijima: It seems to me, as an ordinary mother, that the Ministry of Education always bases its judgements and its statements on the assumption that the most extreme case is the typical one. But there are not so many extreme cases, either among teachers or textbook writers. Even if there were a few wild textbooks and a few wild teachers, they would soon disappear by a process of natural selection. If teachers were given more freedom they would surely put more effort into their job. When it comes down to it, the Ministry is just like the rest in trying to impose its own views on the whole nation.

Miyaji: You talk of extremes, but that is just what this case was about—an extreme case. He as good as said that "all" of the *Kojiki* was invented for the sake of the Imperial Family. He surely didn't have to be so dogmatic about the "all"—that's what the argument was about.

The Ministry of Education appealed to the Tokyo Higher Court on 24 July,[2] citing other High Court and Supreme Court judgements in support of the contention that the people's fundamental right to educate was entrusted to the State and could only be entrusted to the State, and that the constitutional guarantee of academic freedom did not apply equally to school teachers. A common view is that, given the difference in composition of the District Court and the High Court—judges with a reputation for being "liberals" like Judge Sugimoto who delivered the present judgement are very rare phenomena in Japanese High Courts—there is a very strong likelihood of the judgement being reversed and everything then continuing as before. It is also suggested that the Ministry feels so strongly about the matter that everything will be done to ensure that the case is entrusted to a "reliable" judge.

An alternative view suggests that at least a minority within the Ministry does not see the matter in quite such apocalyptic terms. They too are in favour of the appeal, but not so much because they think it would be a disaster if the judgement were not reversed as because they see it as a means of buying time. If the appeal is rejected and a further appeal is made to the Supreme Court, the whole process could take ten years. Ten years from now, according to this view, the Japan Teachers Union will no longer be a serious contender for power and ideological divisions within the country are likely to be less extreme. At that point it would be quite safe to remove controls over textbooks. It is impossible to say whether such a minority in fact exists, or if it exists how influential it is.

University of Sussex, September 1970   R. P. DORE

---

[2] This was followed on 8 August by a "directive" (*tsūdatsu*) issued by Bureau Chief Miyaji to all prefectural governors and directors of education. The directive forcefully reiterated the Ministry's objections to the judgement and declared that no changes of any kind were to be made in the textbook system pending the appeal.

The History of the Textbook Controversy

IRIE YOSHIMASA

With the start of the new school year this April, the history textbooks for middle schools will contain references to *jūgun ianfu*, the "military comfort women" who served as prostitutes for the Japanese armed forces before and during World War II. On June 27 last year the Ministry of Education announced the results of its review of the textbooks for use starting in 1997. It became known at that point that all the history texts approved for use in middle school social studies classes would include passages about these women, who are said for the most part to have been assembled against their will by brokers and government authorities at the request of the military and forced into prostitution.

When the results were announced, various groups immediately protested against the publication of the new texts. Ultrarightists sent sound trucks to the Ministry of Education, where they blared out denunciations. The publishers of the texts also became targets of these groups' noisy attacks.

On October 3, Sakurai Yoshiko, a prominent journalist known for her advocacy of HIV-infected hemophiliacs in their battle with the Ministry of Health and Welfare, addressed a group of about 200 teachers in Yokohama at the invitation of the city's Board of Education. In her speech, she expressed misgivings about the new books. Sakurai, while noting that some of the comfort women were certainly pressed into service against their will, declared that given the lack of documentary evidence, it was premature to assert that forced recruitment had been the policy of the military or that the government was involved, as assumed by the authors of the texts.

After this speech, Sakurai received some angry messages by fax at her office. One member of the Yokohama Teachers' Union wrote that her comments "were not only a distortion of the historical facts but also a slander against the women who have courageously declared that they were military comfort women." Another local teachers' group, declaring that her statement was contrary to the city's educational policy and had "severely injured" its teachers, demanded that she issue a correction and an apology.

Sakurai was taken aback at these reactions: "I'm quite ready to receive counterarguments, but it's most inappropriate for people concerned with human rights to take their own value standards as absolute and force them on others, unilaterally demanding that those who differ revise their statements without any attempt to enter into discussion with them. This is a terribly dangerous approach."

MASOCHISTIC HISTORY?

On December 2 a group calling itself the Society to Make New History Textbooks had its inaugural meeting. The group's initial declaration included the following passage:

"The middle school textbooks by seven publishers that recently passed the review process present a description of modern and contemporary history in which even the Sino-Japanese War of 1894–95 and Russo-Japanese War of 1904–5 are taken to be merely wars of aggression [by Japan] against [the rest of] Asia. Not only that, but they take the Meiji state [the government of Japan during the 1868–1912 Meiji era] itself to have been evil, and their entire account of Japan's modern and contemporary history is a condemnation of a history of crimes. For example, their uniform adoption of the position that the 'military comfort women' were recruited by force, despite the inadequacy of the evidence, may be seen as a result of the facile self-denunciatory view of history that they have adopted."

University of Tokyo Professor Fujioka Nobukatsu, one of the main organizers of this new group, has long been calling for reform of the history curriculum. He has called the contents of the Japanese history taught in schools since the end of World War II "masochistic" and "anti-Japanese," suggesting that what is being presented is the "Comintern view" or the "Tokyo War Crimes Trial view" of Japan's past; "dark history" is another term he has used in describing the current curriculum. Here is part of a comment from him published in the *Sankei Shimbun* on June 28, 1996:

"The textbooks from the seven publishers that have passed the review process cannot by any means be called textbooks written for Japanese. The 'indirect aggression' of foreign countries that begrudge Japan's prosperity has reached virtual completion in the field of the history texts that form the framework for the nation's common store of knowledge. Using government funds to pay for textbooks so full of hatred against our own country and forcing them on schoolchildren represent a grievous violation of the people's right to education."

I read through the seven textbooks that have become

IRIE YOSHIMASA
Born in 1952. Studied at
Waseda University. Is a
reporter at *Bungei Shunjū*.
Author of *Shi e no tobira*
(Door to Death) and co-
author of *Tochi no majutsu*
(The Magic of Land).

the target of such ire. My impression is that they do seem to be written in such a way that children are likely to draw a dichotomy between the "good," namely the masses, the weak, the victims of discrimination, the Koreans, and so forth, versus the "bad," namely the Japanese government. The question is whether this should be taken to represent the authors' loss of pride in their own country's history or merely the permeation of a pacifist view that innocently opposes war.

Still, I must say that judging the worth of textbooks simply on the basis of whether they contain the word *ianfu* is tantamount to a witch hunt.

THE REVIEW PROCESS

Not just any publisher can come out with a textbook. To become a "textbook company," it must meet certain conditions set by the Education Ministry. The major requirements are that it have a capital fund of at least ¥10 million and at least five people with experience as textbook editors.

Before the war, elementary school textbooks were designated directly by the national government, though middle school texts were prepared independently and screened. Now, however, all texts from elementary through high school are subject to the review system established in 1947 and overhauled in 1989, at which point the standards were revised considerably and the review cycle was lengthened from three years to four.

A publisher seeking to issue a textbook first prepares a "white-cover text" in line with the school course guidelines and official review standards, and submits it to the Textbook Division in the Education Ministry. The text next must await the verdict of the Textbook Authorization and Research Council, an advisory panel affiliated with the ministry.

Drafting a "white-cover text" is an extremely expensive and time-consuming task. Since failure to pass the screening process means that the contents cannot be published as a textbook and the company will be unable to recoup its investment, publishers tend to be very obedient to the suggestions made by the Education Ministry. Each text is checked by one textbook inspector inside the ministry and by three outside inspectors. Their findings are submitted to the Textbook Authorization and Research Council, where specialist members in various fields check the contents and a recommendation is made to approve the text

or not. This goes to the minister of education, who makes the actual decision. In practice, however, the council's recommendation is final.

Sometimes the council draws up a recommendation that calls for revisions in the text. The publisher then prepares a list of changes in line with the council's opinions and submits it, together with the revised text, for reconsideration. The council will then take another look and decide one way or the other.

That, in general terms, is how the textbook review system operates. The textbooks used in compulsory education (six years of elementary school and three years of middle school) are distributed free of charge to pupils, in line with the provision in Article 26 of the Constitution that "compulsory education shall be free." In fiscal 1996 (April 1996 to March 1997), about ¥43.8 billion in tax revenue was used for this purpose. Under a 1963 law, the choice of what textbooks to use is in the hands of the district groupings of local boards of education. At present the local boards are grouped into 478 such districts, generally encompassing several municipalities.

In years gone by, the review process could be quite difficult. The Education Ministry and Nikkyōso (Japan Teachers' Union) were constantly at loggerheads over the approval or disapproval of particular texts. But at some point the tensions relaxed—or perhaps it would be more accurate to say that the standards changed. The roots of this transformation, which has produced the situation where all the middle school history texts have suddenly added passages about the military comfort women, can be traced back to 1982, when the first "textbook flap" occurred.

THE TEXTBOOK FLAP OF 1982

On June 26, 1982, various newspapers and television stations reported that the Education Ministry had required the rewriting of passages in proposed history textbooks that referred to Japan's pre–World War II expansion onto the Asian continent as *shinryaku* (invasion), demanding that the word *shinshutsu* (advance) be used instead. On the basis of these reports, the Chinese government lodged an official protest on July 26, accusing the ministry of having distorted the historical record of Japanese militarism. The South Korean government subsequently followed suit.

The year 1982 happened to coincide with the tenth anniversary of restored diplomatic relations between Tokyo and Beijing, with a visit to China by Prime Minister Suzuki Zenkō scheduled for that autumn. The prime minister's senior staffers were therefore anxious to settle this diplomatic problem quickly. Miyazawa Kiichi (who later became prime minister himself) was serving as chief cabinet secretary, the prime minister's official spokesperson; on August 26 he issued a statement aimed at defusing what had turned into a serious issue in relations with Beijing and Seoul. Miyazawa, on behalf of the Suzuki administration, declared that the government would have the textbook council reconsider the present review standards and would see to it that they were modified in response to the complaints of Asian neighbors.

This Miyazawa statement cast something of a spell over Japan's subsequent foreign policy. In the view of Nishio Kanji, another organizer of the New History Textbook Society, it marked the start of a policy of "diplomacy by apology" in a "diplomatically inept Japan." He has commented as follows:

"There's a commonly accepted myth that Germany has rightfully apologized for its past and Japan has wrongfully failed to do so. This myth is convenient not just for victors who dropped atomic bombs but also for the Germans. It allows them the comfort of putting Japan's war crimes in the same category as the crimes against humanity committed by Nazi Germany. It has also turned into the only way China and South Korea can rock Japan's boat. That textbook incident was symbolic as an indicator of Japan's position in terms of diplomatic coordinates."

The textbook review standards were subsequently revised in keeping with Miyazawa's comments. A new requirement was added, namely, that proposed texts for use in compulsory education should "show the necessary consideration for international understanding and inter-

"OUR COMPANY HADN'T USED

'INVASION' IN ITS TEXTBOOKS FROM

THE START. AFTER THE 'ASIAN

NEIGHBORS' CLAUSE WAS ADDED,

. . . HOWEVER, WE STARTED USING

'INVASION' OURSELVES."

national harmony in their treatment of the events of modern and contemporary history between [Japan and its] Asian neighbors."

MISTAKEN REPORTING

The June 1982 media reports upon which the Chinese and Korean governments based their protest were in fact mistaken. The Education Ministry had not, it turned out, required the word change (though it had often "suggested" such a change for some time). The source of the error was in the press club of reporters assigned to the Education Ministry. When a set of text review results came out, the practice in this club at the time was for each major subject to be assigned to a separate reporter, who would compose a report and share it with the other club members. A reporter from the Nippon Television Network, assigned to cover world history, wrote that in one textbook the authors had been required to replace the phrase "invaded northern China" (*Kahoku ni shinryaku*) with "advanced into northern China" (*Kahoku ni shinshutsu*) in reference to the Japanese military incursion. This factual error was picked up by the media without any double checking, leading to the diplomatic flap.

The upshot of this incident and the subsequent addition of the "Asian neighbors" clause to the textbook review standards was that at least one textbook company revised its editorial policy. Here is a comment from an editorial staffer at Osaka Shoseki: "For several years before the official protest from the Chinese government to the Japanese government in 1982, textbooks reviewed by the Education Ministry frequently came back with the recommendation that *advance* be used instead of *invasion*. Our company hadn't used *invasion* in its textbooks from the start. After the 'Asian neighbors' clause was added and the contents of the school course guidelines were revised, however, we started using *invasion* ourselves."

This was just the beginning of the textbook issue as a source of friction between Japan and its neighbors. In 1986 a second textbook incident occurred. On May 27 of that year, the screening council gave its approval to a history text for high schools drafted by a group called the National Congress to Safeguard Japan, headed by Kase Shun'ichi, a former ambassador to the United Nations, and slated for publication by Hara Shobō. By the end of the month the South Korean government had come out with a criticism directed at Tokyo, and the case then spread to China, Taiwan, and countries in Southeast Asia.

Domestically the controversy started with an article that appeared in the daily *Asahi Shimbun* three days before the review results were announced, under the title "Japanese History Textbook with a Reactionary Tone."

Nakasone Yasuhiro was prime minister at the time, and his administration was facing an election for both houses of the National Diet on July 6, barely a month away. The government was therefore determined to avoid a diplomatic fracas. The Ministry of Foreign Affairs sought

68

SURELY THE CHILDREN WHO ARE THE

OBJECTS OF INSTRUCTION WOULD

LIKE TO HAVE A CLEAR EXPLANATION

OF THIS DISAGREEMENT.

either to have the text in question disapproved or to have the publisher withdraw the request for review. The Education Ministry, however, refused to back these proposed solutions. At the prompting of the prime minister's staff, a senior bureaucrat at the Foreign Ministry (Fujita Kimio, director general of the Asian Affairs Bureau, now president of the Japan International Cooperation Agency) went to see Kase and the president of Hara Shobō to suggest withholding the book from publication. In the end it was in fact published, but only after an extraordinary four rounds of revisions.

THE 1993 APOLOGY

On August 4, 1993, just before Miyazawa Kiichi stepped down as prime minister, Chief Cabinet Secretary Kōno Yōhei announced the results of an investigation into the issue of the "comfort women" conducted by the Cabinet Councilors' Office on External Affairs starting in December 1991. With Kōno's statement the Japanese government acknowledged for the first time that there had been cases in which women were assembled against their will by the military, government authorities, and others and forced into prostitution.

Kōno offered the following words of apology: "Undeniably this was an act with the involvement of the military authorities of the day that severely injured the honor and dignity of many women. The government of Japan would like to take this opportunity once again to extend its sincere apologies and remorse to all those, irrespective of place of origin, who suffered immeasurable pain and incurable physical and psychological wounds as comfort women." He also stated, "We hereby reiterate our firm determination never to repeat the same mistake by forever engraving such issues in our memories through the study and teaching of history."

Concerning the manner in which the women were recruited, Kōno declared, "The Korean Peninsula was under Japanese rule in those days, and their recruitment, transfer, management, and so forth were conducted generally against their will through such means as coaxing and co-

ercion." But he did not officially provide a precise definition of what was meant by "generally." This was the source of subsequent vagueness in foreign policy.

It is not hard to imagine how this train of events has caused the textbook review standards to change. The Kōno statement had a substantial impact on those preparing history texts. An insider from Nihon Shoseki, one of the textbook companies, comments:

"Some of the comfort women took their case to court, and in 1993 the chief cabinet secretary came out with an apology for the matter. We figured that the other publishers would probably include the issue in their textbooks and that if we didn't include it in ours, it might affect their prospects. So in our high school history books, we carried references to the comfort women from 1994 on."

Yasuda Tsuneo, a professor at the University of Electro-Communications, who is one of the authors of a middle school history text published by Kyōiku Shuppan, explains some of the process of deciding whether to refer to this issue: "When we're writing a textbook, we have a number of authors' conferences. Sometimes we invite twenty or thirty active teachers to attend and express their opinions. In a case like that of the military comfort women, for example, we would tell them 'This is now a public issue, and we're planning to cover it in our new text.' If, as Professor Fujioka claims, the topic is unsuitable for middle school students, I would expect the classroom teachers to have spoken up. But to the best of my memory we heard no remarks like that. And so it was decided to go ahead with reference to the matter."

The head of the Education Ministry's Textbook Division, Takashio Itaru, has this to say on the subject: "Given the Kōno statement, the U.N. report [drafted by Radhika Coomaraswamy and made public in January 1996], and the 'Asian neighbors' clause [in the textbook review standards], it seems inevitable to me that the issue of the so-called military comfort women be covered in textbooks."

The popular *manga* (comic book) author Kobayashi Yoshinori, who, like journalist Sakurai, has been active in the cause of the HIV-infected hemophiliacs, is another of the organizers of the New History Textbook Society: "I see textbooks as the landmark for moves to change trends in society. If you rewrite the texts, you rewrite social trends. I think of them as the symbol. People whose brains are still infected by leftist ideology are extremely sensitive to issues like the comfort women or the word *invasion*. And the conservatives overreact because of their own fears. So touching on the textbook issue has come to be taboo. If other people are afraid to deal with it, I will."

Kobayashi drew quite a response when he wrote about the comfort-women issue in his serialized *manga*: "The letters from those who assert that there was no forced recruitment are very logically presented. By contrast, those on the other side are truly emotional with their assertions that the women were recruited by force and must receive an apology. Their thinking runs like this: 'War is bad. Japan went to war, so it was evil. And because it was evil, it probably recruited the women by force.' They're hysterical about the matter. Aggression is bad; never mind trying to explain the causes or processes leading to the war. Japan is bad. My question to them is 'What if you had been alive then?' I'm quite happy to offend those idiots who think they can label Japan a barbarian country and be pure and blameless themselves."

Professor Nishio is also impatient with the authors of schoolbooks that have nothing good to say about Japan's modern history: "History needs to be reproduced just as it happened, but Japan's textbooks apply today's value standards to yesterday. The authors attack everything. But you can't see things clearly if all you do is oppose them. What they write is not really textbooks but merely pamphlets in the style of activists' propaganda flyers. The existence of mistakes and contradictions in Japan's past should be acknowledged. But at the same time we have to recognize that Japan has been a success as a country. . . . The current set of textbooks don't explain this success. Not only do they fail to acknowledge it, but they actually portray it as more of a failure. The same can be said of their treatment of Japan's postwar recovery. Surely no other country has textbooks that don't affirm the country itself."

A DEEP RIFT

What do the authors think? Yasuda, for one, disagrees with the "liberalist" view of history advocated by Fujioka, claiming it amounts to no more than a history centered on the state and the deeds of great people. He asserts that history should allow for multiple views. Another textbook author,

Professor Obinata Sumio of Tokyo Metropolitan College, also takes issue with Fujioka's position: "Professor Fujioka often talks about 'history to be proud of.' That's a typical example of prejudgment. Unfortunately the facts include some things that we can't be proud of. Is it wrong to teach about them? I don't think so.

"Contrary to the idea that today's textbooks are an uninterrupted display of masochism, they include many bright passages. Faithfulness to the facts naturally means inclusion of both the good and the bad. History education isn't ethics, and it's not a matter of saying, 'Read this and be uplifted.' The factual record includes some bitter parts, but they're historical facts, so pupils need to deepen their understanding of them."

Ironically, schools in fact devote little time to teaching this period of history whose textbook treatment has become the focus of all this debate. One reason is that teachers are too busy preparing students for entrance exams to high schools and colleges.

In any case, the rift between the authors of the texts and their critics runs deep, involving different approaches to viewing the past and different ideological stances. Surely the children who are the objects of instruction would like to have a clear explanation of this disagreement.

Translated from "Rekishi kyōkasho daisensō," in Bungei Shunjū, *February 1997, pp. 306–15; abridged by about one-third. (Courtesy of Bungei Shunjū.)*

Language and Politics:
The Reversal of Postwar Script Reform Policy in Japan

NANETTE GOTTLIEB

T HE PERIOD SINCE THE END of the Allied Occupation of Japan has seen a number of attempts to reverse several Occupation policies. Some, such as the revoking of administrative decentralization of education and the police force, have been successful, while others, such as constitutional revision, have not. In general, the period since the 1950s has seen a pattern of conservative social change backed by the Liberal Democratic Party. An area that illustrates this trend is that of language policy, specifically the policy toward script. The partial revision of the immediate postwar script reforms that occurred over a twenty-year period from the mid-1960s to the end of the 1980s, most notably the revision of the 1946 list of recommended characters, is an example of a policy that, while not imposed by the Occupation authorities, had been arrived at during the Occupation and was later reversed to some extent in a conservative direction through direct LDP intervention.

Government language-planning and policy-formulation initiatives in Japan date back to the establishment of the first National Language Research Council (*Kokugo Chōsa Iinkai*) in 1902. Since that time, the process has been driven by a number of imperatives. In chronological order, these have been modernization in the Meiji period, imperialism during the war years, democracy in the immediate postwar period and conservatism from the 1960s on. The tension between the last two of these imperatives, in relation to the 1981 revision of the list of characters recommended for use in general public writing, forms the subject of this article. The events surrounding the formulation of postwar language policy as it relates to the written language and its later partial reversal have been described by Christopher Seeley (1984, 1991) using a chronological historical approach. The present study examines the intellectual attitudes that contributed to both events, in particular the way the democracy-based argument that had been used to push through the more rigid 1946 character restrictions was turned back on itself to support the later relaxation of the policy.

Nanette Gottlieb is Senior Lecturer in the Department of Japanese and Chinese Studies, University of Queensland.

Research for this article was carried out with the assistance of a grant from the Australian Research Council.

The Journal of Asian Studies 53, no. 4 (November 1994):1175–1198.

A potted history of postwar script reform policy runs as follows: would-be reformers on Japan's National Language Council (*Kokugo Shingikai*) and its predecessor, the Interim National Language Research Council (*Rinji Kokugo Chōsa Iinkai*), had been attempting since 1923 to introduce both limits on the number of Chinese characters in use and modernization of *kana* usage to a system based on contemporary rather than archaic pronunciation.[1] They had been thwarted by entrenched conservatism and ultranationalism, which viewed attempts to tamper with the traditional orthography as an attack on national values. When the war ended, however, so did the political and social domination of the ultranationalists. The Council, basing its arguments on the close connection between script reform and the efficiency of education, in view of the urgent need to rebuild Japan quickly, was able in 1946 to push through a restrictive list of 1,850 characters and effect a change from historical to modern *kana* usage. This was followed by a string of other reforms, which included simplification of character shapes and rationalization of the various readings that could be assigned to characters in different contexts (*on* and *kun* readings, depending on whether the character was being used to represent a word of Japanese or Chinese origin), of how much *hiragana* should be appended to the character representing the first part of an inflected word (*okurigana*), and of how many characters from the main list were to be taught during the period of compulsory education.

During the 1960s, however, increased national prosperity and resurgent conservatism led to a confrontation over the direction of future language policy between the traditionalists, who had been overshadowed but always present since the war, and the reformers. An often-heard argument during this period was that the character limits represented an unacceptable infringement of the freedom of expression guaranteed in the 1946 constitution. As the result of a change in intellectual attitudes and political stances since the end of the Occupation, the Education Minister in 1966 requested the Council to re-examine the entire cycle of postwar reforms. Over the next twenty-five years, many of the postwar reforms were partially reversed. In those areas where restrictions had been firmly applied in an attempt to contain and control the prewar situation of 5,000–6,000 characters with complex shapes and numerous readings, the limits were both quantitatively and qualitatively relaxed, with a shift in nature away from *seigen* (limit) to *meyasu* (guide) being spelled out in the official policy documentation. The outstanding example of this, of course, is the 1981 List of Characters for General Use (*Jōyō Kanjihyō*), which increased the number of characters from 1,850 to 1,945 (see Seeley 1991 for details). While the actual extent of the reversal was not particularly dramatic—the character list increased by only 95 items—the repudiation of the postwar declaration that the list was to be used as a limit on the characters that could be used in government and educational texts in favor of a more relaxed status as a "guide" to usage represented a negation of the spirit of the original reforms. The only reforms left substantially untouched were the system of modern *kana* usage and the simplified character shapes, which by that time were so firmly entrenched that it was not considered possible to reverse them.

Democracy and Script Reform

Immediately after the war, then, the major motivation for language policy initiatives came from a push for "democratization" coupled with the economic incentive

[1] The Interim National Language Research Council in 1923 proposed the first character list, the 1,962-character List of Characters for General Use. The Interim Council was replaced in 1934 by the National Language Council, the body responsible for language policy-formulation today.

of national reconstruction. Society at large evinced a desire to break with past ways of thinking, which had led to a crushing national defeat, and this combined with the new concept of democracy imposed by the Occupation forces to provide a powerful argument in favor of rationalizing the way Japanese was written. Carol Eastman points out that orthography reform in the absence of any social, cultural, or political turnover is unlikely to succeed (1983:23), and in Japan the tremendous social and political upheaval following defeat and the accompanying change in intellectual climate provided the impetus for script reform. A promising new era began for those who had formerly been repressed; this group, referred to as "reformers" in this article, included both radicals whose ultimate goal was the total abolition of characters (or even *kana* in the case of romanizers) and those who prevailed in the string of postwar reforms described above—moderates who advocated streamlining of the existing orthography. The new constitution removed sovereignty from the hands of the emperor and placed it squarely in the hands of the people. How were those people to participate effectively in the public life of a democratic state, ran the argument, if a large character set and outdated *kana* conventions prevented them from achieving levels of literacy sufficient to read complex political debate, the text of the constitution, and other legal and government documents?[2] Given the circumstances of the time— the obvious physical destruction that had resulted from the policies of the ultranationalists, and the presence on Japanese soil for the first time of an occupying army—it was difficult to rebut this argument without being tarred with the same brush as the disgraced former leaders. Those in favor of script reform were quick to see the advantages of using the democracy argument, although they were not arguing from expediency alone but from long and deeply held convictions. Background support was provided by the presence of the Americans, whose observations on the difficulty of the existing script system and tentative suggestions that romanization be adopted as Japan's national script galvanized the Japanese into action to counter the perceived threat (never a real possibility) that they might lose their own script if they did not modify the way it was used (Trainor 1983:300–12).

Whether the Occupation reforms can be said to be genuinely democratic in the manner some were imposed is not the issue here. What is of interest is the way the leading figures in the script-reform camp latched on to the fashionable term "democracy," using it to sanctify their aims and assume moral superiority over their opponents. In language-reform terms, their strategy translated to the statement that complex Chinese characters belonged to the former ruling class and that script and the remaining vestiges of archaic styles should be changed so the entire nation could understand the written language with ease. The slogan *"kokugo wa kokumin zentai no mono"* (our language belongs to *all* the people) was often heard from reformers such as Yamamoto Yūzō (1887–1974) and Toki Zenmaro (1885–1980), whose activities are detailed below. Simplifying the written language would play an important role in disseminating an understanding of democracy and of science, and would result in an increase in scientific knowledge among the general public as opposed to only specialists being seen as essential to reconstruction. An editorial in the *Yomiuri Hōchi Shinbun* in November 1945 suggested that the abolition of characters

---

[2] The literacy survey carried out by the Supreme Commander for the Allied Powers' Civil Information and Education Section in 1948 found that, although the rate of total illiteracy was low, only 6.2 percent of Japanese were literate as loosely defined by the survey (i.e., able to answer all the questions correctly), and all groups performed badly in the *kanji* dictation section. These findings verified claims of supporters of script reform (Unger 1987:91–92).

would clear away the remaining feudal mentality and enable Japan to achieve American-style efficiency. Use of the Western alphabet instead of characters, it was suggested, would result in an increase in national intellectual standards that would lead to maturity as a democratic government and a civilized nation.

The advocates of abolishing characters in favor of romanization or *kana* as the national script, who had been active since the Meiji period (see Twine 1991a:224–50) but had been suppressed during the war, now found that their arguments to a certain extent carried new weight and were, at least, no longer dismissed out of hand. Matsusaka Tadanori (1902–86), an energetic supporter of *kana*, recalled that after Japan's defeat there occurred a re-evaluation of the belief, hitherto considered sacrilegious by purists, that reshaping the written form of the national language to a more effective norm was an acceptable activity (1970:67). The story is told of Matsusaka silencing criticism of proposed reforms by pointing out the window at the ruins of Tokyo and asserting that the devastation had come about because the people of Japan had not had the words to criticize the military—what they saw before them was hardwon evidence of the need to democratize the language. The strength of Matsusaka's commitment to the concept of democracy is revealed by the conversation between Matsusaka and conservative Tokieda Motoki (1900–67) during a Council meeting, when Matsusaka commented on how the difference in their backgrounds had shaped their dissimilar views of the written language—Tokieda, he asserted, who had been brought up as a bourgeois youth whose family owned a villa in the resort town of Karuizawa, could afford to see script as worth retaining unchanged because of the tradition it enshrined, whereas he, Matsusaka, with his working-class background, fought for script reform on behalf of all those unlearned young people who harbored a desire to learn but were frustrated by the orthography (Uemae 1975:166–67).

This was a powerful argument in a period when, for the first time, sovereignty was passing into the hands of the people. In December 1945 the Kokugo Kyōkai (National Language Association), the Nihon Rōmazikai (Japan Romanization Society), and the Kanamojikai (Kana Society, a group dedicated to promoting *katakana* as the national script) joined forces and presented a proposal for the solution to language problems to the Supreme Commander for the Allied Powers, and in June the following year the *kana* and *rōmaji* groups issued a joint statement that they would cooperate in working toward the abolition of characters by disseminating horizontally written *katakana* and Japanese-style *rōmaji*[3] (Kitta 1989:56, 58). The general mood in these unsettled days of the immediate postwar period, as described by Sugimori Nagahide, was one of revulsion against the xenophobia, reactionary conservatism, and ultranationalism of the war period; the people had a yearning for that which was modern, Western, and rational. With the coming of the Occupation forces, street signs, station names, and other public signs that had hitherto been written in characters came to be written in *rōmaji* and English, and many English words such as "mama," "papa," and "OK" entered daily conversation. All over Japan examples of horizontally written *kana* appeared, and it seemed to many that written Japanese was undergoing

---

[3] Supporters of romanization were polarized around the issue of which of the two versions of spelling should be used: the Hepburn system, developed by medical missionary James Hepburn (1815–1911), which employed the letters of the alphabet as they were used in English, and the Japanese-style (*Nihonshiki*) system developed in 1885 by physicist Tanakadate Aikitsu (1856–1952) and others who wished to use the alphabet for a more faithful representation of the sounds of Japanese.

74

a historically determined and desirable process of rapid change toward use of phonetic script (Sugimori 1983:106).

This change did not take place, however, as the majority of members of the reconvened National Language Council supported a continuation of the use of characters, albeit with limits imposed. In his opening speech to the first postwar Council meeting in November 1946, the Vice Minister of Education stressed that script reform was necessary for the construction of a new Japan and was fundamental to all other reforms. The unrestricted use of characters and their complexity were seen as hindrances to cultural development, and the Council was requested to begin work toward reform. Subsequently, an 1,850-character List of Characters for Interim Use (*Tōyō Kanjihyō*) was accepted at the November general meeting of the Council, along with the recommendations for Modern Kana Usage (*Gendai Kanazukai*), both of which were ratified by the government the same month. The Education Minister declared in announcing the two lists that the problems of characters and *kanazukai* had been the biggest of Japan's language problems and as a result of the solutions now proposed, Japan could look forward to the thorough implementation of democracy, the further development of the cultural level of the people, and a rise in efficiency in day-to-day living. All these would contribute greatly to the reconstruction of the nation.

The reforms were announced in two forms: a Cabinet *kunrei*, or decree from a higher government office to those below it, that made it binding on all government offices to follow its contents, and a more general *kokuji*, a notification or bulletin put out by the Cabinet to inform the public that did not carry any element of legal compulsion. This form, in which all future language policies would be announced, brought bitter criticism from conservatives who argued that the government ought not to interfere in language issues. It was, of course, pointed out in rebuttal that the *kunrei* was binding only on government offices and the *kokuji* not at all, but this did not satisfy the critics, who countered that as the *kunrei* made it compulsory for the Education Ministry to follow the new lists in compiling textbooks, a de facto element of duress was involved. Council chairman Toki Zenmaro, defending the Council against criticism from Tokieda Motoki that the list was being enforced in newspapers and textbooks, pointed out that the press was observing the limits for reasons of increased efficiency of production and that, far from adopting the recommendations in school texts because of compulsion on the part of the Council, the Education Ministry believed the change would increase the effectiveness of education. Tokieda remained unconvinced, however, and his supporters during this discussion agreed with him that a request from the Ministry authorization committee to the textbook printing firms was, in fact, a form of compulsion (Toki, et al. 1952:15–16). This argument over the validity of government intervention came to be one of the main points held against reformers in the coming years, although conservatives did not hesitate to use the same procedures in implementing the later round of revisions.

The issue at stake in *kana* usage was a relatively simple matter of whether to base spelling on historical convention or modern pronunciation. In the case of characters, however, much more was involved. Over the years since the Meiji period, characters had been variously criticized for the educational burden they imposed, the fact that, despite their long history of adaptation in Japan, they had not originally been developed to suit the requirements of the Japanese language, the obstacle their unlimited use presented to the smooth functioning of democracy, the role they played in perpetuating homonyms, and, until recently, the hindrance they presented to office automation. On the credit side, characters had been presented as repositories of cultural tradition, offering the advantages of conciseness and visual clues to meaning (particularly with regard to distinguishing homonyms), allowing the formation of neologisms as need arose and thereby contributing to the swifter absorption of new knowledge, and permitting an extra dimension of visual richness in literary expression that was not possible with a phonetic script. During the Occupation, it was the democracy argument that was most often heard: the continued existence of a large character set with unrestricted readings would prevent the people from arriving at a critical understanding of political problems in a democratic society. Conservative Ōno Susumu, one of the most vocal opponents of the postwar reforms, reflected later that the claim that characters would obstruct the development of democracy was demonstrably untrue, as in China a revolution (surely one form of democracy) was achieved while using them, and Japan itself had managed to catch up with the West in this political sense despite retaining characters (Ōno 1962:246).

The tension between democratization and elitism in the writing system had been evident since the Meiji period. Whereas the traditional orthography had been championed first by those who had enjoyed a Confucian education in the days when class conferred that privilege or later had had the luxury of higher education, the prewar reform proposals had been backed by the Education Ministry to eradicate the difficulties caused by the length of time needed to teach the old writing system. The social class and economic circumstances of the conservatives enabled them to better deal with the things of the past, while the working class fared less well because of less schooling. Despite the much-touted period of Taishō democracy, during which the newspapers pressed for character limits to enable wider social comprehension of the news as well as for more pragmatic reasons, the rise of ultranationalism had tarred concepts such as democracy and liberalism with suspicions of treason against the state.

One of the strongest advocates of the need to democratize written Japanese was novelist and language activist Yamamoto Yūzō, who had been advocating character limits since before the war. Yamamoto had spent part of the war in Tochigi, and had been made even more keenly aware of the need for script reform by the difficulties factory workers there had with characters (Matsusaka 1962:81). In January 1946 he arranged a meeting of representatives from twenty-five private language-related groups, among them phonetic script advocates and educators, to discuss whether the Japanese might collaborate among themselves to solve the language problem, given the somewhat threatening interest from the Occupation authorities. This resulted in the formation of the Kokumin no Kokugo Undō Renmei (Federation of Private Japanese Language Movements), a body known in its early days as the League for the Democratization of the Japanese Language, which was to be instrumental in having the draft of the new constitution rewritten in modern Japanese rather than in the traditional Sino-Japanese (see Twine 1991:125–37). In his opening speech at the exploratory meeting, Yamamoto argued strongly that Japan could never attain true democracy unless its language problems were solved.

Others who supported Yamamoto in this endeavor included Andō Masatsugu (1878–1952), Nishio Minoru (1889–1979) and Matsusaka Tadanori. Matsusaka in particular was indefatigable in stressing the connection between language reform and democracy over and over again during the years that followed. Defending the postwar reforms in later years against often-heard complaints from the intelligentsia that modern youth "did not know characters" as a result of them, he produced figures to show that there had actually been an increase in rates of character acquisition compared with the prewar period, pointing out that the vast majority of people had not known many characters before the war. Those who criticized the literacy skills of today's university students, he claimed, were usually comparing them with the elite few who had attended a university before the war, prior to the advent of mass higher education, which, of course, resulted in a lower average. Postwar university students, however, came from a much broader social spectrum than before, had mastered the List of Characters for Interim Use and could both read and write them, the most that could be expected of an ordinary person. As long as Japan aimed at a democratic society, Matsusaka argued, language policy must take as its target what could be realistically expected of an average citizen. The language should belong to the people as a whole, and it was through this democratic form of language that higher culture must be created (1978:45).

Momose Chihiro, another *kana* advocate, likewise credited the postwar character limits and adoption of phonetic *kanazukai* with closing the previous great gap in literacy levels between the elites and the rest of the populace. After the defeat, the power of the traditionally educated elder statesmen who had blocked earlier attempts at script reform had been dissipated, enabling the implementation of democratic language policies that permeated throughout society to elites and average citizens alike. The result was that thirty years later many young people had no conception of the difficulties that characters had caused society previously (1980:5). It may have been this lack of understanding of the earlier problems mentioned by Momose that contributed to the smooth acceptance of the later revisions. Although the revisions were bitterly contested by those who had been involved in the postwar reforms and saw all that they had fought for being overturned, they were generally accepted by society at large, perhaps because thirty years of the post-reform writing system had induced either an amnesia or a lack of comprehension (depending on the age of the person concerned) as to the realities of the earlier system. The spread of mass higher education also meant that many more people than before were now accustomed to expecting higher levels of literacy.

The utilitarian approach to script espoused by reformers contributed substantially to ignoring the warnings of certain scholars that script reforms ought not to be rushed, that Japan was not a new country with a superficial literary tradition but an old society with a long and complex cultural history. Such a view was not popular in those postwar days, smacking as it did of the defeated ultranationalist ideology. Fukuda Tsuneari, author and opponent of the reforms, however, asserts that he had met often with scholars of Japanese language and literature during the war, as well as government officials in language-related positions, and knew that many of them had opposed script reform not from any overblown concept of nationalism but from honest opposition to the proposals themselves. If, as reformers charged, it was true that using historical *kanazukai* would endanger the future of Japanese culture, it was odd that many people had not noticed this until their sudden realization on the day of defeat (Sugimori 1983:134–35). The views of the conservatives were ignored, however, in the sudden freedom afforded the reformers after decades of suppression. Traditionalist Funabashi Seiichi, who along with a few other writers became a Council member around this time, said that he gained the impression they were there only to act as a kind of window-dressing for the Council; when he spoke out against the proposed changes to characters and *kanazukai*, other members were surprised that he should actually say something instead of merely sitting and listening, lending legitimacy to the decisions by his presence (1975:202).

77

There was vocal criticism of the fact that, although newspapers and government offices had been consulted, a broad spectrum of public opinion was not sought before the character list was made official. Council members were portrayed as huddling in closed rooms in secret, devising policies that would affect the entire nation on the members' personal whims, excluding the general public from the decision-making process despite their fine talk of democracy. Journalist Uemae Jun'ichirō takes this line, asserting that Council members were under the illusion that what they were doing was construction, while suppressing opposition with their rallying cry of democracy; just as in prewar days nobody had dared oppose nationalist objectives, so now people were coerced by not wanting to seem to oppose the new ideology (1975:168). To a certain extent, this criticism, particularly when one considers the extensive public consultation that took place in the later revisions of the postwar reforms, is valid: the records do show that at one of the meetings Yamamoto had suggested approaching the major publishers and writers before announcing the list, but the suggestion had been rejected because it was felt that if opinions were sought before the event, things would never be brought to a conclusion (Kokugo Shingikai 1952:86). The report of the Japanese Education Reform Council, however, states that the National Language Council collaborated with it in making a careful study of the simplification of the written language before submitting its proposals to the Education Minister for approval (1950:139). Consultation with the education authorities did occur, then, but the chance for open public input was not offered. This is probably due more to the nature of the social upheavals and more pressing matters of survival in the immediate postwar period than to any overt desire for dictatorship on the part of the Council, although it may have been that the desire for urgent reform blinded those involved to the contradiction of pressing through changes under the banner of democracy while denying the people at large an opportunity to comment.

Moderate Andō Masatsugu defended both the reforms and the manner of their implementation. Whereas some objected to the concept of character limits as an unreasonable application of government pressure in an area of personal liberty, he said, it was generally accepted procedure for proposals in any field to be put forward by the government, debated by the Diet, and then made public as law (although the language reforms were certainly not binding as laws). Language change occurred naturally over time in all societies; in highly developed societies, however, the normal tendency was for intervention by political authorities or cultural agencies through policies designed to guide that change in a desired direction, always with the aim of improving the culture regardless of opposition from a conservative minority. The final decision on whether the changes were acceptable lay with society itself, and some indication of the tenor of public opinion on the new character limits was evident in the enthusiasm with which most of the major newspapers had hastened to implement them (Andō 1975:108–29).

What the conservatives lacked during this period was a coordinated power base. Meanwhile, those favoring a move toward rationalization of the writing system had the support of an influential clique headed by Hoshina Kōichi (1872–1955, tireless advocate of script reform and influential member of all government language committees since the first in 1902) inside the Education Ministry (Sugimori 1983: 105–6 and Shioda 1965:176), the tacit approval of the Occupation authorities, an increasingly stronger position within the Council, and the advantage of being in tune with the temper of the times. Their successes followed one upon the other, backed by Cabinet approval and government implementation.

The reforms represented a major disjunction with the past as to the way script was regarded. No longer was the prevailing view that of characters and *kanazukai* representing some sort of sacred manifestation of the essence of Japanese spirit, sanctified by time and custom to inviolable status, although certainly there was still a substantial, if temporarily subdued, conservative element who held to this view. In its place had risen the ideology of reformers trained in Western linguistics who believed in the supremacy of the spoken language with script being merely a tool for its recording, unencumbered with metaphysical baggage. The reforms were also, over time, to lead to a change in the reading and writing ability of the general public. Their supporters saw them as enabling a rise in general literacy skills; to conservatives, they represented a lowering of standards, albeit standards that had applied only to certain sections of society prewar. In place of profusion, complexity, and tradition now reigned restrictions, simplicity, and convenience. The reforms polarized two opposing worldviews: tradition versus reform, conservative versus progressive. While the psychological background for the reforms thus lay in a desire to get rid of the chains of the past, there was a double edge to this restricting of characters: while it was touted as opening up the way for true universal literacy, it created a new generation of Japanese who could not read prewar literature and documents unless they were rewritten according to the new standards.

In December 1948, a National Language Research Institute (Kokuritsu Kokugo Kenkyūjo) was set up as an affiliated organ of the Education Ministry to carry out scientific surveys of aspects of the Japanese language and its function in Japanese society with the purpose of providing the basis for informed decisions in the formulation of policy by the National Language Council. Here, too, the government's main concern was that any such organization should be democratically run, given its close connection with a basic aspect of national life, and accordingly a committee was set up to discuss its goals and staffing. With the setting up of the Institute as the trigger, the Council underwent a period of reorganization in 1949, culminating in the issuing of a revised National Language Council Ordinance in April 1950. The aim of the reorganization was to free language policy from control by bureaucrats and politicians by allowing it to pursue other avenues of exploration than those dictated by the Ministry and to prevent stagnation by establishing finite terms of membership. A major change was its metamorphosis from a *shimon kikan* (an advisory body that acts upon requests from the Minister) to a genuine, more influential *kengi kikan* (one that could autonomously take up and investigate matters and then make recommendations to the Minister and other related ministers concerning the result). Although, in theory, the Council had had the power to make recommendations resulting from its investigations into Ministry-instigated matters since its inception in 1934, in practice the intellectual climate of the years before 1945 had meant that it was never given the chance, as its proposals were never accepted. In a further bid to have as wide a cross-section of input into decisions as possible, the system of members being chosen by the Education Minister was replaced by one whereby prospective members from a variety of fields were to be recommended to the Minister at the end of each term after a consultative process within the Council itself. The general meetings, which had previously been closed, were also to be open to the public at the insistence of Matsusaka Tadanori. Membership terms, hitherto open-ended, were set at three years, later reduced in 1951 to two.

The new chairman was Toki Zenmaro, a well-known and active advocate of romanization, and this gave rise to suspicion on the part of conservative members that those whose aim was the eventual abolition of characters were gaining a much stronger hold on the Council than they had had before. Toki made no bones about his personal agenda: in a 1947 article, he had spelled out his belief that until the language was democratized, not only would people experience difficulty in communicating thoughts and feelings on an equal basis, but also Japan would suffer in international terms because it would be unable to absorb new developments easily and increase trust of the Japanese worldwide. It was undeniable, he asserted, that many of the words that were hard to understand or invited misunderstanding were written with characters. The sooner that hindrance was done away with, the sooner the reconstruction of a democratic country would come about ("Kokugo to Kokuji Mondai," cited in Uemae 1975:168).

One criticism of the character list frequently heard after its inception was that it did not allow enough freedom of choice in the characters used in personal names. The Family Registration Act of December 1947 had stipulated that only characters from this list be used, and a few name characters, such as that for the often-used male suffix -rō, had been included for that purpose. This was based on the premise that to use noncurrent characters in an area of such basic social importance as names was disadvantageous both to the individual and to society. It was felt to be unnecessarily restrictive of the personal freedom of parents to choose children's names, however, and caused such concern that the issue was taken up in the Lower House of the Diet in early 1951. A subcommittee then set up by the Council produced a list of 92 additional characters, announced in May 1951. From that time on, name characters could be taken either from the main list or the new supplementary list.

The Beginnings of the Conservative Backlash

For over ten years, the conservatives were unable to oppose the reforms to any substantive effect. Then, in 1959, the new "Rules for Using Okurigana" were announced, which recommended in sum that more rather than fewer kana be used in writing various inflected forms commonly written in a character-kana mix (e.g., in the case of the verb tasukeru, -keru to be written in kana rather than just -ru). This was interpreted as just one more attempt to erode the status of characters. With the new rules as the fuse, opposition crystallized into action. The debate on tradition versus modernization broke out with renewed ferocity, this time with the reformers seriously under siege from a now coordinated conservative attack as private groups were formed to lobby for the repeal of their policies. At issue was the meaning of "kokugo no kaizen," the improvement of the language, laid down in the Council's charter as the first of its responsibilities: had the reforms really improved the language by removing prewar sources of difficulty as their supporters claimed, or had they led to serious disorder and in the process cut off the Japanese people from their cultural heritage? To conservatives, improvement of the language meant retreat from the reforms themselves. It is clear that the interpretation of the significant terms that shaped the debate varied according to the intellectual attitudes of the user, in particular in the matter of what constituted improvement, and the Council was about to be riven from within in a confrontation over these issues.

The use of bureaucratic measures, such as Cabinet directives to all ministries to see that the reforms were implemented during the Occupation, represented to conservatives a particularly unacceptable form of state intervention in private matters, and they made one of their major themes in this period the argument that the freedom of expression guaranteed by the constitution was being infringed by current language policy. Fukuda Tsuneari and Yoshida Tomizō, who played important parts in bringing about the eventual reconsideration of the reforms, remarked in 1965 that the use of characters had to a certain extent decreased without any enforcement through a natural process of attrition since the decline of education conducted in Sino-Japanese; there no longer existed fools who deliberately used difficult characters in the conceit that others would not be able to match their erudition (1965:227). Why, then, it was argued, was it necessary for the government to intervene by imposing irksome policies that infringed on an individual's right to freedom of expression? To this the reformers' reply was that the individual was under no such restraint. The Cabinet directives applied only to government departments; while cooperation was requested from the private sector, there was certainly no element of compulsion involved, and people were free to criticize the policies as they pleased. Freedom of expression was in no way restricted, as claimed.

Despite such denials, the "freedom of expression" argument gained ground to such an extent that it was still being heard even after it became apparent that the character limits were on the way to being relaxed; a petition from the Phonetic Society of Japan to the Education Minister and the Diet in 1980 cited the constitution in this respect and asked why there was still considered to be a need to limit and reduce the cultural treasure of language (Nihon Onsei Gakkai 1980:22–23). Matsusaka Tadanori attributed this mistaken impression in part to the statement in the remarks prefacing the first proposal for an expanded list in 1977 that the new list was to be a guide to characters to be used in the public domain and was not intended to be a rigid limit. People reading this, he commented, would naturally gain the impression that the earlier List of Characters for Interim List had restricted the characters a person could use in writing in general social life, and further that this was a violation of the individual's "freedom of expression." Most of those opposed to the 1946 character list had used this argument to attract sympathizers, and it was apparent that the new proposal was seeking public sympathy on a platform of this kind of flawed understanding of the issue. Despite the publishing boom that had resulted from the widening of the reading class consequent upon the adoption of the character limits in the press, writers were vocal in complaining that they were no longer free to use the characters of their choice. Matsusaka dismissed these complaints. Publishers always made demands on writers in regard to theme, sentence length, and so on, and were likewise free to make similar requests about the characters used with their readership in mind. Writers, on the other hand, were free to request that they be allowed to use unlimited characters and to negotiate by putting forward compromise proposals. If no compromise could be reached, they had the freedom to refuse to write in the specified way, and all this was as it should be in an open society (1978:44–45).

The issue of freedom of expression was, of course, linked to that of democracy in an attempt to show that the people, far from being served by the reforms, were, in fact, at risk because of them. Uemae, musing on the intellectual and political climate of the postwar period, observed that although, no doubt, many nostalgic and beautiful things were jettisoned in the name of democracy at this time, when something is inevitable, people—and in particular the Japanese people—are apt to look upon it as reconstruction rather than destruction. Reforms made in the name of democratization, however, he continued, are apt to go wrong once implemented, as in the case of socialized medicine. This is not to imply that democracy itself is bad, just that its name is invoked to sell inferior goods; postwar reforms based on that concept, therefore, caused confusion when they were put into practice (1975:168–69). As well as attracting outright criticism of this sort, the democracy argument was later to be recycled into the service of those who brought about the reversals of the policies adopted under its banner. Language belonged to the people, the reformers had often said in 1946. Language belongs to the people, the LDP subcommittee which recommended the overturning of their policies also affirmed in 1968, and the LDP as the "people's party" had a duty to examine the problems that had resulted from earlier policies and show the way for the future correct direction of language policy (Jiyū Minshutō Seimu Chōsakai Bunkyō Seido Chōsakai 1968:10).

Prior to this, those working toward this end had accused the reformers of having a stranglehold on language policy and argued that it was not right that language, the property of the entire nation, should be manipulated in this way. Writers such as Koshimizu Minoru called for a stop to Council interference with characters; control over the written language should be returned to the people, who should be left to work out autonomously their own individual ways of using script without outside direction (1976:92), a stance supported by the Japan Writers' Association (*Nihon Bungeika Kyōkai*). Many of the articles published by conservatives stressed that the decisions of the Council were not taken democratically enough, with sufficient consideration of "the will of the people," despite the reformers' counterclaim that the policies were worked out for the sake of that same people and that the conservatives would like to return to the undemocratic prewar writing system. The democracy argument was thus turned against the reformers, with claims that their policies infringed on individual freedom of expression and had contributed to disorder in the language that belonged to the whole populace.

The debate was not limited to the confines of the Council. Concern over the direction of postwar policy manifested itself in discussion in newspapers and magazines on the nature of language itself as a cultural treasure and of script, with both sides cogently putting their case. As well, many books on language appeared around this period, among them Kindaichi Haruhiko's famous *Nihongo* (*The Japanese Language*, 1957). Whereas in the immediate postwar period the economic argument linking reductionist script reforms with national reconstruction had carried great weight, and the major character and *kanazukai* reforms had been pushed through in a very short period of a few months, improved economic conditions now meant a degree of comparative leisure to reflect on the changes. The next two decades were to see a backpedaling in all areas except modern *kana* usage, and the eventual marginalization of supporters of the abolition of characters despite their previous position of strength during the Occupation and the years that followed.

As the debate intensified, two private pressure groups, both containing members of the Council, were formed to lobby for their various stances in the wider arena. These were the Language Policy Discussion Group (*Gengo Seisaku o Hanashiau Kai*, April 1958, later renamed the Language Policy Group [*Gengo Seisaku Kai*]), set up in support of the already-achieved reforms, and the Council for Language Matters (*Kokugo Mondai Kyōgikai*), formed in 1959 by those who saw language as a cultural treasure not to be debased lest the nation itself be debased. The latter was formed by conservatives to give themselves a platform from which to launch a coordinated attack on the Council's policies and procedures; feeling themselves outnumbered and ignored in the Council itself, they determined to fight back from outside. As well as engaging in vocal antireform and anti-Council rhetoric in its journal *Kokugo Kokuji* (*Our Language and Script*), this group carried on research activities and compiled its own manifesto on language problems. This document dealt with the broad concerns of modern linguistic theories that had supported language reforms since the Meiji period, the important affective factors that should also have a bearing on policy, and a host of related matters.[4] A third group active in the dispute was the Japan Writers' Association, which was highly critical of the National Language Council's philosophy and activities.

The effect of all these activities and their subsequent press coverage was to bring the language policy debate increasingly to the attention of the public. The event that focused public and press attention firmly on the Council and on language policy in general, however, was the highly publicized 1961 walkout of five conservatives from the final general meeting of the fifth term. Funabashi Seiichi, Uno Seiichi, Naruse Masakatsu, Shioda Ryōhei, and Yamagishi Tokuhei resigned in protest at the system of internal recommendation to the Minister by which the membership of each successive term of the Council had been determined since the postwar reorganization, claiming that this process allowed the reformers to maintain a stranglehold on the makeup of the Council. The procedure was that a selection committee (suisen kyōgikai) of between seven and fifteen members of the current Council would choose the names to be recommended for the next term. Because the number of Council members who supported the reforms had increased after 1949, it was a relatively simple matter for them to preserve their domination of the Council by ensuring that the names put forward were those of candidates who either supported or, at least, would not oppose their stance, often with the same people being recommended for successive terms. The dispute therefore centered on administrative procedures as much as policy, since the one to a large extent controlled the other. What appeared in principle to be democratic, claimed its opponents, was, in fact, autocratic.

What Funabashi and his supporters wanted was a reorganization of the Council, and they had mounted a carefully orchestrated campaign to achieve this. The term of membership of the fifth session of the Council was to expire on March 23, 1961. On March 17, the final general meeting of that session was held, with membership of the selection committee for the next term's members to be decided by general vote that day. Funabashi and the others spoke against what they perceived as the rampant inequity of this system. Discussion was lively and no resolution was reached that day, the meeting being adjourned until March 22. When it reconvened, the conservative group requested that the chairman rather than the meeting choose the members of the selection committee to enable a fairer resolution. This request is somewhat difficult to take at face value, given that Funabashi and Naruse had in the earlier meeting launched personal attacks on Toki for his advocacy of romanization. Their suggestion was strongly endorsed by Tanaka, head of the Ministry's Research Bureau within which the Japanese Language Section was then located, who passed the chairman a list of possible candidates, a move that hinted that at least some of the Ministry's bureaucrats supported Funabashi's group. Toki, however, balked at this suggestion on the grounds that it was not in accordance with the procedure stipulated by Education Ministry regulations. After further heated discussion from both sides, Funabashi led the rest of the dissidents from the room for a five-minute conference. On their return, Naruse announced that since the election procedure precluded any change in the mix of members, their group of five would now resign,

---

[4]This was Kokugo Mondai Kyōgikai (Tokieda Motoki), *Kokugo Mondai no Tame ni: Kokugo Mondai Hakusho*, Tokyo Daigaku Shuppankai, 1962. The original manifesto of this group may be found in *Kokugo Kokuji Kyōiku: Shiryō Sōran* 2nd. ed., Kokugo Kyōiku Kenkyūkai, 1969, pp. 534–35.

and without further ado they left the meeting (see Editorial Staff of *Kotoba no Kyōiku* 1961:10–18).

After this dramatic departure, the Council continued with its appointed business of choosing the members of the selection committee in the usual way. This was by no means the end of the matter, however. The next day, four of Funabashi's group, together with two other representatives of the private Council for Language Matters (to which all the retirees belonged), visited Education Minister Araki and explained the circumstances surrounding their withdrawal, blaming the postwar reforms for what they saw as the present parlous state of the language and at the same time requesting that he revise the regulations governing the Council in a way that would amend the membership selection process. On March 24, the Minister announced at a press conference that to give him greater responsibility in the selection of Council members the present regulations would be amended, and that future Council proposals should not be implemented immediately but re-examined after a twelve-month period of public scrutiny.

Questions on the furor were raised in the Diet four days later by two LDP members, Kajiwara Shigeyoshi and Otani Yoshio, later to become members of an LDP special committee on language policy, who questioned the Minister on behalf of Funabashi and Fukuda Tsuneari. Kajiwara argued against any form of state interference in language and script, displaying an anti-Council outlook, while Otani sought advice on the precise nature of the authority vested in the Council, suggesting it should be returned to the status of a *shimon kikan* rather than a *kengi kikan*, and even quoting Funabashi to the effect that the Council's hidden agenda of abolishing characters was a strategy to make the Japanese people illiterate and turn Japan into a Communist state. This is the first indication I have been able to uncover of the interest in language of several reactionary LDP politicians, which later culminated in 1968 in the report of a special committee lending support to the reversal of the Council's policies, and it is clear from the above comments that people such as Funabashi and Fukuda had a hand in fostering it. The editorial staff of the journal of the Japan Rōmaji Education Society saw this as a deliberate ploy, one tactic of the conservatives being to gain the support of LDP members in a propaganda campaign branding script reform as a scheme to set the stage for a Communist revolution; by this means they hoped to succeed in labeling the reformers as "reds" and thereby estranging the public from them (Editorial Staff of *Kotoba no Kyōiku* 1961:15). To advocates of romanization this was a particularly sensitive area, as much of the prewar and wartime persecution of such groups had revolved around the charge that their theories were motivated by communism.

Public interest in the Council reached an all-time high with the wide press and media reporting that followed the walkout. Funabashi's group published a statement the same day in all major newspapers except the *Asahi*, which again suggests that the withdrawal had been carefully planned in advance for maximum impact. The *Mainichi Shinbun* made it the top story on its city news page that day. All the major papers with the exception of the *Nikkei* carried editorials over the next week, as well as essays and columns dealing with the matters at issue and public statements from various private groups supporting their choice of sides. There was even a mock trial conducted on television during which an important part of the conservatives' "written indictment" centered on the charge that the Council's policies had led to linguistic confusion. The media attention focused on the walkout and its aftermath brought home to the Ministry the realization that public confidence in the Council had been severely undermined. Its plan, therefore, as reported by the *Asahi Journal*, was to restore both faith in and stability to the Council through the selection of members for the next term. To this end, representatives of the two feuding factions would be asked to leave the Council. New members should be undisputed leaders in various fields who would be asked to rethink language problems in a higher dimension.

When the sixth term of the Council first met in November that year, under the chairmanship of Abe Shinnosuke (1884–1964, head of the Japan Broadcasting Association), Education Minister Araki in his opening address requested that, rather than pushing through a string of specific policies as it had done to date, the Council now pause to reflect on public opinion on its past performance and at the same time give due consideration to the overarching issues affecting language problems. Between then and the following April, five meetings were held, at which the pro- and anti-reform views were aired. In April, three subcommittees were set up to begin investigations of specific problems: one to decide the criteria for future improvement of the language, one to carry out an overall evaluation of the results of the council's policies to date, and one to consider those matters where improvement should be planned for the future.

When the National Language Council Ordinance was partially revised by the Ministry in April 1962, three of the earlier regulations were changed. Meetings were no longer open to the public, membership selection was no longer in the hands of an internal committee, and the Council's Rōmaji Research Division was abolished. The Council was divested of its power to decide autonomously how it would approach its tasks and was returned to the system whereby its investigations were to be directed by requests from the Education Minister. Members were henceforth to be appointed by the Minister, a move that led many to suspect that political interference in the makeup of the Council would be forthcoming before long. Tōdō Akiyasu recalled that, when he questioned the Vice Minister on the reason for the change in selection procedure at the Council meeting where it was announced, he was told that no deep significance was attached to it, that the Ministry was merely bringing the Council into line with the procedure used in other *shingikai* (deliberative councils). Tōdō found this argument odd: the business of the Council was to formulate farsighted, long-term national policies, not to suit the convenience of the government of the day. If the Minister were to select members to suit some agenda of his own, there would be a risk that these policies would be distorted (Tōdō 1982:179 and Unger 1987:96). And, in fact, it did become apparent within a short time that supporters of reform were not being "appointed" and that the Council was becoming heavily weighted with members opposed to character limits (Ōkubo 1978:120).

Uno Seiichi, one of Funabashi's group who along with Shioda Ryōhei re-entered the Council for its seventh term, remarked of the atmosphere then that he noticed many more members sympathetic to the conservatives' opinions, which he attributed to the shake-up after the walkout. During this term, Uno resurrected a proposal that had already been rejected in the controversial fifth term, to the effect that the status of the 1946 list be changed from that of a compulsory limit (*seigen*, the word that appeared in its accompanying documentation) to that of a guide. Were this proposal to be accepted, Uno said, the 1946 list could be left as it was. Many felt, however, that the list should instead be overhauled to remove what were perceived as its deficiencies. A character subcommittee was established: it was also suggested that the word *seigen* be replaced with *kijun* (standard). Despite majority agreement, however, two members opposed this very strongly on the grounds that such a change would result in a return to unlimited use of characters and so the proposal was presented simply as a progress report (Uno 1977:36–37). The concern over the descriptive terminology used to define the nature of the list reflected a desire to move away from the impression held by many that its use was compulsory for the private citizen. It was also claimed by many (particularly authors) that having to write within a fixed framework of permissible characters led to unnaturalness in writing, and that because some characters and *on-kun* readings widely used in society were not on either list, society's wishes were obviously not being respected. The move away from "limit" to "standard" was thus an attempt to deal with this issue, and the nature of the list became a matter for widespread discussion.

The LDP Intervenes

The reactionary interest of certain LDP politicians at the time of the walkout began to crystallize over the next few years into a concrete plan of action that was to have a direct bearing on subsequent language policy. In January 1966 the media reported that Prime Minister Satō Eisaku had expressed concern about rumors that the current seventh term of the Council was considering dropping from the 1946 list those characters that appeared in the constitution but were not otherwise widely used in daily life. Soon after, on January 28, a subcommittee on language was set up within the LDP. This committee was continuing its deliberations on language policy when, in June 1966, Education Minister Nakamura Umekichi delivered to the first meeting of the eighth term of the Council its instructions for the future. As we shall see, this LDP committee was to have a bearing on the subsequent partial reversal of postwar policies.

The Minister's formal request (*shimon*) noted that various problems that had arisen since the postwar reforms now required a period of reflection and readjustment. The specific areas where re-examination was requested were the character list (handling, policy, and practice of selection), *on-kun* readings (policy on rationalization, practice of selection), character shapes (overall and individual criteria), *okurigana* (policy and content) and modern *kana* usage (problem areas). His opening speech included a reaffirmation of the three-script system as the Japanese writing system and as the basic premise for future Council deliberations. The Council thereupon began the task of revising the entire cycle of postwar reforms. Realizing that the character list, shapes, and modern *kana* usage were already fairly firmly entrenched after twenty years of use and would therefore prove the more taxing of the tasks, it began by re-examining both the *okurigana* rules and the *on-kun* list at the same time.

All these events taken together—the setting up of the LDP committee, the comments of various politicians, and the request from the government in the person of the Education Minister for a halt to further reforms—indicate a political backing away from the postwar reforms in general that was now manifesting itself in the language arena. The constitution, which to many was the symbol of an alien system imposed by the conquerors, came under attack during this period, with an LDP attempt to revise it in the late 1950s–early 1960s. The growing conservatism and anti-Communism evident during this period worked in favor of people like Fukuda Tsuneari who wished to foster an LDP view that language policy was being dominated by Communist sympathizers. There was also a desire to get rid of what were seen by many as the products of Occupation control, given Japan's increased economic security.

The LDP committee was meanwhile continuing its investigations. Known as the Subcommittee on Language Problems, it was a thirteen-member offshoot of the LDP's Education System Research Committee (*Bunkyō Seido Chōsakai*), which, in turn, was an arm of its Political Affairs Research Committee (*Seimu Chōsakai*). Members included former Education Minister Araki, the chairman of the Language Policy Group, and former Education Vice Minister Naitō. Between January 1966 and the release of its report in May 1968, it carried out various research projects and called in specialists to hear opinions from both sides on whether or not the Japanese language was in a state of confusion. The professed aim of the committee was to investigate from the standpoint of "the people's party," the LDP, whether the postwar reforms had been undertaken too hastily, whether the resulting policies really benefited the people, and whether there had been too much bureaucratic intervention. The final report was entitled *Kokugo no Shomondai* (*Problems in the Japanese Language*), and its preface made clear that this was the official government stance on language matters, to be used as a reference for others with an interest in this area. Japan's language, it stated, had for long ages carried the culture and thought of her race. It noted the view that a disordered language leads to a disordered nation. The committee found that a conspicuous lowering of reading ability had resulted from the postwar reforms, which had been undertaken in response to a mistaken emphasis on the part of the Occupation forces on simplifying Japanese, thereby bringing about the destruction of language traditions. Language and script ought not to be artificially fitted to human convenience but entrusted to the process of natural evolution. The human head is not a bucket that overflows if too much is put in—the basic assumption behind the reforms, that people could not remember difficult things, was in error, the committee wrote.

In general, the report found, the statement in Minister Nakamura's 1966 instructions to the Council that the three-script system was basic to written Japanese should be respected. Then followed a list of particular suggestions for change: character limits should be relaxed; the older forms of the characters should be considered the norm; historical *kanazukai* should be respected; *okurigana* should be reduced and *on-kun* readings increased; official documents should be written vertically; and the tendency to use both foreign loan words and also Sino-Japanese words written half in *kana* and half in characters should be corrected along with the relaxation of character limits. The correct use of honorifics should also be encouraged. All Cabinet directives and announcements relating to the previous reforms should be either repealed or revised in line with the above suggestions (Jiyū Minshutō Seimu Chōsakai Bunkyō Seido Chōsakai 1968:8–16). Much was made of the fact that this review was done for the sake of the people, who were allegedly suffering as a result of Occupation initiatives. After the report was presented to and accepted by the party's executive committee, the subcommittee was disbanded. Significantly, the chairman of the Education System Research Committee at the time was the current Education Minister, Sakata Michita. Sakata had earlier written to Education Minister Arita Kiichi in November 1966 on receipt of the subcommittee's interim report, containing in essence the same recommendations as those of the final report, requesting Arita's consideration of these matters.

The Japan Socialist Party's reaction to the report was to point out the inconsistencies within its findings and proposals. An article in *Gekkan Shakaitō* (*The Socialist Monthly*) accused the LDP of claiming that the alleged drop in reading ability was the result of language policies when blame could really be laid at the door of its own educational policies. To express concern about lowered literacy levels and at the same time recommend a relaxation of character limits was nonsense—with more characters to learn in a finite number of language-curriculum hours, levels would drop even further. The whole document was viewed as aiming at restoring a greater measure of control to the ruling class by reinstating semi-feudal conditions in language which restricted access to information through reduced literacy levels. In one thing only, the document was right—language should *not* be artificially shaped to human convenience when that meant the convenience of the ruling class! (Yabe 1968:136–38)

The proreform party was equally outraged. Matsusaka Tadanori, who had been one of those called before the committee to speak, commented that his experience there had shown him that its members were indeed sincerely motivated by the desire to make Japan a culturally outstanding nation. What many of them understood by the term "culture," however, involved a nostalgic harking back to the way things were in the days when prewar intellectuals were educated, when the tendency was to stress taste in writing rather than the transmission of information. Certain aspects of language use in those days, while certainly tasteful in aesthetic terms, had proven great hindrances in mass education and in machine production of documents. The primary function of script and language, Matsusaka warned, should not be overlooked in favor of this affective aspect. Those who were now responsible for language policy must not be influenced by those who had political power but were amateurs in language matters (1970:69). To Ōkubo Tadatoshi, who wrote an entire book criticizing the subsequent expanded character list, the report was always intended to overturn everything that the Council had achieved to date, despite the committee's pretense of democratically listening to the views of both sides in its deliberations, and in this it reflected the aim of its party (1978:127).

The executive committee of the LDP accepted the subcommittee's report on May 27, 1968. That same day, the report at the last general meeting of the eighth term of the Council included four important points to be passed on to the next term: that the nature of the 1946 list of characters should be changed from that of a limit to a standard, with use of other characters not proscribed; that on-kun readings should be increased; that the trend to using too many *okurigana* should be reversed; and that the public should be made aware that the general impression that Cabinet directives were binding on the entire populace was mistaken (Fujii 1968:8–9). Given that the LDP had already indicated to the Education Minister the drift of its policy and requested cooperation at the time of its interim report two years earlier, it was no coincidence that the first three of these points were in line with the findings of the subcommittee. Momose Chihiro reports considerable pressure on the Council and government offices as a result of the LDP's adoption of the report (1980:7).

When the LDP document appeared, the Council was partway through its review of two earlier policy documents, the List of *On* and *Kun* Readings for Characters for Interim Use and the Rules for Using *Okurigana*, with individual subcommittees set up for each task. The influence of the LDP suggestions on both *on-kun* readings and *okurigana*, backed by the enthusiasm of the many conservatives now in the Council, is clearly indicated by the content of the revisions. The new list of *on* and *kun* readings added a further 357 permissible readings to the 1948 list. The preface to the document addressed several contentious points. Of particular importance was the statement that while the earlier list had been compiled in a spirit of restriction (*seigen*), with readings not appearing on the list banned in areas where the list could be enforced, the new list was to be more loosely construed as a guide (*meyasu*). It was also made clear that the list was meant to be applied to the general public life of society, for example, in laws, official documents, and the press, and not to personal documents or to specialist areas, such as science and the arts. This was important, as much of the criticism of earlier lists of characters and readings had come from scientists who required a larger range for scientific terminology and from novelists and other literati who resented what they saw as a restriction on artistic expression. This statement was also intended to dispel the impression that the immediate postwar reforms had been somehow compulsory for the private citizen. It was emphasized that the list was intended to apply to modern Japanese only. The new rules for *okurigana* likewise involved a backing away from earlier policy: in many words the number of syllables to be written in *hiragana* after the character was decreased, and hence a corresponding increased importance attached to the character itself.

The eleventh term of the Council, which began in November 1972, took up two more of the points on the Minister's 1966 list, embarking on a reconsideration of the List of Characters for Interim Use (including the Separate List for education) and the List of Forms for Characters for Interim Use. In contrast to the speed with which the 1946 list had been compiled, the plan was to spend that term hammering out the basic policy to be followed, the next term preparing a draft policy on both issues for public perusal and comment, and a third term continuing its investigations and preparing the final reports to be sent to the Minister. It was made clear from the outset that the task would be approached with a view to easing rather than increasing limits on characters.

In addition to the political motivations described above, this backpedaling in language policy may also be attributed to the change in intellectual climate consequent upon improved economic conditions since the days the reforms were enacted. Once released from the imperative of getting the country back on its feet, there was leisure to consider other matters, and the increased economic and political stability allowed conservative ideas to resurface. It was during this period that the current crop of *Nihonjinron* literature—speculating on the nature of Japanese society and the Japanese people in all their aspects, with a particular emphasis on the "uniqueness" of Japan and its language—made its appearance (see Miller 1982:73–75). Whereas advocates of replacing characters with a phonetic script in the late 1940s had taken as one of their major platforms the economic argument that characters slowed down development because the time spent mastering them could be better spent learning other useful skills, by the 1970s it had become apparent that Japan could, in fact, make significant economic progress despite the use of characters, a point not lost on conservatives who crowed that Japan's success proved characters were not inefficient as claimed and, in fact, aided progress. Within this environment of increased reflection it was only natural that a reassessment of the need to limit characters should take place. Many opponents of relaxed limits, however, continued to insist that it was precisely *because* of the postwar reductions that economic growth had been accelerated, a claim dismissed by Ōno Susumu for whom the real cause of growth was the Ikeda income-doubling policy rather than any script reform policy (1977:108).

Public reaction to the expanded list of 1,945 characters was, in general, positive after the eventual announcement of the Council's final report in March 1981. The change was widely reported in the television news that night, with prominence given to the increase of ninety-five characters and the restoration of the nineteen from the Interim List. All morning editions of the newspapers carried the report on the first page the next day as well as on the city affairs page, with supplements giving the characters and their readings. Editorials varied: most expressed the hope that the change from "limit" to "guide" would not lead to unrestricted use and that care would be taken to see that the increase did not become an additional burden on students. Much of the criticism of the new list came from educators concerned at just that prospect: the extra burden the additional ninety-five characters and their associated on-kun readings *would* impose on students and teachers in the classroom. Another tack was taken by critic Kuwabara Takeo (1904–), supporter of the earlier limits, who wrote that Japan was now entering an era where its language would no longer be used by Japanese alone; those in favor of relaxing the limits on characters lacked breadth in international vision. While nobody spoke up for the romanization groups, Matsusaka and Momose represented the *kana* camp in opposing the additions and the nature of the list.

There was much bitter invective from those irate at the political machinations behind the changes. Ōkubo Tadatoshi, for instance, had, as mentioned earlier, written a book, *Ichiokunin no Kokugo Kokuji Mondai (The Language and Script Problems of One Hundred Million People)*, in 1978, criticizing the first of the two drafts of the new list as being evidence of a plot by the LDP to overthrow the democratic language reforms of the Occupation and return to the prewar situation. He was no less critical of the final product, pointing out that of the 1,945 characters seventy were shown by the National Language Research Institute's survey of newspapers to be of low frequency, so there had been no real need to go outside the earlier frame of 1,850. The new list was contradictory, he claimed: while making the criticism that young people could not write characters, it contributed to the worsening of that situation by increasing the number they were expected to learn (Nomura 1981:38). Koizumi Tamotsu likened the reversal of the postwar policies to the 1942 cave-in of Education Minister Hashimoto to right-wing pressure when he watered down the Council's wartime proposals for character limits, denouncing the latest developments as setting at naught all the efforts put in by advocates of script reform since the Meiji period (1981:26). Marxist scholars Suzuki Yasuyuki and Miyajima Tatsuo likewise denounced all the revisions as products of an increasingly rightist and reactionary government and Council (Suzuki 1977:70). Suzuki, in particular, saw these developments as the culmination of the reactionary education policies of the LDP, aimed at producing people capable of working for the prosperity of companies, particularly monopolistic corporations, and at pursuing imperialistic education that would foster conservative morals, sentiments, and feelings conducive to justifying Japan's own development. Although the LDP had made use of the banner of democracy, he claimed, the revisions had nothing to do with democracy but everything to do with manipulating language policy to create a complicated, elitist education system that would serve the ends of a monopolistic capitalist system (1977:20–46).

With the issue of a policy document, "The Writing of Foreign Loanwords," in 1991, the twenty-five year cycle of reflection on and revision of the postwar revisions requested by the Minister came to an end. While modern *kana* usage remained unchanged, in all matters relating to characters there had been a definite reversal of previous policy, confirming the central importance of characters to written Japanese, removing strict limits on their use, and sidelining those, such as the romanization groups and the Kanamojikai, who had hoped to see the eventual abolition of characters. The major change in direction and philosophy was in the nature of the policies, from prescriptive limits to flexible guides. It was a limited victory, however, because although the conservatives argued that the prewar character and *kanazukai* practices should be respected as the legitimate forms of the written language, no really significant return to them occurred as a result of the modifications to the postwar reforms. Despite the pivotal role played by the concept of time (as in "time-hallowed custom") in their arguments as to the sanctity of the old script system, time in this instance was their enemy. It was simply too late to engineer a radical reversal of language policy without the supporting social environment provided by the rise of ultranationalism before the war. While the drastic change in policy during the Occupation had been possible because of the desire to break with the past and the extreme social upheaval that followed defeat, no such equivalent social trauma existed later to which conservatives could link their arguments for a return to the unrestricted system of the past.

Language policy in Japan, as indeed anywhere else, has always been formulated to suit the agenda of those in power at the time. Prewar, the dominance of ultranationalism ensured that attempts to challenge the existing orthography were defeated on grounds of national security. Postwar, most of the reforms that were finally achieved during the Occupation period, while their basic structure remains unchanged in that there still exist official policy documents on various aspects of the writing system, have been reshaped both qualitatively and to a lesser extent quantitatively to reflect an increasing conservatism with the active encouragement and intervention of the LDP. The prevailing mood in language policy with regard to script remains one of relative conservatism. With the current success of the Foreign Ministry policy in promoting the study of Japanese overseas, the advent of the word processor, which has revolutionized document production in Japan, and the re-establishment of economic security despite the continued use of characters, it is generally believed that many of the earlier arguments for script reform are no longer valid. This outcome may be attributed in large part to the use of the political and affective arguments outlined in this article.

Glossary

hiragana	平仮名, ひらがな	meyasu	目安
kana	仮名, かな	okurigana	送りがな
kanazukai	仮名遣い	on reading	音読み
katakana	片仮名, かたかな	rōmaji	ローマ字
kengi kikan	建議機関	seigen	制限
kijun	基準	shimon	諮問
kokuji	告示	shimon kikan	諮問機関
kun reading	訓読み	shingikai	審議会
kunrei	訓令	suisen kyōgikai	推薦協議会

hiragana	one of the two phonetic scripts, used today to write those sections of a text where characters cannot represent Japanese grammatical features
kana	the term used to refer collectively to the two phonetic scripts, *hiragana* and *katakana*.
kanazukai	the way *kana* are used, specifically refers to the historical usage or the modern usage
katakana	one of the two phonetic scripts, used today mainly for writing words of foreign origin (except those of Chinese origin)
kengi kikan	government body that autonomously investigates matters and makes recommendations to the Minister and other related ministers concerning the result

91

kijun	standard
kokuji	public announcement
kun reading	the way a character is pronounced when it represents a word of Japanese origin
kunrei	Cabinet directive to ministries
meyasu	guide
okurigana	*kana* added to characters to represent the inflected part of a word
on reading	the way a character is pronounced when it represents a word of Chinese origin
rōmaji	the Western alphabet
seigen	limit
shimon	formal request from a Minister
shimon kikan	advisory body that acts upon requests from a Minister
shingikai	deliberative council
suisen kyōgikai	selection committee that makes recommendations

List of References

ANDŌ MASATSUGU. 1975. *Gengo Seisaku Ronkō* [A Study of Language Policy]. Tokyo: Yūzankaku.

EASTMAN, CAROL. 1983. *Language Planning: An Introduction.* Novato, Calif.: Chandler and Sharp.

Editorial Staff of *Kotoba no Kyōiku.* 1961. "Kokugo Shingikai no Kūdetaa" [Coup d'Etat in the National Language Council]. *Kotoba no Kyōiku* 132:10–18.

FUJII, TSUGUO. 1968. "Shinbun to Kokugo Seisaku" [Newspapers and Language Policy]. *Gengo Seisaku* 10:8–12.

FUKUDA TSUNEARI and YOSHIDA TOMIZŌ. 1965. "Kokugo Shingikai o Shikaru" [Chiding the National Language Council]. *Shio* 63:220–30.

FUNABASHI SEIICHI. 1975. "Sengo Sanjūnen no Kokugo Seisaku" [Thirty Years of Postwar Language Policy]. *Kokugo Kokuji* 86:19–24.

Japanese Education Reform Council. 1950. *Education Reform in Japan: The Present Status and Problems Involved.* Tokyo: Japanese Education Reform Council.

Jiyū Minshutō Seimu Chōsakai Bunkyō Seido Chōsakai. 1968. *Tokushū: Kokugo no Shomondai* [Special Release: Language Problems]. Tokyo.

KITTA HIROKUNI. 1989. *Nippon no Rōmazi Undō 1789–1988* [The Romanization Movement in Japan, 1789–1988]. Tokyo: Nippon no Rōmazi-sya.

KOIZUMI, TAMOTSU. 1981. "Nihon no Moji Seisaku" [Japan's Script Policy]. *Gengo* 10 (11):20–27.

KOKUGO SHINGIKAI. 1952. *Kokugo Shingikai no Kiroku* [Proceedings of the National Language Council]. Tokyo: Monbushō.

KOSHIMIZU MINORU. 1976. "Sengo Kokugo Seisaku no Risō to Genjitsu" [Postwar Language Policy: Ideal and Reality]. *Asahi Jaanaru* 9/4/1976:90–93.

MATSUSAKA TADANORI. 1962. *Kokugo Kokuji Ronsō: Fukkoshugi e no Hanron* [The Language and Script Debate: The Argument against Reactionism]. Tokyo: Shinkyo Shuppan.

———. 1970. "Jidai Gyakkō no Kokugo Shingikai" [The National Language Council: Out of Step with the Times]. *Seikai Ōrai* 36(9):64–69.

————. 1978. "Shinkanjihyō ni Jisshi o Kuitomenakereba Naranai" [We must not Allow the New Character List to come into Effect]. *Sakubun to Kyōiku* 1978:42–45.

MILLER, ROY ANDREW. 1982. *Japan's Modern Myth: The Language and Beyond*. New York: Weatherhill.

MOMOSE CHIHIRO. 1980. "Kokugo Seisaku o kaeru Riyū wa Nanika" [Why Change Language Policy?]. *Kana no Hikari* 695:3–7

NIHON ONSEI GAKKAI. 1980. "Kasekika shita Kokugo Seisaku: sono Konponteki Hansei to Shinkyōiku Seisaku e no Tenkan" [Fossilized Language Policy: A Thorough Reconsideration and the Implications for Education]. *Onsei Gakkai Kaihō* 163:22–23.

NOMURA, MASAAKI. 1981. "Jōyō Kanjihyō no tōjita Mono: Masukomi no Hankyō o otte" [Media Reaction to the List of Characters for General Use]. *Gengo Seikatsu* 355:32–39.

ŌKUBO TADATOSHI. 1978. *Ichiokunin no Kokugo Kokuji Mondai* [The Language and Script Problems of a Hundred Million People]. Tokyo: Sanseidō.

ŌNO SUSUMU. 1962. "Shin Kokugo Shingikai no Kadai" [Problems with the New National Language Council]. *Sekai* (193):243–250.

————. 1977. "Shinkanjihyō wa Moji no Katsuryoku o Kaifuku saseru ka" [Will the New Character List Restore the Vitality of Characters?]. *Asahi Jaanaru* 11/2/1977:106–111.

SEELEY, CHRISTOPHER. 1984. "The Japanese Script since 1900." *Visible Language* XVIII (3):267–301.

————. 1991. *A History of Writing in Japan*. Leiden: Brill.

SHIODA RYŌHEI. 1965. *Kokugo Zuihitsu*. Tokyo: Sekkasha.

SUGIMORI NAGAHIDE. 1983. "Kokugo Kaikaku no Rekishi (Sengo)" [The History of Language Reform: Postwar]. In Maruya Saiichi, ed., *Nihongo no Sekai 16: Kokugo Kaikaku o Hihan suru* [The World of Japanese Language 16: Criticisms of Language Reform]. Tokyo: Chūō Kōronsha, pp. 95–168.

SUZUKI YASUYUKI, ed. 1977. *Kokugo Kokuji Mondai no Riron* [The Theory of Language and Script Problems]. Tokyo: Mugi Shobō.

TŌDŌ AKIYASU. 1982. *Kanji no Kako to Mirai* [Characters: Their Past and Future]. Tokyo: Iwanami Shoten.

TOKI ZENMARO, SAWADA KINJI, KINDAICHI KYŌSUKE, TOKIEDA MOTOKI, NAKAMURA MUNEO, and NISHIO MINORU. 1952. "Kokugo Shingikai wa dō iu koto o shite iru ka" [What is the National Language Council Doing?]. *Gengo Seikatsu*, March 1952:2–24.

TRAINOR, JOSEPH. 1983. *Educational Reform in Occupied Japan: Trainor's Memoir*. Tokyo: Meisei University Press.

TWINE, NANETTE. 1991. "Language and the Constitution." *Japan Forum* 3.1:125–37.

————. 1991a. *Language and the Modern State: The Reform of Written Japanese*. London: Routledge.

UEMAE, JUN'ICHIRŌ. 1975. "Shōwa Nijūichinen: Kokugo Shingikai" (1946: The National Language Council). *Shokun* 7 (7):156–80.

UNGER, J. MARSHALL. 1987. *The Fifth Generation Fallacy: Why Japan Is Betting Its Future on Artificial Intelligence*. New York and Oxford: Oxford University Press.

UNO, SEIICHI. 1977. "Sengo no Kokugo Kaikaku—Watashi no Taiken o Chūshin toshite" [My Experiences with Postwar Language Reform]. *Kokugo no Kenkyū* 10:33–42.

YABE, H. 1968. "Jimintō no Kokugo Seisaku ni miru Handōsei" [Reactionism in the LDP's Language Policy]. *Gekkan Shakaitō* 140:136–38.

Lessons from the *Kokugo*
(National Language) Readers

ELAINE GERBERT

Kokusaika, or "internationalization," has been one of the most frequently used words in the Japanese media since the early eighties. Japan's increasingly active presence in the world economy has given rise to an active debate over the ways in which the citizenry of Japan will function as participants on an international stage in the twenty-first century. In Japan, as in other countries, awareness of the growing importance of international relations in national life has refocused attention on education. Official initiatives to meet the challenge began in August 1984 when Yasuhiro Nakasone, the prime minister at the time, established an ad hoc Council on Educational Reform to review existing educational practices and make recommendations for their reform.[1] Since then, efforts to enhance internationalization have focused largely on absorbing the increase in the numbers of foreign students, mostly from Asia, studying in Japan; providing for the education of Japanese children living overseas; instituting study abroad for upper secondary school students; and improving communication skills in foreign languages, primarily English.[2]

Thanks are due to Patricia Weiss for enabling me to share my thoughts on Japanese textbooks with the participants of two Mid America Japan in the Schools Seminars, and to Margaret Childs and the anonymous *Comparative Education Review* referees for reading and commenting on earlier versions of this article. I would also like to express appreciation to Vickie Doll, Endō Kenji, Joan LaValle, Rieko Nagamasa, Nobuko Narita, and Yagawa Sumiko for helping me to secure needed materials.

[1] Government of Japan, Ministry of Education, *Mombushō 1990 Ministry of Education, Science and Culture* (Tokyo: Ministry of Education Science and Culture Publications, 1990), p. 56. The council, consisting of forty-five representatives from elementary, secondary, and higher education, business, industry, and organized labor identified eight issues of pressing concern. Three of these were "basic requirements for an education relevant to the 21st century," "coping with internationalization" and "coping with various changes in our society, including internationalization in different sectors," and the promotion of wider and more efficient use of the information media.

[2] Ibid., pp. 58–59. These efforts have been made under the auspices of the Mombushō (Ministry of Education) Headquarters for the Implementation of Educational Reform, a group organized for the purpose of executing recommendations made by the Council of Educational Reform and headed by the minister of education himself. In the newly revised course of study issued by the Mombushō in March 1989, *kokusaika* appears alongside *koseika* (individualization) and *jōhōka* (informationization) as a national educational goal. *Koseika* implies the promotion, not of individualism, as the term may imply, but of structural reorganization of university programs for the purpose of promoting greater flexibility and creativity, particularly in the area of scientific research. *Jōhōka,* undertaken to better cope with the "information age," calls for the infusion of more computers and other information technology into technical high school and university programs and more training for teachers in information science and technology. For information on research on the incorporation of *kokusaika,*

Comparative Education Review, vol. 37, no. 2.

At the same time that the government encourages "internationalization," elementary school readers, written and produced under the guidance of the Mombushō (Ministry of Culture), reinforce a sense of national identity. The culturally coded images and themes in these readers create an image of a world that is immediately and unmistakably "Japanese." While social studies textbooks teach young Japanese about the world, Japanese language readers preserve a core of native values and perspectives that serve to anchor the child *in* the world.

At the other end of the spectrum from the monocultural Japanese reader stands the multicultural American elementary school reader. This reader, often regarded as a model of cultural tolerance, focuses heavily on the varied ethnic and racial backgrounds of young people in the United States and, one may assume, in doing so, prepares young Americans to feel at home in a world made up of diverse others. In addition to stories featuring American children from different cultural backgrounds, there are many stories based on folktales from around the world (especially Africa) and stories about young people in different national settings. So varied are the characters and experiences depicted in these textbooks that one is often left wondering what nation their audiences might be living in. Cultural diversity, so absent in the Japanese reader, is everywhere present in the American reader. By contrasting the Japanese textbooks with American textbooks, I hope to show how Japanese materials are designed to create a common singular consciousness in their youth.

Fostering a sense of belonging to the Japanese nation through the readers is in keeping with the tenor of a 1984 address to the Council of Educational Reform by Prime Minister Nakasone, who said that educational reforms are to be guided by the principle of *preserving and further developing traditional Japanese culture* while at the same time cultivating in children universally accepted "moral and behavioral standards" for the purpose of enabling future Japanese citizens to "contribute to the international community *with a Japanese consciousness*."[3] That Japanese language readers should play a critical role in shaping the self-image of the Japanese is not surprising when one considers the ways in which the Japanese language has been viewed by many in Japan. There is a huge body of literature in

---

koseika, and *jōhōka* into the curriculum, see Nihon Kyōiku Nenkan Kankō Iinkai (Japanese Education Yearbook Publication Committee), *Nihon kyōiku nenkan* (Japanese education yearbook) (Tokyo: Gyōsei, 1991), p. 167.

[3] Italics are mine. See Robert Leestma, ed., *Japanese Education Today* (Washington, D.C.: U.S. Department of Education, 1987), p. 64. This position was also articulated in the Mombushō's newly revised 1989 course of study, where one of four recommendations reads: "To put more value on developing in children an attitude of respecting Japanese culture and traditions, as well as an increased understanding of the cultures and histories of other countries in the world. Thus children should be helped to develop the qualities required of a Japanese living in the international community" (Government of Japan, Ministry of Education, p. 24).

the country that claims the essence of being Japanese to be inextricably linked to speaking the Japanese language and asserts the uniqueness of both the Japanese identity and the Japanese language.[4]

This study explores some of the ways in which readers in the past 8 years have fostered the sense of a "Japanese consciousness" in children who will reach adulthood around the year 2000. Citations and examples are taken from readers published by leading textbook publishing companies between 1984 and 1992 for grades 1–6.[5]

The National Language and the National Language Reader

The study of the Japanese language in the Japanese educational system is known as *kokugo,* the "national language." The word used to designate the Japanese language when it is studied as a foreign language by a nonnative Japanese, or when the Japanese language is distinguished from other languages in the world, is *nihongo.* One might say that *nihongo* is comparable to the face Japanese show to the outside (*soto*), while *kokugo* is comparable to the face reserved for the members of one's ingroup (*uchi*).

Kokugo study occupies more classroom time than any other subject in the 9 years of compulsory education: an average of 1,987 classroom hours are spent studying *kokugo* in grades 1–9, as opposed to 1,496 spent on mathematics, 943 on social studies, and 908 on science.[6] In defining educational standards and procedures to be followed in the study of *kokugo,* the Mombushō prescribes a specific list of Chinese characters (*kanji*) to be learned at each grade level of compulsory education and the proper stroke order to be followed in writing each of about 2,000 characters. In elementary school, in addition to 996 characters, students must learn two phonetic syllabaries and the roman alphabet. *Hiragana* (the cursive phonetic syllabary consisting of 46 signs), is introduced in volume 1 of the two-volume first-grade reader. *Katakana* (the 46-letter angular phonetic

---

[4] The semimystical attitude toward the special nature of the Japanese language propounded in *nihonjinron* writing (literature that explores and asserts the "unique" character of the Japanese people) is by no means a recent phenomenon. Nationalist scholars of the seventeenth century, for example, undertook painstaking philological analysis of the Japanese language in order to support their claims of Japan's uniqueness. See Yamazaki Ansai, "Lectures concerning the Chapters on the Divine Age," in *Sources of Japanese Tradition,* trans. and ed. Ryūsaku Tsunoda, W. Theodore de Bary, and Donald Keene (New York: Columbia University Press, 1958), 1:358–60. More recent assertions of the inseparability of "Japaneseness" and the Japanese language have led the American linguist Roy Andrew Miller to comment that "the Japanese language has gradually been elevated to the position of one of the major ideological forces sustaining Japanese society, at the same time that it helps that society to close its ranks against all possible intrusions by outsiders" (Roy Andrew Miller, *Japan's Modern Myth: The Japanese Language and Beyond* [New York and Tokyo: Weatherhill, 1982], p. 283).

[5] The readers surveyed in this study were published by Mitsumura Tosho Shuppan, the leading publisher of *kokugo* textbooks in Japan. I also discuss stories in readers published by Kyōiku Shuppan, Nihon Kyōiku, Nihon Shoseki, and Gakkō Tosho.

[6] Hitoshi Kaneko et al., *Kyōiku Shōroppō* (Guidelines for education) (Tokyo: Gakuyō Shobō, 1984), pp. 96–97.

syllabary used to transcribe non-Sinitic foreign loanwords and onoma-topoeia) is introduced in volume 2. The study of *rōmaji* (roman letters) begins in the fourth grade.

The use of *katakana* to transcribe words borrowed primarily from Western languages (mostly English) suggests the strength of the outside (*soto*)/inside (*uchi*) dichotomy that underlies virtually all social transactions and speech forms in Japan. Transcription in *katakana* (as opposed to *kanji*, used to write words of Sinitic origin, or a combination of *kanji* and *hiragana*, used for words of Japanese origin) marks as different (alien) even words of Western origin that have been in use since the sixteenth century. A quick glance immediately determines the "foreign" provenance of a loan-word. Of the thousands of European loanwords taken into the language, virtually none have made it to native status—that is, none are written in *hiragana*. This is comparable to a situation in which Americans would write "hurricane," "igloo," "croissant," and thousands of other words in upper-case letters to show that they are not original English words. The distinction between the Japanese language and foreign linguistic elements enters the consciousness of Japanese children from grade 1.

Six years of *kokugo* education in elementary school are followed by 3 years of *kokugo* classes in junior high school and another 3 years of *kokugo* study in senior high school. Junior high school students learn an additional 300, 350, and 252 characters in the 3 years of study, respectively. Senior high school students concentrate on reading modern and classical Japanese literature in their classes of *Kokugo* I, *Kokugo* II, *Kokugo hyōgen* ("national language expressions," basically a course in composition), *Gendaibun* (modern literature), and *Koten* (an introduction to classical Japanese grammar and literature and to *kambun*—a Japanese system of glossing classical Chinese texts).[7] Elementary school *kokugo* texts may be said to develop "Japanese" attitudes toward self-expression, nature, the self in relation to nature and to others, and the past—in other words, to lay the psychological foundation on which the appeal of the literary canon introduced at the higher grade levels will rest.

Six commercial publishing companies produce textbooks for the elementary school system, in contrast to the situation in the United States, where over 100 companies engage in publishing elementary school readers. Prefectural and local school boards determine which publishers' textbooks will be adopted for a given school system in the case of public schools, and faculty make the determination in many private schools. All textbooks, however, must be certified by the Mombushō before they can be placed on the market. Because the Mombushō established guidelines regarding the style and content of the textbooks, and determines the constitution of the committees of scholars and educators who examine and license

---

[7] Ibid., p. 97.

them, there is a high degree of uniformity among the series issued by the different publishing houses; what differences do exist are largely cosmetic in nature.

Mombushō control in fact extends to even the physical size and length of the textbooks. All are in paperback format, unlike the hardcover format of American textbooks, and all conform to the same dimensions. Textbooks for *kokugo*, social studies, mathematics, and science for grades 2–9 measure exactly 5¾ inches wide by 8¼ inches long. All elementary school textbooks are thin, light and pliant, easy to slip into a book bag and transport. (Children are generally not allowed to keep books in their lockers at school and must carry them home.) Small, light, and extremely portable textbooks would seem to be an incentive for their use at home by Japanese children, just as the heavier weight and more cumbersome dimensions of the larger, graphically more lavish American readers might militate against their use at home by American children (the 1989 Macmillan Press series "Connections," e.g., measures 8 by 9½ inches). The *kokugo* readers are also compact: reading, writing, vocabulary, and the introduction of Chinese characters are all integrated into a single thin volume. The Macmillan texts, by contrast, are supplemented by as many as eight large-size elective paperback workbooks per grade containing exercises on spelling, word meaning, reading, creative writing, story analysis, oral presentation, and drama activities, plus a workbook written in English and in Spanish for parents who wish to work with their children at home. Japanese textbooks are inexpensive and—unlike the far-costlier American textbooks, which are used for several years by succeeding classes of students—are not returned to the school after use. They are personal possessions of the children and, as such, can become extensions of the children themselves.

The World as a Limited, Safe Place

Elementary school readers in the United States today expose children to a view of a world made up of persons of diverse cultural and racial background with a wide array of problems and personalities, a world far removed from the safe, narrow, predictable vision of life presented to youngsters in the Dick and Jane readers 40 years ago. As early as the first grade, children read about youngsters their own age who have physical and social problems far more challenging than anything that ever confronted Dick and his sisters. There are characters who are blind or confined to wheelchairs; characters who are prey to the feelings of insecurity and inferiority created by sibling rivalry or parents who are socially disadvantaged; children who suffer or are self-conscious because they are too fat, or too tall and thin. There is an emphasis on caring for and assisting others, and children are depicted befriending and helping not only peers and equals, but members of the family and the community who are old, frail, sick, or handicapped.[8] Indeed, one of the principles determining the selection of stories seems to be diversity. Being different is a positive value, and textbooks feature characters who exemplify a kind of individuality by virtue of some physical or psychological feature that makes them stand out.

In contrast to the current American emphasis on exposing children to the challenging complexities of life, Japanese elementary *kokugo* textbooks present the world as a safe, predictable place, a secure, protected environment where man and nature interact harmoniously. While the American reader presents difficulties children encounter and provides many examples of how children overcome their fears and their dilemmas, the Japanese reader seldom even acknowledges that children might have problems. Nor are children shown to harbor strong emotions. In comparison to the significant role it plays in American stories, desire, for example, as a motivating force is much more muted in Japanese stories. Japanese children are not often shown to have conflicting feelings or to struggle with their emotions, as children often do in American stories. Human figures in those stories are moreover usually depicted in rough, abstract fashion with little attention paid to individual differences. Children frequently all look alike, except for differences between girls and boys.

What is highlighted and celebrated instead is the natural world. In place of the large color photographs of children of different races found in the 1989 Macmillan readers, for example, the 1989 second-grade Mitsumura Tosho reader opens with colored photos of plants and insects, which give way to photos of landscapes in the upper grades. The most common perspective is the ground level perspective of the child. Attention is focused downward on the small forms of life that inhabit the grasses, seashore, and ponds of the child's world, as opposed to the images of flight (e.g., planes and trapeze artists) and ascent (mountain climbing) so often favored in American readers. The low ground-level line of observation places the child in a position of control over the bit of nature that he or she is taught to observe and write about. And within that narrow scope, the emphasis is on the same close observation of detail and procedure that characterizes Japanese elementary and junior high school science textbooks. Plants and insects that the child is likely to encounter close to home are presented in all their generic individuality, and children learn to distinguish and name three kinds of dragonflies, for instance, or name the stages in the life cycle of an *akiakane* (a kind of dragonfly). The focus on the natural world close to home nurtures a sense of familiarity and confidence vis-à-vis the surrounding environment.

[8] See the volumes *Look Again, Friends Aloft, Adventuring,* and *Observing* in the 1989 Macmillan "Connections" reading series, ed. Virginia A. Arnold et al. (New York: Macmillan, 1989).

Whereas the inspirational messages that introduce the themes of the units of American readers are frequently related to themes of adventure and invention, those introducing Japanese readers emphasize the close interrelationships between people, plants, and animals. Eight-year-old children are likened to "young leaves" who, like the leaves of trees, prosper under the sky and the sun.[9] The fluid ease with which natural forms interpenetrate each other is emphasized from the very first grade. A first-grade reader, for example, begins with a story in which a class of children and their gym teacher mount a cloud that "looks like" a whale.[10] The whale-cloud carries them out to sea but turns back when the school whistle signals the end of recess, as responsive to school rules as the children themselves. Nature as the ground of being is underlined in the titles of the textbooks (e.g., "Dandelion," "Dragonfly," "Blue Sky," "Young Leaves") and in the color photo frontispieces of dandelions, dragonflies (an ancient symbol of Japan) and flowers that are tied thematically to the stories.

The suggestion that children dwell in a protected space, at home in nature, is conveyed on the first page of the third-grade reader: "The sky is bright / above me here too / over that cow too / it lives over that mountain / over the pine tree too / everywhere the same clear blue."[11] Third-grade youngsters in America open to page 1 of the 1989 Macmillan textbook, *Adventuring,* and find a message that is not only considerably more sophisticated but that implants a warning that all may not be well in the child's world: "Our language is full of surprises. In this unit, you will read about how communicating, or not communicating clearly, can lead to confusion."[12]

Children in American textbooks are depicted as highly goal-oriented individuals who assume new responsibilities and gain mastery over themselves by facing new challenges. Children in Japanese stories tend not to have pivotal experiences that catapult them onto new stages of maturity. The world is a not a place of accident, motion, and change so much as a place in which the child is safely at home. The *kokugo* textbooks bring before the child familiar, positive features of the world. Some American stories (such as the numerous ones about blindness in the 1989 Macmillan "Connections" series), on the other hand, seem to be designed to bring the child face to face with what he or she may not know directly but may privately fear.

---

[9] Nobuo Ishimori et al., *Kokugo san-ue Wakaba* (National language grade three, vol. 1, Young leaves) (Tokyo: Mitsumura Tosho, 1989), p. 1.

[10] Nobuo Ishimori et al., *Kokugo ichi-shita Tomodachi* (National language grade one, vol. 1, Friends) (Tokyo: Mitsumura Tosho, 1990), p. 10.

[11] Nobuo Ishimori et al., *Kokugo san-shita Aozora* (National language grade three, vol. 2, Blue Sky) (Tokyo: Mitsumura Tosho, 1986), p. 1. Translations from Japanese are mine unless otherwise noted.

[12] Arnold et al., eds., *Adventuring,* p. 9 (see n. 8 above).

This tendency to prolong the state of early childhood is a well-known facet of life in Japan.[13] Like the Chinese, the Japanese have traditionally held the view that man's nature is inherently good, that human instincts can be trusted. Children are thought to come into the world unblemished, amenable to teaching. The notion that inborn selfishness and greed make it necessary that children subordinate their wills to the authority of their elders lest their characters be spoiled is alien to traditional Japanese views. Today as yesterday, young children are accorded special indulgences in the home and are rarely subjected to physical punishment at the elementary school level.[14]

As the scope and complexity of the world of the *kokugo* reader is limited, so too is the number of selections it contains. For each grade, 1–6, there are two *kokugo* textbooks: volume 1 (*ue*) and volume 2 (*shita*), with seven to nine units in each. A unit consists of one or two reading selections followed by a skills developing section. Together the two volumes amount to fewer than 300 pages, less than half the number of pages in a typical hardcover reader of a basal reader series published in the United States, which may contain up to 36 units, with several reading selections and a skills developing activity in each. The teacher working with the *kokugo* textbook proceeds systematically, spending a week on each chapter. The broad selection of stories in readers such as the Macmillan "Connections" series requires the teacher to select some stories and skip over others.

The reading samples in the *kokugo* readers are not only fewer but represent a more modest array of text types than readers for comparable grade levels in the American series. Volume 1 of a 1988 fourth-grade Japanese reader published by Kyōiku Shuppan, for example, contains an essay (*zuihitsu*), two stories (*monogatari*), a student composition (*sakubun*), poetry (*shi*), two expository prose pieces (*setsumeibun*) on insects, a record of a scientific investigation (*kirokubun*), and a composition summarizing the results of a classroom experiment. Volume 2 contains two stories, two expository prose pieces, a children's story (*dōwa*), a poem, a composition, and the biography (*denki*) of a nineteenth-century village headman who engineered the construction of a famous stone bridge. (While the essay is labeled a "biography," its focus is not on the man's life but on the technical details of the water transport system that he devised.) A typical

[13] Joy Hendry, *Becoming Japanese: The World of the Pre-school Child* (Manchester: Manchester University Press, 1986), pp. 15–17. A more recent study of education at the preschool level is Lois Peak's *Learning to Go to School in Japan: The Transition from Home to Preschool Life* (Berkeley and Los Angeles: University of California Press, 1990).

[14] This all changes quite suddenly and radically, however, when the child enters junior high school. For accounts of physical punishment (*taibatsu*) meted out in junior high schools, see Ken Schoolland, *Shogun's Ghost: The Dark Side of Japanese Education* (New York: Bergin & Garvey, 1990).

fourth-grade American reader, the 1989 Macmillan *Landscapes,* contains stories, biography and autobiography, historical fiction, folktales, riddles, fantasies, book reports, tall tales, ballads, social studies articles, science articles, legends, historical stories, a fine arts article, a play, a photo essay, a science story, and a narrative poem: 49 different entries altogether, as opposed to 17 in the Kyōiku Shuppan reader. Japanese readers are organized according to principles of simplicity, uniformity, and a conservative estimation of children's needs and abilities. The American readers are inclined toward multiplicity, diversity, choice, and as becomes clear when one examines the rhetorical appeals of the texts, to an enlarged view of children's abilities and a desire to challenge them to expand their horizons and capabilities.

Emphasis on Empathy and Feeling

In addition to length and variety of text types, there is also a significant difference in the types of reaction that American and Japanese textbooks seek to draw from their readers. The American textbook places significantly greater emphasis on logical analysis, formal statements of principles, verbal definition of terms, and critical evaluative thinking. Children are introduced to activities such as distinguishing between true and false statements, reality and fantasy, fact and opinion; comparing and contrasting; and making judgments about whether actions are just or unjust, right or wrong.[15] Analytical thinking is encouraged as the child is instructed to distinguish between main idea and supporting details, order a sequence of events, and analyze a story in terms of the elements of plot, setting and mood, character, and character's motives. Thinking involving cause-and-effect relationships is emphasized. (There are even visual aids to cause-and-effect thinking, such as a diagram with a column of causes joined to a column of effects.)[16] The concept of first-person narration is defined, and children are instructed to "write in the first person." The notion of figurative expression is introduced and then refined with definitions of idiom, simile, and metaphor in the fourth-grade Macmillan reader (whereas the fourth-grade Kyōiku Shuppan textbook stops with the concept of an idiomatic expression). American children are invited to think in hypothetical terms, whereas the attention of Japanese children is fixed more on the concrete situation at hand.

---

[15] A fifth-grade instruction manual, e.g., includes for each lesson a section on guiding children in critical thinking. Ten-year-olds are asked to consider problems such as, "Did the emigrants have a right to settle on land that belonged to Mexico and Great Britain? Explain your answer," and "Do you think it was right of Mr. Edwards to have started a fight with the man from Huron? Explain your answer" (Virginia A. Arnold et al., eds., *Landscapes: Teacher's Edition,* "Connections" series [New York: Macmillan, 1989], pp. 189, 211).

[16] Virginia A. Arnold et al., eds., *Sketches* (New York: Macmillan, 1989), p. 481.

Writing activities in the American readers are sequentially structured and involve a fair amount of formal reasoning. American children are taught to outline the development of an idea. They are taught the concepts of sentence and paragraph and are told that "the main idea is often stated in a sentence which is many times the first or the last in a paragraph."[17]

The emphasis in *kokugo* texts on empathy and subjective feeling is readily apparent in the titles to the introductory units of the texts at all grade levels. Children learn to "think about feelings" (*kimochi o kangaete*), to be aware of the ways in which "heart speaks to heart" (*kokoro no kayoiai*), and to "attune their hearts" (*kokoro o kayowaseru*). Children are taught to examine their emotional reactions to stories, and to do this on the basis of close self-observation. They write descriptions of their impressions (a genre known as *kansōbun*) and the ways to do this are carefully enumerated, as in this set of instructions following one frequently anthologized story about a man and a fox:[18]

> 1) First introduce a summary of the story and then write about what you felt and thought when you read it.
> 2) Introduce the events of the main scenes and then write about what you felt and thought at each scene.
> 3) Focus on the scene that left an especially strong impression and write about what you felt and thought.
> 4) Without introducing either a rough summary or the scene, gather together your impressions and opinions regarding the whole of the story.[19]

While American textbooks tend to encourage the child to step away from the story and to analyze the situation and the actions of the characters and to evaluate the effectiveness of their actions, *kokugo* textbooks often invite the child to imagine the feelings of another and to merge his or her identity with that of the character, even if that character should happen to be an animal. Children reading the story "Gon the Fox" are instructed to "become Gon the fox and address Heijū [the farmer who accidentally shoots Gon], and then become Heijū and talk to Gon."[20] They are not so much encouraged to distinguish between fiction and fact as to enter imaginatively into the fictive world. "Write a letter in which you write as if you were talking to Heijū," read the instructions following the story.

[17] Ibid., p. 170.

[18] *Kokugo* textbooks contain not only detailed instructions for writing but also many models of student compositions. This is in keeping with the traditional Japanese way of teaching an art or a skill through close modeling and repeated practice. See Victor Nobuo Kobayashi, "Tradition, Modernization, Education: The Case of Japan," *Journal of Ethnic Studies* 12, no. 3 (Fall 1984): 106–14. See also Catherine C. Lewis, "Creativity in Japanese Education," in *Japanese Educational Productivity*, ed. Robert Leestma and Herbert J. Walberg, Michigan Papers in Japanese Studies no. 22 (Ann Arbor: University of Michigan, Center for Japanese Studies, 1992), pp. 224–45.

[19] Junji Kinoshita et al., *Shōgakkō kokugo yon-shita* (Elementary school national language grade four, vol. 2) (Tokyo: Kyōikyu Shuppan, 1988), pp. 24–25.

[20] Ibid., p. 23.

Children are furthermore taught to share their impressions and feelings. They are instructed to read a story aloud in a way that brings the scene under description vividly alive to their listeners and to discuss their impressions of the story together with their friends. The role of the *kokugo* textbook in promoting group harmony and molding a common consciousness is reflected especially in this emphasis on oral reading and discussion. The group effort is underlined by instructions that are cast in the presumptive "let's . . ." and "shall we . . . ?" sentence patterns that involve both speaker and listener in a mutually cooperative mental effort. Children also receive instructions on how to modulate their voices to fit different types of speech acts (inquiring, inviting, encouraging, urging, etc.).

Language in these textbooks is treated as a means of expressing affective states of mind. Children are taught to be sensitive to the emotional effects of the words they use, such as the effect of writing a message using Japanese words, as opposed to Sino-Japanese words ("Kotoba no Kanji" [The feeling of words], fifth-grade reader, vol. 2, Mitsumura Tosho, 1991). There is almost no grammatical analysis. When an analytical approach is summoned, it is directed to the exploration of the behavioral phenomenon of plants, insects, or fish, or it is focused on a practical physical experiment rather than on a social situation. Human actions are not analyzed and critiqued from a perspective of right and wrong, just and unjust. Children are taught instead to observe closely, to be sensitive to the nuances of feeling in others, to imagine and to empathize with those feelings, and to be understanding and cooperative. The basis of the reading activity is not so much the commonality of logical thought as it is the commonality of feeling as children are exhorted, "Let's manage to read so that we convey to the listener the appearance of the scene and the feelings of the character."[21] The *kokugo* textbooks teach children to attune their sensitivity not only to the feelings of other people, but also to nature.

A Nature-centered View of the World

In the midst of the ongoing debate in the United States about whose experiences and what kinds of experiences should be represented in textbook literature, coming face to face with the world of *kokugo* stories in which human protagonists drop out of the picture altogether can be startling and disconcerting. Instead of stories about courageous, innovative, individualistic people who surpass physical and psychological limitations, one encounters stories about plants, insects, frogs, fish, foxes, and monkeys. Oftentimes the human observer, while present at the beginning of the story, will have faded away by the story's end. The specific consciousness

---

[21] Junji Kinoshita et al., *Shōgakkō kokugo yon-ue* (Elementary school national language grade 4, vol. 1) (Tokyo: Kyōiku Shuppan, 1988), p. 4.

of the individual self, so central and consistently present from beginning to end in American stories, becomes a neutral, general consciousness that presides over but does not intrude into the world of the *kokugo* story.

The relative insignificance of the human figure in the world of the *kokugo* reader is not surprising when taken within the context of traditional Shinto and Buddhist views of the unity of all forms of life. Here one might recall that Japan is a nation where priests once debated whether plants possessed a Buddha nature and where poet-priests like Saigyō (twelfth century) and Bashō (1644–94) polished their craft composing poems about plants and insects. A glance through a list of modern Japanese stories by leading authors turns up titles such as "Rain Frogs," "The Wagtails' Nest," "The Grasshopper and the Bell Cricket," "The Red Frog," "The Centipede," "The Wasps," and "The Red Cocoon."[22] The very sign for "word" is written with the characters, "speech-leaf." Stories about nature in the elementary grade *kokugo* readers mark a route that will eventually lead young readers in the junior and senior high school years to the *Manyōshū* (A.D. 759), popularly known as "The Collection of Ten Thousand Leaves," an anthology of poetry that celebrates the natural beauty of the lush botanical environment in which the early Japanese found themselves, and to classical works such as *Hōjōki* (A.D. 1212, A record of my hut) and *Oku no Hosomichi* (A.D. 1689, Narrow road to the back country) in which aesthetic and spiritual encounters with nature are central.

Traditional religious and philosophical teachings of Japan encouraged a passive attitude toward nature; people gained spiritual depth through the contemplation of natural phenomena. Characters in *kokugo* textbooks act within this tradition of contemplation and meditation and by example teach young readers to be sensitive to small changes in the environment. A sick boy spends an entire day watching the play of light on a chair left out on a beach from the window of his hospital room in "The Chair at the Beach" ("Hamabe no Isu," third-grade reader, vol. 1, Mitsumura Tosho, 1987). A boy hopes for good weather on his birthday in "The Birthday" ("Tanjōbi," fifth-grade reader, vol. 2, Mitsumura Tosho, 1988). When the awaited birthday finally comes around, anticipation is heightened by the jingling of a tiny bell that he carries in his pocket (a gift from his sister), and the highlight of the day is a beautiful falling leaf, an event which is experienced privately, poetically, and in extraordinary quietude.

The 1988 fourth-grade (vol. 1) Kyōiku Shuppan reader begins with a *zuihitsu* essay entitled "The Little Mud Flat" ("Chiisana Higata"), in which the first-person protagonist records his emotional reactions to the

---

[22] From *Stories by Shiga Naoya, The Paper Door and Other Stories*, trans. Lane Dunlop (San Francisco: North Point Press, 1987); and *A Late Chrysanthemum: Twenty One Stories from the Japanese*, trans. by Lane Dunlop (Tokyo: Tuttle, 1988).

migrating birds that come to a mud flat near his home. The speaker describes a small mud flat near his house which exists only during low tides; the rest of the time it is an indistinguishable part of the ocean. It is home to crabs, shells, shrimp, and small fish. The "I" informs the reader that, when he has time, he shoulders a telescope and sets out for the shore of the mud flat to look at the birds that gather there. Viewing and the personal reaction to what is seen constitute the content of the essay. "*The sight of birds* hunting for food, quarrelling, and flying about *fills me with happiness*." In traditional Japanese essay style, the narrator situates his point of view within a season. "In March the water of the mud flat looks cold and the grass and the earth on the shore still wear wintry colors. The winter birds are lined up and are basking in the sun, and the seagulls are flying slowly." The tone is subdued; the only suggestion of drama is the appearance of brightly colored sandpipers that fly in from the south to give the mud flat an appearance of spring. "The sandpipers are messengers that bring spring to Tokyo Bay." The narrator describes the bird's size ("a bit bigger than a pigeon but with its long bill and legs it looks quite large") and describes the peculiar shape of its bill, which lends it the name, "bent-bill sandpiper." The narrator talks about the bird's diet, its migratory habits, and the way its chest and stomach turn bright brick red. Toward the end, the focus broadens to include the sight of other birds.

"The Little Mud Flat" is very much in keeping with the Japanese tradition of essay writing. A *zuihitsu* is not a logical exposition of a position, but a personal miscellany or lyrical evocation, often a recollection, of nature scenes. This *zuihitsu* is typical in the quiet, understated presence of the narrator, whose activity is limited to observing, and whose absorbed observation carries him into the very being of the bird itself: "I too tried imitating it by standing on one leg, but I got tired right away. . . . I admired them for being able to remain standing on one leg for a long time."[23] The self identifies with and merges with nature. It never become a fully constituted "personality," the way it does in a fourth-grade Macmillan reader nature story, "The Living Desert," where the narrator is grounded in a social context and interacts continuously and vigorously with other characters who have names and sharp-edged personalities. Although ostensibly about nature, this story is filled with a medley of voices that seem to drown out the sounds of nature:

> I began to have a feeling that something was missing. I finally realized what it was. "There's nothing here," I remember blurting out to Jan.
> Jan didn't get my point at all. For her, there was plenty there—all kinds of low-growing plants and grasses, cacti, and bushes. She could have spent a year and still not investigated all the plants in that desert.

[23] Kinoshita et al., *Shōgakkō kokugo yon-ue*, p. 8.

"I mean there are no *living* things," I said.

She was annoyed. "What do you think all those plants are?"[24]

Other stories about animals and nature in this American reader are even more striking for the active intervention of human beings in the lives of animals. In "Elisabeth and the Marsh Mystery," the unexpected appearance of a stray sandhill crane prompts a family to enter a swamp in the middle of the night to stalk it, catch it, and transport it by truck to an airport so that it can be shipped to a wildlife refuge in Indiana to join a large flock of sandhill cranes due to arrive there. In the prize-winning story, "The Trumpeter Swans," a pair of trumpeter swans are saved from a fox by a boy who suddenly appears on the scene to intervene in their lives. Like many American children's stories, this story is marked by a strongly anthropocentric view of nature; the male and female swans are referred to as husband and wife and are invested with human perceptions and reactions: "The cob's wife pretended not to notice that her husband was showing off, but she saw it, all right, and she was proud of his strength and his courage. As husbands go, he was a good one."[25] In Japanese stories about animals, people are not only less energetic about helping animals; sometimes, as in "Gon and the Fox," people are definitely inferior to animals, which come across as more understanding, more generous, and wiser; in short, more humane, than humans.

The active, as opposed to contemplative, orientation toward nature in American readers can also be seen in the nature of the questions posed at the ends of the stories. Children reading the story about the sandhill crane are asked, "What extraordinary thing did the sandhill crane do? Why wasn't the crane frightened by all the people who had come to find it? Do you think the sandhill crane could have found its way to Indiana without help? Explain your answer."[26] These questions reveal the tendency to analyze and dramatize events in nature, which contrasts with the Japanese tendency to quietly lose the self in the contemplation of nature. Japanese children are told at the end of "The Little Mudflat" to "read while paying attention to the parts where the mood of the season is described," and "to read aloud in such a way that the appearance of the sandpipers is clearly conveyed to the listener."[27]

In the *kokugo* reader, small forms of life emerge with crystalline clarity in a setting emptied of human need and intention. One reads about camouflages used by fish; the growth of a gourd plan, the life cycle of a frog; how a dandelion propagates seeds; stages in the life cycle of a dragonfly; the life stages of a salmon, and the behavior mechanism of

[24] Arnold et al., eds., *Sketches*, p. 422.
[25] Ibid., p. 514.
[26] Ibid., p. 509.
[27] Kinoshita et al., *Shōgakkō kokugo yon-ue*, p. 9.

ants that enables them to find their way back home. One sixth-grade reader (vol. 2, Mitsumura Tosho, 1990) features a story narrated by baby crabs at the bottom of a stream. The drawings accompanying the story, which reproduce with geometric shapes the impression of sunlight refracted on the surface of the stream viewed from below the water's surface, are striking for the abstract unanthropocentric perspective they give of the crabs' world.

Nature provides not only setting and subject but lessons for living in the *kokugo* textbook. Second graders begin the new school year, in April, by reading (in the 1989 and 1992 Mitsumura Tosho readers) "Fukinoto" ("Swamp Cabbage"), a little parable about symbiotic cooperation and harmony in nature. Tree tops obligingly sway their heads to allow sun rays to melt the snow and enable a young struggling swamp cabbage to expose its head to the sunlight. Sacrifice for another is taught by the *hirugao* (literally "daytime face") flower, in the third-grade story "Hirugao" (Kyōiku Shuppan, 1984). The protagonist is a convolvulus or *hirugao* that lives on the beach. A recent storm has swept sea water containing a small fish into the rock crevice by which the flower dwells. "Hirugao" has become good friends with the fish, and realizing that the fish will die if the trapped water evaporates, prepares to sacrifice its life by asking the human narrator to wrench it from its soil to prevent the sun from coming out and drying up the pool of water. (According to popular folk belief the sun will come out when the *hirugao* blossoms.) A slightly less extreme degree of solicitude is displayed by a lizard in the story "Spring Bicycles" ("Haru no Jitensha") in a 1984 Kyōiku Shuppan third-grade reader. The lizard enjoys sunning itself on the steps of a shrine on an early spring afternoon, but worries about the fate of its cousins, the frogs, when it hears the bells on the bicycles of the village children. In an interesting twist, inhabitants of the animal world that traditionally serve to signal seasonal change for humans, are here the readers of signs, and human beings, the signs to be read. These bicycle bells are for lizards and frogs, harbingers of spring, and with spring comes the danger of being squashed to death by bicycle wheels.

Currents of sympathy flow not only between people, plants, and animals in these textbooks; even inanimate things can become objects of empathetic concern. In "Sedge Hat Jizō's" ("Kasako Jizō," second-grade reader, vol. 2, Kyōiku Shuppan and Mitsumura Tosho, 1991), statues of Jizō, the guardian deity of children whose cap-and-bib clad image can be seen throughout Japan, come to life and bring food to an old man who covered their heads with sedge hats to protect them from a snowstorm. Stories like this teach the moral value of returning a favor (*on-gaeshi*) and present the world as a safe, predictable place where even inanimate beings may return kindness with kindness. Not even death marks a rupture in the continuity of relationships that constitute the child's safe, happy world in the story "Suho's White Horse" ("Suho no Shiroi Uma," second-grade reader, vol. 2, Mitsumura Tosho, 1991), a Mongolian folktale about the origin of the horsehead fiddle retold by Yūzō Ōtsuka. Suho's white horse makes its way back to him after it has been shot by arrows, and with its dying breath instructs Suho to fashion a lute from its bones, sinews, skin and hair. By playing the lute that is magically invested with the spirit of the white horse, Suho will be with his horse forever after.

It is significant that the nature featured in *kokugo* textbooks is mostly the nature of the Japanese islands. There have been to date relatively few stories about nature outside of Japan. An appreciation of the splendours of the globe and the inculcation of a sense of awe toward the physical universe do not appear to be the goals of the *kokugo* reader.

The Image of the Happy Yamato Family

The attention devoted to nature in the *kokugo* textbooks, together with the pronounced focus upon the growth of plants and insects in the science textbooks in grades 1–6, provides urban children with a link to a natural environment that is rapidly being eroded in today's highly urbanized Japan and contributes to the creation of the image of a common agrarian past (until the end of the nineteenth century, 80 percent of the population was rural). Nature, and the experience of a particular kind of nature— that is, the plants, insects, meadows, fields, streams, and mountains of the Japanese islands—become touchstones for life as a Japanese person. Children dissect the same plants that their parents and grandparents knew as children, fashion boats from the same leaves, plant the same seeds, and catch the same insects. And in repeating the childhood experiences of their ancestors, they are led to "discover" an enduring common identity, rooted in nature, amid the alienating environment of the larger cities. Growing urbanization and modernization in Japan has been accompanied by growth in the idealization of the agrarian past of the Japanese people, of which the commercialization of the image of the *furusato*, or old home village, now used to sell food products and promote tourism within Japan, is but one obvious example. The *kokugo* textbook contributes to the construction of this mythic communal past through its images of nature and through traditional folktales and nostalgic stories about childhood visits to ancestral villages in the countryside that transport the young reader back to the rural past with the now grown-up urban narrator whose perspective she or he shares.

The Japanese children who are members of this idealized amorphous family with roots in the countryside tend to be vaguely suggested, tentatively adumbrated sketches of girls and boys. The faces and bodies are faintly illustrated with light ink and paint washes and are frequently depicted in

111

a manner that abstracts and flattens their phyical features to cartoon-like dimensions. Unlike characters in American readers, unique individuals with unique problems whose distinctive features are illustrated with strong line and color in large-size pictures, Japanese *kokugo* children seldom have surnames and often not even first names.

When a child's uniquely individual circumstances and proclivities are stressed, the child is likely to be a character in need of remolding to fit the norm; for example, a girl named Sawada Tamiko in "Sawada's Mole" ("Sawada no Hokuro," fourth-grade reader, vol. 1, Kyōiku Shuppan, 1988) who bears a distinctive large mole in the middle of her forehead and whose figure is, uncharacteristically, well-defined in pen-and-ink drawings accompanying the text. Sawako's physical blemish creates a character flaw. She is inordinately self-conscious (the ideal Japanese child is a happy, energetic, and unself-conscious), and, to hide the mole, she grows long bangs that hang curtain-like down to her nose. Whereas many American stories follow a script in which a child's attempts to solve a dilemma constitute the events of the narrative, typically, in this Japanese story, the solution is not worked out by Sawada but is imposed from without by a figure in position of authority. And the problem is not simply the boys in the class who tease Sawada by calling her "Daibutsu no osekkai" ("Great Buddha busybody"), an allusion to her mole, which resembles the *urna* on the forehead of the Buddha, and to her habit of officiously taking classmates to task for breaking rules. On the contrary; Sawada herself is seen to be at fault because her self-conscious behavior disrupts social harmony. Her long bangs, which she holds to her forehead even when she works out on the parallel bars and does vaultjumping exercises in gym, prevent her from participating according to form and call undue attention to herself.

The teacher in this Japanese story does not reprimand the boys and teach them to tolerate other people's differences, as she might were she a character in an American story. When Kimura Sensei finally intervenes, it is not to spare Sawada's feelings, but to make Sawada an object lesson in mutual support and group unity. "If a friend were uncomfortable about something and it made her very sad, what would you do?" she asks the class. "Wouldn't you want to help her?" In a dramatic gesture, Kimura Sensei makes all the students close their eyes while she brings Sawada to the front of the class, combs her hair, ties back her bangs with a barrett and a blue ribbon, and then turns her around to face all her classmates. The children are instructed to open their eyes to view the new Sawada. The teacher invites a response from all those who promise to never tease Sawada again and the children cry out, "Yes" as they raise their hands.

At the end of the story there are instructions that urge young readers to identity themselves with Sawada:

Let us try to read the following sections as we imagine ourselves in Sawada's stead

1. when she was told by Kimura Sensei to cut her hair;
2. when she had her bangs parted by the teacher in front of everyone;
3. when Mitsuo called her "Great Buddha Busybody."[28]

While Sawada is singled out by others because of her aberrant appearance and behavior, considerations such as her right to privacy or the integrity of her inner self that might be injured when she is put on display by the teacher do not enter the picture.

If one of the goals of textbooks is to develop constructive social attitudes in children, the *kokugo* textbooks have only barely begun to address the problem of bullying (*ijime*) that has plagued Japanese junior high schools for some time. Much of this bullying is directed against children who are perceived as being different from the majority. Children who are physically weak, who do poorly in school, who dress differently, or have different accents may be subjected to bullying, which may range from name calling to physical attacks that end in death.[29] While some folkloristic stories in the textbooks do contain dialogue written in regional dialect, one kind of diversity, the textbooks have been slow to treat the idea of diversity itself. Insofar as they seldom acknowledge that differences do exist, the textbooks cannot be said to contribute to the tolerance of individual differences. They are in fact striking for their seeming insistence on a unified homogenous people residing on the four main islands of Japan. While regional customs and festivals are noted, they are those of regions within the four main islands; peoples living farther south, on Okinawa, or on any small island, are not mentioned. And while stories about American Indians are almost obligatory in American textbooks today, the aboriginal Ainu, for example, do not appear in *kokugo* textbooks. Nor is the existence of minority Korean, Chinese, or burakumin (members of communities of social outcastes), or children of mixed-race marriages, acknowledged. Unlike American textbooks, where young people are often shown helping and comforting older people, Japanese textbooks seldom acknowledge the existence of the elderly, other than as characters in fairytale settings.

In spite of the fact that Japanese children are made keenly aware of the ways in which success in school leads directly to coveted positions in the adult world, children in *kokugo* textbooks are not depicted competing in school, nor are the social differences that result from school performance alluded to.

[28] Ibid., p. 23.
[29] For an extended report on cases of bullying (*ijime*) as well as corporal punishment in Japanese schools see Schoolland (n. 14 above). A rather unusual dramatization of the dynamics of bullying is found in a story in a 1991 sixth-grade Gakkō Tosho reader entitled "Roshia Pan" (Russian bread), in which a village schoolboy is heckled by junior high school classmates for "harboring a spy" because he is on friendly terms with a Russian family living next door.

Unlike social studies textbooks, the focus of the *kokugo* texts is not on society, and, for a country as densely populated as Japan, the stories tend to be very thinly populated. Unlike American stories where children are often shown making new friends, *kokugo* textbooks contain few stories in which a child confronts a stranger; when such stories do occur, they are often set in the past, where, for example, a city child encounters a group of village children. Before 1992, stories in which foreigners appeared were rare.[30] One interesting exception is the story of a man's posting to India and his children's successful adjustment to life there, which appeared in the second volume of the 1990 sixth-grade Mitsumura Tosho reader. The frontispiece of the text departs from the usual scenes of Japanese nature and introduces photos of Jainpura and Indian children. But the story is entitled "Connecting Hearts" ("Kokoro o Tsunagu") and significantly dwells on the importance of feelings. The author writes that his elder son was able to communicate successfully with Indian friends not only because he could speak Hindi and English, but, more important, because he had cultivated the "Japanese" skill of communicating "heart to heart." He goes on to say that forgetting about the heart and attempting to persuade someone with words alone just will not work; indeed, the important thing is the heart (p. 89).

Memories of the Pacific War

Of all the subjects contained in the *kokugo* readers, the Pacific War is probably the single most rhetorically powerful means of creating a national consciousness and sense of belonging to a people with a common history. The war has occurred with significant frequency as a theme especially in the third and fourth grades. (In the 1992 Mitsumura Tosho reader, however, the war story appears in the sixth-grade reader.) In the 1988 and 1989 Mitsumura Tosho readers and the 1988 Kyōiku Shuppan reader, the central significance of the story about the war is underlined by the frontispiece color photograph of cosmos flowers, the kind featured in the story, "One Flower," which appears in all three readers.

As if to emphasize the helplessness of the Japanese citizenry that suffered the bombardments, the hunger, and the defeat, most of these stories are about young girls. Through these small girls Japanese children

---

[30] The story "Roshia Pan," alluded to above, is an exception. The incidents of the story take place in the early thirties, around the time of the Manchurian Incident, soon after which the Russian family leaves the boy's village for an unknown destination and is never heard from again. The narrator and his family know almost nothing about the Russians or why they have come to Japan. And while the remarks of the Japanese school children about the family are rendered in a vivid, realistic manner, the narrator's account of playing with the Russian boy gives no indication of the boy's personality, nor do his comments about the Russian family ever make the foreign individuals "come alive." Despite physical proximity and frequent contact, the family remains isolated and cut off in the narrator's consciousness.

are led to see the war as an event that overwhelmed the Japanese nation, much as any other natural catastrophe, an event in which they were helpless victims swept up by forces that they could neither understand nor control. By shifting the focus at the end of these stories from war time to the present or near present, the authors invite contemporary school children to identify with the children in the story. The war becomes a national event that all Japanese shared; as part of each Japanese person's past, it becomes integral to the Japanese identity. The wartime stories' focus is on the deprivations suffered by the citizens on the main islands of Japan (excluding Okinawa, where civilians perished or, as some would say, were sacrificed by the Japanese military, in great numbers in the last days of the war). Men are generally absent from these stories. They are away at the front or have already died in battle. When present, they are depicted as gentle, weakly men who are good to their children, often wear eyeglasses, and are among the last to be conscripted.

The suffering caused by lack of food is a common theme. In "One Flower" ("Hitotsu no Hana") little Yumiko has learned that the words "please give me just one" will often yield a single potato or a piece of squash to quell her gnawing hunger. The planes come daily and the city is reduced to rubble. The day comes when even her sickly father is called up. Yumiko is carried on her mother's back when the family goes to the station to see him off. Not wanting to send her husband off to war with the image of his child's crying face, Yumiko's mother gives her the last riceball in her knapsack. By the time they arrive at the station where the recruits have congregated Yumiko is clamoring again for "just one." She begins to cry, and her father disappears to find something to appease her hunger. He returns with his farewell gift, a single cosmos flower which he has found growing on a garbage heap. At the sight of the bright flower Yumiko forgets her hunger and wriggles with delight. The father boards the train wordlessly, with his gaze fixed on the flower in his daughter's hand, and smiles as the train pulls away. Ten years later, we are told, Yumiko no longer remembers her father's face, or that she even had a father, but the small hut in which she and her mother live is surrounded by cosmos flowers.

The flower exchanged at the moment of farewell in this story resonates with significance. The image of the single flower harks back to the story of the origin of Zen Buddhism, the moment when the Buddha silently held aloft a flower, a gesture to which Kāshyapa, one of his close disciples, reacted with a smile of recognition, and thus marked the first transmission of the dharma. The cosmos flower growing in the garbage also recalls the lotus, symbol of Buddhism, rooted in the mud. The association between flowers and the passing on of a tradition lives on powerfully today as a central ritual of the contemporary wedding ceremony, where the bride and groom present their parents with flowers to acknowledge the ties that bind children to parents.

The episode of the giving of the flower in "One Flower" is also linked to past aesthetic traditions through the sensibility of *aware*, the sensitivity to fragile perishable beauty that recalls the ephemerality of life. Of all the images in classical literature associated with *aware*—moonlight, snow, dew on autumn grasses, the cries of insects, the flight of birds—none was used as frequently as flowers. The story also recalls literary conventions of the past in its elliptical linkage of events and use of images to communicate situation and state of mind. That Yumiko's mother feeds her daughter in the postwar reconstruction era by doing piece work at home is conveyed by reference to the sound of a sewing machine. That this little family will survive is suggested through the image of the many cosmos flowers surrounding the hut, flowers through which Yumiko, now playing at being the "little mother," passes on her way to market. The absence of explicit narrative explanation and the communication on the level of symbol and suggestion are in keeping with the traditional emphasis on feeling and intuition and is yet another way in which the textbooks help to mold a sensibility that will be further reinforced through the classical literature encountered in the junior and senior high school *kokugo* textbooks.

Many of the stories about the war are thus centered on a humble object that provides a link between the prosperous present and the war years. Keepsakes fashioned by the hands of those who suffered and sacrificed during the war are prized far more highly than any goods that can be purchased with money today. Dolls carved from pencil stubs by a rough country boy and given to a city girl who was evacuated to his mountain town are such objects in "The Pencil Dolls" ("Empitsubina," second-grade reader, vol. 1, Nihon Shoseki, 1989). Having given her two pencil dolls, representing the emperor and the empress dolls of the traditional girls' day festival, the boy, who tries to make the newcomer feel welcome, promises to bring the rest of the court dolls to school the next day, but that night, the part of the town where he lives is bombed, and he perishes along with the rest of his family. The girl, grown up, treasures the priceless pencil dolls and tells their story to the current generation of elementary school children.

The travails of their owners invest such objects with a spiritual quality that becomes a legacy left by the generation of children who lived during the war. These stories convey traditional moral virtues such as sacrifice, effort (*gambare*), and endurance (*gaman*). In "Mother's Paper Dolls," ("Okaasan no Kamibina," third-grade reader, vol. 1, Kyōiku Shuppan, 1984) a woman tells her young nieces the story of the paper dolls that her mother made for the dolls' festival during the war. Growing up during wartime, the narrator is always hungry, and her mother sells the court dolls that have been in the family for generations to buy white rice for her to eat. When the girl sees her mother folding origami paper dolls to display on the festival day, and learns that the dolls that have been evacuated along with the family have been sold, she calls the paper dolls hateful and throws a tantrum. The mother weeps silently and continues to fold the paper into dolls. The shock of seeing her mother's body shaking with grief jolts the girl into an awareness of her selfishness. Overcome with a feeling of shame, she resolves to do her share and sets to folding paper dolls alongside her mother. The father never returns from the Pacific Islands, and the paper dolls become her most treasured possessions. Now she shows the dolls to her young nieces and tells them the story of "mother's paper dolls" to teach them the way her mother struggled through difficult times during the war.

Continuity of life during and after the war is suggested by recurring visual and auditory images of the river in "The River and Norio" ("Kawa to Norio," sixth-grade reader, vol. 1, Kyōiku Shuppan, 1983) and the sound of the mortar used to grind soybeans in "The Song of the Mortar" ("Ishiusu no Uta," sixth-grade reader, vol. 1, Mitsumura Tosho, 1989 and 1992). Both stories are set in the countryside around Hiroshima in the summer of 1945. The gurgling sound of the stream and the grinding of the pestle against the mortar are images of homey comfort that contrast with the unarticulated horror of the bombing that runs as a subtext throughout the stories. The bombing is never described directly, but alluded to through its effects: the mothers of the child protagonists never come back from visits to the doomed city and the children are left behind with grandparents. Norio's father who went off to war as a soldier does come back, eventually. Father, we are told with breathtaking understatement in the next sentence, "was a little box." The idea that the father's ashes were contained in the box, which would normally be expressed with the words *hako no naka ni arimashita* ("were in the box") or *hako no naka ni irete arimashita* ("had been placed in the box"), is condensed to *hako deshita*, "was a box," a formulation that summarizes Norio's loss with startling abruptness. At the end of the story, the orphaned Norio cuts grass for his pet goat alongside a river that seems to repeat the refrain, "mother come back, mother come back."

If the story about Norio emphasizes a boy's dependency on a lost father and mother, the story about a girl emphasizes the need to be strong and to carry on. The different messages for boys and girls is consonant with the general tendency in Japanese society to indulge young boys and to make girls more responsible for controlling their impulses. Chieko is selfish and bored at the beginning of "The Song of the Mortar" as she and her grandmother grind the soybean flour for the observance of the annual August festival of the dead, but she becomes filled with resolve

117

to live for others after her parents perish in Hiroshima on August 6. "Study, study—stand up no matter how hard things get," sings the mortar at the end of the story. The legacy of the war is redoubled effort for this young female child.

The war is never depicted in its early days of euphoric victory, but in the last days, when the very weakest and unfit of the men were conscripted and women and children ran for their lives into bomb shelters. The drawings that accompany these stories are rendered in ink and light washes of brown and grey, so that the wartime events seem to transpire in the dim shadows of distant memory. The war years constitute a yawning void into which fathers stepped, never to return, and entire families disappeared. At times the message of victimization in the war comes across in a sudden shocking way.

In "Chiichan Casts a Shadow" ("Chiichan no Kageokuri"), anthologized in third-grade readers published by Mitsumura Tosho in 1987 and 1991, the world of innocent children's play and the world of death come together with astonishing suddenness. On the way home from visiting the ancestral graves, a father teaches his daughter Chiichan, her older brother, and his wife a game that he played when he was a boy. The family of four hold hands, stare hard at their shadows, and at the count of ten look up at the sky where their shadows appear to leap up. The father jokingly calls the shadows their "commemorative photograph." The next day "even this man with the weakly physique" goes off to war. Chiichan and her brother continue to play games with their shadows until planes loaded with incendiary bombs transform the once wide pleasant sky into "a fearful place." One night Chiichan is awakened by air raid sirens. A strong wind blows and fires dart up all around. Mother, son and daughter flee their home and in the melee, Chiichan becomes separated from her mother and her brother. She spends the night with a group of refugees under a bridge and the next morning makes her way back home, where she waits all day for her mother and her brother to return. That night she eats a little dried rice from a cloth bag and sleeps inside the crumbling dugout. A cloudy day dawns, and another dark night comes. Chiichan eats a bit more of the dried rice and falls asleep inside the dugout. On the third morning bright sunlight strikes her face. She feels hot chills and her throat is terribly dry. The sun is in the sky when, "The sky is just right for sending your shadow," her father's voice comes down from the blue sky. "Yes, let's all do it together," her mother's voice also comes down from the blue sky. Chiichan stands up on shaky legs and staring hard at her shadow, begins to count. "One, two, three." Soon her father's low voice is counting along with her. She hears her mother's high voice joining in. And then her brother's laughing voice chimes in, "T-en."

When Chiichan looks up at the sky, there are four white shadows clearly outlined in the blue sky. She calls out, "Father, Mother, brother." At that moment she realizes that her body has become completely transparent and that she is being sucked up into the sky. The color of the sky stretches out before her. Chiichan is standing in the middle of a sky-colored field of flowers at the top of the sky. "I've floated up here because hunger made me so light," she says. At that moment she sees her father and her mother and her older brother walking toward her. They are laughing. "So that's why you didn't come for me. You were all up here." Chiichan begins to laugh brightly and runs through the field of flowers.

The author ends the story with the statement: "And thus the life of a little girl disappeared into the sky one morning in early summer." And adds in a postscript: "Ten years later, many more houses than before filled the town. The spot where Chiichan sent her shadow up has become a small park. Today beneath the blue sky a boy and a girl about the age of Chiichan and her brother are laughing as they play."

Some images of the war take a more violent, graphic form. "The Angry Jizō" ("Okoru Jizō," third-grade reader, vol. 1, Nihon Shoseki, 1989), is set in Hiroshima itself on the day the bomb falls. The main protagonist is a statue of Jizō, the guardian deity of children, who stands by the wayside in a neighborhood in Hiroshima and is affectionately addressed as "Smiling Jizō." It is the morning of August 6. In most of the stories about the war, the bombings are treated as more or less apolitical natural catastrophes, and information about with whom or why the Japanese are at war is not given. In this story, however, 8-year-old readers are furnished with the explicit information, "an American B29 bomber was sighted in the air" and there was a blinding flash of light, "as bright as if the sun had fallen." "It was an atom bomb." Its effects are described vividly: windows, pillars, and people are blown into the sky, catch fire, and rain down upon the earth. The Jizō statue is swept into the air, splits in two, and his trunk is buried in "hot burning" sand. Only his laughing face remains.

The story departs from the usual treatment of the war by describing the wounds and burns suffered by the victims. People wrapped in burning clothes run by. Mothers with scorched hair carrying dead babies, children with faces swollen with burns stumble past the head of the Jizō. They cry out: "Run!—" "It hurts—" "Help!—" Looking up from the sand, the head of the Jizō sees the columns of fire rising into the sky. The next day the head is among the many dead bodies that lie scattered about the burned out landscape. A little girl in a blue dress who used to pat the Jizō now reappears in the distance looking ever so much like a rag blown by the wind. Only a bit of faded blue is discernable on the charred cloth

119

that hangs from her body. She totters toward the Jizō and falls to the ground. A large red burn "shaped like a peony" covers her back (and is rendered in one of the almost abstract drawings that illustrate the story). She calls for her mother ("*kaasan*") and begs for water. The head of the Jizō strains, and his laughing expression disappears, replaced by the ferocious expression of a heavenly guardian king.[31] As the girl continues to call for water in a voice that grows fainter and fainter, tears from the Jizō's glaring stone eyes flow faster and faster, roll across the sand, and fall into her mouth. Aided by the Jizō's tears, she dies peacefully (even managing to sing a soft song before drawing her last breath). The head crumbles into tiny pieces and mixes with the sand.

Days later people return to Hiroshima. An old man who appeared in the beginning of the story discovers the body of the Jizō, finds another stone for his head and tells him how his wife and son died in the bombing. Thereafter, the new head takes on the same expression as the old one did when it had to watch the horribly burned little girl in her death throes. As time passes more and more people notice with amazement the transformation of the facial expression of the Jizō. His smile has not only disappeared but has been replaced by a scowl, and the kind look in his eyes has turned into a savage glare. A postscript informs the young readers that this statue of the Jizō still stands where it once stood . . . in Hiroshima.

Recent Developments

In April, 1992 elementary school children throughout Japan began using the new *kokugo* textbooks written according to the guidelines issued by the Mombushō in 1987. The new 1992 Mitsumura Tosho textbooks (vol. 1, for the first semester; the second semester texts were not available at the time of this writing) bear the same titles and the same inspirational messages on the first pages as the 1989 edition.[32] Many stories have been carried over from the previous Mitsumura Tosho series with minimal changes; for example, the new textbooks introduce 1,006 as opposed to 996 Chinese characters. Moreover, themes identified in previous *kokugo* textbooks are retained and reemphasized. Nature comes to the fore again,

---

[31] The Shitennō (Four Heavenly Kings) defended the four directions surrounding the Buddhist realm. The Heavenly Kings were originally gods of Indian folklore that were later amalgamated into the Buddhist pantheon. They have fierce, uncharacteristically Japanese, expressions, bear weapons and crush demons underfoot. Representative images of the Heavenly Kings are often found guarding entrances to temples and shrines.

[32] The Mitsumura Tosho textbooks were selected for this most recent survey as well because they are the most widely used series in Japan. The titles of the first volumes of the 1992 set are *Kazaguruma*, "Pinwheel" (first grade); *Tampopo*, "Dandelion" (second grade); *Wakaba*, "Young Leaves" (third grade); *Kagayaki*, "Radiance" (fourth grade); *Ginka*, "Silver River" (the equivalent of the English, "Milky Way"; fifth grade); *Sōzō*, "Creation" (sixth grade). Size and format remain basically the same, although covers, photographs, illustrations and artwork have been redesigned; vol. 1 of each grade reader now contains 7 or 8 as opposed to 9 units; and the lengths of the books vary somewhat from that of the 1989 series.

both in stories repeated from earlier editions (e.g. "Swamp Cabbages" and "The Wisdom of the Dandelion," to name two that were referred to earlier in this study) and in new stories. Attractive color photos of plants, seascapes, and landscapes grace the frontispiece of virtually every textbook in the new series. Animals, as opposed to people, figure in most of the stories, as before.[33] Even a fantasy introducing the possibility of "other worlds" that operate according to different physical laws does so through the character of an animal: a whale that walks, talks, and eventually manages to fly ("The Day the Wind Is Strong," [Kaze ga tsuyoi hi], sixth-grade reader). People and animals care for each other in stories such as "The Rolling Riceball" ("Musubi Kororin," first-grade reader), in which a peasant gives rice to field mice and is rewarded with gold in turn. Even stories that would appear to be about people and their concerns turn out to center around subjects that are about nature or that evoke traditional responses to natural beauty. For example, a young boy's grandfather dies but remains with him in spirit through the beautiful blossoms of the grandfather's magnolia tree in "The School of Goodbye" ("Sayōnara no Gakkō," fifth-grade reader). A boy's favorite uncle, a magician who leaves Japan for parts unknown, communicates with him from afar through flowers in "Flowers and the Magician" ("Hana to Majutsushi," sixth-grade reader).

The poetical treatment of nature continues to figure prominently. In "The White Hat" ("Shiroi Boshi"), anthologized in both the 1989 and 1992 editions of the fourth-grade reader, magical transformations take place on a sunny afternoon in early summer, and "poetic logic" is exemplified in the delicate shifts of image to image (white shirt, summer orange, white cap, summer orange, white butterfly, summer orange, boy and mother with a butterfly net, girl, field, white flowers, white butterflies) that link its parts, as well as in the synesthesia of scent, color, and warmth. Each of the 1992 textbooks contains a section on poetry, as before, and there is once again a special feature article on classical *tanka* and *haiku* in the sixth-grade reader, with an emphasis on the longevity of these ancient, yet vital and flexible, Japanese poetic forms, which (in the case of *tanka*) have been practiced for over a thousand years.

Natural beauty, poetry, and the theme of the continuity of the Japanese "race" are conjoined in the frontispiece photograph of the "Jōmon sugi" and the poem about the tree that appear in the fourth-grade reader. The cryptomeria tree in Kagoshima Prefecture, designated a natural treasure (*tennen kinenbutsu*) of the nation, is celebrated in a poem that asks children to compare their ages and the ages of their parents with the tree that stood (and still stands) for a thousand years—that is, "the equivalent of

---

[33] Roughly a third of the stories feature human characters; the rest are dominated by images of plants, animals, landscapes, and other natural features.

7,200 years of human life." The message of the continuity of life on the
Japanese islands is brought home audibly as well as visually, when children
recite the poem aloud, imaginging that they themselves are the tree, as
they are asked to do in the exercises following the text.

The collective experiences of the Yamato family continue to be emphasized in a variety of ways, including through references to the Pacific
War, such as in Tsuboi Sakae's well-known story ("The Song of the Mortar"
[Ishiusu no uta]) about the war orphan Chieko who survives the bombing
of Hiroshima and pledges to work ever harder to secure a better future
for her people. This story was in the 1989 sixth-grade reader and reappears
in the 1992 edition, accompanied by updated illustrations.

Factual articles about features of life in the different regions of Japan
(e.g., "The Snow Country Today" [Yukiguni wa ima], traditional Japanese
folktales (e.g., "The Rolling Rice Ball" [Musubi kororin]), stories with
traditional premodern rural settings (e.g., "The Story of Kitchomu"
[Kitchomu banashi]), and stories set in country villages (e.g., "Crossing
the Suspension Bridge" [Tsuribashi o Wataru]), as well as articles on
Japan's remote past, seem to stress the importance of *wareware nihonjin*":
"we, the Japanese people." For example, "The Discovery of the Nagayaō
Wood Strips" ("Nagayaō mokka no hakken"), a report of an archeological
excavation that leads to the reconstruction of life on an eighth-century
nobleman's estate in Nara, the country's first permanent capital, reminds
sixth-graders of Japan's long and special history.

This concern with the preservation and promotion of a Japanese
identity does not preclude in the 1992 series (as it did not in the 1989
series) reaching beyond Japanese borders. The theme of nature within
Japan seems to lead perforce to worldwide concerns about the environment.
In fact, mankind's existence on earth and the life of the planet are subjects
treated in the fourth-, fifth-, and sixth-grade readers: in "Searching for
Dinosaurs" (Kyōryū no saguru) and "Visiting an Incineration Plant"
(Shōyaku kōjō no kengaku) in the fourth-grade reader; "I Am Grass"
(Ware wa kusa nari), "Treasuring Nature" (Shizen o taisetsu ni), "The
World the Map Shows" (Chizu ga miseru sekai), "Continents Move" (Tairiku
wa ugoku), "Flour and Life" (Kona to seikatsu), and two stories about
nuclear arms in the fifth-grade reader; and "The Blessings of the Sun"
(Taiyō no megumi) and "Ozone Destroyed," (Ozon kowareru) in the sixth-
grade reader.

However, what might be called a more dramatic international dimension
is brought to the fore in five stories translated from English and one story
written on a Korean subject by a second-generation Korean author born
in Japan. Three of these stories appear in the new third-grade reader: a
translation of Anita Hewitt's "Kangaroo Joey Finds His Shadow" ("Kage
o mitsuketa kangarū bōya"); a translation of "Elmer Meets the Tigers"

122

("Eruma, tora ni au") from Ruth Stiles Gannett's book *My Father's Dragon;*
and a re-creation in Japanese of the Korean folktale, "The Three Year
Mountain Pass" ("Sannentōge") by Yi Kum Ok. The fourth-grade reader
contains a translation of Eve Titus's story, *Anatole,* about a self-employed
mouse named Anatole who works as a cheese taster in a French cheese
factory. The British writer Allison Uttley's story, "The Cornfield" (translated
into Japanese as "Mugibatake"), is the seventh foreign story and appears
in the fifth-grade reader. Though only five in number, the new stories
mark a significant increase for the first-semester third-, fourth-, and fifth-
grade readers, in which previously there were none.

"The Three Year Mountain Pass" appears to be the first Korean story
to ever appear in a *kokugo* textbook. It is set in a traditional Korean village
and makes no reference to Koreans in Japan, but its presence nonetheless
constitutes a minor landmark, given the long history of difficult relations
between Japan and Korea and the highly controversial status of Koreans
living in Japan. It is a fantastic but optimistic story that dramatizes the
capacity to adopt a new point of view, to change. The legend of the "three
year mountain pass," which is taken to mean that a person has but 3 years
to live should he or she stumble and fall while going over a certain
mountain pass, is reinterpreted by a young miller to mean that one will
live for 3 more years if one stumbles once, for 6 more years if one should
fall twice, 30 more years if one should fall ten times, and 300 more years
if one falls a hundred times. The old villager in the story, who stumbles
and falls and falls into a deep depression thinking that he will die within
the next 3 years, is rejuvenated and revitalized by the young miller's ironic
lesson. The message of change is impressed on the young readers through
exercises following the story that urge children to repeatedly compared
the old and new interpretations of the "three year pass."

The themes of challenge and change are ever present throughout the
third-grade reader. The young kangaroo in "Kangaroo Sonny Finds a
Shadow" is reluctant to leave the warm security of his mother's pouch
but, led by the desire to "have" his own shadow, eventually leaves it to
explore the world on his own two feet. This may also be read as an
illustration of an urge to overcome the desire to be indulged and protected
by a parent or other care giver (a psychological phenomenon common
among young Japanese children, who are said to *amaeru*, to cling to their
parents with the expectation of being indulged by them).[34] This same
reader also features a story about a third-grade boy who conquers his
fear of heights and succeeds, howsoever timidly, in climbing a ladder at
school. "Elmer Meets the Tigers" similarly conveys the message of rising

[34] See Takeo Doi's *Anatomy of Dependence*, trans. John Bester (Tokyo: Kodansha, 1973), for an
extended analysis and discussion of the kinds of behavior associated with *amaeru* and its nominal
form, *amae*, which he regards as characteristically Japanese.

to meet challenges and emphasizes as well relying on self-confidence and inventive thinking to overcome unexpected difficulties. (Elmer, in the episode translated here, gives the tigers chewing gum and thus prevents them from exercising their teeth on him.) The science article at the end of the third-grade reader is entitled "Changing Colors of Soap Bubbles" and is followed by a short essay on "things that change."

That this textbook may have been designed with the aim of encouraging a more open attitude to change would seem to be borne out by the inclusion of the one story that has been carried over from the 1989 edition. In "Crossing the Suspension Bridge" ("Tsuribashi o wataru"), a city girl visiting a mountain village overcomes her fear and works up the courage to cross a suspension bridge spanning a ravine in order to play with the local children. Equally significant, it seems, is the fact that stories that have not been repeated are the ones that depict children in more passive, reflective moods, for example, "The Chair at the Beach" ("Hamabe no isu"), or that focus on the child as the passive recipient of another's child's kindness in a traditional rural setting, for example, "Tarō Cricket" ("Tarō kōrogi").

A new interest in meeting challenges can also be seen in the story, "Anatole Goes to the Factory" in the fourth-grade reader. This story about the mouse who is not caught in a trap baited with cheese but instead wins accolades and wealth by serving as the discerning cheese taster of a cheese factory introduces a kind of energetic irony that is also new to the *kokugo* reader.[35]

If, at this point, we asked ourselves the question, How closely did the designers of the new textbooks follow Mr. Nakasone's recommendations? we could answer without hesitation, in part, Very closely. They do indeed promote the preservation and development of traditional Japanese values, as did the designers of the 1989 textbooks. They do, however, in addition, albeit to a considerably lesser degree, introduce the notion of "change" as a universal human experience and the need to develop some of the qualities required to successfully meet "change" and its attendant challenges—for example, self-confidence and inventive thinking. This may well be, although small and cautious, the most important step those designers have taken in the direction of the internationalization of the *kokugo* (national language) readers.

---

[35] One may, however, note that the French setting in the original American story has been de-emphasized; characters in the Japanese version do not intersperse their speech with French words and phrases (*ma chere, c'est la vie, magnifique,* etc.), as they do in the English version. And Anatole is congratulated on winning the status not of a businessman, as in the original, but as a *sarariman* (a salaryman, someone who works for a company rather than a quasi-independent entrepreneur).

Education

●

EDWARD BEAUCHAMP

A major problem in discussing education and democracy in Japan or, indeed, in any other country is one of definitions. Although providing a clear and rigorous definition of what is meant by democracy and democratic education is theoretically desirable, this approach often leads to other difficulties. For example, if democratic education is defined in terms of an idealized version of democracy, it becomes nothing more than a paradigm existing only in the minds of political theorists. Under these circumstances it is difficult to suggest that a system of democratic education can exist anywhere in the world. Perhaps democratic education, on the other hand, should be pragmatically evaluated as to how well it compares with the somewhat imperfect and different democratic systems found in places like the United States, England, or France. If a country's educational system contains both democratic as well as undemocratic elements (as many do), should it be classified as democratic or undemocratic? At what point does it become one or the other? Finally, we should recognize that democratic institutions can exist in a variety of configurations resulting from unique historical and cultural circumstances. Democratic institutions are not monolithic, and viable variations can be found in both decentralized and highly centralized societies, as well as in states on all but the extremes of the political spectrum.

In this essay, I assume only that the educational system in Japan, as in all other countries, to some extent reflects and to some extent creates the democratic and undemocratic aspects of the wider society and political system. One of the purposes of this essay, therefore, will be to discuss how the accomplishments and problems of Japanese democracy and society impinge upon education, and another will be to show how education contributes to those strengths and weaknesses.

Two of the most important ways in which education and the wider society are connected is through *access* to education and through the *process* and *content* of education. Access to education in all modern societies is one of the prime means by which social and economic status is distributed in society and therefore is closely related to the problem of equality in democratic society. The process and content of education constitute some of the major means by which societies socialize their young to important shared values and behavior, including political values and behavior. What pupils learn, and how they learn, is therefore crucial for the kind of democratic citizens they will become as adults. This essay will focus on these problems of access and equality, and eduaction and democratic citizenship. In the course of the essay, it should become increasingly apparent that the Japanese, despite the many serious problems facing their educational system, have fundamentally solved the ancient contradiction between democratic access and the maintenance of world-class standards of quality of education.

Prewar Education

There is no doubt that the Occupation of Japan (1945–1952) was a watershed of gigantic proportions in modern Japanese history and that it triggered significant changes in that nation's life. It is important, however, to recognize that democratic elements in the educational system did not emerge only from the seven years of American Occupation. Indeed, despite the overwhelmingly authoritarian character of prewar Japanese education, one can discover some potentially democratic elements at least as early as the Meiji era (1868–1912) when Japan opened herself to the world and consciously set about learning from its more advanced nations, some of whom were themselves in various stages of democratic evolution.

The influence of these Western democracies on Japan was especially strong in the first dozen years of the Meiji period. Japan's new leaders realized that a modern educational system was an essential tool for transforming Japan from a weak, feudal state into a strong modern one. This is not to suggest that the Japanese oligarchs were motivated by democratic principles, but rather to point out that their actions served democratic ends by increasing literacy, expanding the number of people possessing at least a basic education and opening up people's minds to Western learning.

One of the most significant actions taken by the early Meiji authorities was the so-called imperial Charter Oath (1868) which laid down the aims of the new government and insisted that "knowledge shall be sought throughout the world." In response to this clarion call, many Japanese students journeyed, at government expense, to the United States and Western Europe to pursue their studies, and several thousand foreign experts, the so-called *oyatoi gaikokujin,* were brought to Japan to teach, to advise the government, and to promote Japan's rapid development in a wide variety of fields.

Although usually hired to teach such "practical" subjects as science, technology, or English, it was not possible to restrict the foreigner's teaching to narrow channels. One of the earliest and most influential *yatoi,* William Elliot Griffis, for example, spent a year teaching science in the castle town of Fukui, deep in the interior of Japan, and found that some of his most exciting teaching was done during informal evening gatherings in his home with several of his students and local townsmen anxious to learn not only about science and manufactures, but also about life in the United States, its religion, history, and constitution. Griffis' experience was not unusual; other *yatoi* recount similar experiences. Many of his students went on to become political, business, and academic leaders, and it seems reasonable to suggest that Griffis' informal teaching had an influence on at least some of them.

A large percentage of the foreign educators were Americans, many of whom urged their employers to design Japan's new educational system on the American model. In fact, Americans held many responsible positions, including Professor David Murray of Rutgers who served as Japan's National Superintendent of Education (1873–1878), and Marion Scott who established the first teacher training institution in Tokyo in 1872. French and German influences were also present in the creation of Japan's education system, and at least some of them were not hostile to democratic education.

The school system was highly differentiated with elementary school being the common experience providing both a general education and a moral education for all. The amount and kind of education a youngster received after completing elementary school was based on the needs of the state. Admission to post-elementary schools, especially those leading to higher education, was extremely selective and usually based in large measure upon entrance examinations. Although girls as well as boys received the benefits of compulsory education (ultimately extended to six years), public secondary schools catered primarily to boys. The women who went on to secondary and higher education did so mostly at private schools.

From about 1880 a conservative reaction to the earlier liberal decade emerged, and authoritarianism clearly became the dominant characteristic of prewar Japanese education. The educational system became highly centralized, unabashedly elitist, and strongly state-centered. Ideologically the system was driven by Confucian principles, especially the version propounded by the followers of Chu Hsi (1130–1200) and expressed most eloquently in the 1890 Imperial Rescript on Education which, until 1945, was the guiding document for Japanese education. This rescript emphasized the five human relationships considered necessary by Confucians for a good society: loyalty to the emperor (as a symbol of the state), filial piety, affection among siblings, harmony between husband and wife, and trust among friends. Chu Hsi's thought was congenial to Japan's conservative leadership in that it emphasized the need for unswerving loyalty to the state and one's superiors. The educational philosophy expressed in the Imperial Rescript, and the required moral education courses, was hostile to democratic education. It was expected that the individual submerge himself in service to the emperor as symbol of the state.

There is little doubt that Japanese schools generally succeeded in inculcating loyalty, obedience and the technical skills needed to produce efficient workers and loyal, unquestioning citizens. Thus, it is also likely that the educational system established and developed after the 1880s contributed greatly to creating a Japanese public eventually susceptible to the ultranationalism and authoritarianism of the military, once it took power it the 1930s.

The prewar educational system, therefore, presents a mixed picture. In terms of access to education, prewar Japan was in many ways remarkable. Educational opportunity was relatively widespread, especially compared to many European democracies of that era. A universal compulsory education system was quickly developed, leading to almost universal literacy by the turn of the century. Males at least could advance to secondary and higher education based on ability, and there were some private schools and other facilities for women. Financial support for students, and tuition-free education in the case of teacher-training normal schools, decreased the cost of education for many. Upward mobility through education, therefore, was probably greater in Japan than in many other industrialized nations by the first quarter of the twentieth century. By providing universal access to primary education, creating basic literacy, and exposing some Japanese at highter educational levels to rational, secular knowledge, the system contained elements which, if not automatically democratic, nonetheless provided the potential for positive integration with a democratic system after the war.

On the other hand, the system itself was thoroughly undemocratic in its goals (to serve the state), its processes (hierarchical, authoritarian, and centralized), and its content (a curriculum guided by an emperor-centered and nationalist ideology). Ironically, the combination of relative equality in distribution but undemocratic process and content of education probably contributed to nondemocratic politics in prewar Japan. The imperial state ideology was broadly disseminated, and support for the elite inculcated, to a significant extent through a broad-based educational system.

The American Occupation and Education

Almost fifteen years of unbridled military rule at home and aggression overseas culminated in Japan's unconditional surrender following the atomic horrors of Hiroshima and Nagasaki. The experience of the 1930s and the 1940s left Japan devastated physically and spiritually, and the nation searched for an organizing principle that would offer hope for the future.

One of the primary goals of postwar American policy was the democratization of Japan, and democratic education was believed to be vital in this quest. Before Japan could be democratized, however, the American policymakers believed that it was necessary to dismantle those elements of the existing Japanese educational system which were antidemocratic or militaristic in nature, and to replace them with components that would foster the desired democratic tendencies. These initial steps were, of necessity, negative ones—the clearing away of the old to make way for the new.

Democracy Imposed: Occupation Reforms

The negative period consisted of two separate but related stages. One was the steps taken by the Japanese themselves. Even before the

Occupation authorities made any demands upon it, the Ministry of Education abolished the old Wartime Education Law, and on September 15, 1945, promulgated a new "Educational Policy Towards Construction of a New Japan." Although "democracy" was not specifically mentioned, the general thrust of this policy was clearly toward the elimination of militarism and its replacement with a democratic educational system. It is significant that the Japanese not only anticipated the overall direction of American educational policy, but also made an early effort to accommodate themselves to it.

The Americans followed through with the second stage by issuing four basic directives in the autumn and early winter of 1945. These directives cleared away much of the foundation of prewar Japanese education by purging teachers with "militaristic and nationalistic" tendencies, abolished state supported Shinto, and suspended all courses in moral education, history, and geography. These actions essentially completed the negative phase of educational reform and forced American authorities to think seriously about what the new structure they were committed to build would look like. Fortunately, presurrender planning for the Occupation had begun in 1943 and was based on several assumptions which were particularly relevant for the reform of Japanese education. The United States, for example, did not envision the destruction of Japan's cultural heritage and the imposition of American values and institutions. American planners, in fact, believed that rather than destroying Japanese culture, they could "use it, as far as possible, in establishing new attitudes of mind conforming to the basic principles of democracy and fair-dealing." In addition, these same planners assumed that a peaceful postwar Japan "presupposed the existence of those in the country who would be predisposed to accept the [liberal American] vision and carry out the task of reconstruction along liberal lines."[1]

One of the first steps taken by the relatively inexperienced Americans put in charge of reforming Japanese education, most of whom were not professional educators, was to request that a high-level educational mission be sent to Japan to provide advice and, perhaps more important, a legitimation of their plans for reform. A twenty-seven-member mission under the chairmanship of Dr. George Stoddard (former New York State commissioner of education and president-elect of the University of Illinois) arrived in Japan in March 1946. Consisting primarily of school administrators and education professors, the First United States Education Mission to Japan (USEMJ) can

be fairly described as representing the mainstream of American progressive educational thought, but it had virtually no knowledge of
either Japan of Japanese education. The report which it issued, under
the imprimatur of General Douglas MacArthur, was widely viewed
as a blueprint for reforming Japan's education. Both its tone and
recommendations faithfully articulated the fundamental tenets of
America's notion of democratic education. Given the composition of
the USEMJ, and the brief time it spent in Japan, this document with
its stress on decentralization, demilitarization, and democratization
could have been written in New York, Chicago, or San Francisco
with less trouble and expense.

Decentralization was viewed by the mission, as well as by the
Civil Information and Education Section of MacArthur's headquarters (CI&E), as the key to reforming Japanese education along democratic lines. The centralized power of the ministry of education was,
in the mission's words, "the seat of power for those who controlled
the minds of Japan." After all, local control of American schools had
kept them "close to the people" and out of the hands of the machinations of national government. The Americans, however, failed to
consider that their decentralized system was an organic outgrowth of
an enormous geographical expanse and the "rugged individualism"
which flourished on the frontier. Japan was a small, heavily populated
island nation which placed great emphasis on cooperation and harmony. Throughout their modern history the Japanese had had a centralized educational system that reflected the belief that education's
function was clearly one of serving the needs of the state, not to fulfill
the potential of the individual.

To achieve decentralization, the USEMJ strongly urged that the
role of the Ministry of Education be reduced from a controlling organ
to one providing only advice and assistance to local educational entities. Although abolishing the Ministry of Education had been seriously considered, the combination of the ministry's political influence
and the need of the Occupation authorities to use the ministry's administrative skills to implement Occupation policy made this option
impractical.

Given the assumptions inherent in the argument for decentralization, the next logical step was to enhance local decision making by
advocating locally elected school boards. In 1948, the required legislation was put in place. It was a very controversial experiment from the
outset and did not last long. Four years after the end of the Occupa-

tion, the Local Education Administration Act was passed which eliminated the popular election of school board members and their power over the educational budget.

Among its other major recommendations the 1948 legislation urged curriculum and methods of education be expanded beyond the old pattern of a single textbook and teacher's manual. Moreover, it proposed that individualization according to student needs and abilities be instituted, that the content and approach of moral education be overhauled and no longer treated as a separate subject in the curriculum, that a 6-3-3 system be installed and compulsory schooling be extended to nine years, that normal schools be transformed into four-year institutions to better prepare teachers in content and democratic pedagogy, that the educational opportunities of women be expanded, and that guidance be stressed in the schools. For good or ill, all these recommendations spoke to a faith in dominant American educational theory and practice, and almost all were to be adopted by the men and women of the CI&E and eventually imposed.

Meanwhile, the legal foundation of educational reform was being constructed. After much discussion a new constitution came into effect on May 3, 1947. Unlike the American constitution, which fails to mention education, the Japanese document specifically states that "all people shall have the right to receive an equal education correspondent to their ability, as provided by law. All people shall be obliged to have all boys and girls under their protection receive ordinary education as provided by law. Such compulsory education shall be free."

In the spring of 1947 the Diet passed two basic pieces of educational legislation, the School Education Law and the Fundamental Law of Education, which effectively codified the Occupation's educational reforms and set Japan's schools on a democratic course. The former set down detailed administrative regulations, from kindergarten through university education, while the latter was a bold policy statement articulating democratic objectives. "Having established the Constitution of Japan, we have shown our resolution to contribute to the peace of the world and the welfare of humanity by building a democratic and cultural state. The realization of this ideal shall depend fundamentally on the power of education." The several provisions of this law called for the full development of personality, respect for academic freedom, equality of educational opportunity for all without discrimination of any kind, coeducation at all levels, education for citizenship, and the separation of church and state.

When American control was withdrawn in the spring of 1952, the educational reformers had succeeded in clearing away the old undemocratic structures, replacing them with ones more to their liking; they had replaced those individuals identified as ultranationalists or militarists with Japanese who seemed committed to democratic values; they had provided Japanese educators with new curricula, textbooks, and methodologies. In short, they had given their best effort and now, as they withdrew to the sideline, they could only hope that their best effort had been enough.

Democracy Revised: The "Reverse Course"

It should not be surprising that with the return of sovereignty in 1952, the Japanese began a careful examination of the reforms of the previous seven years and modified or changed those things which they believed were not in harmony with the nation's political and cultural traditions. Education did not escape this scrutiny, and by 1956 the government had, for all intents and purposes, scrapped the American-imposed school board system and allowed the Ministry of Education to regain control over the educational system, particularly in the areas of administration, curriculum, and textbook selection.

These changes did not, however, signal a rejection of democracy as a concept and a return to "the bad old days." If the Japanese were to have democracy, they were determined to have a variant that was consistent with their traditions and culture. The Japanese penchant for centralization reasserted itself, but this was not necessarily undemocratic. Local control over education, as the study of American education amply demonstrates, can result in a greater sensitivity to the needs of the area, but can also lead to racial discrimination, religious bigotry, textbook censorship, and other undemocratic acts. One can also argue, and many Japanese did, that a centralized system ensured that every child— from Okinawa to Hokkaidō—enjoyed "equality of educational opportunity" because of the relatively equal physical facilities throughout the country, a uniform curriculum administered by the Ministry of Education, equal access to the same textbooks, teachers of relatively equal competence, and a uniform set of national standards.

Postwar Education: Access

Three decades after the United States relinquished its authority over Japanese life, the results of American efforts to democratize

Japanese education are more clearly visible. There is no question that democratic education exists in contemporary Japan, but it exists in a form quite different from the the model that the United States advocated in the postwar years. In examining its structure, one finds elements that resemble those found in European as well as in American education. This pattern is not unlike that found in Meiji and prewar Japan in which aspects of French, German, English, and American systems were part of a mosaic uniquely Japanese.

A careful examination of several key elements found in any definition of democratic education provides a measure of the fundamental health of Japan's system in terms of access to education and standards of quality. There can be little doubt that postwar Japan has made enormous strides in providing expanded educational opportunities for its young people. In the thirty-five years between the end of World War II and 1980, the number of students attending school in Japan increased by over 80 percent, from 15 million to over 27 million. Virtually all young people now complete the nine years of compulsory education (99.98 percent in 1980), and an impressive 94.2 percent of these graduates go on to the noncompulsory senior secondary school. Perhaps most significantly, the Japanese have demonstrated that mass education does not have to be purchased with diluted standards. Time and time again, international achievement tests have placed the Japanese at, or close to, the top in a variety of subjects. Furthermore, in 1980, 37.4 percent of the senior high school graduates attended some kind of institution of higher education.

The Examination System

Japan's remarkable achievement of accessible, high quality education has not been without its problems and costs. One of the most widely criticized elements of Japanese education is the examination system which not only determines one's educational future, but also one's lifetime career opportunities. Ezra Vogel has commented that "no single event, with the possible exception of marriage, determines the course of a young man's life as much as entrance examinations, and nothing, including marriage, requires as many years of planning and hard work."[2]

Japan is an intensely education-oriented society, and graduation from a university is a prerequisite to success in that society. This, however, tells only part of the story, for university graduation is not enough—the real test is found in the question, "From *which* university did you graduate?" Japanese universities are ranked according to prestige and, while this element is found in other countries, the fine gradations between universities, faculties within universities, and professors studied under is often difficult for outsiders to comprehend. If viewed as a pyramid, the apex of Japanese higher education is firmly occupied by the University of Tokyo, and the most prestigious faculty within that institution is its Faculty of Law (in Japan a combination of political science and public administration). Just beneath Tokyo are a handful of other former imperial universities such as Kyoto, and Kyūshū, closely followed by a gaggle of prestigious private universities such as Keiō and Waseda. The broad base of the pyramid contains hundreds of other institutions, most of which are perceived as second or third rate.

In nearly all Japanese universities success on the entrance examination is, if not the sole criterion, by far the most important one for admission. Those who are able to pass the examination for a prestigious university, preferably Tokyo, can look forward to an assured future, because once the student enters the university, completion of the degree is virtually automatic. Competition for the best universities is, in a word, fierce. It is not uncommon for only one of every fifteen or twenty applicants to be admitted to the best schools. This statistic takes on added meaning when one realizes that only the best students are encouraged by their teachers to aim this high. In other words, a preselected elite take the Tokyo University examination and only a small minority can expect to pass it.

Getting on the escalator to career success is, therefore, dependent upon passing the entrance examination to one of a handful of elite schools. This results not only in high school education being distorted by an undue emphasis on passing examinations, but also in lower education being distorted by these pressures. An important consequence of this preoccupation with passing exminations is a lack of emphasis on creativity or the noncognitive aspects of education. Students desiring to compete in the university examination war know that they must start preparing by the lower secondary level or earlier. It is not uncommon to find weary youngsters riding home on the subway or commuter trains at 10 P.M. after having attended supplementary lessons from late afternoon. Parents, notably, the *kyōiku mama* or "education mama," work very hard to help their children pass entrance examinations, even for preschools or kindergarten. There are many bizarre, but often true stories about the sorting process at this level. For example, one preschool was unable to devise a suitable entrance test for two-year-olds and after much discussion decided that, under the circumstances, they could best determine the children's ability by testing the mothers instead!

This distortion of lower education is also reflected at the high school level. Since the reputation of a school and its teachers is, in large measure, dependent upon the number of its students who go on to prestigious universities, it is not uncommon for teachers to spend a great deal of time drilling their students to pass examinations. Junior high school teachers, taking their cue from the higher level, often become similarly absorbed, and it is not unheard of for some primary school teachers to conduct mock examinations to accustom their charges to the reality of the system.

At least from junior high school, ambitious students are committed to extra study, extra texts, and practice examinations which will rule their lives until they either succeed or admit failure in the university examination competition. Assisting students to prepare for examinations is big business. A visit to virtually any large bookstore in a Japanese city illustrates both the centrality of entrance examinations to student life and the vast profits being made by entrepreneurs. These bookstores are filled with students of all ages. They flock to the shelves appropriate to their interests where they discover books and pamphlets on techniques to help them pass the ubiquitous examinations. Shelves are conspicuously marked with signs such as "For Secondary Entrance Preparation." Provocative titles include *The Complete Study Guide for Passing University Entrance Examinations,* or *English Vocabulary Most Likely to Appear on the Entrance Examination,* and so on. Pamphlets containing past examinations and sample questions fill the shelves.

A few years ago a government *White Paper on School Children and Youth* linked examination pressures with personality changes in children, pointing out that because study takes up virtually all of a youngster's waking hours little time is left for play. As a result, children do not have sufficient opportunity for socializing. The report complained that "gregariousness which used to be a hallmark of school children can no longer be taken for granted." Related to this are increasing reports of health problems in youngsters that are attributable to examination pressures.

Another problem related to the examination system, challenged by some researchers, is the widely perceived causal relationship between examination pressures and teenage suicide. No one doubts,

however, the so-called *rōnin* phenomenon. This term, which originally referred to the "masterless samurai" of feudal days, is now used
to describe students who, having failed to pass the entrance examination to the school of their choice, spend an extra year (and sometimes
much longer) studying to pass the examination. Thus, today's *rōnin*
are "students without a university." In at least one important sense,
Japan's entrance examination system is eminently democratic. Success on these examinations is based on merit, that is, one can succeed
regardless of one's station in life so long as one has the basic intelligence and is willing to work as hard as necessary to master the material that appears on the examinations. Perhaps most important, the
cost of attending the most elite national universities—which are supported by the state—is only a fraction of the tuition of third-rate
private universities. This fact takes on great significance when we
reflect that in the United States the best universities are generally
perceived to be expensive private institutions. In Japan most people
feel that the best education is obtained in the public sector.

One cannot argue, however, that there is no correlation between
success on the examinations and one's social and economic circumstances. As elsewhere, the child from a middle-class home will not
only have greater resources enabling him to attend supplementary
schools, benefit from private lessons, and purchase learning aids, but
also will be the recipient of a much richer cultural experience.

Despite a good if somewhat flawed access record, an increasing
number of scholars are recognizing that a significant area of inequality
in Japanese education is represented by the fact that approximately 75
percent of students attending four-year institutions are in the expensive
private sector. Therefore, although access to relatively inexpensive
national universities is reasonably democratic, the access problem is
much more complicated. In the past several years the children of the
affluent have begun to dominate entry to the public institutions at a
significantly greater rate than two decades ago, and poorer families find
it increasingly difficult to pay the higher costs of private education. In
addition, unlike the United States and other industrial nations, the
Japanese government has not recognized the need to provide financial
aid to deserving students, making their plight even more difficult.

Women

Prior to 1945, Japanese females had very limited access to advanced education. The secondary education alternatives that were

available to them heavily favored domestic education, while university preparatory schools were a male preserve. Today, however, things have changed for the better: girls outnumber boys by 94.5 to 93.1 percent at the senior high school, and one out of every three female graduate advances to some form of higher education. It should be pointed out, however, that the vast majority of these women graduates enroll in junior colleges and most of those who go on to four-year colleges major in fields such as English literature.

While teaching in International Christian University and Keio University in the mid-1970s, I was impressed by the contrast between the numbers of female students attending ICU, a good university, and Keiō, which is among the most prestigious in Japan. It was striking that a seemingly high percentage of the ICU women, daughters of international businessmen and diplomats, had received much of their secondary education in North America, Europe, or Australia, while the few Keiō women had spent their lives in Japan. Upon being asked why they chose ICU rather than applying for more prestigious universities, it was clear that unless one not only attended a rigorous Japanese high school, but also attended so-called cram schools and supplementary schools, there was little chance of passing the requisite entrance examinations to the elite schools. ICU, of course, places much importance on its entrance examination, but also takes into consideration a variety of other factors in making admission decisions.

A second reason, mentioned almost as often by ICU female students, suggests that despite thirty years of democratic education, there still exists a widespread ingrained prejucice against women. It is rare in Japan for a young man to marry a woman graduate of a more prestigious university than the one he attended. Therefore, a young woman graduating from Tokyo University has in effect significantly narrowed her pool of eligible suitors. The other side to this coin, in the ICU case, is its well-deserved reputation for effectively teaching English to Japanese students, and Japanese to foreigners. A female graduate of ICU is, therefore, presumed to have a high level of English-language ability, is accustomed to dealing with foreigners and, therefore, is an attractive potential wife to ambitious young male graduates of elite universities planning careers in international business, diplomacy, or any field in which such an internationally oriented wife is an asset. Educational decisions are still made in the 1980s on such assumptions.

Another example of the widespread attitude toward the education of women is seen in a recent policy implemented by the Kyoto Pharmaceutical University which announced in late 1983 that it would give preferential treatment to *male* applicants for admission. As the number of young men successfully passing the entrance examination declined over the past several years, more women were accepted. School officials felt threatened by what they called the "feminization" of their institution and sought to reverse this trend. Their justification, according to the school's officials, was that Japanese companies overwhelmingly prefer to hire men and that the university saw no point in producing graduates who will not be hired by industry. It is clear that although Japanese women have made important educational progress since the end of World War II, they still have a long way to go to catch up with their brothers.

The important point, however, is that the political process does allow for change to occur within the system. Several examples of this process can be seen in the contemporary media. Japanese families have forced the Ministry of Education to set up a commission to study whether the present regulation making home economics a required secondary school course for girls should be retained, modified, or abolished. In another case, women and teachers' groups are agitating for the elimination of what they consider sexist biases in a number of widely used textbooks. Although change occurs slowly, it does occur. One can present many examples of educational discrimination against Japanese women, but viewing their situation in the broad historical sweep since 1945, it is difficult not to be impressed with the progress made.

Minority Groups

One of the most widely known facts about Japan is that its population is an unusually homogeneous one. On the other hand, relatively few non-Japanese are aware that this homogeneous population contains several relatively small, but significant minority groups, including approximately 3,000,000 former outcastes called Burakumin, more than 1,000,000 Okinawans, and close to a million indigenous Ainu, Koreans, Chinese, *hibakusha* (atomic bomb victims), *konketsuji* (offspring of interracial parents), Indochinese refugees, Southeast Asian "entertainers," and resident foreigners (including several thousand Americans and Europeans). This essay will not deal with this wide range of peoples because of space constraints, but will concentrate on the Burakumin and Korean minorities.

The Burakumin, literally "hamlet people" because they lived in *tokushu buraku,* specially designated hamlets, are descendants of the outcasts of Tokugawa Japan (1603–1868). They are the largest minority group in Japan and are heavily concentrated in the west, with more than half found in the western parts of the main island of Honshū (Kinki and Chūgoku regions). Legally emancipated in 1871, the Burakumin made no significant educational gains until their agitation for governmental attention succeeded in 1969 with the passage of the "Law of Special Actions" for Dōwa Policy, which provided a legal framework for actions promoting the welfare of Burakumin. Although it contained no specific educational provisions, it did require that both national and local officials identify Burakumin educational problems and take the necessary steps to solve them. In the same year the government announced a Long-term Dōwa (Integration) Policy Program effective to March 1979, later extended to March 1982. Upon expiration, this law was replaced, after much debate, by the compromise Area Improvement Measures Law, valid for five years.

The results of these actions have been mixed. On the one hand, whereas only about 30 percent of Burakumin children attended senior high school in 1963 (compared to 64 percent of non-Burakumin children), studies by Nobuo Shimahara of Rutgers University conclude that the situation has significantly improved. The current national high school enrollment is about 95 percent and Shimahara suggests that "the difference in high school enrollment between the eligible minority and majority populations has narrowed to less than 10 percentage points." In fact, Shimahara provides evidence suggesting that important gains have also been made by Burakumin at the college level. He is careful to point out, however, that "there is still a significant difference between Burakumin and majority youths in educational attainment at the postsecondary level," although the gap has diminished somewhat.[3]

Another Japanese student of the Burakumin educational problems, Fumiko Okamura-Bichard, contends that although attending senior high school in increasing numbers, Burakumin youngsters are "deprived of equal *opportunites* within school, requiring compensatory measures."[4] For example, in a country of virtually universal literacy, the rate among Burakumin is only 80 percent. Indeed, the dropout rate for Burakumin students ranged from a high of 5.4 percent in Okayama Prefecture to only 1.6 percent in Nagano Prefecture. Among majority students the *highest* dropout rate was 2.7 percent, in Kōchi.

Japanese reactions to this minority problem vary. Some recognize the need for social justice, others see such demands as a sign of deleterious social change. The majority are disinterested because it has no direct impact on their day-to-day lives. The Burakumin and their supporters have tried mightily to educate the broader public to the problem, but their success has so far been limited. For example, the director of the Justice Bureau, in 1982, was quoted as telling a group of local government officals that "the rather unsavory parallel has been drawn . . . that public servants are as much a fact of life as the Tokushu Buraku. But public servants are, after all, just human beings." It is attitudes of this sort, not only among government officials who should know better, that need to be changed if Burakumin are to overcome their historic disability.

Another group that has traditionally faced discrimination is Japan's approximately 700,000 Korean residents. In discussing the problems of Koreans in Japan, Thomas Rohlen concludes that "it is not a question of barriers existing within the school system itself," but rather obstacles which spring up when Koreans "seek employment in the Japanese labor market."[5] That a Korean problem exists in the school system is, however, widely recognized. There have even been some efforts, in cities with large Korean populations, to inject into the public schools what one might call "ethnic studies" for Korean students.

Although Japanese education is highly centralized, especially by American standards, it is wrong to assume that there is no differentiation among schools. Not all Japanese school boards are the same. For example, Kobe, a city with historic foreign ties and controlled by political progressives, has confronted its discrimination problem. The school board has published various antidiscrimination materials for use in both junior and senior high schools in an attempt to deal with discriminatory attitudes toward both Burakumin and Koreans. Although not entirely successful, because many teachers feel uncomfortable discussing such issues, this is an approach that may lend itself to long-term improvements in the situation.

On the other hand, as in the case of the Burakumin, anti-Korean prejudice is often deep-seated. Some Japanese parents will change their residence or send their children to private schools in order to avoid having them attend school with Korean youngsters. The irony is that these young Koreans have usually been born in Japan, speak Japanese as their native tongue, and have taken on Japanese cultural patterns. Many have even gone to the extreme of hiding their Korean roots by using a Japanese name. Some Koreans, however, remain wedded to their Korean heritage. In September 1983 there was a heated public controversy over an alleged attempt of school officials in Nagoya to pressure Korean parents into enrolling their son under a Japanese name. The school officials claimed that they "suggested" this to the parents for educational reasons, that is, the child was apt to be teased by his classmates because of his "strange" name. Korean organizations and other opponents of discrimination refused to accept this explanation and charged that it was reminiscent of the Japanese occupation of Korea when all Koreans were forced to adopt Japanese names.

Koreans, however, do have the option of sending their children to two sets of Korean schools in Japan, one subsidized by the government of North Korea and the other by South Korea. The major problem with attending a Korean school, however, is that their graduates are not allowed to take entrance examinations for the prestigious national or public colleges and universities. This is a contributing cause to the fact that, according to Rohlen, Koreans in Japan "have statistically half the average chance of going to a university." Despite this, however, Rohlen argues persuasively that there is "little evidence that the difference in outcome stems primarily from discrimination in the education and matriculation process itself."[6] This conclusion is scant comfort for Japanese educators because the Korean minority does have legitimate grievances which, if not satisfied, contain the potential for serious social discontent.

Democracy in the Schools: Process and Content

Access to education is only one part of the issue of democracy in education. Another important aspect is the role that schools play in educating pupils to democratic citizenship, that is, in performing the function of political socialization. Schools may influence beliefs and behavior in several ways, among the most important of which are (1) direct teaching about democracy and politics (that is, the intentional inculcation of beliefs and values); and (2) the authority structure and students' experience in the classroom (that is, providing models and training in democratic decisionmaking and participation).[7]

There is no doubt that democracy as a political doctrine to guide conduct is widely accepted by an overwhelming majority of Japanese youth. The reverse side of this, however, is a widespread acceptance of the thesis that the democratic creed is the only vehicle with which peace and prosperity can be secured. Thus, unlike many other countries, democratic education has a very strong orientation toward peace and world order. As Joseph Massey has concluded, "there is substantial and consistent evidence to indicate that democracy has become established in the attitude structure of young Japanese, and indeed of their elders as well, as the preferred system of government."[8]

The question arising from this is an important one. What caused this widespread faith in democracy among postwar generations? Certainly a large part of the answer can be found in the trauma of defeat in World War II (compounded by the nuclear conflagrations in Hiroshima and Nagasaki) and the subsequent East-West cold war. But the radically reformed postwar educational system is also at least partially responsible. Another significant cause, if one accepts the premise that the political orientation of the nation's teachers does make a difference in the ideological tenor of the classroom, is the emergence of the Japan Teachers Union (Nikkyōso).

One of the major results of the American Occupation of Japan was the creation of a strong teachers' union which, since its birth in the years following World War II, has consistently been politically to the left of center. Less interested than their American counterparts in bread-and-butter issues, the Japan Teachers Union is committed to a socialist model of an egalitarian society as part of a peaceful world order. Inculcating democratic values is, therefore, an important part of the union's ideological commitment.[9] If, indeed, an important part of what a child learns in school is a result of what educators refer to as the "hidden" or "latent" curriculum, then it seems not unreasonable to suggest that teacher attitudes and behaviors have exerted an important influence on the political socialization of young people.

During the "reverse course" of the 1950s the Japan Teachers' Union fiercely resisted the conservative politicians's efforts to undo the democratic educational reforms imposed by the Americans, and during the turbulent 1960s and 1970s, its members were in the forefront of opposition to the Vietnam War, Japanese rearmament, U.S.-Japan security arrangements, and so forth. One knowledgeable and perceptive student of Japanese education, William K. Cummings, in his valuable study of Japanese elementary education, has concluded that there is a close correlation between "the extent to which teachers of a school are unionized" and those schools where "egalitarian educational themes are paramount."[10]

Classroom atmosphere and teacher-student authority relations in the postwar period also no longer resemble the stiff, rigid, and authoritarian conditions of the earlier period. Although teachers are respected and clearly in charge, pupils interact relatively freely in an informal and relaxed atmosphere. Ronald Dore, writing about his observations of Japanese classrooms in the late 1950s, found an absence of inflexible discipline and widespread free expression by students. He concluded that "what was to be seen in these schools certainly did not suggest the educational system which one associates with an authoritarian society."[11] This was reaffirmed by Benjamin Duke in the 1960s when he concluded that "today the Japanese student has greater freedom than students in most countries," and they "have little inhibition in asking questions, and usually in only some of the classrooms of the older 'pre-war' teachers does one find an atmosphere of strict obedience."[12]

Perhaps the single most telling characteristic of Japanese teachers is that they are not only democratic, but they are highly professional in their approach to their work. The organization of Japanese schools, with morning and weekly faculty meetings, biweekly research meetings, and quarterly public research seminars, provides strong incentives for teachers not only to systematically discuss classroom problems with their colleagues, but to actually conduct important educational research. While it is undoubtedly true that American teachers also spend a substantial amount of time in faculty meetings, it is the rare faculty meeting that goes beyong the principal's agenda.[13] In addition, the concern of many Japanese teachers for their charges goes far beyond the classroom. It is not uncommon to find teachers checking up on their students in coffee shops, or spending time in after-school club activities. More than a formal student-teacher relationship exists in the Japanese educational context; teachers are often more like older brothers or sisters, as much concerned with the youngster's total development as with classroom performance.

Another important dimension of the democratic changes which have taken place in postwar Japan is the dramatic increase in parental and community involvement in school matters. Parent-Teacher Associations are common, but tend to leave pedagogical questions to the principal and the teachers to address. Most schools have some type of student government, usually with at least some autonomy, and many homerooms are democratically organized. Ronald Dore believes that "it seems safe to say that the products of postwar schools, as compared to their fathers, are more like citizens than subjects, are better capable of forming public opinion . . . and are more certain of their right to hold and express such opinions."[14]

Furthermore, both in the classroom and outside it, the Japanese child is constantly embedded in a network of relationships with adults and peers that emphasize cooperation in a "community." This can best be illustrated through the experiences of my son when he attended a typical Japanese elementary school in the mid-1970s. From the very outset, it was clear that one of the major goals of his teacher was to create a "community" from the fifty children assigned to her second grade class. As a result several interesting things occured. Immediately an open line of communication with the home of each child was established through a class newsletter, a telephone tree, home visits by the teacher and so on. Group activities requiring cooperation and harmony were stressed over individual activities. A sense of belonging and loyalty to the class were encouraged in a myriad of ways. This group orientation may not be the typical American's idea of democracy, but it is very Japanese. The individual in Japan seeks self-fulfillment not as an autonomous individual, but as part of a group. This is not only true in the classroom, but also in the worlds of business, government, sports, and crime.

Stress on cooperative and harmonious behavior is also reflected in nonacademic activities. For example, most elementary schools do not have a cafeteria where the children eat lunch. Rather they eat their noon meal in their classroom *with* their teacher. The food is either prepared at the school or brought from a central location, and each class sends a delegation, complete with white aprons, face masks, and chef's hats, at a specified time, to pick up the food for their classmates. The youngsters then serve the food to each student. The teacher eats with the students to set an example of the correct way of eating and to ensure that things run smoothly. When lunch is completed the class cleans the classroom in preparation for the resumption of formal teaching.

The democratic lessons of this exercise are clear. The class is a group in which everyone shares the food and the work involved in getting it and cleaning up. The implicit lesson demonstrated is one of the dignity of labor and everybody's obligation to do their fair share for the good of the group. This principle is also carried out at other times during the year when teachers and students will embark on clean-up projects to improve the appearance of the school. This also serves to give both teacher and taught a sense of shared pride in their school.

The process of democratic education is, however, only one half of the picture. The content of democratic education, or what is taught about democratic education also needs to be examined. Social studies and moral education are the courses most relevant for inculcating democratic values and what follows is a summary of their content at the elementary, lower secondary, and upper secondary levels.

At the elementary level (grades 1–6) among the overall objectives of the social studies curriculum is the cultivation of "a fundamental awareness of being citizens in a democratic and peaceful nation and society." With this in mind, first graders are taught that the school's physical plant and equipment, as well as surrounding parks, are "owned jointly by the people." The second grader learns that all jobs in his community are important for the community's well-being and worthy of respect. By the third grade, students are taking "geography" with an emphasis on knowing their local area and community. Fifth graders are exposed to more sophisticated democratic concepts such as popular sovereignty, parliamentary and representative government, constitutional guarantees, and the like. The amount of time devoted to social studies begins in grade one with a modest 68 forty-five-minute class periods per year, increasing to 70 periods in grade two and jumping sharply to 105 class periods per year in grades three through six.[15]

Moral education at the elementary school is a constant 35 class periods per year from grades two through six, but only 34 class periods during grade one. The content of moral educaion classes is a far cry from prewar Japan when moral education was a synonym for unrestrained nationalistic propoganda. Today, moral education "is aimed at realizing a spirit of respect for human dignity . . . , endeavoring to create a culture that is rich in individuality and to develop a democratic society and state, training Japanese to be capable of contributing to a peaceful international society, and cultivating their morality as the foundation thereof."[16]

At the lower secondary level (grades 7–9) the social studies curriculum is designed to "develop basic qualities of a civic nature essential to the builders of a democratic and peaceful nation and society." At this level, geography, history, and civics are taught and, although there is democratic content in the former two subjects, the civics course is undoubtedly the single most important vehicle for transmitting democratic values. In this course, usually taught in grade nine, and meeting for 105 class periods per year, a wide variety of relevant topics are treated. These topics include "Respect for man and the constitution of Japan." "The individual and society," "Foreign trade and international cooperation," "Democracy and law," "International society and peace," and so forth.[17]

Moral education classes in the lower secondary school meet for 35 class periods per year in grades 7, 8, and 9 (private schools may substitute religious education for all or part of the moral education courses). The objectives of moral education at this level are identical with those postulated at the elementary level, and the content of the course, although its treatment is more sophisticated than that of the elementary schools, is not significantly different in its nature.[18]

The objectives for upper secondary (grades 10–12) social studies are basically similar to the lower levels, but reflect a greater complexity. The aim remains, however, to develop in the students the "qualities necessary as citizens which are essential for competent builders of a democratic and peaceful nation and society." At this level electives play a greater role than in the earlier years enabling students to choose from courses in contemporary society, Japanese history, world history, ethics, geography, or politics and economy. A student's choice of electives depends upon what kind of program he or she is pursuing in high school (general, vocational) and upon the student's future academic plans. In any event, the objectives and content of all of these possible electives reflect varying degrees of democratic content.[19]

How effective are these classes in instilling democratic values? Political socialization studies find it extremely difficult to separate out the various influences that form a young person's political identity, so it is impossible to say with any precision. Massey did find that Japanese students were very positively oriented toward the symbol of democracy and toward democratic institutions such as the diet and elections.[20] Classroom teaching probably helps to inculcate, or at least reinforces, these attitudes. On the other hand, Massey also found that Japanese school children, even in early grades, were extremely cynical about their national political leaders (much less so toward local leaders) when compared to children in other democratic countries. Whether these cynical attitudes toward politicians derive from school experiences or from the transmission of attitudes in the family or media is difficult to say. It is clear, however, that whatever contribution civics and social studies courses may make toward positive attitudes toward democratic institutions, they are not able to overcome or counteract an early developed cynicism toward politicians and political leaders.

Democratic Education: Recent Problems

Because education performs such a crucial function in modern society—the transmission of values and behavior to the young—educational systems everywhere are subject to constant pressures and problems, some of which are political. Japan is no exception, as some recent controversies show.

One of the universal problems afflicting Japanese education is the increasing bureaucratization of school administration. The enormity of the educational enterprise in Japan can be seen by the facts that there are almost half a million teachers at the primary level and another quarter million each at the middle and high school levels. The relative centralization of education in Japan also adds to bureaucratization: the largest ministry in the Japanese government is the Ministry of Education, employing over 132,000 persons. Even with this large staff, the number of pupils per class is relatively large, in 1983 averaging over thirty-three per class at the primary level and thirty-eight per class at the middle school level.[21] As a result, alienation of both students and teachers is not completely absent from Japanese education.

Despite the "community" aspects of Japanese education, increasing bureaucratization of the school system, alienation, and the fierce pressures for educational attainment through examinations have probably contributed to a recent phenomenon that has caused consternation in Japan: rising incidents of school violence. Police records indicate that incidents of school violence nearly doubled (1,292 to 2,125) in the five years between 1978 and 1983, with those involving violent attacks on teachers showing a nearly fivefold increase (from 191 to 929 cases) during the same time period.[22] Compared to some American urban school systems where violence is endemic, these figures may not seem too disturbing; but in the Japanese context, where education and teachers are so respected and harmonious social relations so valued, these trends have caused tremendous alarm and controversy.

Another recent issue reflecting problems in Japanese education explicitly involved questions of democratic control over educational content and Japan's relations in the international community. In Japan's centralized system, the Ministry of Education must still approve the limited range of textbooks used in the schools. The ministry thus may request authors to make changes in text content prior to approval. In one such case that became a major political issue, the ministry requested that a text describing the Japanese invasion of China in the late 1930s not use the word "invasion" (*shinryaku*) but rather the word "advance." This change was greatly criticized, both at home, where many are concerned about the tendency for the government to want to emphasize national pride in the curriculum, and abroad, where other Asian countries are still very sensitive to Japan's aggression in World War II. This issue caused a major diplomatic controversy with the People's Republic of China.

Conclusion

Japan's postwar record in democratic education is a good one, but by no means perfect. Japan shares the problems of most modern democratic nations of bureaucratization and alienation in the school system with consequent problems of maintaining feelings of purpose and value among teachers and students. Japan also has particular problems of excessive pressures for examination achievement and of preventing education from becoming a political football in the conflicts between left and right. Some problems of discrimination against women and minorities remain. Finally the high degree of centralization of the system, while providing uniform nationwide standards, creates issues of academic freedom, as the recent textbook controversy illustrates.

On the other hand, the successes of Japanese education are undeniable. The prewar authoritarian and ideological system has been thoroughly revamped, although retaining and expanding its relatively egalitarian access and meritocratic standards. Postwar education provides relatively easy access at most levels; it bases competition for the most elite schools not on the accident of birth but on merit; it provides experiences—academic and nonacademic—that reinforce basic democratic principles; it maintains world–class standards, and, for the most part, strives to strengthen democratic elements, but within the context of Japanese culture with its emphasis on educational achievement and "community" norms. It is clear, therefore, that the Japanese have considerably democratized postwar education and, in doing so, have socialized the younger generation to life in a democratic polity. If we set Japan's democratic education next to that of the United

States, England, West Germany, or Switzerland we will find that they have different contours, but contain a common core of democratic values. To have accomplished both relatively egalitarian access to basic education *and* the maintainance of very high academic standards in the context of providing training for democratic citizenship is no mean achievement.

NOTES

1. SWNCC, "Directive—Positive Policy for Re-Orientation of the Japanese," National Archives of the United States, Record Group 319, Records of the Army Staff, ABC 014, Japan (13 April 1944).

2. Ezra F. Vogel, *Japan's New Middle Class* (Berkeley and Los Angeles: University of California Press, 1963), p. 40.

3. Nobuo Shimahara, "Toward the Equality of a Japanese Minority: The Case of Burakumin," *Comparative Education* 20, 3 (1984): 347–48.

4. Fumiko Okamura-Bichard, "Promotion of Equality Through Education: The Cases of Japan's Burakumin and India's Scheduled Castes," paper presented at the 28th Annual Conference of the Comparative and International Education Society, Houston, Texas, March 24, 1984.

5. Thomas P. Rohlen, *Japan's High Schools* (Berkeley and Los Angeles: University of California Press, 1983), p. 133.

6. Ibid.

7. For a discussion of the political socialization process and a case study of the family, school, and adult political socialization of Japanese student activists, see Ellis S. Krauss, *Japanese Radicals Revisted: Student Protest in Postwar Japan* (Berkeley and Los Angeles: University of California Press, 1974).

8. Joseph A. Massey, *Youth and Politics in Japan* (Lexington, Massachusetts: D. C. Heath, 1976), p. 68.

9. On the teachers' union see Donald R. Thurston, *Teachers and Politics in Japan* (Princeton, N.J.: Princeton University Press, 1973); Benjamin C. Duke, *Japan's Militant Teachers: A History of the Left-Wing Teachers Movement* (Honolulu: University of Hawaii Press, 1973).

10. William K. Cummings, *Education and Equality in Japan* (Princeton, N.J.: Princeton University Press, 1980), p. 107.

11. Ronald P. Dore, *City Life in Japan* (Berkeley and Los Angeles: University of California Press, 1958), p. 240.

12. Ben C. Duke, "American Education Reforms in Japan Twelve Years Later," _Harvard Educational Review_ 34 (Fall 1964): 534.

13. Cummings, _Education and Equality in Japan,_ p. 12.

14. Ronald P. Dore, "Education: Japan," in _Political Modernization in Japan and Turkey,_ ed. Robert Ward and Dankwart Rustow (Princeton, N.J.: Princeton University Press, 1964), p. 198.

15. Ministry of Education, _Course of Study for Elementary Schools in Japan_ (Tokyo: Ministry of Education, Science, and Culture, 1983), pp. 27–35.

16. Ibid., p. 111.

17. Ministry of Education, _Course of Study for Lower Secondary Schools in Japan_ (Tokyo: Ministry of Education, Science, and Culture, 1983), pp. 14–34.

18. Ibid., pp. 121–25.

19. Ministry of Education, _Course of Study for Upper Secondary Schools in Japan_ (Tokyo: Ministry of Education, Science, and Culture, 1983), pp. 23–39.

20. Massey, _Youth and Politics in Japan,_ p. 185.

21. PHP Research Institute, _The Data File, 1984_ (Tokyo: PHP Kenkyujo, 1984), pp. 346–50.

22. Ibid., p. 361.

Postwar Japanese Education:
A History of Reform and Counterreform
Ikuo Amano

Japanese education is now at the center of a heated debate on reform. The discourse itself is nothing new. Since World War II there has never been a time when calls for change have not been voiced. The current round of debate, however, which got underway in the latter half of the 1980s, differs markedly from earlier ones in three important ways: The need for reform is no longer a point of contention, agreement has been reached on the direction reform should take, and the debate has begun to be coupled with real action. The party platforms for the October 1996 House of Representatives election provide a clear indication of this change. The policy objectives of all parties except the Japanese Communist Party included deregulation of education and gave impetus to Ministry of Education reform initiatives, which since the mid-1980s have been grounded in the concepts of liberalization, individuality, and diversity.

The current chorus of calls for educational reform grows out of a broad-based realization that Japanese politics, the economy, and society need to be restructured. The participants in the debate are not just politicians, bureaucrats, and educators. Major Japanese business organizations, such as Keidanren (Japan Federation of Economic Organizations), the Keizai Doyukai (Japan Association of Corporate Executives), and Nikkeiren (Japan Federation of Employers' Associations), have come up with their own reform proposals, and newspapers and other media have

IKUO AMANO is a professor at the Center for National University Finance.

JAPAN REVIEW OF INTERNATIONAL AFFAIRS   Winter/Spring 1997

begun actively covering educational issues, thus playing a major role in shaping public opinion. For many years the postwar debate on educational reform unfolded along ideological lines, with the Education Ministry pitted against Nikkyoso (Japan Teachers' Union), conservatives against progressives, management against labor. The upshot was lots of talk but no action. In this regard, too, the situation today represents a departure from the past.

Until now education has been held up as one of the main reasons for Japan's remarkable economic success since the war. The country's egalitarian elementary and secondary schools, with their good educational conditions and outstanding teachers, produced a high-quality work force whose members were diligent, intelligent, and steeped in the ethos of teamwork. In the early 1980s, however, attention began to focus on the "blight" of elementary and secondary education; the deterioration of education, a major support of the Japanese economy, was viewed as a serious social issue. The National Council on Educational Reform, set up in 1984 as an advisory body reporting directly to the cabinet, helped stimulate a national debate on educational reform, with "educational blight" a central topic. The spread of hitherto rare pathological phenomena—children's violent behavior at home and, at school, bullying, declining scholastic ability, refusal to attend school, dropouts—stirred up public fears of an educational crisis.

Initially these problems were linked to excessive emphasis on academic credentials and ruthless competition in entrance examinations, features of Japanese society and education since prewar times, and the council came up with a number of recommendations aimed at alleviating the situation. In the course of subsequent deliberations, however, the council members realized that the problems were products of Japan's affluent, egalitarian postwar social structure. They also became aware that the deterioration of the country's postwar supports was not confined to the economic, political, and administrative spheres. Various social systems were also foundering and in need of reform, and the problems in the schools were symptomatic of this.

In 1987 the council disbanded without having produced a

clear agenda for the future of education. Nevertheless, the debate showed no sign of abating, and demands for liberalization,
individuality, and diversity continued to emanate from business
groups, the media, and the general public. By this time all sides
had become convinced that Japanese society faced a structural
crisis of which educational problems were symptomatic.

The Beginnings of the Postwar System

The history of postwar Japanese education can be said to have
begun with a report issued by a U.S. education mission that visited Japan in the spring of 1946, when the country was under
Allied Occupation. This report served as the foundation for reforms carried out between 1947 and 1949. The mission, formed
in response to a request by the Supreme Commander for the
Allied Powers, comprised educators and other experts from the
United States. At the end of a month-long stay, the mission submitted a report containing a blueprint for a postwar Japanese
educational system. The underlying philosophy was the democratization of education, with the basic model for change provided
by the American system. This was not surprising, given the background of the members and the international acclaim the U.S.
system enjoyed as the most advanced and successful in the world.

Questions remain, however, as to whether the mission's members were able to acquire an adequate understanding of the basic
structure of the Japanese system during their short stay and how
far they realized that the success of the U.S. model depended on
conditions unique to their own country. At the time of its defeat,
Japan had nearly 75 years of experience operating a modern educational system. Following the Meiji Restoration of 1868, which
brought to power a group of reform-minded leaders, the government set to work creating a system that integrated aspects of
French, German, and other Western models with indigenous
social and cultural elements. The basic structure differed notably
from that of the United States. The reforms undertaken after
the war were based on a report that did not pay adequate attention to the differences between the Japanese and American
structures and were pushed through on the strength of SCAP's

authority. Over the next 50 years Japanese education developed in a process fraught with conflict caused by the pull between acceptance and rejection of this arbitrarily imposed American model.

The main objective of the Occupation reforms was to dismantle the centralized, multitrack educational system that Japan had developed over the past three-quarters of a century and replace it with an American-style decentralized, egalitarian, single-track system. To this end the Education Ministry, which had enjoyed immense authority, was weakened, a system of public elections for boards of education was introduced, textbook publication was liberalized, and schools were given more freedom in curriculum planning. Dramatic changes were made to the school structure. The prewar class-based, multitrack system of secondary and higher education was reorganized into a simpler, more accessible single-track system. The highly variegated secondary schools were consolidated into middle and high schools, and institutions of higher education, which had included a variety of institutions with differing terms of study and systems, were consolidated into four-year universities and two-year junior colleges. The reforms did not end there, however. High schools were made coeducational, and small school districts were reorganized on the American model. It was even planned to transfer control of national universities to prefectures, following the example of U.S. state universities, though in the end this was not done.

Nearly all these bold proposals were implemented. But as soon as the San Francisco Peace Treaty went into effect and the Occupation ended in 1952, a "counterreformation" got underway, with the Education Ministry pushing through new policies to revive and reinforce its control. The shift from election to appointment of boards of education, a more rigorous textbook authorization system, stricter ministry curriculum guidelines, separation of general and vocational high schools, and introduction of medium-sized and large school districts were all part of this reversal, which ushered in an era marked by fierce clashes between Nikkyoso, which supported the ideals of the American model, and the ministry, which sought to undo some of the Occupation reforms. This confrontation also represented a "proxy war" between postwar Japan's two political forces, the conservatives and the progressives. The ministry's goal was not wholesale rejection of the American model. The battle was above all an ideological and political struggle over control of educational content. No changes were made to the egalitarian, open structure of the school system. Because of this, the American model became an extremely powerful force shaping and changing postwar Japan.

The Egalitarian Impulse

Under the Occupation reforms compulsory education was lengthened from six to nine years, six years of elementary school and three years of middle school; in addition, many new educational opportunities were made available at the high school level. At the end of the 1950s, when the economy entered a period of rapid growth, the ratio of students going on to high school began to surge. The proportion, which had stood at 52% in 1955, rose to 58% in 1960, 71% in 1965, 82% in 1970, and more than 90% in 1975. Just 30 years after the inauguration of the new school system, the vast majority of children were now attending school until the age of 18. The spread of high school education was followed by the popularization of higher education. The proportion of 18-year-olds going on to two- or four-year colleges remained at 10% between 1955 and 1960, then rose rapidly to 17% in 1965, 24% in 1970, and 38% in 1975, a level that put Japan second in the world, behind the United States. These figures present a striking contrast to those before the war. In 1935, for example, just 40% of all students completing elementary school continued to secondary school, and a mere 3% went on to higher education. The Education Ministry's response to the rapid rise in the proportion of students continuing to the next level of education was to promote rather than contain the trend. In this regard Japan was able to create an egalitarian society in an extremely short period.

Equal opportunity in education was also the result of the social and economic reforms implemented under the Occupation. The liberalization of farmland, dismantling of the zaibatsu, and reform of the family (*ie*) system played especially important roles in transforming the class structure, creating opportunities for social and economic upward mobility and firing people's desire for education. Demand for education had been strong since the start of modernization in the late nineteenth century, and the tendency toward intense entrance-exam competition and excessive emphasis on academic credentials had begun to emerge at that time. The democratization of education, the economy, and society after the war had the effect of further fueling educational aspirations while creating the conditions necessary for achieving them. As the economy moved through its rapid-growth phase, it continued to provide opportunities for employment and advancement to the growing ranks of high school and college graduates. The trend toward more schooling mirrored the migration from rural to urban areas, the shift from primary to secondary and tertiary industries, and social and economic upward mobility.

The postwar educational system not only provided equal educational opportunity but also ensured that the same quality was offered by all schools. After restoring its administrative authority, the Education Ministry focused its efforts on reducing regional disparities so that all children could receive an education under the same conditions. Clear standards were established on what school facilities were necessary, as well as teacher qualifications and pay, and fiscal measures were undertaken to enable schools to meet the requirements.

The push for curricula in accordance with ministry guidelines and reinforcement of the textbook authorization process can be considered part of the ministry's overall policy of achieving equality in the schools. Nikkyoso and the progressives strongly resisted moves to limit or usurp teachers' academic freedom, but ultimately children up to the age of 15 received the same level and type of education based on standardized curricula and textbooks. Even at the high school level, about 70% of students attended nonvocational schools providing a uniform curriculum of academic subjects, including English. Academic subjects were also compulsory at vocational schools, though less time was devoted to them.

This educational system was a key factor in the "middle-class consciousness" that took root among the Japanese, with almost 80% eventually identifying themselves as middle class. The social and economic reforms carried out immediately after the war and Japan's subsequent rapid economic growth paved the way for an open, egalitarian society offering substantial upward mobility and minimal income disparities. Egalitarian education was not only a product of this society but also a major factor in its formation.

Entrance Examinations and the School Hierarchy

The egalitarian education system did not eliminate competition but actually encouraged it. One of the most striking differences between the American and Japanese systems is the method of screening applicants. Public high schools in the United States do not screen applicants, nor do universities administer their own entrance exams. By contrast, all high schools and universities in Japan select entrants on the basis of achievement tests. The entrance exam system is a major component of the prewar period that was not abolished by the postwar reforms, and it has been the main force fostering egalitarianism and competitiveness in education.

Entrance exams for public high schools are administered in medium-sized and large school districts, which sometimes include more than 10 schools. Because applicants are placed in schools in accordance with their test results, inevitably people rank schools by their students' scholastic ability. This hierarchy exists in all school districts. Middle school students compete to get into schools as close to the top as possible. Private high schools, which account for 30% of enrollment, are not part of the school-district system, but they too screen applicants with entrance exams. With more than 95% of middle school graduates now continuing to high school, students find themselves obliged to study for the entrance exams not only in school but also at privately run after-hours cram schools known as *juku*.

A similar hierarchy exists among universities. The ranking is essentially a legacy of the prewar system of higher education, in which institutions were differentiated and organized into numerous strata based on such factors as the term of study and the secondary schools with which they were affiliated. This order, reorganized into a hierarchy based on universities' prestige as institutions of education and research, directs the flow of applicants. The internationally known pyramidal hierarchy of Japanese universities, with its broad base and narrow apex, generates fierce competition among students aiming for one of the schools at the top.

The university screening process is based primarily on the results of entrance exams. For this reason, the higher the university is in the hierarchy, the more preparation is required. Students hoping to reach the top must first get accepted by a high school that attracts the brightest students and does a good job preparing them for exams. In addition to their regular school studies, they must attend preparatory or cram schools to acquire the knowledge necessary for the entrance exams. Many find that they need to spend a year or two after high school preparing for the exam of the university of their choice. The Japanese academic year begins in April, and every spring the press lists the number of successful applicants to each university from each high school, thus indicating the position in the hierarchy of both universities and high schools, as well as which high schools send the most students to which universities. To the public, a university's prestige depends less on its merits as an educational and reearch institution than on the academic prowess of its entrants.

The British sociologist Ronald Dore has said of this screening process and system for progressing to the next level of education, "The school system functioned as a general intelligence testing device."[1] To be sure, the postwar Japanese system has achieved great success in screening students by their level of scholastic ability and producing a generally high-quality work force by means of the skillful blending of equality and competition. The postwar reforms made the educational system more American, democratic, and open, and that led to a steady increase in users of this "general intelligence testing device." In other words, the

1. *The Diploma Disease: Education, Qualification, and Development* (London: Allen and Unwin, 1976), p. 45.

hierarchical structure of education played a role in the upward spiral in the number of people aiming for schools as close to the top as possible. As more students sought to continue their education, the competition to get into prestigious schools spread from the high school level to the middle school and even the elementary school. In this regard education centered on preparation for entrance exams can be considered the inevitable outcome of the Americanized education system adopted by Japan after the war.

Corporate Hiring and Academic Credentials

Corporations have probably been the main beneficiaries of the postwar educational system. When hiring, companies lay more stress on general ability than on specialized knowledge and skills. Because of the standardized curriculum, high school graduates have a good grounding in such academic subjects as English, mathematics, and science. And university graduates, products of a system that functions as a general intelligence testing device, not only have proved they are smart enough to have passed the demanding entrance exams but also bring with them knowledge of a specific field. Until recently, such graduates were just what companies were looking for.

The hierarchical structure of high schools and universities makes it easy for firms to obtain information on the general level of ability they can expect of graduates. Based on this, they regularly recruit groups of graduates from particular high schools and universities, train them in various company-run programs, move them around from position to position to give them experience, promote them as they gain seniority, and guarantee them a place in the firm until retirement. This personnel policy has worked well for Japanese companies, but it also leads to preoccupation with academic credentials, since firms tend to give priority to graduates of top-ranking high schools and universities when hiring. The spread of "credentialism" affects the choices made by students, who aspire to get into a school as close to the top of the hierarchy as possible to improve their odds of getting a good job, and thus exacerbates entrance-exam competition.

The vicious circle of academic credentialism and entrance-exam competition has been a major headache for postwar education. The main victims are the children and the schools. As the number of students continuing to high school and college rises, middle and high school education increasingly revolves around preparation for entrance exams at the next level, and excessive emphasis is put on rote learning and test-taking skills. Children spend a substantial amount of time studying for these exams, since getting into a high school or college of even slightly higher standing will give them an edge when job hunting. But they lose all desire to study once they are accepted by the university of their choice and liberated from the intense competition of exams, since they know that most companies do not care what they have learned and what grades they have received but focus only on the position of their school in the hierarchy.

Although the relationship between education and the economy and between academic credentialism and entrance exams has always posed numerous problems for schools, until recently it was neither irrational nor unproductive from the standpoint of corporate personnel policies. Companies only began to join the chorus of criticism in the early 1990s, a development that reflected a structural shift in the economy and intensification of international economic competition, especially in cutting-edge science and technology. This changing environment forced companies to review their personnel policies, since it was becoming increasingly difficult to continue hiring large numbers of new graduates, training them in-house, and guaranteeing them jobs until they reached retirement age. Many firms had to adopt new measures—putting increased emphasis on practical and specialized expertise when hiring, recruiting experienced personnel, using outside firms to train recruits, and encouraging surplus employees to switch jobs.

At the heart of these changes was a shift in the types of workers companies wanted. It is no coincidence that all the educational reform proposals drawn up by business organizations emphasize the need to create a work force endowed with independence, individuality, originality, and creativity. In an age of rapid change and intense competition, companies cannot survive with workers who are merely obedient, fiercely loyal, and capable of conscientiously carrying out appointed tasks. In short, the business community's dissatisfaction with the state of education and its reform proposals are motivated by the need for new kinds of human resources.

The Drive Toward Liberalization, Individuality, and Diversity

The problems with Japanese education today, as identified in the business reform proposals and elsewhere, have caused stress to be placed on the three concepts that have served as the pillars of the Education Ministry's reform initiatives since the mid-1980s: liberalization, individuality, and diversity. The very basis of the system the ministry created after regaining its strong regulatory authority in the 1950s—an egalitarian but uniform system in which schools and students lack diversity and individuality—is being called into question. By skillfully blending equality and competition, the system achieved major successes, including the creation of an affluent and egalitarian society. But the nature of this society was also the root cause of the pathological school phenomena that began to emerge in the 1980s.

Societies in which poverty and inequality exist afford people the dream of upward mobility. Japan after the war was such a society. Study and hard work held out the promise of good academic credentials, economic remuneration, and social status, and this in turn triggered a surge in the number of students continuing their education, raised the level of their scholastic achievement, and supported the rapid growth of the economy. By the 1980s nearly all of postwar Japan's dreams had come true. Almost the entire population had achieved a uniformly high standard of living and level of education and income. When Japan became an affluent, egalitarian, middle-class society, however, education began to face a range of new problems. Student violence against teachers and other students, bullying, an aversion to school or even refusal to attend school, poor academic performance, and dislike of studying were all held up as serious social issues. At the root of these problems was a decline in children's aspiration for education and learning. Born and raised in an egalitarian and affluent society, they had no "golden dreams." Educational and employment opportunities alone could no longer provide them with sufficient motivation for studying hard. A hierarchical structure continued to exist among schools, compelling children to compete for a place at the top. But although they took part in the competition, they could not work up any real enthusiasm for it, since they knew that the differences in position and pay they could expect following graduation were minimal.

The pathological phenomena mentioned above attest to the growing power of antiacademic values and culture among students. Liberalization, individualism, and diversity, the basic goals of the current educational reforms, are the way to suppress this antiacademic culture and revive the aspiration for education.

A Return to the American Model?

In the late 1980s the Education Ministry began easing the strict controls on education under the pressure of public opinion. For example, in the name of diversification it actively encouraged the adoption of methods other than achievement tests for evaluating and selecting applicants, such as the principal's recommendation, essays, interviews, athletic ability or artistic talent, and volunteer activities. Diversification in high schools was also promoted, with schools accorded considerably more latitude to design their own curricula and students provided with more electives. At the same time, a growing number of idiosyncratic or specialized high schools were established, bearing names including the words *international, information,* or *comprehensive.* Such schools bridged the divide between general and vocational education and also transcended vocational schools' traditional concentration on the fields of agriculture, manufacturing, and commerce. At the level of higher education, the standards for chartering universities were revised, and faculties were handed control over their curricula, leading to the founding of new colleges and faculties bearing names including such words as *international, information, environment,* and *policy.* In addition, grade skipping for especially bright students, which had long been taboo, was permitted in special cases. In this way liberalization, individuality, and diversity began to be translated from mere slogans into action.

Underlying these reform initiatives was the Education Ministry's painful acknowledgement that it was responsible for creating a system that, while egalitarian and efficient, was also uniform and lacking in freedom and diversity. The ministry, together with a majority of the participants in the reform debate, became convinced that the only way to raise students' flagging motivation and eradicate the pathological phenomena in schools was to emphasize students' individuality, allowing them greater independence and free choice and making the educational system more open, flexible, and diverse.

This initiative bears an uncanny resemblance to that of the Occupation-imposed American model. After half a century, postwar Japanese education seems to be moving back to its starting point. But the similarity is merely superficial. In the repeated process of acceptance and rejection of the American model that was the springboard for the postwar period, Japan has created a thoroughly "Japanese-style" educational system. This is evident in the ironic fact that the present reforms, aimed at creating a system endowed with the salient features of the U.S. model— freedom, individualism, and diversity—are being directed by the authoritarian Education Ministry.

Until recently Japan's egalitarian, efficient elementary and secondary schools attracted international praise. The achievements of Japanese children in science and mathematics, as revealed in international surveys, were regarded as important forces behind the country's rapid economic growth. While it is true that pathological phenomena have emerged in the schools, the problems Japan faces are common to the United States and Europe and in this sense can be considered pathologies of the developed world as a whole. The number of dropouts, incidence of school violence, and number of children who refuse to go to school may be rising, but the levels remain low in absolute terms. For this reason there has been no rush to push through reforms at the elementary and secondary levels. The ministry seems to be focusing its efforts on finding the right balance between control and freedom, individuality and collectivism, uniformity and diversity.

Unlike elementary and secondary education, however, Japanese higher education has long been the target of intense criticism both at home and abroad. By its very nature, higher education should be the least susceptible to control, uniformity, and rigidity. The biggest problem with the postwar reforms lay in the Education Ministry's application of the principles of equality and control not just at the elementary and secondary levels but also in higher education. Utterly failing to emulate the U.S. model, the ministry made higher education even more rigid than before the war. The pyramidal hierarchy among universities is thus the product of the postwar reforms.

Once again the Japanese are looking to the United States for a model for higher education. Today, as half a century ago, the U.S. system abounds in openness, freedom, fluidity, and diversity and continues to be the most successful in the world. The international consensus is that the phenomenal growth of the Japanese economy is the product of elementary and secondary education, while America's strength in state-of-the-art science and technology is due to the high level of U.S. university education and research. Likewise, it is generally held that Japan's universities have failed to cultivate human resources with the originality, creativity, innovation, and independence needed to prevail in international economic competition, let alone competition in high technology.

The chorus of demands within Japan for educational reform is motivated primarily by a strong sense of crisis over the state of higher education. This has spurred various steps toward reform in the 1990s. Aiming to make university organizations and higher education systems more open and flexible, the Education Ministry has taken various deregulatory measures, foremost among them a revision of the university chartering standards. American higher education has clearly served as a model for the reform initiatives, which range from diversification of the methods of screening applicants to liberalization and reform of university faculties, facilitation of the admission of mature-age students to graduate schools, establishment of lifelong learning programs, encouragement of joint research with industry, an increase in government funds allocated to universities on a competitive basis, enhancement of the postdoctoral fellowship system, and the introduction of tenure criteria for teachers (traditionally, all full-time faculty members have automatically had tenure).

Japanese universities have finally taken it upon themselves to study and learn from their American counterparts. But the result will not be a mere imitation of the American model that disregards the traditions and achievements of Japanese universities in the postwar period, or more precisely since the Meiji Restoration. Universities must work within the context of both the conditions in the elementary and secondary schools that provide them with their students and the conditions in the corporations and society that utilize and enjoy the fruits of university education and research. The major issue at stake is actually the fundamental relationship among Japanese education, the economy, politics, and society. Thus today's loud calls for educational reform, especially in the area of higher education, are both a healthy development and an extremely difficult challenge for Japan.

WHAT IS A SUCCESSFUL SCHOOL?

The more the school cares about students, the more students care about matters of schooling.
Thomas Sergiovanni, *Moral Leadership*

Japanese children learn a lifelong lesson that is the cornerstone of the efficiency and success of modern Japan: Each person has a role to fulfill as best he or she can.
Deborah Fallows

DELIBERATELY OR NOT, SCHOOLS PROFOUNDLY SHAPE children's social and ethical development. Schools can motivate children by rewards and punishments or by an appeal to what is right. Schools can allocate opportunities for leadership to all children equally or to the best-behaved and highest-achieving children disproportionately. Schools can emphasize competition among children or shared goals accessible to all: persistence, doing one's best, friendliness, helpfulness. Since schooling profoundly shapes children's social and ethical development, it's odd that we so often define successful schools purely in terms of academic achievement.

JAPANESE SCHOOLS: DO THEY FOSTER SOCIAL AND ETHICAL DEVELOPMENT?

Japanese schools are often lauded for their academic achievements. But do they also foster children's ethical and social development? We find sharp differences of opinion on this question. Childhood and youth indicators of failed social and ethical development – such as delinquency, school dropout, and self-destructive behavior – generally appear to be substantially lower in Japan than in other industrialized countries, including the United States. As the U.S. Study of Education in Japan notes, "by comparison with various other industrialized nations, including the United States, delinquency in Japan is mild and infrequent."[1]

School-Related Problems

In contrast to this relatively optimistic American assessment, Japanese educators and the Japanese public are profoundly concerned about problems of elementary and secondary students, including *ijime* (bullying), *ochikobore* (students who fall behind academically), *tōkōkyohi* (school refusal), and school violence. Many of these problems begin in elementary school, and common sense suggests a connection between these problems and the downward pressure exerted by the examination system.

Figure 2 provides data on *tōkōkyohi* (school refusal), the term applied to students absent from school more than 50 days during the year because of "dislike of school." The rate of school refusal in Japan has increased more than threefold among junior high students since 1966 and now amounts to 7.5 students per 1,000. During the same period, the rate has nearly doubled among elementary students but is still relatively low, affecting fewer than 1 student per 1,000. Comparable statistics are not available for the United States, but principals of American elementary schools tell me that it's not unusual in an elementary school of 400–800 students to have 1 or more students who persistently stay home from school. Such a very rough reckoning suggests that the American experience may not be greatly out of line with the nearly 1 in 1,000 Japanese elementary students who miss more than 50 days a year of school because they dislike school. Comparisons are complicated, however, by the fact that 40% of parents of Japanese school refusers do not push unwilling children to go to school;[2] in many U.S. states, truancy laws would not permit leniency. On the other hand, the Japanese rate may underestimate the problem, because many school refusers attend special counseling centers where they may continue their

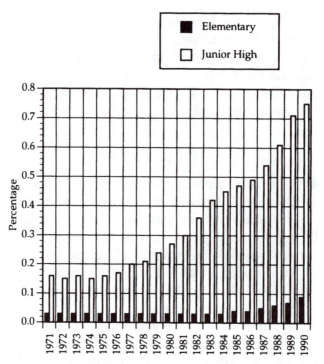

Figure 2. Percentage of Japanese students refusing to attend school 50 days or more per year, 1971–1990.

Source: Monbushō Shōtō Chūtō Kyōikukyoku, 1992.

schooling and thus escape the school-refusal statistics. Research suggests that a variety of events precipitate school refusal in Japan, including problems with classmates, teachers, and schoolwork (37%); personal circumstances such as illness (26%); and problems in family life such as family discord or a sudden change in family circumstances (26%).[3]

Violence in Schools

In his book *Shogun's Ghost*, Kenneth Schoolland describes several horrifying incidents of bullying that have occurred in Japan's middle schools and high schools. Figure 3 provides data on bullying, a

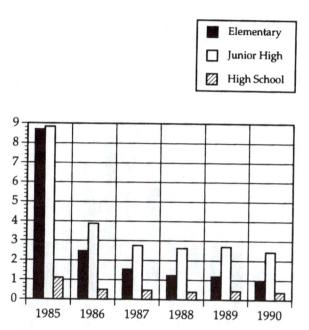

Figure 3. Incidents of bullying per 1,000 students.

Source: Sōmucho, Seishōnen Taisaku Honbu, 1991, based on data from Ministry of Education, Science, and Culture

problem that was the focus of intense national concern and intervention in the mid-1980s. For 1991, the figures shown amount to a little less than 1 incident of bullying for every two Japanese elementary schools and 1.2 incidents per middle school. As shown, reported bullying has declined sharply since the mid-1980s, when national statistics were first collected. The decline is sometimes attributed to increased awareness and intervention on the part of educators.[4] Unfortunately, we do not know how much bullying goes unreported. As shown in Figure 4, bullying peaks at junior high and occurs at a much higher rate in larger schools (Figure 5). Table 8 breaks down by type all reported incidents of bullying in Japanese elementary schools during 1990.

Unfortunately, the seriousness of the reported incidents is difficult to judge. What proportion are the kinds of teasing, threats,

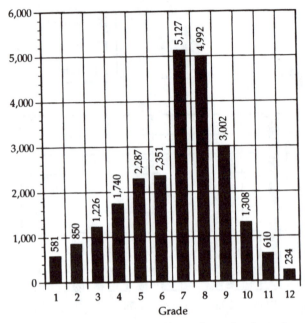

Figure 4. Incidents of bullying by school grade.

Source: Sōmucho, 1991, p. 257, based on data from Ministry of Education.

and exclusion that are also familiar, if unpleasant, features of life in many American schools? What proportion represent the kind of intense, ongoing cruelty that has led several Japanese students to take their lives? Only about 16% of the reported bullying incidents in elementary schools involve use of force. Insults, exclusion, and humiliation account for the majority of incidents.[5] Principals – who report the information that ultimately becomes the statistics – have told me that they report only repeated, systematic attempts to humiliate or coerce a classmate, not one-time incidents. A low rate of police involvement suggests that relatively few of the incidents are serious. In 1989, police provided "guidance" (*hodō*) to a total of 314 students as a result of bullying incidents: 278 middle school students, 35 high school students, and 1 elementary student.[6]

Shogun's Ghost also describes use of corporal punishment in Japanese middle schools. Although prohibited by law, corporal punish-

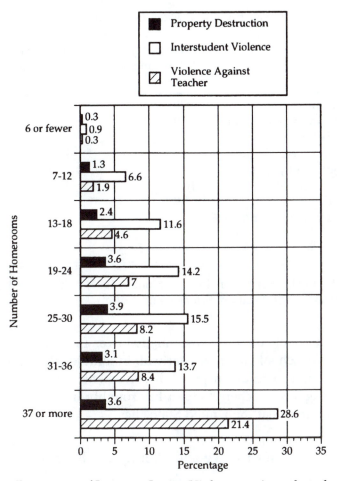

Figure 5. Percentage of Japanese Junior Highs reporting selected types of violence, by school size.

Source: Sōmucho, 1991, based on data from Ministry of Education.

ment is practiced by some Japanese middle school teachers, according to many sources.[7] In 1991, 331 teachers were disciplined for using corporal punishment.[8] Ministry of Education statistics for 1991 report 713 incidents of violence against teachers, 1,859 incidents of violence among students, and 518 incidents of property destruction in Japan's 11,290 middle schools. The number of inci-

Table 8. *Bullying Incidents in 1990, by Type*

	Elementary (11,999 incidents) (%)	Junior High (17,651 incidents) (%)
Verbal insults	15.9	19.8
Being teased, made fun of	24.0	22.4
Having belongings hidden	8.6	6.8
Being ostracized	23.0	12.8
Being ignored by group	6.3	6.0
Physical force	16.9	22.7
Blackmail	1.9	6.2
Forced, intrusive friendliness (*osekkai shinsetsu*)	1.5	1.3
Other	1.9	2.1

Source: Sōmucho, Seishōnen Taisaku Honbu, 1991, p. 258, based on data from Ministry of Education, Science, and Culture.

dents in high schools was substantially lower. In the same year, 780 incidents of school violence, nearly all in middle schools, were serious enough to result in police involvement; 466 of these were violence against teachers.[9] Japan has roughly half the number of schoolchildren that the United States has.

Self-destructive and Delinquent Behavior

Figure 6 provides statistics on the arrest of American and Japanese minors. Once again, statistics suggest a relatively low incidence of serious offenses by Japanese youth. Other data suggest, however, that Japanese youth manage to engage in some self-destructive behavior even without easy access to illegal drugs. Police detained more than 22,000 minors for "guidance" (*hodō*) for thinner sniffing in 1990.[10] Once again, it's difficult to know what to make of the statistics without knowing more about how they are collected. Do they underestimate problems to create an impression of a harmonious society, as some critics suggest, or overestimate problems to obtain increased funding, as others have conjectured? The fact that

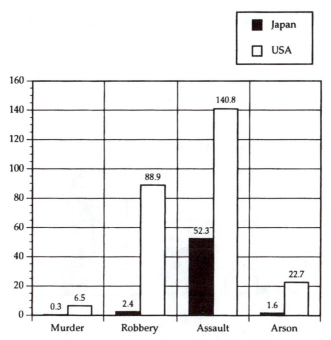

Figure 6. Arrests of persons under 18 per 100,000 for 10- to 18-year-olds.

Source: Hōmushō Hōmusōgōkenkyūjo, 1990, pp. 408–409, 452–53 (1988 data).

police even bother to collect and publish statistics on minors' pedestrian crosswalk violations may say a great deal about the frequency of serious crime – or about the tolerance for deviations from proper conduct.

Youth suicide – one of the few problems for which reasonably objective comparable data are available – is often thought by Americans to be very common in Japan, an impression that probably stems from the Japanese media's intense coverage of examination-related suicides. As Figure 7 shows, however, the most recent international comparisons indicate that the suicide rate for American 15- to 19-year-olds is nearly three times that of their Japanese counterparts. A survey of 3,000 high school students found that Japanese students reported *fewer* feelings of stress, academic anxiety, depression, and aggression than their Chinese and American peers.[11]

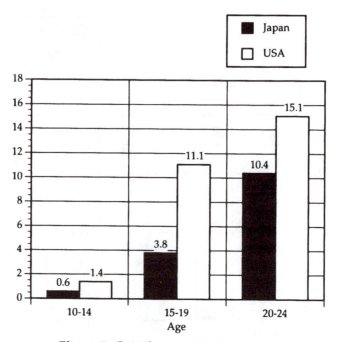

Figure 7. Suicides per 100,000, by age.

Source: Sōmucho, 1991, and U.S. National Department of Health and Human Services, National Center for Health Statistics, Hyattsville, MD, 1992.

Japanese teen pregnancy and abortion rates are among the lowest in the world, despite the fact that most Japanese teens (60%) approve of sexual relations among their peers with appropriate contraception.[12]

Liking for School

Of course, the relatively low rate of various problems among Japanese youth may not be attributable to schooling; it may be attributable to family influences or other qualities of the society. Yet observers who have actually spent time in Japanese preschools and elementary schools, including schools serving less advantaged populations, uniformly comment on children's eagerness, involvement, and active role in school life.[13]

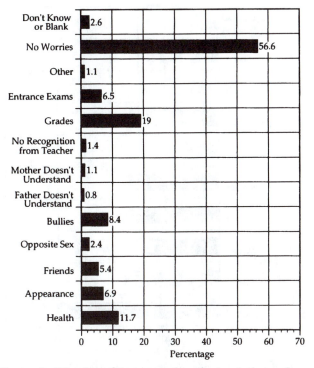

Figure 8. Worries of Japanese fourth- to sixth-graders.

Source: Sōmucho, 1991, p. 54 (data from NHK Broadcasting Research Institute, "The Activities and Attitudes of Elementary Students," 1989).

More than 80% of Japanese fifth- and sixth-graders report that they are completely satisfied or mostly satisfied with their school life. (The comparable figure for Japanese middle school students is only 60%.) Similarly, over 85% of Japanese fourth- to sixth-graders describe themselves as happy.[14] As Figure 8 shows, over half of the fourth- to sixth-graders polled by the NHK Broadcasting Research Institute said that they had no worries or problems; about one quarter worried about grades or entrance examinations, and only 8% worried about bullying. As Figure 9 shows, the picture is strikingly different for Japanese junior high students, only 8% of whom say they have no problems or worries; 75% of junior high students report worrying about school and examinations. In their study of

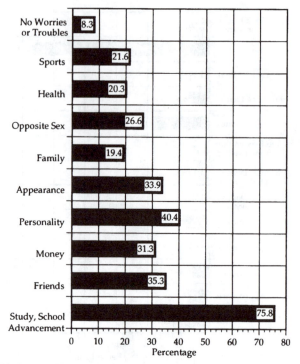

Figure 9. Worries of Japanese Junior High students.

Source: Sōmucho, 1991, p. 55 (data from Nihon Seishōnen Kenkyūjo, Primary Panel Study of Junior High Students, 1988)

Chinese, Japanese, and American students, researchers Harold Stevenson and James Stigler found that Asian elementary students liked school more than their American counterparts did.[15] Ineko Tsuchida's study of Japanese and American fourth-graders also found greater liking for school among the Japanese students.[16]

Summary

A few conclusions seem justified from the various data. First, Japanese education, even at the elementary level, is not free of problems. The bullying, school refusal, and school violence that have so disturbed the Japanese public and press do extend beyond the inci-

178

dents reported in newspaper headlines. Second, most problems increase dramatically at junior high (the final stage of compulsory education in Japan and the peak of cram-school attendance), echoing the recommendation of Japanese educators that education for this age group needs reform. Finally, for serious problems (such as suicide and major crimes), for which cross-national data are most likely to be comparable, Japanese rates do appear to be substantially lower than those in the United States. Japanese rates of youth suicide, drug use, and violent crime have generally remained steady or fallen over recent decades.[17] Without minimizing the seriousness of problems such as school refusal, bullying, and school violence, the numbers suggest that Japanese schools do "succeed" socially with a very high percentage of students, losing relatively few students to school dropout (see chapter 1), delinquency, and self-destructive behavior.

Because of the many ways Japan and the USA. differ, it will never be possible to prove that elementary schools in one country or the other more effectively promote children's commitment to schooling. In any case, differences between the two countries mean that strategies that are effective in Japan might not work, or might not be regarded as appropriate, in the United States. Yet the strategies used by Japanese preschools and elementary schools are remarkably similar to approaches that have been successful in promoting children's academic and social development in U.S. schools. In fact, American educators interested in promoting children's fullest social and ethical development *independently* came up with many of the practices routinely used in Japanese schools. A subsequent section of this chapter describes the Child Development Project and other homegrown American approaches that rest on principles similar to those widely found in Japanese elementary schools.

MEETING CHILDREN'S NEEDS: A KEY TO EDUCATIONAL SUCCESS

American research and theory suggest that when schools meet children's needs, children come to care about school. Three basic psychological needs – belonging, autonomy, and competence – may be particularly important to children's attachment to school.[18] Let's look briefly at each of these basic psychological needs.

"Belonging" refers to the child's need for close, supportive relationships. That such relationships are fundamental to children's healthy emotional and social development is basic to Western, as well as Japanese, theories of human development.[19] As we have seen, Japanese elementary schools foster such relationships in many ways. They make friendliness and cooperation central, clear goals of classroom life. They emphasize *everyone's* belonging to the class and the school community and scrupulously avoid ability grouping, individual awards, and other practices that imply that some members are more valued than others. Teachers expend much effort nurturing familylike small groups where children feel comfortable and able to speak up.

"Autonomy" describes the child's need to feel some control over the environment and to be free of undue or arbitrary restraint. As we've seen, Japanese schools provide for young children's autonomy in many ways. All children assume leadership in rotation. Children help shape the goals and rules by which they live. Discipline emphasizes self-evaluation rather than evaluation by the teacher, and self-management rather than adult control.

"Competence" is the child's need to pursue activities regarded as worthwhile. Children naturally explore the world and try to make sense of it – even without rewards or encouragement from others. Much research shows that children are young scientists, constantly trying to explain the physical and human world around them. Children are likely to find school gripping and important if it helps them in their quest to make sense of the world. As noted in chapter 7, lessons in Japanese schools are often driven by children's own thinking and by their involvement in tasks that are likely to be inherently interesting – crafting boats that float, designing the ideal playground, exploring each room of the school, using measurement to understand the world around them. Such meaningful child-driven activities are much more likely to meet children's need for competence than would a focus on isolated "basic" skills. The breadth of the Japanese curriculum and the emphasis on effort and participation rather than on competition further increase the likelihood that *all* children – not just an academically able few – will find areas of competence and feel themselves to be valued members of the school community.

In summary, Japanese preschool and early elementary classrooms have many qualities that help them effectively meet children's basic needs for autonomy, belonging, and competence. In response, children are likely to come to care about school and about the values emphasized there. I have pointed out, in prior chapters, aspects of Japanese educational practice that I think many Americans would find troubling, such as allowing children to fight or to handle dangerous tools. Yet none of these is central to Japanese education. What *is* central is a set of values deeply consonant with widely held American values. The next section briefly spotlights successful American approaches that are based on some of the same fundamental principles as Japanese elementary schooling.

AMERICAN APPROACHES: THE CHILD DEVELOPMENT PROJECT

At a California elementary school, kindergarteners are planning a class aquarium. They brainstorm all the plants and animals they would like and then discuss which ones are feasible: Which need salt water, rather than fresh? Which fish might eat each other? They list their top choices and talk about how many they can buy within the $20 budget. At the end of the class meeting, they reflect on how the meeting went: Did they show respect for one another?

To the Japanese teachers who have watched this California class on videotape, the setting is exotic: a carpeted classroom where children can gather cross-legged on the floor around their teacher. But the lesson is familiar: a class project that invites children's ideas, joins children in planning a shared project, and melds social and intellectual development as children both think about marine biology and reflect on whether they showed respect for one another's ideas.

This California classroom was videotaped as part of the Child Development Project (CDP), a school change effort developed by American researchers and teachers. CDP's aim is to help students become good learners *and* good people, with an emphasis on qualities such as concern for others, responsibility, thoughtfulness, and motivation to learn.

The Child Development Project targets many facets of schooling: what is taught, how it is taught, how students relate to one another and to teachers, how norms for student and adult behavior are developed and enforced.[20] Interestingly, this project – based in American basic research and theory – *independently* arrived at many of the same practices that are at the heart of Japanese elementary education. Central to the Child Development Project is the effort to make the school a "caring community of learners" in which:

- All children are valued, contributing members.
- Students are motivated by a personal commitment to responsible, caring behavior rather than by rewards and punishments.
- The curriculum is meaningful and engaging to children.

How do elementary schools pursue these goals? Table 9 lists major components of the Child Development Project and examples of each component. The similarities between the Child Development Project and the Japanese practices outlined in chapters 2–7 are striking. Both emphasize a school-wide sense of community and discipline that promotes personal commitment to values. Both emphasize explicit discussion of values, such as kindness and responsibility, and methods of instruction that capitalize on children's intrinsic motivation.

I chose the Child Development Project for Table 9 because of my own familiarity with it and because of the careful longitudinal research demonstrating its positive effects on American children in their academic as well as social and ethical development. But I think many other homegrown approaches, successful in American settings, fit some of the same basic principles outlined for the Child Development Project. For example, James Comer's School Devel-

182

opment Project and New York's innovative Central Park East schools emphasize caring, supportive relations among students and between students and adults and opportunities for all students to contribute to the life of the school.[21] These projects draw on American traditions and research – including Dewey's vision of progressive education; "attachment" theory, which recognizes emotional bonds as fundamental to development; and intrinsic motivation. Albert Shanker, president of the American Federation of Teachers, recently wrote:

> The problem is that [American] schools are not organized in a way that gives teachers and students a chance to develop close and caring relationships. . . . Elementary school children spend one year with a teacher – just long enough to *start* feeling comfortable – and then they move on to a new teacher. Why shouldn't elementary and junior high school students stay with the same group of kids for three or four years? Why shouldn't . . . the class be broken down into small groups so each group can . . . get to know one another?
>
> These ideas are sound in educational as well as emotional and moral terms. Students who are connected with another adult, and with one another, are less likely to drop out. And they are more likely to work and shape one another up – and thus to enjoy a measure of success in school work.
>
> Mentoring [outside of school] can fill an important need for the many youngsters who have no close or caring relationship with an adult. But we are kidding ourselves if we think we can make a dent in this enormous problem with ad-hoc arrangements. We should stop working around the edges of the main institution concerned with children – the schools – and concentrate on making our schools moral communities.[22]

Despite the growing awareness that close relationships are crucial to children's development, educators who would make this happen must swim against other very strong currents in U.S. education: an obsession with achievement test results, an assumption that academic excellence requires competition, and the notion that learning occurs most efficiently when children are grouped by ability.

Table 9. *Major Goals and Practices of the Child Development Project*

Caring, supportive relationships	Students and teachers get to know one another as people through daily opportunities to share ideas and experiences as part of class meetings, class "unity building" activities, shared planning, literature discussions, etc.
	Much collaborative learning; deemphasis of competition
	Shift away from techniques that stigmatize or reward individual children (e.g., names on board, reprimands) toward discussion of "what kind of class we want to be" and reflection on progress
Intrinsic motivation	Emphasis on values, not rewards and punishments, as the reason to behave responsibly
	Subject matter that is intrinsically interesting: literature instead of textbooks, hands-on activities, choice
	Shift away from praise and criticism by teacher and shift toward questions and comments that focus students' attention on the learning
	Teachers draw out children's questions and thinking; learning is meaning-centered
Attention to ethical and social dimensions of learning	Students explore what it means to be a principled, caring person as they study history, literature, and other subjects
	Children help shape class and school norms based on their desire to be treated with kindness, fairness, etc.
	Children frequently reflect on whether they are showing kindness, responsibility, fairness, etc., in their daily work and lives together

184

THINKING ACROSS CONTEXTS: LIMITATIONS OF JAPANESE IDEAS IN AMERICAN SETTINGS

I can think of two major reasons to reject Japanese practices as a source of ideas for our own educational practice. First, they may run counter to widely held American values. Second, they may be impractical here. Prior chapters have explored some aspects of Japanese preschool and early elementary education that may run counter to American values. This section explores conditions that may make it difficult to use ideas drawn from the Japanese context.

Children's Status

Japanese children live in what one American researcher has called a "privileged world." By all the usual indices – infant mortality, malnutrition, child abuse, family stability, parental drug abuse, poverty – Japanese children are extraordinarily fortunate, even compared with children in other advanced industrialized nations.[23] Few Japanese teachers, but many American teachers, must somehow educate children whose families – poor, alienated, or stressed – do not always meet children's basic need for food, shelter, and adult attention.

The disciplinary practices used in Japanese schools aim to develop stable, trusting relationships between adults and children and among children. Would Japanese teachers be able to use these techniques if many students came to school – by virtue of their early experience – mistrustful of adults? As noted in chapter 6, much research suggests that young Japanese children are given wide latitude for misbehavior and that the focus of maternal efforts during the preschool years is on building a warm, close relationship to the child, not on obedience.

In contrast, it's likely that conflict with adults and punishment are much more common experiences in the lives of young American children. This raises the possibility that Japanese disciplinary approaches, if used with American children, might not work as readily. Yet disciplinary practices focused on building stable, caring relationships may be especially critical for children who have had disrupted or difficult relationships outside of school. James Comer, a distinguished psychiatrist who has worked to restructure schools serving poor minority children in the United States, writes:

> All the money and effort expended for educational reform will have only limited benefits – particularly for poor minority children – as long as the underlying developmental and social issues remain unaddressed. Yet most teachers and administrators are not trained to organize and manage schools in ways that support the overall development of students.[24]

The importance of stable, caring relationships in children's development is a central principle in much American theory and research on child development and is the crux of some of the best-regarded American programs for educating poor minority children. Even in Japan – where children lead a "privileged" early life that includes strong parental support, universal health care, and a high proportion of stable, two-parent families – schools devote considerable time and attention to building trusting, sustained relationships between children and adults. Doesn't it follow that this effort deserves even more attention in American settings?

Curriculum

As noted in chapter 2, Japan has a national curriculum, with tight control of textbooks. The national control of curriculum and textbooks means that the same content – often the same lesson – is taught to schoolchildren throughout Japan. So, for example, I saw quite similar "Mothers' Work" lessons taught in first-grade classrooms in three different Japanese schools. In all three schools, the students had investigated, as homework, the mother's activities over a 24-hour period. Although the three teachers introduced the lesson using different personal examples and had the children engage in different activities (e.g., drawing and writing), the basic point of the lesson was more or less the same across classrooms: to develop an appreciation of the mother's work and a specific commitment to help her.

The complete sets of lessons in all subject areas that Japanese teachers have at their disposal are, I think, an extraordinary resource. Typically, each lesson is dominated by a single important goal for children's learning – for example, to discover that heat rises or that measurement is useful – and a single problem to explore in depth. Information provided in the teacher's manual often illuminates the thinking children are likely to bring to the problem, supporting teachers' treatment of children as active, thoughtful participants whose ideas should help drive the lessons. Supported by such frugal, carefully crafted lessons and examples, Japanese teachers are free to focus on how they will interest and motivate students – not on culling important concepts and information from textbooks and teachers' manuals jam-packed with lists of new concepts, information, vocabulary, and application problems. A critique of American science textbooks has noted that the average American science lesson contains more new vocabulary than a foreign-language lesson and that textbooks feature attention-grabbing sidebars worthy of *Ripley's Believe It or Not* but irrelevant to the science concepts under study.[25]

The focused, coherent lessons experienced by Japanese students may help them develop habits of mind that are important to learning. One study suggests that Japanese fourth-graders have a coherent, organized mental "script" of a mathematics lesson that enables them to attend selectively to important information, whereas American children attend equally to important and unimportant information – presumably because they have not developed clear expectations about what mathematics lessons include.[26] The pressure on American teachers to create original curriculum materials, rather than to provide skilled interpretations of standard curricula, may be broadly detrimental to American education:

> In America, teachers are judged to be successful when they are innovative, inventive, and original. Skilled presentation of a standard lesson is not sufficient and may even be disparaged as indicating a lack of innovative talent. It is as if American teachers were expected to write their own play or create their own concerto day after day and then perform it with expertise and finesse.

These two models, the skilled performer and the innovator, have very different value in the East and West. It is hard for us in the West to appreciate that innovation does not require that the presentation be totally new, but can come from thoughtful additions, new interpretations, and skillful modifications.[27]

One lamentable gap in our knowledge of Japanese education is how Japanese *teachers* feel about the curriculum they teach. Do they wish for more latitude in choosing the content and goals of their lessons and in selecting topics of interest to the particular children they teach? Japanese elementary teachers do have some room for innovation, both within regular subjects and within the nationally designated periods for class-chosen activities. For example, elementary classes I observed studied local pollution-related diseases, took oral histories of local weavers, and read novels outside the standard curriculum. In all cases, however, these activities received relatively little time, and teachers had to submit lesson plans in advance to the principal, noting the titles of nonapproved texts. Japanese teachers interested in a "whole language" approach to reading told me they envied American teachers' freedom to choose books and focus on interesting issues raised by books rather than on recall of information.

I have mixed reactions to the calls for a national curriculum in the USA. Japan's national curriculum ensures that all children study subject matter of agreed-upon importance but still allows teachers, principals, and local boards of education some room to pursue particular local and personal interests. A strength of the Japanese curriculum is its focus on subject matter from children's daily lives: potatoes and cabbage worms from the class garden as examples of growth and development; mapping the school as the introduction to geography. A paradox of the standardized Japanese curriculum – at least in the areas of mathematics and science – may be that it supports and frees teachers to be *more* responsive to the individual thinking of the children they teach, because lesson plans highlight students' thinking. Too, Japanese teachers are largely free of the onerous task of locating and reviewing good curricula. Yet in reading and social studies, the Japanese curriculum is less impressive, particularly in the upper grades. As children get older, language instruction tends to focus on factual recall and detailed analysis of texts rather than on the important ideas raised by a work of literature. Social studies – in the early years an opportunity to map the neighborhood and study the local sewer system – becomes increasingly focused on memorization of names and dates in the upper elementary years.

My guess is that a national curriculum would prove too confining for many American educators, whose freedom to study particular issues of interest – local conflicts, problems of concern to students, topics in the news, the literature and culture of newly arrived class members – can help create a curriculum meaningful to students and responsive to their needs. Japan's national curriculum creates friction even in that relatively homogeneous country. For example, teachers from Kyushu have complained to me that the science curriculum is not appropriate to the seasonal changes and local biology of their very southern climate.

Yet Japanese practices underline a striking gap in American elementary education: a sound *process* for defining what is important to teach children and bringing this to bear on the taught curriculum. Although professional groups in the United States regularly debate what is central to education in various subject areas, their deliberations have limited influence on the de facto curriculum, which is defined in great part by standardized tests and commercial textbooks. So in a sense there is already a national curriculum in the United States – but not one that lays out, thoughtfully and frugally, the knowledge, thinking, and attitudes central to children's development.

Status

As discussed in chapter 2, Japanese teachers enjoy a great deal of prestige, as measured by compensation and by other indices. They also report more influence on school policy and more help from their fellow teachers than do American teachers.[28] Japanese families tend to place great importance on education and imbue teachers with an almost sacred status.[29] How different the situation is for many American teachers, who daily find evidence that they are not regarded as professionals: poor compensation, endless paperwork, "teacher-proof" curricula, incentives and accountability systems that equate learning with factory production, major school redesign efforts that largely exclude the teacher's voice. Such offenses may be more than unpleasant; they may destroy the very conditions needed, within a school, to create and sustain excellent teaching.

American research suggests that school improvement hinges on a sense of community and collaboration among teachers – conditions easily undermined by top-down control and a focus on "accountability."[30] For teachers as well as students, learning requires the emotional safety needed to take risks and to recognize and learn from mistakes. When high status and professional treatment are lacking, so too may be the safety to learn. In the current climate of education bashing in the United States, who can blame the American math educator who said, "I'm sick and tired of hearing about the Japanese"?[31] Yet who can see such attitudes as fertile ground for educational improvement?

Comparative studies of Japanese and American families suggest that Japanese parents are more indulgent of young children but that they also emphasize respect for authority more strongly.[32] Hence Japanese teachers, bolstered by a strong cultural emphasis on respect for authority, may have an easier job than their American counterparts. Perhaps it's easier to focus on warm, friendly relations with children, "educational love," and "playing with children" when the status and authority of teachers is firmly established, as it appears to be in Japan.

Assessment

Few systematic data are available about testing practices in Japanese elementary schools. Many teachers I studied gave short tests at the end of units in mathematics, social studies, and other areas to check on whether students had mastered important concepts – "to test my teaching," as one Japanese first-grade teacher phrased it. Many Japanese teachers use unit tests produced by publishers, but there is also a national organization of Japanese teachers opposed to commercially produced tests.[33] What can be said with certainty is that standardized tests play nowhere near the role in Japanese elementary schooling that they do in the United States, where school funding, real-estate prices, and legal sanctions may all hinge on standardized test scores.

Having read many horror stories about the downward pressure exerted by Japanese college entrance examinations, I was surprised to find that Japanese teachers individually, or with grade-level colleagues, chose whether and how they would evaluate students' progress. Although education during the upper elementary grades may become more focused on the entrance examinations to junior high taken by the small percentage of students (5%) who attend private or national schools, what is striking in the early and middle years of elementary school is teachers' freedom to focus on children's social and ethical growth and on children's understanding of subject matter, not on their performance on externally imposed measures.

That standardized testing can be the enemy of good teaching is hardly a new point, but it is one that needs to be emphasized in comparing Japanese and American schools. Although some researchers have argued that entrance examinations positively influence Japanese educational achievement, exactly the opposite case can also be made: that elementary achievement is high because Japanese teachers are free from the pressure to teach to standardized tests. Japanese teachers are simultaneously supported by clear national objectives that emphasize social, ethical, and intellectual development and free to teach for understanding rather than drill students for test performance.

SUMMARY

In this chapter, we've explored differences between Japanese and American early elementary education that may make Japan's "lessons" difficult to apply in the United States. As we've seen, Japanese children are well cared for. Teachers enjoy high status, support from a coherent and generally thoughtful curriculum, and relative freedom from the tyranny of standardized tests, at least during the early years of elementary school. They are supported by a national curriculum that emphasizes social and ethical, as well as intellectual, development. Given these differences, what lessons can we reasonably learn from Japan?

Most striking, I think, is the attention Japanese schools devote to children's social and ethical development. In a society often described as homogeneous, teachers spend a great deal of time helping children build friendships and a sense of shared purpose within the classroom and school. In a society where most children are well cared-for economically and socially, children's social and personal development is nevertheless central to the elementary curriculum. If children's social and personal development demand so much attention in a society like Japan, shouldn't they demand even more in the United States?

Second, Japanese schools do not "just" nurture children's social and personal development. They also pursue an ambitious academic agenda. But this agenda is pursued without emphasizing competition among students. Lessons and all other school activities are carefully designed with an eye to students' social, personal, *and* intellectual development. And so Japanese schools are able to escape the pendulum swing between social development and academic rigor that has blemished American educational history.[34]

Like some American schools, Japanese schools find the key to success in meeting children's own needs – for belonging, friendship, contribution, exploration of the world around them. The quest to meet children's needs is integral to some of America's most successful educational programs and yet strongly antithetical to other powerful forces in American education. What, then, should we be looking for as we look at education for our children?

WHAT IS A SUCCESSFUL SCHOOL?

1. U.S. Study of Education, 1987.
2. Homusho Jinkenyōgokyoku, 1989, p. 38.
3. Monbushō Shōtō Chūtō Kyōiku Kyoku, 1992, p. 9.
4. Sōmucho, Seishōnen Taisaku Honbu, 1991.
5. Ibid., p. 258.
6. Ibid. (These statistics exclude incidents that occurred outside school within youth gangs.)
7. Fukuzawa, 1989; White, 1993.
8. Reported in White, 1993, p. 86, based on Asahi News Service report of December 26, 1991.
9. Monbushō, 1992.
10. Sōmucho, 1990, p. 271. Police provided *hodō* to 21,552 minors for thinner sniffing and to 986 for stimulant use *(kakuseizai)* in 1989.
11. Stevenson, Chen, & Lee, 1993.
12. White, 1993, p. 191.
13. See, for example, Easley and Easley, 1983; Sato, 1991; Tobin et al., 1989; White, 1987a.
14. Somucho, 1991, pp. 52–55, 60–61, 88–89.
15. Stevenson and Stigler, 1992.
16. Tsuchida, 1993.
17. Somucho, 1991, p. 240.
18. I am indebted to Marilyn Watson for pointing out the connection between meeting children's needs and internalization of values. Watson, Solomon, Battistich, Schaps, and Solomon, 1989, and Connell and Wellborn, 1991, provide data on educational application of the attachment theory developed by Deci and Ryan, 1985.
19. Bowlby, 1969; Doi, 1973.
20. Solomon, Watson, Battistich, Schaps, and Delucchi, 1992.
21. See, for example, Comer, 1988, on the School Development Project and Bensman, 1987, on the Central Park East schools.
22. A. Shanker, "Where we stand: Mentoring reconsidered," *New York Times*, March 20, 1994, p. E7.
23. Boocock, 1987. See also Shwalb, 1993, for a discussion of the connection between Japanese childrearing and preschool life.

24. Comer, 1988, p. 48.
25. Linn, Songer, and Eylon, in press.
26. Yoshida, 1993.
27. Stevenson and Stigler, 1992, pp. 167–68.
28. Sato and McLaughlin, 1992.
29. White, 1987a.
30. McLaughlin et al., 1990.
31. Stigler and Perry, 1987, p. 1.
32. Kobayashi-Winata and Power, 1989; Power and Kobayashi-Winata, 1992.
33. Nihon Kyoshokuin Kumiai, 1974.
34. Kliebard, 1987.

Higher Education in Japan

LOUIS D. HAYES*
University of Montana

Higher education has not been an important element in Japan's rise to the status of an economic superpower. While education through high school is rigorous and demanding, that of colleges and universities is not. Despite the lack of academic rigor, institutions of higher education are highly selective in their admission standards especially the prestigeous "national universities". Once admitted, students are virtually guaranteed a degree which serves as their passport to success in life. The higher the status of the university, the better the employment prospects for students. This system is causing growing concern in Japan as the intellectual demands of modern society require a large pool of well-educated manpower, a need that higher education is not meeting.

It took less than fifty years for Japan to rise from complete political and economic prostration following defeat in World War II to become one of the most dynamic if not yet the largest economic system in the world.[1] Today, a wide variety of sophisticated industrial products made in Japan dominate markets worldwide. This "economic miracle" is the result of a combination of a focused commitment and the efforts of a highly skilled work force. In international rankings, Japanese students collectively score at or near the top on standardized math and science exams. Japan's population in general is almost totally literate in a language of daunting complexity. These accomplishments are a credit to the enterprise of the Japanese as a people and to the effectiveness of their educational system, at least through high school. Given the importance of learning in Japan's economic success, it is perhaps paradoxical that very little credit for the nation's postwar attainments is attributable to the system of higher education.

*Direct all correspondence to: Louis D. Hayes, Department of Political Science, University of Montana, Missoula, Montana 59812. Telephone: (406) 243-4707.

The Social Science Journal, Volume 34, Number 3, pages 297-310.

Until the reforms introduced after World War II and the economic prosperity that followed, higher education was small in size, very selective in its admissions and elite in its product. Before the Restoration in 1868, there were a variety of teaching and research institutes including one The Institute for the Study of Barbarian Documents. Private academies and Buddhist monasteries in some ways resembled higher education in the modern sense. But the first real university was not established until 1877 in Tokyo. Tokyo University was given the designation Imperial University in 1886 and assigned the exclusive responsibility of enquiring into "abstruse principles of learning in accordance with the needs of the state." The preeminence of Tokyo University Law Faculty graduates among the bureaucratic elite, a phenomenon that continues today, was established when such graduates were exempted from the civil service exam under the Imperial University Order of 1886. Other Imperial Universities were soon established in Kyoto and elsewhere and in 1903 "professional schools", another type of university, were authorized with their mission limited to providing advanced instruction in the arts and sciences. The University Order of 1918 granted university status to private and prefectural or municipal institutions. Few men and even fewer women had the opportunity to pursue advanced learning at these institutions.[2] Only the intellectually gifted were chosen and, after completing their university studies, graduates assumed important positions in society. This practice was not unlike that followed in Europe, upon which it was in fact patterned. The European and Japanese systems were designed to produce educated manpower to meet political and economic needs, not to create broad opportunities for social development.

During the 1920s, students were attracted to leftists philosophies inspired by the Russian Revolution and economic problems at home. The government meanwhile was moving in the opposite ideological direction. In an effort to promote orthodox beliefs, the Ideological Control Bureau was created in 1934 followed by the Nationalism Instruction Bureau in 1937. To promote a proper public orientation toward the state, a Research Institute for National Spirit and Culture and an Educational Reform Council were created. These efforts were augmented during World War II by even more vigorous attempts to promote ideological orthodoxy.

Educational philosophy underwent fundamental transformation after the war. As part of their commitment to change Japanese society away from its imperial roots and toward democracy, the American Occupation authorities addressed themselves to an overhaul of the system of education. The philosophy behind this undertaking was expressed in the *Report of the First U.S. Education Mission to Japan*. It contained three basic principles: equal opportunity, broad knowledge aimed at personal enlightenment, and respect for academic freedom and autonomy. In higher education, this meant curriculum revision—greater emphasis was placed on social science and humanities, for example. In an effort to make access to higher education available to a broader range of students, additional universities were created mainly by reorganizing and upgrading existing colleges. Enrollment at the university level increased slowly, however, until it began to accelerate in the 1960s stimulated by rapid economic growth.

Changing the curriculum by shifting away from the speciality emphasis that characterized university education before the War and adding emphasis upon general education together with the expansion of enrollment from 1960 onward resulted in two problems. One was an overall decline in the quality of higher education. Much of the newer curriculum was less demanding and the expansion of enrollment meant students of lesser ability were being recruited. The other was the survival of the elitist aspect of higher education through a differentiation among institutions based on prestige. The more established institutions had greater prestige, especially the old imperial universities, and they attracted the better qualified students. University status correlated with employment status; the more prestigious the university, the better the jobs its students could expect upon graduation. Thus competition for admission intensified. Attaining the opportunity to attend the institution of one's choice is an onerous and frustrating process for the university student of today, but the experience of higher education itself is considerably less so.

Postwar reforms brought an end to rigid centralized control over higher education. Private universities were encouraged to develop their own individual characteristics free from government interference. As a result, the control of the Ministry of Education over private universities was substantially reduced. The government was encouraged to end its preferential treatment of public institutions. By the 1960s, however, the link between liberal, democratic ideals and higher education had been replaced with an emphasis upon meeting the nation's manpower requirements. Career opportunities and a college education became more closely joined. Despite the important role of higher education in social and economic affairs, the government has never developed a comprehensive policy that has effectively dealt with the problems of education (*Japan's Private Colleges and Universities*, p. 33).

For students, higher education is not a continuation of the intense learning environment that they experience through high school. The role of universities in generating and imparting knowledge is less important than their capacity to define social status. Accordingly, the prestige of a university is more important than the quality of the service provided. Among other things, this situation tends to marginalize the contribution of faculty. While it is attempting to change higher education through reform efforts, the government does not have the degree of control over universities that it has over the schools at the K-12 levels. It does have considerable financial influence, but using the power of the purse to change the character of higher education has not been effective.

STUDENTS

As of May 1993, there were 2,389,651 undergraduate and graduate students (724,520 female) enrolled in 534 universities. These institutions are divided into three categories: national universities (98), other public universities (46) and private universities (390). There are also 530,295 students (486,811 female) enrolled in 595 junior colleges (37 national, 56 other public and 502 private). The high percentage of female students in junior colleges is a reflection of an educational philosophy which stresses "finishing" type courses for women and also the restricted employment opportunities available to them (*Ministry of Education*, pp. 62–63).

Pressure to gain admission to an institution of higher education, particularly to one with high status, is tremendous. Parents begin preparing their children for university at the preschool level. Competition to get toddlers into the right kindergarden can itself be ferocious. The ultimate test of the student's academic preparation and intellectual ability, to say nothing of his or her subsequent position in life, comes at the time of university admission exams. Two exams are given: one general exam is used mainly by public universities and by some private institutions. The second exam is one devised by each university. In 1993, 513,000 students had applied to take the standardized exam, an increase of 8.6% over the previous year. The standardized test in effect determines who is qualified to take the specific university tests. To increase their chances of admission, students summon all manner of aid to the cause. The assistance of the gods is enlisted through prayer, written examples of which can be found at local shrines. A more practical approach is to take the exams for several universities or departments within the same university.[3] It is typical for students to take 8-10 or more such tests.[4] This can be very expensive as the private universities charge 30,000 yen (more than $300 at current exchange rates) to take each exam. Universities whose prestige is in the lower ranks give their exams first. Some students aspire no higher than such schools while others take these exams in order to guarantee themselves admission of some kind. They then take the exams of higher-prestige universities at a later date. Once admitted, students have a short period of time (approximately 10 days) to pay admission fees which are not refundable. Students are also expected to pay tuition although most private universities now permit delaying this charge until the results of national university exams are known. Nonetheless, admission fees can be $2500 or more and tuition is twice that for arts students and three times for engineering students.

Those students, called *ronin*, who fail to gain admission anywhere or to the university of their choice spend a year or more cramming in preparation to repeat the tests. There may have been as many as 400,000 such nonmatriculating students in 1993. New applicants and those repeating the exam constitute a larger number of students than there are places (*The Japan Times*, 17 January 1993, p. 2). In 1993 there were places for approximately two-thirds of the applicants.

The disparity between the number of applicants and the number of spaces available in universities should soon begin to diminish. For one thing, the number of people in the university-entering age group (18) is declining. There will simply be fewer students seeking admission because of demographic trends and the younger student is not being replaced by persons in older age categories. The "non-traditional" student is a phenomenon that has not yet begun to appear in any significant numbers in Japan. Another factor contributing to the decline in the student population pool is the high cost of education which is making it increasingly difficult for families to carry the burden, especially if they have more than one child to educate. There was a substantial drop in the number of applicants in the early 1990s which was associated with the weakening of the economy.

By the time they have been admitted to a university, Japanese students have spent a good part of their lives in rigorous preparation for that event. Compared to the time and effort spent qualifying for advanced study, once having entered an institution of higher learning students discover that the demands made of them are diminished substantially. "...[T]here is undoubtedly a persistent feeling that university life may provide a moratorium on overtaxing one's intellect" (Buckley, 1985, p. 90). The course work is not demanding and once admitted, a student is virtually guaranteed a diploma. "Social constraints put the school administration and faculty in a position where they feel obliged to permit graduation of students who worked so hard to get into college." (Woronoff, 1980, p. 120) The years of higher education for students are more like a vacation than a time of serious study. It is a welcome pause before entering the pressured environment of employment or married life.

Universities and colleges vary in their academic standards as do departments and programs within them. But generally speaking, expectations are less than for the higher education systems in Europe or North America. Students attend class irregularly, some hardly at all. Lecture notes are copied and sold, a process facilitated by the fact that some professors make few changes in their courses from year to year.[5] Course exams are not demanding, if they are given at all, and students who do not pass can retake them. In some courses, there are few if any requirements apart from class attendance. Of those who enter the various institutions of higher education, 95 percent ultimately receive degrees.[6] In the United States, getting into college is easy but getting through is another matter. Fewer than 50 percent of those who enter American colleges and universities ever receive a degree. Graduation from college in Japan, in and of itself, is not looked upon as a particularly significant accomplishment. It is not an achievement in which the student takes much pride nor does it confer much status. The status is achieved from having gained admission—particularly to an institution with a good reputation—in the first place (Dore, 1976, pp. 48–49). Moreover, there is a strong feeling that having failed to gain admission to a national university and thereby elite status, students join a private university which they regard as a leisure center with no incentive to study. This is a view that private universities are at some pains to dispell (*Japan's Private Colleges and Universities*, p. 52).

There are, of course, exceptions to this broad generalization. After the first two years of "general education," a select few students, mainly those at the major national universities, need to establish good academic records in order to compete for choice career assignments in business or public service. For these students, there is also the prospect of rigorous exams for admission into government service, a reality that creates a seriousness of purpose for many students.[7] For the great majority of students, while competition for jobs is intense, the quality of college work is of little significance. Technical schools—engineering for example—are more demanding of students than liberal arts schools. Here the connection between formal education and vocational aptitude is more readily apparent.

Being substantially liberated from the demands of study, many students find themselves in the unfamiliar situation of having a great deal of spare time on their hands. In the 1950s and 60s, a popular outlet for student energies was politics particularly of the radical left-wing variety. Many activities, including mass public demonstrations, were directed at a wide range of issues, a favorite being American foreign policy which was regarded as imperialist. Today politics has less attraction for students most of whom have turned their attentions elsewhere. The radical student movement has all but disappeared in Japan, reflecting a worldwide phenomenon. Students have turned to more mundane diversions including social clubs which, appropriately, emphasize group loyalty and personal discipline. These social clubs usually involve athletics or various kinds of recreational activities. Few have anything to do with academics. Japanese students have only begun to discover the attraction of drinking and other social diversions and are limited in doing so by the fact that universities do not have on-campus student housing which makes it difficult for students to spend considerable time together. Socializing is also limited by the fact that many students at universities in the larger urban areas may spend as much as four hours per day commuting between their homes and campus.

THE PRESTIGE FACTOR

Located on the top of the higher education status hierarchy are the old imperial universities such as Tokyo and Kyoto. These are followed closely by a select group of private institutions that also have good reputations. Other public and private universities follow. The academic demands of private universities are generally lower than those of the public institutions. Private schools tend to be crowded and understaffed. There are 26 students per professor on average in private universities compared to 8 per professor in public universities (Michiya, 1978, p. 291; *Japan's Colleges and Universities*, p. 137).

Despite an economic slowdown in the early 1990s which created delays in hiring, students who gain admission to one of the top universities can be confident of good jobs upon graduation. Especially coveted is employment with big corporations or powerful government agencies such as the Ministry of Finance. While ability and performance are increasingly important criteria for advancement, educational pedigree remains the decisive criterion. "It is still the case that the university one has succeeded in entering is likely to determine one's chances of getting the security of an elite position in a government department or large firm" (Fukutake, 1982, p. 210). For university graduates, especially from institutions of lesser standing where there is greater competition, job hunting can be a trying process involving long trips, more exams and lengthy interviews.

Most universities have placement services which work hard and generally are effective in obtaining employment for their graduates. Also there are connections between certain universities and specific companies involving alumni who provide links to the job market, donate money to the school and sometimes interfere in the institution's affairs (*Japan's Private Colleges and Universities*, p. 52). Employers look for more than intelligence and aptitude in their applicants; they are also interested in compatible personnel. Companies want people who will fit into their system. "A good employee is one who is a blank page on which the company can write what it wants" (Mason, 1972, p. 126).

American universities, and to some extent those in Europe, make an effort to include foreign-born scholars in their various faculties. American universities also go to great lengths to recruit talented athletes for their student bodies. In both cases the intent, among other things, is to enhance the visibility and prestige of the institution and make it more attractive to a diverse group of prospective students. Enriching the faculty by recruitment of foreign professors has been a practice only among Japan's private universities, until recently. Prior to 1983, no foreigners were permitted to hold formal faculty appointments at the national and public universities on the grounds that foreigners were prohibited under the law from engaging in activities that impacted Japanese "policy-making" (Beer, 1984, p. 364). Now, non-Japanese faculty are actively recruited although this is not always welcomed by the more traditionally inclined members of the professoriate. Intercollegiate athletics has assumed considerable importance in Japan and there are now efforts made to recruit well-known and promising student athletes.

Recognizing their parochial nature, Japanese universities have begun vigorous efforts to promote international exchanges. Many student and faculty exchange programs now exist between Japanese institutions and their counterparts abroad. While this is an important development, like foreign faculty, it is not universally supported within Japanese universities. Many, especially the more traditionally oriented faculty, see these programs as a corruption of academic traditions and a drain on resources. Faculty involvement in exchange programs is constrained by the fact that extended stays abroad could mean sacrifice of status within a faculty member's department and loss of non-university related income opportunities. For students, there is concern that spending a year abroad will put them at a disadvantage in the quest for employment. The senior year is devoted to job-hunting and some students think spending time at a foreign university would put them a year behind others of the same age.

FACULTY

Salaries for faculty in institutions of higher education are comparable to those of managers in middle sized companies. However, because of the high cost of living in Japan, the living standards of most professors are somewhat more modest than those of western academics. Japanese faculty salaries have been declining in comparison to the average national income (Pempel, 1978, p. 147). There is little salary difference between professors with the same number of years of service nor is there much difference among academic fields.

The Japanese professor does not confront the kind of job stress that is common for the average "salaryman". They are not victims of *karoshi* or death from overwork, a matter of some concern among middle aged white collar workers. Professors are immediately tenured upon being hired. They really need not do much of anything apart from teach their classes unless they desire promotion which requires demonstration of scholarship through publication. Throughout their careers, professors confront little if any performance evaluation, although the government is pushing efforts to introduce such mechanisms. Publishing is facilitated by the fact that universities have their own journals which publish professor's work. Selection is largely without competition or outside refereeing. The publishing requirement can also be met by editing already published material or by translations. Moreover, financial assistance is made available to conduct research and professors are not faced with the problem of intense competition for limited funds. Research support need not result in published work. Professors can receive research support year after year and produce nothing more than annual reports on the progress of their efforts.

The work load carried by senior professors and those who do not seek promotion is light. While a teaching load may include as many as six courses, some of them usually involve more than one section of the same course and courses meet only once a week. Many Japanese universities have more than one campus and professors may spend considerable time commuting from one campus to another to give lectures. Even with

201

these demands, there is ample time for other pursuits including textbook publishing, involvement in *juku* (cram schools), consulting and administrative work. It is not uncommon for professors (especially part-time lecturers) to teach at more than one university; a few teach at three.[8] This is especially true for professors in large metropolitan areas.

The governing structure of universities is not always transparent. In the case of private universities especially, it is sometimes difficult to identify the persons who exercise real power and the procedures by which they are selected are not always clear. Of course, all education is, nominally at least, under the general authority of the Ministry of Education. The decision making process at the university level is slow, combersome and often ineffective. The consensus based approach, similar to that employed in business and government, is also used by universities. This approach works for business and government, and even for education at the K-12 levels because each has an end product. For business it is goods and services. For government it is policy action and problem solving. For K-12, results are measurable by student performance on exams. In the consensus approach, the cooperation of everyone is enlisted in achieving that end product. Universities have no such product standard. Each unit within the university protects its prerogatives with feudal zeal which means that even routine decisions can take considerable time. Cooperation among departments can be extraordinarily difficult requiring a substantial investment of time and effort. Unlike American universities where the institution is "governed" by "the administration", Japanese faculties play a more direct role. Even administrative offices, for example, have faculty directors in charge. But they usually leave the actual day to day running of the office in the hands of administrative personnel.

Japanese universities are not as concerned about maintaining high academic standards as are their counterparts in the US where it is usually a requirement that professors and senior administrators possess terminal graduate degrees. There is no similar expectation in Japan and as a result, few Japanese professors possess doctorates. Some have completed the course work toward a PhD but have not written a dissertation. A significant number of staff and faculty are recruited directly from other professional areas. Many professors have had full careers doing something other than teaching or other university related work. For example, former journalists find work at universities and employees of large corporations can get second jobs after retirement. This is a good way to broaden and enrich teaching resources, but it does little to enhance scholarship and academic excellence.

A matter of growing concern is the tendency of universities to hire their own people. A significant percentage (sometimes as high as 80%) of the faculty and especially staff are graduates of the university that employs them. This practice denies the institution the enrichment of the experience and training of people from other universities. But of greater importance is the in-group, out-group situation that results. Graduates of the university in which they are working form a network of social, communication and attitudinal links. Those who are not graduates of that university are not part of this network and thus find their ability to function effectively diminished. Outsiders are excluded from the subtle messages that characterize Japanese group behavior. The presence of graduates from other universities can also have the opposite effect. Graduates of more prestigious institutions sometimes think it is somewhat beneath them to have much to do with those products of lower status universities.[9]

The relatively low level of academic achievement in higher education is not limited to students. Members of the faculty are not very productive by western standards although there are exceptions. Limited productivity is due in large part to the fact that research scholarship is not a principal function of Japanese universities. Research and development work more often takes place in private corporate laboratories and research institutes rather than within the system of higher education (Hane, 1986, p. 398). Even at the nation's top institution, Tokyo University, faculty productivity has been declining. Indeed few Japanese academics have won international recognition for their work. Scientists in Sweden, Switzerland and the Netherlands have won more Nobel prizes than have Japanese. Researchers in Japan have not proven adept at research for which there is no predictable outcome (Belassa & Noland, 1988, pp. 44–45). This kind of theoretical work the Japanese have generally left to others. Rather than seek important discoveries "on the frontiers of science," Japanese research efforts tend to be concentrated on the "applied" side which is where human and financial resources are committed (Michio, 1985, pp. 16–17). University based research is constrained by a number of factors: rigid governing hierarchies, inadequate financing especially for facilities, poor programs at the postdoctoral level, weak ties to industry and limited involvement by foreign researchers (Tatsuno, 1990, pp. 224–232).

FINANCING HIGHER EDUCATION

Public institutions receive a substantial part of their financing from the government while private universities rely primarily on student fees. Compared to universities in the US, those in Japan receive little support from private contributors. There are organizations connected to individual universities to which supporters, especially alumni, may contribute and these sums can be deducted from the donor's tax obligation. Endowments established by and in the name of corporations are uncommon.[10]

Private schools must rely upon bank loans for the construction of physical facilities and upon tuition and other fees to pay them off and to maintain the institution. Public institutions, in contrast, receive less than 20% of their operating budget from student fees. Keeping students in college and attracting more of them is thus an economic necessity at private schools (Pempel, 1978, p. 149; *The Japan Times Overseas Weekly Edition*, 14 January 1989, p. 3). It would not contribute to the end of financial survival if students were subjected to a heavy work load and rigorous performance standards. Raising expectations might create a dropout problem, something that does not now exist.

For their part, universities face rising costs which they have no alternative but to pass on to students in the form of higher tuition and fees. In late 1992, private institutions announced their intention to raise tuition and fees. The highest figure (Hosei University Law Faculty) was nearly 1 million yen (*The Japan Times*, 25 December 1992, p. 2). Private universities depend heavily upon student fees for operating expenses, 57% on average.[11] For them, government support amounts to approximately 20% of the budget despite the fact that the Private School Subsidy Law of 1975 calls for a 50% government share of operating costs.[12] The costs for technical schools such as medicine and engineering are considerably higher than liberal arts institutions which means their tuition and fees are higher although they receive proportionately the same government subsidy. As universities compete for students from a shrinking population pool, the result is unlikey to have a positive effect on the quality of the educational experience.

The government is not indifferent to the financial problems facing higher education and has committed to achieving comparability in tuition between national and private universities. Nonetheless, due to budget constraints the tuition charged by private universities remains at least 1.5 times that of public institutions, on average. But the important difference between the two types of institutions is in the amount of money spent per student. The expenditure per student at private universities is less than half that of public ones. This extra expenditure means that public universities have twice the faculty, space and facilities that are available at the average private institution.

One way by which universities, expecially private ones, save money is by hiring a large portion of part-time faculty. On average there can be more than twice as many part-time lecturers as full-time faculty. This saves money in two ways. Part-timers are paid less than regular faculty. Perhaps more significantly, part-timers do not receive benefits such as the annual bonus which can be worth more than seven months of salary.

PROBLEMS OF HIGHER EDUCATION

There is growing concern among educational professionals in both the government and the universities for the quality of higher education. This concern is nothing new, however. In the late 1960s, the highly charged political atmosphere of the time encompassed education and led to riots and campus disruptions. Disorder became so severe that many institutions, including Tokyo University, were closed for more than a year. Among the student grievances was dissatisfaction over higher education. Everything from the curriculum to faculty to administration to admission practices was criticized. The underfunding of higher education in general was a common theme. The government responded with a complete assessment of the educational system which eventually led to specific suggestions for change. In late 1983, the government proposed several reforms. These included, among others, changing the examination system, diversifying and "internationalizing" the curriculum and making education more socially responsive (Hayes, 1992, pp. 40–41; Cummings & Kobayashi, 1985, p. 423). Greater priority was to be given to improvement of social overhead, especially in education, which would benefit society more broadly rather than just emphasize economic growth (Pempel, 1982, pp. 180–181). But the changes were not all liberalization; there was also concern for discipline and citizenship. Acting on the recommendations proposed by a commission set up by Prime Minister Nakasone, the Ministry of Education introduced a new course of study at the pre-university level (the fifth since the end of the War) which, among other things, called for mandatory flag ceremonies and anthem singing by students (*The Japan Times Weekly Overseas Edition*, 25 February 1989, p. 4). Higher education largely escaped the emphasis upon social order and patriotism as the energy of the student-backed reform movement had all but disappeared by the mid 1970s.

Despite the increasing attention given to deficiencies in the system of higher education, some problems remain and tend to worsen as time goes on. The educational system is rigorous and demanding through high school and the entrance exam system allows for the establishment and maintenance of high standards. It also raises the level of performance expectation meaning that students are going to work harder. The system, including higher education, has worked pretty well for those Japanese companies that do not want highly specialized graduates but instead prefer recruits with excellent general skills who can then be trained in company sponsored programs. But business is also beginning to complain that new recruits lack maturity and social skills, aspects of learning and growing up that the educational system does not effectively provide. Higher education in particular has given little if any attention to such matters.

A custom that draws both praise and condemnation is the cram school. Students supplement their regular school studies with additional hours spent at night and on weekends at cram schools. Not all of these institutions are devoted to preparation for taking university admission exams. But for those that are, the purpose is almost entirely directed toward enhancing skills at exam-taking. The nature of the admission exam system itself, with its emphasis upon objective questions, stresses memorization and rote learning, an approach that does not stimulate creative intellectual activity. Having spent so much time, effort and money in getting into college, it is not surprising there is little enthusiasm for further academic effort while there. Moreover, student learning energies have been constrained by the standardized exam system which tends to retard the development of those aspects of intellectual ability concerned with inspiration, innovation and creativity.

The issue of educational quality at the university level is a matter of serious concern for Japan given the fact that the knowledge/information race is not only accelerating but has more participants. Japan has achieved its present advanced industrial status by buying many technologies from abroad and making successful commercial applications out of them. To this end, Japan has invested heavily in applied aspects of education, particularly engineering. But the sophisticated academic resources needed to sustain past successes and to build upon them are underdeveloped. Japan is among the world's leaders in spending on research and development but most of this is done by private industry. Very little theoretical or basic science is done anywhere in the country. In an effort to correct this situation, the Japanese have begun to enter into cooperative ventures with foreign research organizations, especially in the United States. The Japanese were involved in the American "super collider" nuclear physics project, for example. Spending on higher education is low which means there is not enough space and facilities are qualitatively inadequate. The buildings and equipment of even top universities are increasingly rundown. This problem is currently exacerbated by the fact that in the late 1980s and early 1990s resources have been strained by a population bulge of 18-year-olds, a product of the post-war babyboom (Hidetoshi, 1987, p. 180).

The conformity oriented and highly selective university admission process has contributed, in the view of many Japanese, to a growing problem of rebellious behavior and disorder in the schools. Among the criticisms of the Japanese approach to education is its psychological impact on students. It is said, for example, that the emotional tension of "exam hell" and, worse, failure to gain admission to the institution of one's choice, results in some emotional problems and an elevated suicide rate.[13] Violence involving students, and juvenile delinquency in general, although still small by western standards, appears to be on the increase (Rohlen, 1983, pp. 294–301). This youthful violence, much of which is targeted specifically on the schools, reaches a peak just before the testing period in February/March as does the suicide rate among students especially those who have not done well on exams (Hidetoshi, 1987, p.190). Considerable interest and concern over this phenomenon has been generated in the press which has emphasized the growing dimensions of the problem (Yoshiya, 1983, pp. 9–17). It is not clear whether this behavior reflects a weakening of the traditional emphasis upon personal discipline or if it is the consequence of something new, an expression of frustration and alienation brought on by the social and psychological demands of modern urban society. In any event, the educational system in Japan, as elsewhere, is a primary mediator of social stress.

Competition in education has intensified as the numbers of parents who are able to spend extra on their children's education by enrolling them in night schools has grown. This extra study may result in higher average performance on exams, but the number of places has remained fairly constant. Thus while expectations have risen, the capacity of the system to make room for all students at top universities and to provide them with the kinds of jobs they feel entitled to is not keeping pace.

EDUCATION AND JAPAN'S FUTURE

Contemporary youth are less influenced by traditional commitments to personal discipline and hard work for its own sake than were earlier generations. Some Japanese place the blame for this "youth rebellion" on the education reforms introduced during the Occupation. Contemporary education is viewed as corrupting Japanese values and sense of order. Accordingly, education should return to the traditional approaches that existed prior to World War II (Yoshiya, 1983, pp. 9–17). This seems unlikely, however, as education is moving even further away from the traditional.

Contemporary Japanese education faces social changes, particularly affecting the family, associated with modern industrialized and urbanized society. Moreover, ideas and practices found elsewhere, especially in Europe and the US, find favor among Japanese educators. Especially important are philosophies which stress individuality and self-expression over conformity and standardization (Vogel, 1963, p. 143).

Many in the educational establishment are reluctant to accept the changing social and intellectual environment. In March 1986, the newly appointed Minister of Education, Masayuki Fujio, created a political flap which ultimately led to his resignation when he openly criticized Occupation influences on Japanese education suggesting "post-war education has ruined Japan." He also down-played the extent of Japanese brutality during World War II. These ideas were shared by most of his colleagues in the LDP leadership (*Far Eastern Economic Review*, 14 August 1986, p. 28; Masato, 1987, p. 51). Efforts to raise the level of academic expectations and to introduce mechanisms of performance evaluation for faculty are met with spirited opposition. Even though the Ministry of Education has mandated such changes in higher education, implementation has been slow and uneven.

Japan has been generally well served by its system of education; it would be hard to argue otherwise. The particular weaknesses of higher education have increasingly come to occupy the attention of educators and the government. There has been extensive debate on education and numerous reform proposals have been offered designed to make the educational system even more effective in meeting the nation's needs (Schoppa, 1991). By and large, however, efforts to promote educational reform have not been successful (Schoppa, 1991, pp. 251–257).

The shortcomings in the educational system have been overshadowed by its successes, particularly its contribution to Japan's economic development. And there are other benefits to the Japanese approach to education. As Ronald Dore observed, "Japan's approach to education has the added advantage of postponing the youthful self-indulgence that has undermined other societies by keeping adolescents glued to their studies for most of their waking hours" (Dore, 1976, p. 50). Education in Japan, like that in all countries, must be continually responsive to society's changing tastes and needs. However, whether Japanese education possesses the kind of adaptability and initiative necessary to confront the evolving demands made of it is uncertain.

NOTES

1. Except where otherwise indicated, information for this paper has been obtained through interviews and conservations with faculty, students and staff of various Japanese institutions of higher education during 1992–1993. I am particularly indebted to Mr. Kazuo Hosoi, Professor Rieko Yamashita and Mr. Hiroshi Ohta for their efforts in obtaining educational statistics.
2. In fact, higher education was jeolously protected as a male preserve. The mere presence of women in the halls of learning was regarded as pollution. See Barbara Rose, *Tsuda Umeko and Women's Education in Japan*. New Haven: Yale University Press, 1992, pp. 129–130.
3. Students do not seek admission to a university as such. Rather they must apply for admission to a specific faculty or department and thus take the exam designed by that faculty. In turn, admission decisions are made by faculty.
4. Universities have high schools affiliated with them. The top ten percent of the graduates of such high schools are admitted to the affiliated university without all the examinations required of others. Of course, they may prefer to go elsewhere.
5. In short order, students learn of these practices. There are compilations of courses prepared by students describing the approach taken by the professor and the kind of work expected. Some professors take attendance once a month or so and students upon learning these procedures, adjust their attendence schedules accordingly.
6. The graduation rate is lower for engineering students than for those in the arts.
7. "Daily routines for these students consist of going to classes, studying in the library until it closes at night, and returning to the boarding house, where more time is spent in study." See B. C. Koh, *Japan's Administrative Elite* (Berkeley: University of California Press, 1989), p. 166.
8. Professors hold a regular faculty position at one university and are part-time instructors at others.
9. This situation is not unfamiliar to American academics. A PhD from Harvard carries a high currency value, at least in the mind of its holder.
10. The government does encourage donations. Companies giving money to universities incur a 60% tax. See Malcolm McIntosh, *Arms Across the Pacific* (New York: St. Martin's Press, 1988), p. 20.

11.	In addition to tuition/fees and government subsidies, private universities supplement their budgets with revenue from such sources as university owned businesses.

12.	Private universities niew this situation as one of willful neglect. "Once again, the government has made unmistakably clear its low regard for provate colleges and universities." See *Japan's Private Colleges and Universities*, p. 39, 164.

13.	Competition for admission to prestigeous schools is not limited to universities. Admission th the better high schools is also determined by examination.

REFERENCES

Beer, L. (1984). *Freedom of Expression in Japan: A Study in Comparative Law, Politics, and Society*. Tokyo: Kodansha International.

Belassa, B. and M. Noland. (1988). *Japan in the World Economy*. Washington: Institute of International Economics.

Buckley, R. (1985). *Japan Today*. Cambridge: Cambridge University Press.

Cummings, W. and V. Kobayashi. (1985). Education in Japan. *Current History*, (December): 423.

Dore, R. (1976). *The Diploma Disease: Education, Qualification and Development*. Berkeley: University of California Press.

Far Eastern Economic Review. (1986, 14 August): 28.

Fukutake, T. (1982). *The Japanese Social Structure: Its Evolution in the Modern Century*. Tokyo: Tokyo University Press.

Hane, M. (1986). *Modern Japan*. Boulder: Westview Press.

Hayes, L. (1992). *Introduction to Japanese Politics*. New York: Paragon House Publishers.

Hidetoshi, N. (1987). Universities Under Pressure to Change. *Japan Quarterly*, *34*: 180.

The Japan Times: (1993, 17 January): 2

The Japan Times Overseas Weekly. (1989, 25 February): 4.

Japan's Private Colleges and Universities. (1987). 33.

Masato, Y. (1987). History Textbooks that Provoke an Asian Outcry. *Japan Quarterly*, *34*: 51.

Mason, R. (1972). *A History of Japan*. New York: The Free Press.

Michiya, S. (1978). The Sociology of a Student Movement—A Japanese Case Study. In E. Beaucamp (Ed.), *Learning to be Japanese: Selected Writings on Japanese Society and Education*. Hamden, Conn: Linnet Books.

Michio, N. (1985). Developments in Postwar Japan. *Japan Quarterly* 32: 16–17.

Ministry of Education. (1993). *Universities and Students*. Tokyo: Government of Japan.

Pempel, T.J. (1978). *Patterns of Japanese Policymaking: Experiences from Higher Education*. Boulder: Westview Press.

———. (1982). *Policy and Politics in Japan: Creative Conservatism*. Philadelphia: Temple University Press.

Rohlen, T.P. (1983). *Japan's High Schools*. Berkeley: University of California Press.

Schoppa, L.J. (1991). *Education Reform in Japan: A Case of Immobilist Politics*. London: Routledge.

Tatsuno, S.M. (1990). *Created in Japan: From Imitators to World-Class Innovators*. New York: Harper and Row, Publishers.

Vogel, E.F. (1963). *Japan's New Middle Class: The Salaryman and His Family in a Tokyo Suburb*. Berkeley: University of California Press.

Woronoff, J. (1980). *Japan: The Coming Social Crisis*. Tokyo: Lotus Press.

Yoshiya, S. (1983). Changing Patterns of Juvenile Aggression. *Japan Echo*, *10*: 9–17.

Burakumin Protest: The Incident at Yōka High School

At 9:30 A.M. on 22 November 1974, some fifty-two teachers at Yōka Senior High School in southern Tajima, an area in Hyōgo Prefecture, walked off the job, declaring that under the conditions prevailing in the school they were unable to teach. The immediate targets of their statement were members of a local branch office of the Buraku Liberation League (Buraku Kaihō Dōmei, referred to hereafter as the league). The league's student members at Yōka High School had been attempting since May to gain approval for a study group on burakumin problems at the school and at the time of the teachers' walkout were engaged in a hunger strike over the issue. Emerging from Yōka High into the bright sun of that Friday morning, the teachers encountered a large gathering of league members. Shouting that the teachers were abandoning their responsibilities as educators, league members blocked their exit and ordered them back into the school. As one league account later succinctly stated, "The teachers resisted, which resulted in chaos. In this struggle, many people were injured." [1] The "chaos" continued for some thirteen hours, during which time the teachers were forced back inside the school, formally denounced by the league, then compelled in extended sessions to acknowledge in writing that they had behaved discriminatorily toward burakumin. By the end of that long day, as many as sixty people, most of them teachers, had been injured, with forty-eight hospitalized.

---

1. *Yōka Kōkō sabetsu kyōiku kyūdan tōsō: Sabetsu kyanpein o haishi jijitsu o tashikameru tameni* (Kobe: Buraku Kaihō Dōmei Hyōgo-ken Rengō-kai, 1975), 48. The account of events is reconstructed from numerous sources, including *Akahata*, *Mainichi*, the Yōka student newspaper, and league publications. The figure for those hospitalized is from Rohlen, "Violence at Yōka High School," 685–686.

In the conflict referred to as the Yōka High School incident, the objective condition for a protest is located in the terms of status relations that persist between majority Japanese and burakumin, of whom there are an estimated 1.2 to 3 million today in Japan.[2] As in the case of the Untouchables of India, burakumin (literally, "people of the hamlet") were originally assigned outcaste status because of their occupations as butchers, tanners, and leatherworkers—tasks regarded as impure and despicable under the tenets of Buddhism. In Japan, Buddhist teachings on the evils of killing animals and eating meat fused with Shinto conceptions of *kegare* (impurity or defilement) and *imi* (avoidance connected with blood, dirt, and death). Historically, then, the burakumin were "specialists in impurity," in that they assumed occupational roles that protected the rest of society from having to deal with the impure.[3] In some cases they enjoyed elevated status as a result; temple sweepers and landscape architects, for example, "polluted" through their association with dirt, nevertheless had a privileged position in society.

Until well into the medieval period, from the twelfth to the sixteenth century, these "special-status people" were a loosely defined group of persons engaged in a broad range of occupations. During the latter part of the medieval era, however, occupational categories tightened, and those who dealt with pollution now came to be seen as polluted themselves. Laws enacted in the Tokugawa period required burakumin to live in segregated villages, and the deference behavior required of them likewise became increasingly extreme. When burakumin encountered a majority Japanese, for example, they were expected to move away or to prostrate themselves until the other had passed. Extraordinary restrictions on movement were sometimes instituted; in 1820 in the feudal domain of Tosa, for example, they

2. Determining or even estimating the number of burakumin in Japan is both a difficult and a sensitive task. Since the historical aim of at least one wing of the burakumin liberation movement has been for burakumin to merge with the majority population, it is considered inappropriate to ask people who live outside officially designated *buraku* (those villages that have qualified for compensatory measures under laws passed in 1969 and 1982) to identify themselves as burakumin in various government tallies. The Buraku Kaihō Dōmei estimates the number at 3 million, while the official figure from a 1985 General Affairs Agency survey was 1.2 million. The latter figure, however, includes only those burakumin living in officially recognized buraku districts (*Daily Yomiuri,* 6 December 1987, 6).

3. The term is from Dumont, *Homo Hierarchicus*, 48; cited in Emiko Ohnuki-Tierney, *The Monkey as Mirror: Symbolic Transformations in Japanese History and Ritual* (Princeton: Princeton University Press, 1987), 91. Ohnuki-Tierney (pp. 75–100, 140–144) provides an excellent discussion of the historical evolution of the social position of "special-status people" and of the cultural and symbolic meanings of purity and impurity in Japan.

were banned from walking in the street and from entering the city after 8:00 P.M.[4] When burakumin went to a majority person's home, not only were they not invited in, but they were expected to remove their headgear and footwear and to squat in the dirt-floored entryway before stating their business. They were forbidden to wear silk and were excluded from majority temples, shrines, and festivals.[5]

In 1871, in the wake of the 1868 Meiji Restoration, the caste system was abolished and burakumin subsequently could move about freely. Yet they nonetheless continued to be exposed to numerous forms of status-based discrimination. Mikiso Hane cites numerous examples of burakumin maltreatment, even by government officials. A handbook issued by the Ministry of Justice nine years after their "liberation" described burakumin as "the lowliest of all people, almost like animals."[6] In 1919 the government instructed an entire burakumin hamlet in Nara Prefecture to relocate because it overlooked an area considered sacred to the Japanese. Not until World War II was an effort made to end discrimination against burakumin use of majority temples; meanwhile, burakumin continued to be barred from hot springs and bathhouses.

No legal barriers restrict burakumin today. Indeed, article 14 of the Japanese constitution of 1947, which guaranteed equality to women, also forbade discrimination based on social status and family origin—wording designed to extend the measure to burakumin. Since burakumin are ethnically, linguistically, and in every other way indistinguishable from majority Japanese, the basis for discrimination against them is difficult for outsiders to understand. Discriminatory attitudes in the end spring from fears of pollution that have remained long after the religious taboos associated with eating meat and slaughtering animals disappeared, and after burakumin themselves, with all other Japanese, gained occupational freedom and mobility at the outset of the Meiji period.[7] Because of discrimination in employment and other spheres, economic status and educational levels have been lower and the crime rate higher among burakumin than among majority Japanese; these and other handicaps in turn lead to fur-

4. See Hane, *Peasants, Rebels, and Outcastes*, 142–143.

5. Ibid., 139–143; and DeVos and Wagatsuma, *Japan's Invisible Race*, 6–34. See also Harada Tomohiko, *Hi-sabetsu buraku no rekishi* (Tokyo: Asahi Shinbunsha, 1975); and Hijikata Tetsu, *Hi-sabetsu buraku no tatakai* (Tokyo: Shinsensha, 1973).

6. Hane, *Peasants, Rebels, and Outcastes*, 146.

7. According to anthropologist Emiko Ohnuki-Tierney (*Monkey as Mirror*, 100), the "symbolic structure of purity and impurity" that placed burakumin at the bottom of the social stratification system and, figuratively speaking, outside society has not fundamentally changed since the onset of the Tokugawa era.

Table 3. Discrimination Affecting Burakumin

Psychological Discrimination (latent in concept and consciousness)	Actual Discrimination (appears concretely in actual life)
Contempt	Refusal of employment
Prejudice	Low educational and cultural standards
Aversion	Inferior living environment
Refusal of social contact	Low income level
Cancellation of wedding engagement	Unstable occupations
	Petty scales of agriculture and small enterprise

Source: Akio Imaizumi, *Dōwa Problem: Present Situation and Government Measures* (Tokyo: Prime Minister's Office, 1977), p. 7.

ther discrimination, in a vicious cycle that affects disadvantaged groups widely, whatever the national setting.

Discrimination against burakumin is multifaceted (see table 3); however, the two most prevalent forms are in marriage and employment. When a marriage is contemplated with someone whose family is not known to the prospective bride or groom's parents, they commonly will hire a "marriage detective" to do a background check. If the prospective spouse's family is traced to a burakumin village, parents often will oppose or abort the marriage plans.[8] The same discrimination occurs in employment, where a person's burakumin origins may be traced to place of birth. Although the traditional Japanese family registry system included such information, in 1976 groups associated with the burakumin movement finally succeeded in restricting access to these records. Since then, "buraku place-name registers" (*buraku chimei sōran*), published commercially and sold surreptitiously to companies, marriage detectives, and others, have continued to allow interested parties to identify burakumin. Even though such books are outlawed by the Ministry of Justice as soon as they appear, new versions are quickly produced—evidence of the enduring intent to discriminate.[9] Moreover, discriminatory treatment is often quite different from

8. In a 1980s survey of married couples in which one partner was a burakumin and one was not, 37 percent reported that they had faced opposition to the marriage for explicitly discriminatory reasons (*Daily Yomiuri*, 6 December 1987, 6).

9. For an excellent discussion of the legal battles over such books, see Buraku Kaihō Dōmei, *Konnichi no buraku* (Osaka: Kaihō Shuppansha, 1987); and Frank K. Upham, "Ten Years of Affirmative Action for Japanese Burakumin: A Preliminary Report on the Law on Special Measures for Dōwa Projects," *Law in Japan: An Annual* 13 (1980): 39–73.

that experienced by a minority person whose race or ethnic identity is readily visible, and can come unexpectedly when the burakumin origins of someone thought to be a majority Japanese are suddenly discovered. In short, the informal exclusion of burakumin from many spheres of majority social life continues, thereby affirming the stigma that their status carries.

In contrast to youth and women in status-based relationships, burakumin do not confront a calculus of rewards under ideal conditions. Historically, it is true, burakumin did benefit from various protective measures that, in effect, compensated for their status inferiority and exclusion from society. In the Tokugawa period, for example, they enjoyed clear instrumental rewards in the form of an occupational monopoly on leatherwork and certain other "polluted" occupations. Indeed, burakumin were able to use their "polluting effect" to expand the monopoly to occupations that had formerly been neutral, such as straw-sandal making and basket weaving; thus burakumin had work even when other groups, such as *rōnin*, or masterless samurai, could find none. Other material benefits included tax-free use of land, and various benefits accrued as well to burakumin leaders, who were permitted to exercise rather complete control over their own communities, even to the point of having power of taxation.

With emancipation in 1871, however, burakumin lost these various forms of compensation for status inferiority, which Meiji policy considered special feudal rights; these included the tax exemption of their land, as well as the trade monopoly on leatherwork—and just when the demand for leather for boots, saddles, and other equipment for Japan's new conscription army was rising. The special power and prerogatives of burakumin leaders were likewise stripped away.[10]

Certain benefits did accrue to burakumin as a result of their earlier legal monopolies, however. Burakumin continue to figure prominently as butchers and middlemen in the beef industry and as merchants and manufacturers in the shoe industry. Indeed, they have used their political power effectively to lobby for protections of both industries against inexpensive imports.[11] Burakumin have also been aided by *dōwa*, or "integration," legislation of 1969, 1982, and 1987, with funds provided to improve living conditions in qualifying buraku. Yet despite the bitter criticism of many majority Japanese, to whom such measures represent "special treatment," the charge that burakumin as a group are better off than majority Japanese

10. See DeVos and Wagatsuma, *Japan's Invisible Race*, 17–34.

11. See John Longworth, *Beef in Japan* (St. Lucia, Queensland, Australia: University of Queensland Press, 1983), 70–75, for the role of burakumin in the beef imports issue. For their role in the leather and shoe industries, see *Asahi Shinbun* (evening issue), 24 December 1985, 3.

because of successes in a few occupations or the monetary benefits gained from recent legislation has little basis in reality. By virtually every measure, from health to status in the workplace, burakumin are significantly worse off. Few material or affective rewards have come to burakumin in exchange for accepting the status quo; indeed, the benefits they have gained—such as protection for the meat industry or special funds for buraku—have been the reward not of quiescence but of making active claims. Thus, for burakumin, the expectations that operate on women and juniors in a seniority system have not been a constraining factor. With so little to lose, it is no wonder that burakumin have picked up the pace of their protest in this century.

Like many social conflicts involving a large cast of characters and numerous charges and countercharges, the particular conflict that unfolded at Yōka High School is multidimensional. At one level it was the eruption of an ongoing ideological conflict between the Japan Socialist party (JSP), which has links to the Buraku Liberation League, and the Japan Communist party (JCP), to which most of the teachers were connected through their membership in the JCP-allied Hyōgo Prefecture High School Teachers' Union (Hyōgo-ken Kōkyōso). The political ideological dimensions of this conflict were manifest throughout. Indeed, sources identified with the JCP position in the struggle later argued that the real "minority" players in the Yōka incident were not the burakumin people or the league members but the teachers, who found themselves confronted with a JSP-dominated power structure in Yōka Town that backed the league because of its links to the Socialist party; in this view, the league members who participated in the struggle were little more than pawns in a game being played by the JSP.[12] Similarly, some league sources have charged that the teachers were hapless victims of their own JCP-dominated union, which was acting on its own party-dictated agenda. These sources, pointing to the dramatic success of the JCP in the local election held three months after the Yōka High School incident, argue that the Japan Communist party sent the teachers out on that November morning into waiting throngs of angry league members specifically to provoke an attack, knowing that the actions of the league, with its JSP ties, would discredit the town's Socialist administration and so cause its defeat in the upcoming election.

At another level, the Yōka incident was a manifestation of an inter-

12. Fujiwara Toshihiro, interview with author, Kyōto Buraku Mondai Kenkyūjo, Kyoto, 3 July 1978.

organizational conflict within the burakumin movement over who should lead: the Buraku Liberation League, which, with its prewar antecedents, has been the major burakumin rights organization, or a rival organization, the National Liaison Council for Buraku Liberation League Normalization (Buraku Kaihō Dōmei Seijōka Zenkoku Renraku Kaigi), formed in 1969 by communists who broke with the league. These two groups, though they share a commitment to improving the lives of burakumin people, have fundamentally different views on how to achieve that goal. The "normalization group," following the JCP line, sees the plight of burakumin in the context of the working-class struggle. In the key issue at Yōka, for example, they saw the purpose of a high school study group dealing with burakumin problems to be that of teaching the participants about the oppression not only of burakumin, but of labor and farmers as well, all in the context of a discussion of class struggle. The league, in contrast, has argued that a high school study group directed at burakumin problems should be aimed at raising burakumin people's consciousness of their own unique problems as an invisible minority.[13]

The difference in the approach of these two rival groups was even more profound in practice than in theory. A buraku problem study group formed at Yōka High School by the JCP had only one burakumin member at the time of the Yōka incident. According to its league critics, this group approached the problems of burakumin academically and from a historical perspective; its membership, they said, was made up of majority students who were there because of their commitment to the Japan Communist party, not because of an interest in the problems of burakumin specifically. The league-sponsored buraku liberation study group, in contrast, was composed entirely of burakumin, students who, by their own account, wanted a more "human" and personal approach to the problems of burakumin in which they could discuss the discrimination that they and their parents had faced. Yet such an approach, by JCP standards, offered students no real framework for understanding the problems of oppressed groups in general. At this level, then, Yōka High School was one of many arenas in which a long-term struggle between rival organizations with differing goals and approaches was being waged.

Finally, the conflict at Yōka High is a foremost example of a status-based conflict. Leaving aside for a moment the organizational and ideologi-

13. The league's position is well-described in Yoshino and Murakoshi, *The Visible Invisible Minority*; and *Yōka Kōkō sabetsu kyōiku kyūdan tōsō*. Both positions are delineated in Wagatsuma, "Political Problems of a Minority Group"; and Rohlen, "Violence at Yōka High School."

cal dimensions of the struggle, the fact remains that the two groups which
met head on outside the school on that November day were made up of
burakumin people on the one hand and majority Japanese on the other.
The teachers were representatives of a majority culture in Japan that treats
burakumin as social inferiors. Meanwhile, despite the support that the
Buraku Liberation League had managed to gain from groups identified
with the majority culture, it was burakumin themselves who engaged in
the actual physical struggle with the teachers. Indeed, their circle of majority supporters soon fell away when the league suffered severe public
criticism following the episode. The struggle, in short, is comprehensible
only in the context of the problems that burakumin people face as a former
outcaste group in modern Japan.

The problems of burakumin in Hyōgo Prefecture have been particularly acute, perhaps largely because Hyōgo has had the highest concentration of burakumin of any prefecture in Japan.[14] The conflict inherent in
burakumin–majority Japanese relations became manifest in the Yōka High
School case for several reasons. A major factor setting the stage for the
struggle was the broad impact that burakumin liberation group activities
have had in recent decades on the consciousness of both burakumin and
majority Japanese with regard to issues of status. A second factor relevant
to the Yōka case specifically was the special influence that the local Buraku
Liberation League chapter had in the Tajima area owing to its efforts beginning in 1973 to recruit young people and encourage them to explore
their position as burakumin. In a larger sense, the incident at Yōka High
School was but one more episode in a long-term movement in which burakumin activists, their consciousness of discrimination raised long ago,
continue to press for improved conditions. Unlike the two other conflict
episodes described in chapters 3 and 4, the struggle at Yōka High School
is part of a larger drama in which conflict has long been manifest and in
which a highly visible protest movement presses for change.

Yōka High School, in existence for over eighty-five years, has been
considered one of the top high schools in its area of Japan—a senior high
school preparing students for Kyoto University, Tokyo University, or another of the prestigious national universities. Before World War II Yōka
was a prefectural agricultural high school, oriented toward training stu-

14. In 1975 there were 4,374 *dōwa* districts in Japan. Nearly half were concentrated in the Chūgoku and Kinki regions, which include Hyōgo, Osaka, Kyoto,
and Nara prefectures. Hyōgo Prefecture had the highest percentage of burakumin
in the population. Akio Imaizumi, *Dōwa Problem: Present Situation and Government
Measures* (Tokyo: Prime Minister's Office, 1977), 8.

dents for the silk industry. In the postwar period, however, it developed into a general high school, with the general college-preparatory course and vocational courses in such areas as stockbreeding, agriculture, and home economics coexisting under one roof.[15] Each year its best students excel on university entrance examinations that are Japan's entry to elite status, a fact that redounds to the credit of the school's dedicated teachers. To prepare students for the exams is a challenge to teachers and demands a major commitment of their energies. Several Yōka graduates (who were majority Japanese) described to me with great fondness and appreciation the amount of time and personal attention they had gotten from their teachers as the time of the university entrance exams approached. To do well on the exams was to do well not only for one's parents, but for Yōka's reputation and that of its teachers as well.[16]

The Tajima district from which Yōka students came in 1974 has a relatively high concentration of burakumin. Whereas in the nation as a whole an estimated 2 percent of the population are burakumin, in Yōka Town approximately 7 percent are burakumin, and in some nearby towns the percentage is as high as 9–10 percent.[17] Burakumin in the Tajima area have traditionally been concentrated in thirty-one buraku, typically in less desirable areas such as near the river or at the foot of mountains. Unemployment has been high. Those who do work are engaged in agriculture or as laborers or line workers in construction or manufacturing. Because land holdings are small and often far from choice, most agricultural workers engage as well in part-time work such as day labor to supplement their meager income. The buraku, compared to nearby nonburakumin villages, are overcrowded, have narrow roads, and often have drainage and landslide problems owing to their location.

Burakumin in the area have long been regarded—by themselves, by the organizations that represent them, and by the schools—as educationally disadvantaged. According to the league, at the time of the protest few buraku in southern Tajima had nursery schools, despite the high percentage of burakumin women who worked, and there were virtually no cultural or special-education facilities. Only a small percentage of burakumin in the

15. Following the incident the two tracks were separated and a Tajima Agricultural High School was established some two kilometers from Yōka High School. Both league members and teachers held that this action by the Hyōgo prefectural Board of Education was a direct result of the incident.

16. Interviews with graduates of Yōka High School who were students at the time of the struggle, Yōka Town, August 1978.

17. Unpublished data provided by the Office of the Mayor, Yōka Town, August 1978.

area went on to the university; quite the contrary, a disproportionately large number, relative to nonburakumin, ended their education before graduating from high school, and most male burakumin students who did finish went through the vocational course. Burakumin school performance in general lagged well behind that of majority Japanese. Data show that among elementary and junior high school students, 10.5 percent of burakumin students were academically in the bottom group in the schools, whereas only 3.3 percent of majority Japanese students fell in that group. Among second- and third-year junior high school students, 44 percent of the burakumin youngsters had what would be the equivalent of a "below C" average in the United States, as opposed to only 24 percent of the majority Japanese.[18]

In 1974, of the twelve hundred students at Yōka High School, fifty-three were burakumin. Reflecting the educational handicaps faced by burakumin throughout Japan, the students who later became involved in protest activities reported that upon entering Yōka they experienced extreme cultural shock and an educational gap vis-à-vis their majority classmates. The fact that they were burakumin was well known to the other students because of their residence in separate villages. For most, entry into a large high school drawing its students from a broad area was their greatest exposure to date to majority culture. Most of the incoming students, especially the boys, headed immediately into the less prestigious vocational course, whereas exceedingly few became part of that top group of general-course students who are the object of particular teacher interest and attention.

The objective basis for conflict, then, existed in the simple reality of the burakumin students' presence at Yōka High School as a distinct, identifiable minority whose school performance overall was below that of majority students. One of the eight burakumin students central to the Yōka protest, interviewed long after graduation, summarized the situation in explaining why he had wanted to join the league-organized study group when it emerged:

> Those of us who came from Sawa buraku, well, our performance was not too good at the beginning. . . . In middle school the buraku students were very active and had a [league] study group. We developed our self-awareness as burakumin, and we could help each other concretely with lessons and the problems we had being burakumin. Our performance really improved. When it came time to go to senior high school, though, we were scattered. I was the only student from Sawa buraku at Yōka. I felt very isolated. When I was

18. Unpublished data provided by the Hyōgo Prefectural Office, August 1978.

approached by [burakumin] seniors to join the new [league] study group I was happy. I had been lonely and timid up until then.[19]

While the specific grievances of the burakumin students at Yōka High School in 1974 are important for understanding the subsequent protest, the larger environment in which this handful of students became key actors is equally significant. Targeting Yōka for a protest effort was part of an overall strategy of a movement committed to ending discrimination, a movement that has long considered reform of Japan's education curriculum a key goal.

Burakumin liberation groups have been extremely active in postwar Japan. The two groups referred to earlier, the Buraku Liberation League and the JCP-organized "normalization" group, both claim large memberships, have research centers in the major areas of burakumin concentration, and carry on an extensive range of activities. The pace of such efforts increased after 1969, when a Law on Special Measures for Dōwa Projects was enacted by the Diet, making funds available for improving the conditions affecting burakumin. Indeed, much of the conflict between the league and the normalization group has been over which group should apply for and distribute these funds at the local level—in essence, which group is the legitimate representative of burakumin nationwide.[20]

A major area of dispute and competition between the two groups was education. In major cities such as Osaka, one consequence of the Special Measures Law of 1969 was affirmative action measures, backed strongly by the league, designed to improve the educational achievement of burakumin students. These measures, however, met with some resistance; in fact, they led to a confrontation in April 1969 between the league and several middle-school teachers—the "Yata incident"—that in many ways foreshadowed the Yōka conflict of five years later.[21] It was, however, in the

19. Comment by one person in interviews with Yōka graduates who were members of the league-organized study group at Yōka and participated in the hunger strike, Tajima regional headquarters, Buraku Liberation League, August 1978.

20. See Rohlen, "Violence at Yōka High School"; and Upham, "Ten Years of Affirmative Action."

21. The measures included extra counseling, remedial classes, upgrading of facilities, and a prohibition on cross-district registration to prevent majority students from switching out of school districts with large burakumin populations. In the Yata incident, the league forcibly detained and denounced several middle-school teachers for supporting the JCP candidate in the Osaka Teachers' Union election of March 1969 and for repeatedly refusing to meet with league representatives to discuss a pamphlet, which the league said was discriminatory, circulated by the candidate. League leaders forced the teachers to attend a public denunciation session in the citizens' hall of a Yata buraku in Osaka. After the session, which

early educational initiatives that the league's dominant role in assimilation education became well established.

Developments in the Tajima area of Hyōgo Prefecture mirrored the changes and tensions taking place in the major cities where burakumin are concentrated. By 1973 Maruo Yoshiaki, a garage mechanic, had emerged as a key local figure in the Buraku Liberation League, and in February 1974 he set up a league district headquarters for southern Tajima. According to Maruo, some 80 percent of the 1,200 burakumin households in the area were at least nominally league members at that time.[22] The large turnouts during the Yōka protest of burakumin carrying signs and banners associating them with district headquarters attest to the organization's great local influence then.

In the period preceding the Yōka High School incident, the local league, led by Maruo, had turned its full efforts toward the question of burakumin education in the public schools. Maruo's recruitment tactics, according to his critics, involved a combination of persuasion, coercion, and personal magnetism; his focus on the young was fully in keeping with the league's view that liberation for burakumin begins with a change in consciousness through education. As the league states it, the aim has been to force a transition from "education for democracy with little attention to *bu* [*buraku*] and *sa* [*sabetsu*; discrimination], to the democratization of education through the perspectives of the most oppressed."[23] Over the year or so prior to the Yōka incident, then, burakumin students in both Yōka High and surrounding schools had been recruited through an extensive campaign to win them to the league cause. By the time a core group of eight burakumin students within Yōka began to demand recognition for their study group in May 1974, the burakumin youth had developed a strong consciousness of themselves as a minority with a right to demand that the educational system meet their needs. Fully linked with the local

---

lasted all day and until almost 3:00 A.M., two league officials were arrested for unlawful imprisonment, finally to be acquitted by the Osaka District Court in June 1975. Although the Osaka High Court reversed the decision six years later, the case has been regarded as a major league victory, for both courts upheld the league's right to use denunciation as a protest tactic, disagreeing only on the level of violence that was acceptable in its application. See Upham, *Law and Social Change*, 78–103.

22. Maruo Yoshiaki, interview with author, Tajima regional headquarters, Buraku Liberation League, August 1978.

23. Yasumasa Hirasawa, "Buraku Liberation Movement and Its Implications for Dōwa Education: A Critical Analysis of the Literature," Harvard University, Graduate School of Education, March 1984 (photocopy).

chapter of the league and led by Maruo, these students saw their own struggle within Yōka as part of the larger burakumin struggle in Tajima and nationwide.

The struggle at Yōka can be fully understood only in the light of the league-JCP conflict over which approach to burakumin problems was to prevail. For a number of years Yōka High School had had a social science study group devoted to burakumin-related issues; in 1970–1971 it was renamed the Buraku Problem Study Group and was effectively reorganized to continue under JCP guidance; by 1973 all but one of the burakumin student members had dropped out. The burakumin secession and their subsequent moves in early 1974 to form a new group of their own unquestionably were part of the overall league strategy in the southern Tajima region. Yōka High School was singled out by the league as a special target because it was considered a stronghold of JCP control, particularly so since the leader of the local branch of the high school teachers' union, itself a JCP center of power, taught there. The goal of the league was thus to break the JCP's control over burakumin education at the senior high school level, and it targeted Yōka High School as a test case. The league's right to organize study groups in the schools, it may be noted, had already been established at the elementary and junior high school levels, where teachers belonged to union branches not linked with the JCP. To focus on the senior high schools, then, was the logical next step in the league's campaign.

Even if we grant that the Yōka students' campaign to gain approval for their study group was part of an overall league plan, it is a mistake to underestimate their own personal commitment to the struggle. The "group of eight" (as indicated above in the comment of one of its members) stated that they had become deeply committed to the league and fully convinced that JCP-directed education for burakumin was fundamentally wrong in its approach. As in the case involving women workers, the process of distancing, or what Murray Edelman calls "myth-making," can be seen to have already occurred before the actual protest began [24]—in the Yōka instance, almost certainly long before the group of eight, with the league in the wings, tried to place its demands before the school authorities.

If all Japanese, by virtue of being women or junior to others, may occasionally find themselves treated unsatisfactorily or oppressively because of attributes that are beyond their power to change, burakumin experience a far more extreme form of status-based discrimination. Historically, prejudice toward burakumin often denied their humanity entirely; nevertheless,

24. Murray Edelman, *Politics as Symbolic Action: Mass Arousal and Quiescence* (New York: Academic Press, 1971), 53–54.

it is important to note that such discriminatory treatment, while extreme, was on a scale that encompassed all deference behavior—for example, whereas in Tokugawa times all status inferiors were expected to bow deeply to their superiors, for a burakumin this meant prostrating oneself before any majority Japanese. The difference, in other words, was in degree, not kind. In a hierarchically oriented society with the emperor at the apex, some group had to occupy the lowest tier and, in the logic of hierarchy, display the extremes of deference behavior. Likewise, whereas historically women were excluded from many spheres, such as politics or—in the case of the upper classes in prewar Japan—the leisure world of their husbands, burakumin were excluded from most spheres of majority Japanese social life. Exclusion, like various kinds of deference behavior, was designed to preserve hierarchy based on relations between unequals.

Of the three groups whose protest activity this book studies, burakumin are by far the most militant in their rejection of deference and other status-based behavior. But then, the material and especially the affective rewards of deference and quiescence that juniors and women in well-functioning superior-inferior relations reap do not accrue to burakumin today. It is also true that burakumin have had particular advantages in reaching a collective consciousness of the dissatisfactions of status inequality and in organizing to protest. One factor, as noted, is that the discrimination against them has been so extreme. But, as resource mobilization theory establishes so well, the extent of deprivation is far less significant to a group's capacity to successfully mount a protest than are other factors having to do with resource availability. Ironically, the greatest advantage for burakumin, as compared to other status groups, has probably been their isolation and exclusion from the rest of society, for, as noted earlier (and in a way that is consonant with the writings of Coleman, Simmel, Coser, and other theorists), the web of close affiliation in junior-senior and men-women relations in daily life not only constrains overt expressions of conflict but also presses status inferiors to find other solutions to unsatisfactory situations, including self-sacrifice and endurance in the name of preserving harmony, maintaining the long-term relationship, and winning the approval of others.[25] For burakumin, who in many cases have but limited interaction with majority Japanese, no such constraints or pressures operate. Little distancing need occur because distance has been in place all along.

25. Coleman, *Community Conflict*; Lewis A. Coser, *Continuities in the Study of Social Conflict* (New York: Free Press, 1967) and *The Functions of Social Conflict* (New York: Free Press, 1956).

For all status groups in postwar Japan who engage in protest, however, the greatest resource has been ideological change. Democratization, which carries forward a process that was under way on a lesser scale earlier in the century, supports their efforts at many levels. Their exposure to the "official" democratic ideology of postwar Japan, even with simultaneous socialization in behavior based on hierarchy and deference to superiors taking place, contributes to necessary consciousness-raising as they consider how to respond to unsatisfactory treatment due both to their status and to their consequent exclusion. Furthermore, the broader force of democratic ideology in the culture at large—as reflected in media treatment of intergenerational issues in politics, for instance, and in public awareness of ideological contradictions in the treatment of women—becomes an external resource to the status-deprived, supporting changes in their own consciousness and in the worldview of other potential allies. The next chapter will explore how status inferiors, having reached a point at which they are prepared to wage a protest, begin to take action.

Compare, Vol. 26, No. 3, 1996

From School to Work in Japan

LARRY RHODES, *University of Hawaii, Manoa*
MORIMITSU NAKAMURA, *Nagano National College of Technology, Japan*

Introduction

American researchers have put a great deal of effort into identifying the factors responsible for Japan's success in achieving high levels of educational attainment. To date, however, they have shown little interest in student counselling and guidance programmes. Perhaps this is because they are preconditioned to think of such efforts in Japan as routine. After all, it is commonly known that Japanese schools do not employ professionally trained guidance counsellors as do many American schools. None the less, a thorough investigation of the subject leaves no room for doubt that Japanese students receive far more social and academic counselling than Americans and that this leads to results that most Americans have never enjoyed.

It is indeed unfortunate that the roles of Japanese career guidance counsellors and homeroom teachers have been almost completely ignored. Perhaps this is because outsiders assume that the content of the Japanese counsellors' work is at least comparable to that of their counterparts elsewhere. On this assumption, who would consider studying what homeroom teachers do in the ten or fifteen minutes everyday before first period begins?

If such misguided assumptions are responsible for the lack of interest shown in Japanese student counselling, it is, indeed, disconcerting. A little observation would make clear, for instance, that most Japanese students choose their future careers in life based on the guidance they receive from their homeroom teachers and guidance counsellors—their lack of professional training notwithstanding.

The Legal Foundation for Career Guidance in Japanese Schools

It is difficult to obtain statistical information as to what percentage of Japanese students find jobs through the efforts of their high schools. In fact, the Japanese government has never conducted such a survey. Nevertheless, it is common knowledge to the Japanese that an overwhelming majority of their young people entering the workforce immediately upon graduation from high school find jobs through the direct assistance of their schools. This should come as no surprise to anyone acquainted with the circumstances. Japanese schools are required by law to help students in their job-seeking activities. The legal bases for this requirement are provided in the School Education Law of 1947 and its enforcement regulations, the Employment Security Act of 1947, and various directives from the Ministries of Education and Labour. In particular, article 52, item 3 of the

0305-7925/96/030261-08 © 1996 British Comparative and International Education Society

School Education Law Enforcement Regulations states that there must be a chief of career guidance in each school. It further states that, 'under the supervision of the principal, this chief will be in charge of helping students choose future school or job careers and providing assistance in all matters related to career guidance'.

In conjunction with this provision, the Employment Security Act requires its local offices to co-operate with schools in their endeavours to provide vocational guidance to students [1]. Specifically, article 25, item 3 of the act states that local branches of the Employment Security Office shall entrust the following responsibilities to school principals: (a) acceptance of job offers from employers; (b) acceptance of job requests from students; (c) introduction of job-seeking students to potential employers; and (d) continuing guidance to students who have already graduated. It is worth noting that the only institutions in Japan authorised by law to perform vocational mediation are the Employment Security Office and schools which have been entrusted to do so according to the above provision. Private vocational mediation for profit is prohibited [2].

Career Guidance Committees In Schools

While these laws provide the legal foundation for school-directed vocational guidance, they do not provide concrete details regarding its actual implementation. The Ministry of Education's Senior High School Course of Study simply states that vocational guidance must be carried out in a 'carefully planned and organized way' [3]. In theory, therefore, schools are free to carry out this responsibility in any way they choose. But in fact, most schools throughout Japan carry out vocational guidance in a remarkably similar way.

As stated above, in each school there is a chief of career guidance who is chosen from among the teachers. The chief is assisted by other teachers who, together, form the Career Guidance Committee. In Japanese schools every teacher is assigned to a committee, and the Career Guidance Committee is invariably one of the largest and most important. This committee is usually divided into two sections—the Educational Advancement Section and the Employment Guidance Section. The former is concerned with helping students pursue further education; the latter with helping them find jobs. Specifically, the Employment Guidance Section is responsible for collecting information about available jobs and introducing that information to students; finding new areas of employment for students by visiting potential work places; administering practice examinations (to be explained below); and co-operating with the Employment Security Office and private companies in helping students find jobs.

In contrast to the USA, Japanese companies actively recruit prospective employees from among high school students, and they do so in strict accordance to official procedure. Before they can actively begin the process, they must first fill out an official recruiting form that specifies working conditions, salary, social and welfare benefits, necessary qualifications, and so on. The contents of this form must then be approved by the Employment Security Office, whose staff scrutinise the information to ensure its accuracy and its propriety in respect of Japanese labour law [4]. On receiving an official stamp of approval from this office, employers may send the recruiting forms to schools or, as in many cases, deliver a copy in person so that direct contact can be established between the employer and the school.

The Role of Homeroom Teachers

While the work of the Career Guidance Committee may appear prominent, the role of Japanese homeroom teachers in helping students find jobs is equally important and deserving of notice. Traditionally, the Japanese words '*tannin no sensei*' have been rendered into English as 'homeroom teacher'. Such a translation may lead English speakers to assume that the duties of Japanese homeroom teachers correspond to those of homeroom teachers in their own countries, but this is not the case. It may therefore be helpful at this point to explain just who these teachers are before attempting to describe their role in helping students find jobs.

Japanese homeroom teachers usually serve as both academic and social advisers to around forty students under their charge for a three-year period. In fact, they do more than merely advise. To a considerable degree, they are responsible for the social and academic success or failure of each of their students. Homeroom teachers are required to keep a record of all their students' grades in all subjects. When a student appears to be in danger of failing a certain subject, the homeroom teacher frequently arranges after-school study sessions with the teacher of the subject in which the student is doing poorly. To put it simply, in Japan failure is never an acceptable alternative, and homeroom teachers must see to it that their students do not fail—either in academic or in other areas.

Homeroom teachers also visit the homes of their students at least once over the same three-year period. A week is usually set aside for this purpose each year. During the visit, the homeroom teacher meets parents and answers their questions concerning their child's progress. They also take advantage of the opportunity to observe the student's living environment—often asking permission to see the student's room. Because of this close relationship with both students and parents, homeroom teachers are uniquely qualified to provide sound guidance in all areas of student life, and most Japanese students rely heavily on their advice.

Strictly speaking, the role of the homeroom teacher in school-sponsored career guidance activities largely consists of disseminating information to students and otherwise carrying out the programmes of the Career Guidance Committee. But in reality, homeroom teachers usually give a great deal of individual guidance to all their students, and the Committee takes advantage of this important relationship in conducting its activities. With all this in mind, it is easy to understand why a literal translation of '*tannin no sensei*' is 'the teacher responsible for [students]' or 'the teacher in charge of [students]'.

How Students use the Resources of the School to get Jobs

The busiest stage of career guidance begins just before the summer vacation of the senior year. Schools begin to receive official recruiting forms from companies in July [5]. Members of the Career Guidance Committee organise the information from these forms into a list containing the names of companies, job descriptions, number of positions available, and so on. Homeroom teachers distribute the list to all job-seeking students before the summer vacation. Students use the list to whittle down the number of jobs they are interested in to a manageably small number. From there, they can get more detailed information by going to the Career Guidance Office and reading the original recruiting forms. They can also ask for advice from members of the Committee who have had direct contact with someone from the company.

Just before the start of the summer vacation, homeroom teachers make a schedule for meeting parents and students to discuss job possibilities. Before this meeting, students and parents have already had a chance to consider job options by referring to the job list provided by the Committee and by looking at the original recruiting forms. At this meeting, homeroom teachers ask students to express their first and second job preferences, giving their own opinions regarding the student's aptitude and chances of employment in these areas of work. If in this meeting the student, parents, and teacher cannot determine two job options, another meeting may be scheduled later during the summer vacation.

After the vacation, students submit in a form indicating their final preferences. The Committee uses these forms to determine which students to recommend for the jobs on their list. Usually, companies have asked the school to recommend a certain number of students for job interviews and tests. They may even have promised to hire a certain number of students recommended by the Committee. In cases where the number of students who want a certain job exceeds the number of students the Committee has been asked to recommend, the Committee, together with the 12th grade homeroom teachers, must select the most qualified students. The students have already been informed of the criteria for making student recommendations and are aware that they must compete. These criteria usually include grades, participation in club activities, and daily behaviour and conduct. Students who cannot receive the Committee's recommendation for their first preference usually can be recommended for their second.

Also at this time, students are given guidance concerning how to take tests and how to conduct themselves in interviews. In Japan, most mid- to large-sized companies require prospective employees to take an examination which measures their general understanding of Japanese, English, and mathematics (and sometimes science and social studies). In addition, they may also be asked to write a short essay on some simple theme such as life in school, favourite hobbies, hopes for the future, etc.

The purpose of the exam is to test the applicants' general knowledge of core subjects, and the test questions are usually undemanding. The following examples taken from a book of practice exam questions illustrate the general level of difficulty: *Geography*—Name the countries in which the following cities are found: (1) São Paulo and Rio de Janeiro; (2) Detroit and Houston; (3) Alexandria and Aswan; (4) Calcutta and Bombay; (5) Naples and Milan [6]. *World History*—Match the following word or phrase (1)–(5) with the historical figure associated with it (a)–(e): (1) French Revolution; (2) *Decameron*; (3) *Book of Various Experiences in the East*; (4) Eastern Roman Empire; (5) Protestant Reformation; (a) Marco Polo; (b) Justinian; (c) Martin Luther; (d) Louis XVI; (e) Bocaccio [7]. *Biology*—Which of the following animals is a reptile: (1) a pheasant; (2) a lizard; (3) a carp; or (4) a salamander [8]. *Mathematics*—Fill in the blank with the number that fits the pattern: 1, 3, 7, 15, __, 63 [9].

The idea here is that companies want workers who can adapt quickly to changing technologies and working situations rather than those with narrowly concentrated skills. Most employers feel that workers who have a fundamental knowledge of core subjects can more easily adjust to ever-changing working conditions. Therefore, specific work skills are almost always developed on the job.

While most companies design their own examinations, practice test booklets (such as the one from which the above examples were taken) with the answers to commonly asked questions are available in all major book stores, and Committee members usually recommend such study materials to interested students. Throughout the senior year up until the actual test date, a number of practice exams are administered by the Committee.

The results are first made known to the homeroom teachers, who then give them back to the students with some advice. Students who plan careers as civil servants can also take practice exams. In this case, their results are tabulated by computer on a national or local scale (depending on whether the test is national or local) in order to calculate their ranking among all the test-takers. As with other practice exams, the results are forwarded to the homeroom teachers, who interpret the data to the students.

In accordance with notices from the Ministries of Education and Labour, companies begin to administer tests from 16 September [10]. They are strongly discouraged from administering exams before this date so as to avoid disruption to the school year. If students take and pass exams too early in that year, they may lack incentive to actively continue their studies until graduation.

Students are given official permission to be absent from school to take the examinations. In many cases, both the written examination and the interview are given on the same day. In cases where the number of applicants is large, interviews may be conducted on another day. Usually within a week, the results are forwarded to the Career Guidance Committee, which informs students through their homeroom teachers.

Students are only allowed to pursue one job choice at a time. They can pursue other options only after they have failed in their first choice. Such a system discourages risk-taking. Constraints on time lead students to pursue job choices in which their success is relatively secure. Those who are not successful in their first preference usually find employment through the introduction of the members of the Committee, who are usually aware of unfilled vacancies. If not, Committee members will diligently contact companies with which they have developed close relations, so that eventually most students usually are able to get a job of some sort through the efforts of their school.

It is important to note that hiring practices in Japan are highly institutionalised and that most students would not be able to find jobs easily without official help. As described above, Japanese companies almost always insist upon receiving some official recommendation from high schools. It is very difficult for a student to be considered seriously for a job in most reputable or popular workplaces without such a recommendation.

It is also important to note that schools are under pressure to be frank and honest in making recommendations. If in a certain job, for instance, a high level of academic aptitude is less important than a friendly and sociable personality, the Committee will strongly emphasise the latter points. Any dishonesty, however, would damage the prospects of employment for students in the future.

The Committee's work does not end once the students have found jobs. After the recruiting process has ended, letters of thanks are sent to companies that have promised to employ their students. The Committee also begins to prepare students to assume their new roles as working members of society. For instance, it may arrange for those who have found jobs to attend driver's training school (after their regular classes, of course), or the sales staff of a cosmetics company may be allowed to hold classes for female students on how to wear makeup. But most importantly, the Committee will usually ask someone from the Labor Standards Inspection Office or the Employment Security Office to lecture the students on their rights as workers according to Japanese labour law regarding such subjects as wages, working hours, and what to do in cases of sexual or other forms of discrimination. Also important are lectures which may be held in order to teach students about opening bank accounts, buying insurance, and other areas of financial concern. Japanese educators emphasise the psychological value of these kinds of guidance as they instil a sense of awareness in students that they are about to become adult members of society.

A Survey Concerning the Degree of School Involvement in Assisting Students in their Job-seeking Activities

As there are no official data available concerning the number of Japanese students who find jobs through the efforts of school committees, we decided to conduct our own modest survey of schools in Nagano Prefecture. While acknowledging that the survey covers only a small geographical area, we would claim that it provides at least a glimpse of what the big picture probably looks like, since the process as described above is rather uniform throughout the nation.

Out of a total of 106 public and private high schools in Nagano Prefecture, 30 were selected. Our guiding principle was to identify characteristics that would make comparison with American schools easier. For example, roughly a quarter of Japanese high school students attend vocational schools, such as commercial, agricultural, and technical schools. As a large majority of these students find related work immediately upon graduation, such schools have few equivalents in USA and are inappropriate for purposes of comparison. On the other hand, nearly three-quarters of Japanese high school students attend *general* schools, which can be further divided into schools for students seeking higher education (the so-called '*shingakko*') and, for lack of a better term, *ordinary* schools. Although this is not an official distinction, since students in any school are free to take college entrance examinations or to seek employment, Japanese themselves tend to think in these terms because the percentage of students from '*ordinary*' schools who enter universities is relatively small. These schools, however, represent a plurality of Japanese schools and can therefore be considered typical. They also seem most appropriate when making comparisons with American schools because of the diversity of the student body. Some will go to universities; some will go to junior colleges or technical training schools; others will find jobs as soon as they graduate. We, therefore, limited our survey to such 'ordinary' public high schools in Nagano Prefecture in which at least 10% of the students sought employment upon graduation.

In early May of 1994, we administered a questionnaire to school chiefs of career guidance asking them the number of students who found jobs through the direct assistance of the school's career guidance committee, as well as the number of students who found jobs on their own, the kinds of jobs the students found, and the degree to which the committee is involved in counselling students who have already graduated.

Of the 30 schools in our survey, the total number of students graduating in March 1994 was 6657. Of this total, 2237 students (or 33.6%) were job seekers. Of these job-seeking students, 2209 (or 98.7%) were able to find a job even during the on going economic recession. According to our survey, 1964 of these students (or 88.9%) found jobs in the private sector through recommendations of their schools' career guidance committees, while most of the others found work through open application for civil service positions. As we have already seen, however, the school helped these students, as well, by administering practice examinations and by interpreting the mock test scores to them so that they could prepare for the actual test. Obviously, the point to note here is that very few students go through the job-seeking process without the help and encouragement of their teachers. Only a very small number of students find work entirely on their own or through family and other connections.

It was also found that nearly half of the schools provide guidance to students who have already graduated. Fourteen schools stated that they are still providing assistance and/or encouragement to their former students. Twelve schools stated that they make yearly visits to the workplaces of their graduates to ask them how they are adjusting to their new working lives. Other schools stated that they send out questionnaires to their former students asking about specific working conditions. Many of the schools also make some effort to be aware of the number of students who quit or change jobs within the first year or so of employment.

Conclusion

As stated in the Nagano Prefecture Long-range View of Education, the main goal of educational endeavours in Nagano Prefecture is to provide 'total education' to its young people [11]. This requires that teachers perform many duties in addition to merely teaching their subjects. Helping students find a path in life after graduation is considered an important part of this 'total education'.

There is currently a great deal of discussion in the USA concerning how to train young people to work efficiently in order to meet the challenges posed by increasingly competitive workers in developing countries. President Clinton himself has stressed the need to learn from the Japanese in this regard. However, current efforts at revitalising the US educational system to meet these challenges bear little resemblance to the way Japanese train their own workers.

At face value, the expression 'school to work' sounds attractive because it suggests the development of educational skills which are appropriate to the workplace. However, as the idea has been applied in the USA, the phrase has come to mean leaving classrooms at the expense of developing basic academic abilities in favour of learning more 'relevant' work skills at actual work-sites. The problem with this approach, of course, is that when their narrowly developed skills become obsolete, poorly educated US workers are unable to adapt and learn new skills which will move them into higher value-added occupations.

Vocational guidance in Japan rarely includes taking students out of the classroom and bringing them to various work-sites to learn practical skills. Actual work skills are almost always taught on the job to young people once they have been employed. Instead, Japanese vocational counselling stresses close and frequent consultation among students, teachers, and parents. Guidance, however, is not limited to mere friendly advice on an *ad hoc* basis. As we have seen, guidance is provided to all students in a very planned and organised way. As a result, the transition from school to work in Japan seems to be a fairly smooth one.

Like the USA, Japan also faces the threat of losing jobs to cheaper labour in developing nations as more and more companies move their factories overseas. Indeed, the Japanese economy itself faces a number of challenges which will probably result in some important changes in the composition of the labour force. Nevertheless, the Japanese are showing more success in moving their workers up the skills ladder and into greater value-added occupations. The Japanese are able to do this because their students master basic skills in their core courses. Their ability to read, write, and perform mathematics at relatively high levels means that they can be easily trained, and retrained, to do many kinds of work. It is worth noting that very few 'ordinary' schools in Japan are equipped with computers or other sophisticated equipment to give students hands-on experience in technically-oriented fields before they move out into the professional world.

These successes notwithstanding, the Japanese system is not without its problems. While students are not generally forced into making important decisions against their will, they may be discouraged from taking risks or stretching their abilities. In some cases, they may be left wondering what they could have done if only they had taken a chance. Also, teachers often feel pressured into getting their students into *any* job or *any* school so long as they do not become '*ronin*' (a Japanese term which originally meant 'masterless samurai', but which today is used to refer to young people who have been unsuccessful in either finding a job or getting into school). But such criticisms are not frequently heard, suggesting that most Japanese are rather satisfied with the schools' efforts. More frequent are the complaints of teachers who would like to be relieved of such time-consuming duties that take up much of their working time. Whatever problems may exist in the Japanese school-assisted job placement programme however, it is certainly utilitarian in its philosophy. Most Japanese high school graduates continue to benefit from the system, in spite of the on going economic recession.

Correspondence: Professor Morimitsu Nakamura, Nagano National College of Technology, 716 Tokuma Amori, Nagano City, Nagano Prefecture 381, Japan.

NOTES

[1] SHOKUGYO ANTEIHO, Dai 25 Jo, Dai 2 Ko. Employment Security Act of 1947, Article 25, Item 2.

[2] SHOKUGYO ANTEIHO Dai 32 Jo. Employment Security Act of 1947, Article 32.

[3] KOTOGAKKO GAKUSHU SHIDO YORYO—SOSOKU, *Senior High School Course of Study—General Rules*, Notification No. 26 from the Ministry of Education.

[4] SHINKI GAKKO SOTSUGYOSHA NO SHOKUGYO SHOKAI GYOMU TORIATSUKAI NO KIHON HOSHIN, *Fundamental Principles of Occupation Mediation Operations Regarding Students Approaching Graduation*. This notice, issued on 6 March 1971, was addressed to the Head of the Vocational Education Department of the Ministry of Education by the Director of the Employment Security Bureau of the Ministry of Labor.

[5] HEISEI ROKUNEN SANGATSU SHINKI CHUGAKKO/KOTOGAKKO SOTSUGYOSHA NO SHUSHOKU NO TAME NO SUISEN OYOBI SENKO KAISHI KIJITSUTO NI TSUITE, *Regarding Recommendation Procedures and the Fixed Date of Job-screening Activities for Junior High and High School Students Graduating in March of 1994*. This notice was issued jointly by the Director of the Elementary and Secondary Education Bureau of the Ministry of Education and the Director of the Employment Security Bureau of the Ministry of Labor on 31 March 1993 and was addressed to the governors as well as the superintendents of education in all prefectures.

[6] *Kokosei no Shushoku: ippan joshiki taisaku (1994), Employment for High School Graduates: how to prepare for tests* p. 38 (Tokyo, Hitotsubashi Shoten).

[7] Ibid., p. 44.

[8] Ibid., p. 122.

[9] Ibid., p. 84.

[10] HEISEI ROKUNEN SANGATSU SHINKI CHUGAKKO/KOTOGAKKO SOTSUGYOSHA NO SHUSHOKU NO TAME NO SUISEN OYOBI SENKO KAISHI KIJITSUTO NI TSUITE, *Regarding Recommendation Procedures and the Fixed Date of Job-screening Activities for Junior High and High School Students Graduating in March of 1994*.

[11] 'Nagano Prefecture Long-range View of Education', Nagano Prefecture Board of Education document, 1989, p. 1.

Linguistic Minorities and Education in Japan

JOHN MAHER, *International Christian University, Tokyo*

ABSTRACT   *The increasing visibility and assertiveness of language minorities in Japan now pose a serious issue for government policy which has hitherto been committed to the historical ideology of a monoracial and monolingual state. Language education policy in Japan is currently predicated upon the need for 'internationalisation' but nowhere does internationalisation include support, or at least encouragement, for community and indigenous languages, or regional dialects. Nowhere is there official acknowledgment that in the public school system, there are languages and language varieties other than standard Japanese, nor that schools might benefit from recognition of 'Other' languages. It is well-known that the idea of a diverse Japan has been systematically avoided by the so-called* Nihonjinron *theories, an ethnocentrist body of writings which purports to value cultural difference whilst emphasising the uniqueness of 'being Japanese'. This ideology is becoming increasingly challenged as many local communities, urban and rural, re-evaluate their changing composition in the light of cultural diversity. Community languages may include Korean, Ainu, new immigrant languages, Japanese Sign Language and others. However, the notion of contemporary Japan as somehow 'multilingual' still remains radically controversial and contested in descriptions such as Government white papers and approved school textbooks. There is a need for a new paradigm regarding the languages of Japan and there are signs that a new and progressive one is emerging.*

> S'il y a depassement de la vision moderne du monde, ce ne peut etre que dans le mouvement de synthese qui s'esquisse a l'echelle de l'humanite.
> (Berque, 1995)

Past and Present

Centre and periphery, national conformity and individual expression, militarism and pacifism, wealth and power, the world and us. In all of the struggles which Japan has engaged in this century (Steele & Araki, 1995), no forked path is set to cause such a profusion of dilemmas in the next as that of the national effort to maintain, on the one hand, the fortress of modernity and, on the other, the call for personal liberty. However, if the way seems unclear, likewise the path of minority language rights in Japan is rugged and chronically ill-defined, but one at least that carries along its course a fundamental purpose shared by all the various language communities: to reject root and branch Japan's officially cultivated ideology of racial and cultural homogeneity (Maher & Yashiro, 1991; Maher & Honna, 1994a,b; Maher, 1997).

0013-1911/97/020115-13 © 1997 Educational Review

What is the problem and how does it affect educational policies? It runs thus: the Japanese government will not recognise, authorise or accredit any public or private sector school which does not employ *kokugo* (literally, the national language, i.e. Standard Japanese) as the language of all instruction, including textbooks and other pedagogical materials. Those groups seeking to maintain their own language or cultural habits (i.e. Koreans, Chinese Ainu, etc.) are at liberty to establish their own schools, but are advised that neither government financial support not accreditation will be given to those institutions. Therefore, children graduating from such schools are ineligible for entry to all institutions of higher education: this includes 4 year universities, medical and technical universities, nursing schools, 2 year colleges and specialist and vocational colleges. Children wishing to enter such institutions are required to study (either independently or at preparatory school) to obtain the necessary eligibility certificates to sit college entrance examinations. Except in the case of *kikokusei* (returnee Japanese children brought up overseas), the government does not recognise the need for bilingual education.

The official and popular explanation for monolingual/monocultural education is terse and quite unambiguous: there are no minorities in Japan. In 1980 an official declaration was made by the Government stating categorically that no linguistic minorities are present in Japan. This was contained in the Report on Human Rights prepared in accordance with the International Covenant on Civil and Political Rights. Referring to Article 27, which recognises the existence of linguistic minorities and recognises the right 'to enjoy their own culture ... or to use their own language', the government of Japan stated 'Minorities of this kind mentioned in the covenant do not exist in Japan' (quoted in Maher & Yashiro, 1995a).

The current government view of ethnic homogeneity, although widely criticised both within and outside Japan, also suffuses the media, social policy and education. At the heart of it lies a kind of 'modernity', a national convergence of effort and mind, that has brought increasing material success wrought over the last 100 years. The nation that has surely bent its collective will towards this success has done so at the price of the cultural other and cultural pluralism. However, if the fact that the homogeneous Japan of the modernist manifesto has never been even slightly true can be easily demonstrated, it rarely is.

The Other Languages of Japan

The Japanese archipelago, consisting of approximately 1000 islands, contains a variety of languages and dialects spoken by its population of 121,000,000 who mostly live in the densely populated coastal areas along the four main islands of Honshu, Kyushu, Hokkaido and Shikoku. Cultural and linguistic diversity is part of the heritage of the Japanese speaking populations.

It is *de rigeur* nowadays to begin discussion of regional or national multilingualism by looking to, or for, evidence of a multilingual heritage. Likewise in Japan it is a speculative certainty (Kawamoto, 1982; Chew, 1976; Maher, 1996) that the Japanese archipelago has been at least as linguistically diverse in ancient and pre-modern history as it now is at the end of the millenium. The cultural contact lines across the ancient Asian Pacific trade routes are well-delineated and the fact recognised positively in Japan as early evidence of internationalism.

In contemporary Japan the foreign and indigenous minority populations continue to increase. Excluding the very large number of non-Japanese background people, such as Koreans and Chinese who are naturalised, the population of registered foreign residents in 1990 was 1,075,317 (a 9.2% increase compared with the previous year) and the figure stood at 1,189,317 in 1995, thus reaching above 1% of the entire population. It is not only these numbers and the distribution of 'foreigners' that comprises the nation's linguistic diversity and carries implications for education and policy making. As I shall mention below, there are minorities (like deaf signers) who are ethnically Japanese (an admittedly very vague term) but who also belong to a minority language community.

We witness the presence of the cultural 'Other' in various languages such as Ainu, Ryukyuan, Chinese, English, Japanese Sign Language, Korean and others (Maher, 1991, 1993; Maher & Yashiro, 1995b; Maher & Macdonald, 1995). Japan also displays a long history of pidgins some of which have disappeared, whilst others are re-emergent, such as the gastarbeiter pidgins in the metropolitan areas of Kanto and Kansai.

Ainu

Public schools on the northern island of Hokkaido are not permitted to teach Ainu language, culture or history. Local petitions to introduce the Ainu language into the curriculum of a primary school near the Ainu villages of the Saru area of southern Hokkaido were rejected by the Board of Education on the grounds that it would require complicated approval procedures from the Tokyo government. Ainu, an indigenous language isolate of possibly Alaic affiliation, is spoken as a native tongue by an unknown number of probably between 50,000 and 200,000 Ainu people who live mostly on the northern island of Hokkaido. Ainu is divided into three main dialect groups: the Kurile group, the Sakhalin group and the Hokkaido group. As mentioned above, the Ainu language is not taught in schools and has suffered as a result of the assimilation policies advocated by successive Japanese governments following the Meiji restoration.

It is common for Western commentators on Japan to bookmark the Meiji restoration as a point of departure for discussion of modernisation, the awakening of liberal democracy. It must be remembered however, that for Japan's minorities, Meiji signalled, by law and military fist, the first systematic attack on Japan's indigenous cultures and languages. Language prohibition was part of a comprehensive educational package initiated by the Meiji restoration of 1871. It did not give the Ainu any route to consolidate their sense of being a distinct community, which in turn might affirm their language heritage. Compulsory education started in 1886 and was later expanded in the special education programme established by the Education Code for Hokkaido Ainu in 1901. These acts not only prohibited use of the language, but specifically excluded the Ainu from learning history, geography and science on account of the Ainu people's alleged 'emotional and intellectual immaturity'. Compulsory education was 6 years for Japanese and 4 years for Ainu.

The 1901 Education Code was aimed at the complete linguistic conformity of the Ainu and at furthering the elimination of the Ainu language. The learning of Japanese was the central feature of the Code. Japanese was taught according to the following schedule: 1st grade, eight classes a week; 2nd grade, 12 classes; 3–4th grades, 14 classes. A Hokkaido Senator of the period wrote thus.

It is true that the Ainu are an inferior people, but they can understand and use the Japanese language only if we make the education good enough. Of course, we know that their ability is low compared to that Japanese.... (quoted in Hatakeyama, 1990, p. 42)

The Revised Regulations of Education for Former Native Children in 1911 further reinforced the disparity between the Ainu and Japanese people's access to the same education. The spurious reason given for this was that 'the development of the Ainu is slower than that of Japanese both mental and physical' (p. 49). (See Siddle, 1996, for an illuminating analysis of Ainu history.)

Since the 1980s onwards, strenuous efforts have been made to increase the cultural vitality of the Ainu in the form of a revival of traditional rituals, the development of teaching materials, language classes in community centres and some universities and a body of Ainu-sponsored political proposals which touches upon language maintenance. The United Nations' declaration on language rights in the Year of the Indigenous Peoples (1993) was one landmark in the history of language maintenance among the peripheral language communities in Japan. Supported by many language minorities, the Ainu achieved significant progress in their struggle for language protection. There are a handful of universities in the northern prefectures of Hokkaido which offer Ainu language instruction. For many years, language learning classes have been held privately in the Nibutaini Valley area (the main concentration of the Ainu community in Hokkaido) but this has now been joined by a number of other 'Ainugo Kyoshitsu' (Ainu language classes) now operated by local community groups in community centres in Hokkaido, such as Sapporo, Asahikawa, Obihiro, Chitose, Wakkani and elsewhere (Maher, 1994).

Ryukyuan

The Ryukyuan language plays no designated or official role in public education in the Okinawan education system and its use is actively discouraged in some schools, although attitudes are changing, owing to awareness of the rapid decline in general knowledge of the language (Matsumori, 1995). The Ryukyuan language, a close relation of Japanese, comprises a group of dialects, many of them mutually unintelligible, spoken throughout the islands which are situated at the south western tip of Japan. The independent Ryukyuan kingdom was established in the 15th century and came under the control of Japan in 1609. Despite official discouragement of the language, Ryukyuan is widely spoken, the standard variety being the Shuri dialect of Okinawa. There are indications that, in addition to the traditional dialects of Ryukyuan, many of which are declining, there are emergent *shin-hogen* or new dialects and pidgin-like sociolects among the younger generation.

Standard Japanese is the medium of instruction throughout the Ryukyuan school system and school textbooks are published entirely in standard Japanese. The decline of vernaculars is accelerated by the Standard Japanese of the ratio and television, magazines, books, official documents and public signs. Recent years have shown increasing local interest in the language and its ethonolinguistic maintenance. A survey by Agari *et al.* (1983), based on a questionnaire among junior high school students in the Ryukyuus, indicated children's increasing loss of command of vernacular languages: when asked if they 'understand' Ryukyuan, 4–15% replied 'very well', 72–88% replied 'a little' and 3.1% 'not at all'. When asked if they spoke a Ryukyuan vernacular, 1.11% replied 'fluently', 60–86% 'a little' and 3–21% 'not at all'. A language carries a big stick, a dialect waves a feather. What a government dismisses as a 'dialect' one day might be designated for political expediency a 'national language' at 12 midnight. This happens. So is Ryukyuan a language or a dialect? It's both, of course.

Chinese

Chinese is found in the various Chinese communities, with a total population of approximately 50,000 living in the urban centres of Tokyo–Yokohama, the Kansai region and parts of southern Kyushu. There are some bilingual (Japanese–Chinese) schools which serve these communities: principally, Tokyo, Yokohama and Kobe. Mandarin Chinese is taught as a second language in these private schools run by the Chinese communities themselves.

English

In addition to several thousand native English speakers who are permanent or temporary residents in Japan and who are served by several English language newspapers and magazines. English is widely studied, virtually as a compulsory subject, in secondary schools and also in higher education. In terms of language attrition, it is worth noting that the historical notion of a language 'model' (usually British or American) has declined considerably in recent years. Multi-accented English, including Asian Englishes, is increasingly acceptable. Also, as well as oral competency, the increasing importance of literacy in English is another trend. Professional or Occupational English is the working language, especially in its written form, of a number of occupations and professions. In the biomedical sciences, for instance, it has been observed that the volume of research reports and articles published English in Japan alone accounts for more than the combined amount published in Canada, Australia and New Zealand (Maher, 1985, 1986, 1989).

English is found also as the native language of inhabitants in the Ogasawara (Bonin) islands, but numbers have declined drastically in recent years. Ogasawaran English is perhaps the most 'perfect' example of language attrition in Japan in recent times. There are between 40–50 international schools in Japan, most of these employing English as a medium of instruction and providing various measures of entry to higher education. None of these schools are accredited by the Japanese government, but graduates are permitted to apply for entry to a small number of internationally minded universities which follow either an open-door policy or a quota system for international school graduates. Such schools are, principally, the International Christian University, Sophia University and Keio University.

The Japanese Deaf Signing Community

Japanese Sign Language (JSL), the language of the deaf, is used by a cross section of an estimated 400,000 hearing impaired people and is subject to dialectal and sociolectal variation. Major strides in sign language usage have been made in recent years. These include the guarantee of sign language interpreting in court, etc, local government-initiated sign language services and signed television broadcasting. The sticking point is school education. With the inauguration of the Kyoto Prefectural School for the Blind and Deaf in 1873, Japanese Sign Language, a language whose structure differs markedly from Japanese, was adopted as a means of instruction. The turning point in bilingual deaf education occurred in 1925, with the introduction of oralism. With this came the dissolution and in fact prohibition of JSL in Japan's schools. This has been the policy up to the recent present. In 1993, a memorandum on special education policy was issued by the Ministry of Education, acknowledging the use of sign language in deaf schools. Hailed in the popular press as the first statement in the history of educational policy to recognise language diversity in schools, the document was frankly invidious and immediately attacked by many language rights activists in the deaf community. The reason was obvious. The definition of sign language adopted by the government was signed Japanese (based on the structure and lexis of standard Japanese) and not Japanese Sign Language, the indigenous language of the deaf community. As Honna & Kato (1995, p. 282) pointed out, 'there is still a long way to go before the legitimacy of sign language is established in deaf education'.

Recent Immigrant Languages

The rapid expansion in the number of immigrant languages, such as Spanish or Tagalog and other Philippine languages, in both urban and rural areas (the latter, for example, particularly in rural districts like Yamanashi and Tochigi), has focused serious attention on the dynamics of family bilingualism and language maintenance in the next generation of Japanese citizens.

In the 1980s, the period of the so-called 'bubble economy', the economic upturn created a labour shortage, particularly in the construction and manufacturing industry. This drew in *gastarbeiter* to work primarily in what is termed, ironically, *san-K* (3-K) type jobs; in other words, work considered *kitsui* (hard), *kitanai* (dirty) and *kiken* (dangerous). From 1980 onward, the influx of Vietnamese-Chinese and Cambodian refugees or foreign workers from Asia and South America, many of whom as speakers of Spanish and, particularly, Portuguese or other languages, settled in Japan. Several commentators have pointed out the urgent need to deal with the problem of the children of recent immigrants who do not have Japanese language ability and who find it difficult to function in public schools (Yashiro, 1991; Isaka, 1996). Consider the immigrant population in the midi-nineties in the city of Hamamatsu (Table I), an industrial seaside city with a medium-sized population located in central Japan between Tokyo and Nagoya.

There are substantial numbers of minority language children in the public school system in Hamamatsu (Table II). Although it was not possible to obtain figures for the distribution of children by level and type (private or public) of school, it is reliably reported that children under 16 years of age can be found through all educational levels (private correspondence with Hamamatsu city Office): that is to say, Hoikuen (Nursery School), Yochien (Kindergarten), Shogakko (Primary School), Chugakko (Junior High School) and Kotogakko (Senior High School).

The three main methodological approaches to this new situation of the Hamamatsu Board of Education (Kyoiku Inkai), which oversees all public and primary and secondary education, in the city is threefold:

(1) the opening of counselling offices in local schools;
(2) the stationing of native speakers in schools (Kahai Kyoin, 'additive teachers') for instruction in toridashi jugyo ('withdrawal classes');

TABLE I. Ethnic minority population in Hamamatsu by nationality and sex in 1994 (adapted from foreign residents registration data, May 1994, Hamamatsu City Office)

Nationality	Total population	Male	Female
Brazil	6489	3751	2738
Korea	2180	1135	1045
China	634	369	265
Vietnam	226	122	104
Peru	734	435	29
Philippines	624	77	547
Australia	30	20	10
Argentina	14	9	5
Sri Lanka	38	34	4
Indonesia	178	175	3
Britain	26	8	18
Iran	17	15	2
India	82	80	2

TABLE II. Age distribution in the ethnic minority population in Hamamatsu in 1994 (adapted from foreign residents registration data, May 1994, Hamamatsu City Office)

Nationality	Total population	Under 16 years	Over 16 years
Brazil	6489	424 (M) 369 (F)	369 (M) 2369 (F)
Korea	2180	142 (M) 1159 (F)	993 (M) 886 (F)
China	634	35 (M) 22(F)	334 (M) 243 (F)
Vietnam	226	36 (M) 47 (F)	86 (M) 57 (F)
Peru	(734)	40 (M) 32 (F)	32 (M) 267 (F)
Philippines	624	9 (M) 13 (F)	68 (M) 534 (F)
Australia	30	0 (M) 0 (F)	20 (M) 10 (F)
Argentina	14	0 (M) 0 (F)	9 (M) 5 (F)
Sri Lanka	38	1 (M) 0 (F)	33 (M) 4 (F)
Indonesia	178	1 (M) 0 (F)	174 (M) 3 (F)
Britain	26	0 (M) 1 (F)	8 (M) 17 (F)
Iran	17	2 (M) 1 (F)	13 (M) 1 (F)
India	82	0 (M) 0 (F)	80 (M) 2 (F)

(3) the development of teachers' manuals and guides, such as *Gaikokujin Jido Seito Jisssen*, 1991 (*Foreign Student Case Studies: a teacher's guide*, 1992)

Currently there are 19 elementary and junior high schools designated as immigrant intake schools in the city of Hamamatsu. In 1987, there were none (Maher, 1997; Isaka, 1997).

Korean

The Korean language has been in circulation in Japan for several hundred years, at least from the time when monks, artisans and other immigrants from the south western Korean state of Paekche came to Japan in the 6th century. The presence of a large number of Koreans (about 700,000) in contemporary Japan is the legacy of

Japanese colonialism when Japan annexed Korea in 1910. The main concentrations of Korean speakers are in urban areas such as the Kanto (Tokyo) and Kansai (Osaka) regions. In the Ikuno-ku district (Korea Town) of Osaka, for instance, there are second, third and fourth generation speakers of Korean who use considerable code switching between the Osaka-Korean dialect and Standard Japanese. The younger generation shows a greatly decreased fluency in Korean and, broadly speaking, less enthusiasm for language maintenance. The *Chosen Soren* (an association of North Korean residents in Japan) operates a separate system of schools in which Korean is the language of instruction.

The immediate post-war period saw an explosion in Korean medium schools. However, in December 1945, the Korean community's electoral and political rights as Japanese citizens were suspended. By the end of 1946, there were 525 Korean schools in Japan. In May 1947, they were obliged to register as aliens and a short while later, in January 1948, the Ministry of Education ordered that all Korean children must receive Japanese public education. The route to bicultural/bilingual education was thus effectively closed. By Spring 1946 there were 647,006 Koreans remaining in Japan. Their children, *nisei, sansei* and *yonsei* (second, third and fourth generation), who are still there comprise the largest minority in Japan, approximately 1,000,000 (including those naturalised as Japanese).

Why the crackdown and consistent discouragement by the *Monbusho* (Ministry of Education) on Korean language education? Two reasons. First, the School Education Act of 1947 provided for a compulsory 9 years education, devolving power to local Boards of Education in prefectures and cities. However, the establishment of Korean schools seemed to show too dramatic a shift towards education decentralisation and freedom at a time when recovery of control over the nation by a discredited but still authoritarian Tokyo bureaucracy was a political priority. Second, the Korean minority was long stigmatised as troublemakers. Allegations of Korean resident involvement after the Great Kanto earthquake in 1923 and the return of many communist and radical reform forces to political life in Japan alarmed the government. Together with China's 'loss to Communism' in Mao Tse-tung's civil war of 1946 and the building waves of the cold war convinced the government that the Koreans constituted a 'dangerous presence'. Under American GHQ tutelage, repatriation, closure of schools and fingerprinting for aliens (sic Koreans) was rapidly implemented. The Korean presence in Japan is viewed with bitterness and suspicion and statements such as that encouraging the Korean language in schools, which might at least provide a useful asset by enhancing community relations and children's cultural awareness, are greeted with incredulity by government and educational authorities.

Korean is taught in higher education, but on a much smaller scale than the 'big' languages. Let us turn, then, to the number of universities in Japan offering courses in foreign languages, including Korean. Collating assorted data, the picture in 1996 looked as in Table III.

Whereas the first generation of Koreans (15% of all Korean people in Japan) are Korean speakers, language proficiency among the second, third and emerging fourth generations, having decreasing contact with Korean culture, continues to decline dramatically. Koreans born in Japan are increasing and it will not be long before most Koreans in Japan are Japan born. In an attempt to maintain the Korean language and culture and avoid the historical bias against minorities found in the school curriculum in Japan, the General Association of Korean Residents in Japan

TABLE III. Universities in Japan offering courses in foreign languages, including Korean

Language	Number
English	495
German	471
French	396
Chinese	265
Russian	129
Spanish	111
Korean	54

(*Sooren*) and the Korean Residents Union (*Mindan*) run their own highly developed school systems, including the writing and provision of textbooks on Korean language and history (Table IV). These schools employ a mixed bilingual curriculum in Japanese and Korean. The school system operated by the Association (*Sooren*) ranges from a 4 year university in Tokyo and over 150 primary and secondary schools throughout Japan enrolling approximately 40,000 pupils. The Union (*Mindan*) has less schools (only four) and about 2000 students enrolled at any one time.

In addition to the above configuration of ethnic Korean children in the Korean language system there is also, of course, a very substantial number of Korean children attending regular private or public Japanese schools (Table V).

The desire to maintain the Korean language as a heritage language exists. A survey conducted by Kyoto University of 1600 Korean parents in Osaka found that 44% of parents believed Korean cultural maintenance necessarily involved education in the Korean language and 40% asserted that language implementation depends upon individual wishes. Only 1.8% said that no Korean language education is necessary (RAIK, 1991, p. 21). Kim Tong-hun, Professor of Law at Kyoto Ryukoku University, argues for a formal language curriculum established by the Ministry of Education: 'We were deprived of our language and names while Korea was a colony of Japan. I think ethnic education for Korean children by Japanese authorities would be a first step towards internationalising the country'.

In the Osaka area, as in some other urban areas, there are adult literacy classes, including *yakan gakko* (night classes) for the many older Koreans who have never learned to read and write in Japanese. Classes have also been established at

TABLE IV. Ethnic Korean schools in Japan

School	Mindan	Sooren
Kindergarten (no figures)	2	68
Primary School	3	85
Pupils	577	9809
Junior High	4	56
Pupils	354	5201
High School	4	11
Pupils	646	4552
College	None	1
Pupils	None	1000

TABLE V. Ethnic Korean children in Japanese
education

School level	Number
Nursery	22,858
Pupils	(no figures)
Kindergarten	15,211
Pupils	21,284
Primary School	25,064
Pupils	57,269
Junior High School	11,047
Pupils	38,007
High School	5427
Pupils	35,199
Vocational School	(no figures)
Pupils	157
Junior College	(no figures)
Pupils	1089
College	(no figures)
Pupils	6378
Graduate School	(no figures)
Pupils	314

community centres to teach basic Korean. These classes are attended by younger
Koreans and even by some Japanese.

Conclusion

In 1997, the maintenance of minority languages poses a serious issue for government
policy, which has hitherto been committed to the historical ideology of a monoracial
and monolingual state. Language education policy in Japan is predicated on the
concept of 'internationalisation', but nowhere does internationalisation include
support for regional and community or indigenous languages. In the guiding
document on internationalisation which outlined its long-term educational goals,
the Ministry of Education wrote thus.

(1) To improve the teaching methods used in foreign language classes. The goals of
    foreign language teaching and learning are to provide opportunities to better
    understand the distinctive history, culture and customs of other nations in the
    world.
(2) To promote international exchanges as widely as possible in the fields of
    education, culture and sports.
(3) To promote the exchange of students, with the specific aim of accepting 100,000
    students in Japan by the beginning of the 21st century.
(4) To improve and expound programmes for the teaching of Japanese to foreigners,
    thus responding properly to the growing enthusiasm of foreigners for learning
    Japanese.
(5) To improve educational programmes for Japanese children living abroad and
    for those who have returned home from a long stay overseas, so that these
    children may further develop the merits and knowledge which they acquired
    while living abroad.

The notion of contemporary Japan as essentially 'multicultural' hits a raw nerve and becomes radically controversial when we turn to official descriptions of Japan ranging from Government white papers to approved school textbooks. The idea of a diverse Japan is systematically avoided, above all in the post-war period, by the so-called *Nihonjinron* theories, an ethnocentric body of writing which emphasises the uniqueness of 'being Japanese' (e.g. Doi's *Anatomy of Dependence*, Nakane's *Japanese Society*, Lebra's *Japanese Patterns of Behaviour*). Given the intellectual commitment to the myth of monolingualism and monoculturalism provided by the Meiji restoration of 1870, followed quickly by the imperialist and nationalist ideology of the pre-war era, in the 1990s this should come as no surprise.

There is no acknowledgement by the government of Japan in the 1990s in the public school system that minorities have language rights or that schools might benefit from a mere acknowledgement that minority languages exist. If you are an Ainu or Korean or Chinese child sitting at a desk in a junior high school in Tokyo or Nagoya, then you will likely keep your mouth firmly shut about your ethnic background. Consider, hypothetically, three children. Thirteen-year-old Shigeru cannot speak Ainu at all but has recently become interested in reciting an Ainu *Yukar*, an (orally) transmitted epic poem.Only when he entered secondary school did he find out that his mother was Ainu. Yukiko, a fourth generation Japanese-Korean, does not speak Korean; her parents do not speak much either. Naomi knows no Chinese, has a Chinese father and will admit so only if asked. Their names, of course, will not reveal their mixed background either, because their parents long ago changed the family name to an ordinary Japanese one. (Only in the last decade have the name laws changed to allow a child, in the family register, to bear a name which is not written in Japanese kanji, the Sino-Japanese characters.) Children who are of mixed ethnic or national background, more particularly Eurasian children, even if they are Japanese nationals, are popularly marked out by the term *haafu* (half). Widely used and not necessarily pejorative, the appellation is a reminder that there is one kind of Japanese and an 'other' kind.

To give one example of the latter, in 1986 Prime Minister Nakasone made a speech to the Liberal Democratic Party reminding them of the fact that Japan is a 'racially homogeneous nation' blessed with an absence of minorities and consequently possessing a 'high level of intellectual competence', unlike the United States with its black and other racial minorities. Those minorities, alas, contributed to the debilitation of the intellectual level of that nation. Ainu and other minorities in Japan, angered by this statement, reaffirmed the need to assert their cultural, including linguistic, presence. Widely viewed by the Ainu as a watershed in their post-war history, language revival measures began, including the setting up of Ainu *kyoshitsu* (private language schools or other facilities). I will cite one more example. Kiyoshi Furukawa, Minister for the Hokkaido Development Agency, in a speech in 1989 declared: 'There is no ethnic problem in Japan. It is a unique country in that it is racially homogeneous and that only one language is used for the national broadcasting and all the population of one hundred and thirty million can understand it' (Hokkaido Shinbun, 1989).

Language diversity of any form has not been cultivated in 20th century education in Japan. This ought to be borne in mind when discussing bilingualism in Japan. The sociolinguist Takeshi Shibata (1975) writes:

Over a period of almost 100 years, the Japanese people were told that dialects were bad and ugly and had to be eradicated, that good Japanese citizens should not to use dialects under any circumstances and that the very existence of varying dialects around Japan was a shame to the sovereignty of nation.

The history of minority language education is a tale of conflicts and rebounds against official neglect sometimes and sometimes active harassment. As the term bilingualism comes into currency in educational circles, there are signs everywhere of change towards a more linguistically tolerant society, but peace comes dropping slow.

Correspondence: John Maher, Department of Communications and Linguistics, International Christian University, Osawa 3-10-2, Mitaka, Tokyo 181, Japan.

REFERENCES

AGARI, M., OSHIRO, Y., AGARI, Y., MOTONAGA, M., ISHIKAWA, K. & TAKUMA, T. (1983) Chugakusei no Hogen Seikatsu to Hogen Rikaido, University of the Ryukyus, *Bulletin of the College of Law and Letters*, 26, pp. 46–59.

BERQUE, A. (1995) La Temporalité la ville Japonaise et le depassement de la modernité, in: *La Modernisation et la Post-modernisation japonaises* (Asian Cultural Studies Sepcial Issue, International Christian Univeristy, Vol. 6) pp. 24–36.

CHEW, J.J. (1976) The prehistory of the Japanese language in the light of evidence from the structures of Japanese and Korean, *Asian Perspectives*, 19, pp. 13–49.

HATAKEYAMA, S. (1990) Attitudes toward the Ainu and its language, unpublished Senior Thesis, International Christian University, Tokyo.

HOKKAIDO SHINBUN (1989) Report of a speech by the Development Agency Director. 29 March, p. 5.

HONNA, N. & KATO, M. (1995) The deaf and their language: progress toward equality, in: J.C. MAHER & G. MACDONALD (Eds) *Diversity in Japanese Culture and Language*, pp. 270–284 (London, Kegan Paul International).

ISAKA, A. (1996) Possibilities of bilingual education in Japan as a multilingual society: a solution from the case of a language program in Hamamatsu city, unpublished Senior Thesis, International Christian University, Tokyo.

KAWAMOTO, T. (1982) Toward a comparative Japanese Austronesian IV, *Bulletin of Joetsu University of Education*, 1, pp. 1–33.

MAHER, J. (1985) The role of English as an international language of medicine, *Applied Linguistics*, 5, pp. 18–36.

MAHER, J. (1986) State of the art article: English for medical purposes, *Language Teaching*, 19, pp. 1–37.

MAHER, J. (1989) Doctors who write: language preference in medical communication in Japan, *International Journal of the Sociology of Language*, 52, pp. 230–242.

MAHER, J. (1991a) Hashigaki [Preface], in: J. MAHER & K. YASHIRO (Eds) *Nihon no Biringarizumu*, pp. iv–vii (Tokyo, Kenkyusha).

MAHER, J. (1991b) Ainugo no Fukkatsu (the Ainu language revival), in: J. MAHER & K. YASHIRO (Eds) *Nihon no Biringarizumu*, pp. 149–169 (Tokyo, Kenkyusha).

MAHER, J. (1993) The language situation of Japan, *The Encyclopedia of Language and Linguistics*, 4, pp. 452–453.

MAHER, J. (1994) Shigo to iu Shinwa: Ainugo no Renaissance (The myth of language death: the Ainu language renaissance), in: J. MAHER & N. HONNA (Eds) *Atarashii Nihonkan, Sekaikan ni mukatte: Nihon ni okeru Gengo to Bunka no Tayosei*, pp. 116–131 (Tokyo, Kokusaishoin).

MAHER, J. (1996) North Kyushu creole: a language-contact model for the origins of Japanese, in: D. DENOON, M. HUDSON, G. McCORMACK & T. MORRIS-SUZUKI (Eds) *Multicultural Japan: palaeolithic to postmodern*, pp. 31–45 (Cambridge, Cambridge University Press).

MAHER, J. (1997) Community languages in Japan, in: *Kokuritsu Kokugo Kenkyujo, Proceedings of the Conference on Language Treatment* (Tokyo, Bonjinsha), in press.

MAHER, J. & HONNA, N. (1994a) Atarashii Nihonkan, Sekaikan ni Mukatte: Nihon ni okeru Gengo to Bunka no Tayosei (*Towards a New Order: linguistic and cultural diversity in Japan*) (in Japanese) (Tokyo, Kokusai Shoin).

MAHER, J. & HONNA, N. (1994b) Hajime ni (Preface), in: J. MAHER & N. HONNA (Eds) *Atarashii Nihonkan, Sekaikan ni mukatte: Nihon ni okeru Gengo to Bunka no Tayosei*, pp. 7–15 (Tokyo, Kokusaishoin).

MAHER, J. & MACDONALD, G. (1995) *Diversity in Japanese Culture and Language* (London, Kegan Paul International).

MAHER, J. & YASHIRO, K. (1991) *Nihon no Bairingarizumu (Bilingualism in Japan)* (in Japanese) (Tokyo, Kenkyuusha).

MAHER, J. & YASHIRO, K. (1995a) *Multilingual Japan* (Clevedon, Multilingual Matters).

MAHER, J. & YASHIRO, K. (1995b) Introduction, in: J. MAHER & K. YASHIRO (Eds) *Multilingual Japan*, pp. 1–12 (Clevedon Multilingual Matters).

MATSUMORI, A. (1995) Ryukyuan: past, present and future, in: J. MAHER & K. YASHIRO (Eds) *Multilingual Japan*, pp. 16–32 (Clevedon, Multilingual Matters).

RAIK (1991) *Action for Koreans in Japan: handbook* (Tokyo, Korean Christians in Japan).

SHIBATA, T. (1975) On some problems of Japanese sociolinguistics: reflections and prospect, in: F.C.C. PENG (Ed.) *Language in Japanese Society*, pp. 49–59 (Tokyo, Tokyo University Press).

SIDDLE, R. (1996) *Race, Resistance and the Ainu of Japan* (London, Routledge).

STEELE, M.W. & ARAKI, T. (1995) *La Modernisation et la Post-modernisation Japonaises* (Asian Cultural Studies Special Issue, International Christian University, Vol. 6), pp. 1–6.

YASHIRO, K. (1991) Imin no Bairingarizumu (The bilingualism of immigrants) in: J. MAHER & K. YASHIRO (Eds) *Nihon no Bairingarizumu*, pp. 177–210 (Tokyo, Kenkyusha).

CHAPTER 5

Teacher Education Reform in Japan: Ideological and Control Issues

Nobuo K. Shimahara

Introduction

Traditionally, Japanese society has relied on formal education to develop character, to cultivate moral and cultural sensitivity, and, indeed, to advance industrialization and modernization. The Japanese belief that teachers should inclusively enhance the instrumental, moral, and expressive aspects of their children's formation has become so deeply entrenched in that tradition that it has become a virtual cultural expression—one that has shaped the evolution of teacher education itself. Teachers have been viewed as agents of character development and nation-building from the inception of formal teacher education at the dawn of Japan's modernization in the nineteenth century. Japanese teacher education has been distinctly influenced by the predominant national ideologies of particular times.

The purpose of this chapter is to present a critical analysis of the salient issues of Japanese teacher education. These issues have been shaped in the particular sociocultural and political contexts of the nation. They have been closely connected to and have arisen from larger national education reform agendas. Therefore, those contexts and national reform movements will receive due attention in the chapter. I will first explore briefly the development of teacher education in Japan and then focus on salient reform issues of today in teacher education. This chapter

1980s. Thus, the government took advantage of the public's escalating support for improving teacher quality and the union's declining power and, during the 1980s, made inroads with its proposed reforms (Shimahara, 1992). The JTU's influence was declining fast in the 1980s. For example, while it enrolled more than 86 percent of all public school teachers in 1958, its membership declined to 51 percent in 1981 and 47.5 percent in 1987 (Ministry of Education, 1989). As the size of its membership drastically declined, internal ideological conflicts threatened the union's unity, eventually splitting it into two separate unions: one affiliated with the Socialist party and the latter with the Communist party.

Internship and Reform in Teacher Certification

Among the recommendations made by the NCER, legislative attention concentrated on internship and reforms of the certification system. Subsequently, following the NCER's recommendations, the Teacher Education Council (1987) drafted detailed reports for legislative consideration concerning internship and certification. The national legislature took legislative action on the two recommendations in 1988, and funding for internship was approved. The enactment of the two bills unambiguously marked the Ministry of Education's victory after nearly three decades of repeated attempts to implement internship and upgrade certification requirements. Suffice it to point out that internship was part of the conservative government's coveted reform agenda, which finally gained the political support needed for implementation. For the JTU, the passage of the bills meant an immense setback.

In anticipation of legislative approval of the internship bill, the Ministry of Education had already started internships in selected school districts throughout the nation, with funding of over $50 million in 1987 and 1988. The purpose of this trial program was to experiment with the model of internship that it developed. This was a carefully orchestrated attempt to promote the success of internship.

In 1989, the mandatory internship program began across the nation, enrolling all beginning public school elementary teachers. In the first year, the funding from the central government reached approximately $200 million. Beginning lower and upper secondary public school teachers started to participate in the program the following year. Internship is a year-long program designed to develop what is identified as teachers' practical competence, *shishitsu*, as referred to earlier. It is a Japanese concept connoting a broad gamut of skills, knowledge, and orientation to handle classroom management, teaching, lesson plans, student guidance, moral education, extracurricular activities, home relations, and teacher committee work (Shimahara and Sakai, 1992b).

The internship program emphasizes the development of a sense of mission, referring to an awareness of purpose in teaching and a broad social and cultural perspective. The program is organized by each prefectural board of education, based on the model suggested by the Ministry of Education and locally created plans. A full-time supervisor is appointed by a local superintendent of schools from among experienced teachers to provide mentoring for beginners, if there are more than one, in a given school. Where there is only one beginner in a school, a part-time supervisor is appointed. In essence, the program consists of three components: in-house, in-service education under the supervision of the mentor, to which about ten hours are devoted a week; a program of about twenty lectures and workshops developed by each local education center; and retreats and summer workshops that total about ten days (Maki, 1993; Shimahara and Sakai, 1992).

What is described here is a skeletal view of internship. Implementation of internship varies considerably depending upon the local cultures of teachers, needs, and resources (Maki, 1993; Shimahara and Sakai, 1992). Ironically, the Ministry of Education has little control over how internship is implemented. In contrast, classroom teachers, who had little influence when internship was legislated, have the capability to control its implementation. Thus, effective implementation of internship by the board of education requires the active participation of mentors and the cooperation of classroom teachers who influence the occupational socialization of beginning teachers, as well as the commitment of school administrators. As David

Hargreaves (1980) aptly points out, reforms must pass through "the teachers' culture as a medium," but they are frequently shaped and transformed in that passage.

Having lost its influence on education policy, the JTU (Socialist-party-affiliated union) has recently become more conciliatory. Given the fact that internship is under way, it has dropped its outright opposition to it and now demands that beginning teachers be mentored by a group of their experienced colleagues, rather than supervisors appointed by the superintendent of schools (Nishizawa, 1992). This represents a significant shift in the union's policy. Incidentally, it should also be noted that supervisors for interns have included union members since the beginning, and the Ministry of Education has not objected.

With respect to the certification system, reformers introduced some significant changes in the preparation of teachers. To improve that preparation, reformers initiated advanced certification and higher requirements for teaching. Japan finally began to place more emphasis on graduate preparation of teachers. Consequently, the numbers of universities and colleges that offer master's programs for teachers have rapidly increased over the past several years. Master's degree holders are now eligible for specialist certification, a newly created category of certification. In 1985, when the latest reform deliberations began, only 3.3 percent of the nation's teachers had master's degrees. Now, Japan has more than forty-three institutions that provide master's-level preparation for full-time teachers, in contrast to the three that existed in 1985 (Ministry of Education, 1992. At last Japan's commitment to graduate education for teachers is contributing significantly to the profession.

Another important change in the certification system is a significant increase in required professional studies for all types of certification, with emphasis on student guidance, management, information technology, and student teaching. Requirements for clinical experience, however, increased only minimally from four to five credits and two to three credits for elementary and secondary teachers, respectively. Additional clinical experience is expected to be provided during the internship year. A final note on the reformed certification system concerns the establishment of *special* certification that enables talented men and women trained outside education to become eligible for teaching through examinations administered by each prefectural board of education. This system broadens the pool of teacher applicants with unique talents.

Teacher Education and Issues of Control

Issues in In-service Education

In the preceding sections, I discussed issues critical to teacher education in postwar Japan. My analysis reveals that teacher education has been subject to a considerable degree of control by the government. The cultural rationale for the state's interest in teacher education is grounded in the Japanese belief that teachers are responsible for nation-building and developing students' character, morality, and cultural sensitivity. Control of education, however, is fundamentally a political issue. Thus, the first fifteen postwar years were a period during which the government and the JTU and its political and educational allies launched a series of political confrontations to gain control over education. The government's control of teacher education, however, started slowly around 1960. The preceding sections elucidate how the government attained control in the succeeding three decades.

In this last section, I will discuss issues involved in in-service education, teacher networks, and the future of teaching in Japan. In-service education for teachers in its broad sense is extensively developed in Japan. The government offers a variety of in-service education programs at its national in-service education centers and prefectural and municipal education centers located throughout the nation (Shimahara, 1991). The government programs enroll public school teachers at various career stages: beginning year, five year, ten year, administrative level, and so on. The programs require targeted teachers to participate in in-service education from three to ten days a year

(Shimahara, 1991). As referred to earlier, the government also established three national universities of teacher education to offer advanced studies to full-time teachers on leave from their schools. In addition, following the Ministry of Education's policy, local boards of education encourage schools to organize in-house in-service education programs. The government's in-service education began in 1960 and had developed extensively by 1980, as prefectural and municipal education centers' participation in in-service education was enhanced (Miyatani, 1979). It is now extended to a one-year mandatory internship program for all beginning teachers in public schools.

Critics of government-sponsored in-service education have raised a crucial political question regarding its purpose: What end does it serve? For example, Teruhisa Horio (1988), a former intellectual spokesperson for the JTU and a former professor of education at the University of Tokyo who represents such critics, criticized government-led in-service education as early as 1971:

> [Government-sponsored in-service training] threatens to make our teachers' desires for personal advancement directly dependent upon the power of a centralized system of administrative control. Thus, to realize their desire for higher positions within the organization of the school, teachers will increasingly have to perform successfully within government-sponsored programs of in-service training (*kenshu*). Moreover, as only those teachers who have already been deemed ideologically deserving of such training will be given the opportunity to participate in the necessary in-service programs [organized at the national level], the organization of elites within the school system will increasingly come under the direct control of the Ministry of Education. (p. 247)

Horio interprets government-sponsored in-service education as a measure of ideological control of teachers by the government. Therefore it, in his view, goes counter to Article X of the Fundamental Law of Education which states: "Education shall not be subject to improper control, but it shall be directly responsible to the whole people." He insists that the autonomy of teachers guaranteed by the Fundamental Law of Education should be recognized and that teachers' right to organize their in-service education is inherent in the concept of teacher autonomy.

The Study Commission on Teacher Education, of the Japan Pedagogical Association (1982), addressed the same issues: the decline of autonomy and the academic freedom of classroom teachers. It expressed a concern that government-sponsored in-service education ignores teachers' autonomy and imposes greater regulations and uniformity upon classroom teachers. In short, the critics' chief concern is government control of teachers and teacher education.

The strongest political opposition to internship came from the JTU, whose ideological leadership still resided in members affiliated with either the Socialists or Communists. As pointed out earlier, the union, which consistently opposed the Ministry of Education throughout the postwar period, has unswervingly rejected teacher internship. The union regards government-initiated internship as a program for training teachers to fit stereotypical official expectations (Miwa, 1988). For the union, internship is nothing but a managerial tactic designed to weaken union opposition to government control of teacher education (Horio, 1988; Miwa, 1988). When the proposal for the current internship was being debated, the union argued: "The government's policy to mold teachers into a uniform type represents illegitimate control over teacher education and fails to develop their competence" (Japan Teachers Union, 1986).

Teacher Networks

As an alternative to government-sponsored in-service education, Japanese teachers have developed numerous self-initiated, voluntary associations and circles to promote teaching. Otsuki (1982) surveyed forty-seven such teacher networks developed since 1948, most of which are currently active. These associations collaborate with the Japan Teachers Union, but do not participate in union activities. They are independent networks committed to a shared purpose: promoting teaching, independent of government control, and a democratic education (Fujioka, 1992; Otsuki, 1982). They are entirely independent from the government and critical of government-controlled education, including in-service education. The Coordinating Council for Voluntary Educational Study Associations was established in 1959 to enhance communication and cooperation among independent networks across the nation. This council also has a branch in each prefecture that coordinates local activities (Otsuki, 1982). These associations were formed in response to teachers' particular concerns and interests that grew in the course of Japan's postwar educational development, and they focus on specific subject areas or other shared interests of teachers. These networks regularly hold conferences and workshops and publish magazines sold at commercial bookstores to disseminate information about their activities. For example, they hold nearly 200 summer workshops, suggesting very impressive participation in self-initiated study activities (Sato, 1992).

At least seventeen teacher networks were formed in response to the climactic 1950s, when the reversal of postwar education reforms occurred. An additional sixteen networks were organized in the 1960s, a decade that created the firm foundations of Japanese education in a postwar era geared to economic growth and industrial expansion. And several new networks developed in each of the succeeding decades. Some of the network activities have had an impressive, lasting impact on the development of Japanese education. For example, such early associations as the Council of History Educators, the Association of Mathematics Education, and the Japan Journal Circle have been exceptionally influential, reaching out to teachers at the grass-roots level (Otsuki, 1982; Fujioka, 1992). A recent, far-reaching network is a considerably popular, loosely knit association of teachers initiated in 1984 by Yoichi Mukoyama, an elementary school teacher. The network is promoting "the national movement to advance the science of teaching," the goal of which is to discover cause and effect relationships in teaching and to generalize these relationships for application (Mukoyama, 1985). Unlike many other teacher associations, this network does not collaborate with the JTU.

In addition, the JTU holds an annual study conference that attracts more participants than do any other educational organizations in Japan. At the local, municipal level, teachers also have many voluntary circles to promote teaching. Moreover, almost every school has an in-house study group that organizes study activities, such as curriculum development, demonstration classes, observation and discussion of teaching, etc. (Shimahara, 1991).

In summary, self-initiated in-service education in Japan is extensive and impressive both nationally and locally. As reported by Sato (1992), a survey of 3,987 teachers in 1981 indicated that more than half of them had been active in some voluntary study groups. Self-initiated in-service education is not financed by national and prefectural governments, but teacher networks constitute substantial support in teachers' commitment to enhancing teaching.

Can Japan strike a balance between government control and teacher initiative? Can such a thing be accomplished in a country where the government inherited the 125-year-old Meiji legacy of shaping teacher education and the national curriculum? The postwar history of Japanese education suggests that it is extremely difficult, if not impossible, to achieve the balance. Teacher initiatives grew rapidly in two different decades. The 1920s gave momentum to very promising teacher initiatives, but they were suppressed under the rise of militarism (Sato, 1992). Likewise, teachers enjoyed a considerable degree of autonomy for nearly a decade from the late 1940s to 1958, during which period many teacher networks were created. Ironically, this was the same period when the postwar reforms were being reversed. The development of teacher networks and other voluntary study circles in Japan is very impressive in spite of the government's control of teachers through legislation, and it suggests Japanese teachers' resilience and tenacious commitment to teaching independent of government support. This development offers evidence that teachers can enhance their autonomy to some degree through their own networks. The history of teaching in postwar Japan suggests that the government does not interfere with teacher networks as long as they do not pose a political threat.

In teaching, as in other professions, there are two spheres of practice whose interactions influence each other. One is the officially sanctioned sphere represented by the national curriculum, teacher education, official in-service education, regulations regarding teaching, etc. The other is the unofficial sphere, where teachers exercise an appreciable degree of independence and freedom, which forms the culture of teaching. The culture of teaching marks the typification of teacher behavior and attitudes: shared interests, commitments, and strategies to cope with external pressures. Teacher networks are part and parcel of the culture of Japanese teachers.

To promote teacher networks, teachers need much greater collaboration than they now have with university professors and researchers. Such collaborations were evident in some of the networks discussed here (Otsuki, 1982) and are recently reported (for example, Sato, 1991), but they are severely limited. Generally, collaboration between teachers and university researchers, and between schools and universities, has been markedly lacking (Shimahara, 1991). This calls for members of the academic community to participate actively in enhancing teachers' self-initiated study activities.

Meanwhile, teachers will have to redefine themselves if they are to acquire professionalism. The JTU defined teachers as "workers" or "proletarians" vis-à-vis the government that employs them and sought to win higher salaries and ideological battles against the conservative government. It is obvious that the union has devoted little energy toward achieving professional status for teachers. I would be remiss, however, if I overlooked the fact that the government has consistently viewed teachers as servants of the state, not as professionals, and that its policy was in significant measure designed to win control over education from the JTU. Consequently, the government has contributed little to the development of teaching as a profession.

Over the past decade, Japanese teachers have been considerably less ideologically bent in response to Japan's economic affluence. That led to the decline of the JTU's membership, and, reflecting the nation's conservative trend, the JTU split into a right-wing and a left-wing union. The JTU represents the right-wing union, which is much larger and by far more influential than the left-wing union. As pointed out earlier, the JTU is now much less militant against the Ministry of Education than in the past. The government, on the other hand, has achieved its anti-union agenda and is no longer confronted by a powerful, militant union. One may speculate if the opportunity exists for both education authorities—Ministry of Education and prefectural boards of education—and teachers to seek a common agenda for promoting teaching as a profession. To reinforce this suggestion, the reader should remember that the first division of the National Council on Education Reform, Education for the 21st Century, initially demanded considerable reduction of the Ministry of Education's authority to regulate public primary and secondary schools in favor of market regulation of schooling (Gyosei, 1985; Schoppa, 1992). That demand was withdrawn in response to the protests of another division of the NCER and bureaucrats of the Ministry of Education.

A Final Word

Japan has regarded formal education as the state's responsibility since 1872, when its first education system was laid out. Likewise, the fledgling state viewed teacher education as its obligation, based on its assertion that teachers were agents of national development and students' development of character, morality, and cultural sensitivity. Japan developed a uniform and efficient school system that immensely contributed to the effective mobilization of its human resources for the development of its industry. Teacher education, especially, was rigidly controlled by the state.

This legacy remains influential and is reinforced by the national creed of enlightenment from above. Postwar legislative initiatives by the government to restore its control of teacher education in the 1950s is testimony to this legacy. But since 1945, teachers have not acquiesced in government policy. Since 1947, the Japan Teachers Union, whose leadership took a left-wing ideological position, was powerful and posed a serious political threat to the government in the 1950s and 1960s. This *in part* prompted the government to take a series of reactionary measures. Indeed, the postwar history of Japanese education can be meaningfully interpreted as a history of struggles between the government and the JTU.

Through education reforms in the 1980s, the government attained more control of teacher education than ever before in the postwar period. Meanwhile, teachers' union membership and ideological intensity measurably declined over the past decade. The left-wing teachers union today can exercise only minor influence over education and the government's policy. There is evidence that relationships between the JTU and the government are beginning to change, at least slightly.

But will the Ministry of Education remain rigid and bureaucratic in the future? Education reforms in the 1980s strove to make the Ministry of Education more sensitive to diversity and to enhance local control. Whether or not the Ministry of Education and university professors are capable of lending support to greater teacher initiatives is a challenging question for Japanese teachers.

REFERENCES

Advisory Council on Culture and Education. 1984. "Report on culture and education" (Bunka to kyoiku ni kansuru kondankai hokoku). In *Education of Japan: Historical Materials* (Nihon no Kyoiku: Shiryo), Osamu Kanda and Masami Yamazumi, eds., pp. 365–371. Tokyo: Gakuyoshobo.

Aso, Makoto and Ikuo Amano. 1983. *Education and Japan's Modernization.* Tokyo: Japan Times.

Beauchamp, Edward. 1987. "The Development of Japanese Educational Policy, 1945–1985." *History of Education Quarterly* 27:302–5.

Central Council of Education. 1958. "Policy for Improving the Teacher Education System" (Kyoin yoseiseido kaizen hosaku ni tsuite). In *Central Council of Education and Education Reform* (Chukyoshin to Kyoiku Kaikaku), Yokohama National Institute for Modern Education (1983), ed., pp. 49–55. Tokyo: Sanichi Shobo.

Central Council of Education. 1971. "Recommendations for Comprehensive Reforms of School Education" (Kongoni okeru gakko kyoiku no sogoteki na kakuju seibi no tameno kihonteki shisaku ni tsuite). In *Central Council of Education and Education Reform* (Chukyoshin to Kyoiku Kaikaku), Yokohama National Institute for Modern Education (1983), pp. 125–187. Tokyo: Sanichi Shobo.

Central Council of Education. 1978. "Recommendations for Improving Teachers' Quality and Competence (Kyoin no shishitsu noryoku no kojo ni tsuite). In *Education of Japan: Historical Materials* (Nihon no Kyoiku: Shiryo), ed. Osamu Kanda and Masami Yamazumi, pp. 329–330. Tokyo: Gakuyoshobo.

Central Council of Education. 1983. *Interim Report on Educational Contents* (Kyoiku naiyo no shoiinkai shingi keika hokoku), November 15.

Fujioka, Nobukatsu. 1992, March. "Self-initiated In-service Teacher Education in Japan." Paper presented at the Comparative and International Education Meetings, Annapolis.

Gyosei. 1985. *The Educational Council of Education and Educational Reforms* (Rinkyoshin to Kyoiku Kaikaku). Vol. 1. Tokyo: Ggosei.

Hall, Ivan. 1973. *Mori Arinori.* Cambridge, MA: Harvard University Press.

Hargreaves, David. 1980. "The Occupational Culture of Teachers. In *Teachers Strategies,* ed. Peter Woods. London: Croom Helm.

Hirahara, Haruyoshi. 1975a. "San Francisco Peace Treaty and Reorganization of Education" (Sanhuranshisuko taisei no seiritsu to kyoikuno saihen). In *Postwar History of Japanese Education* (Sengo Nihon Kyoiku Shi), ed. Kaoru Ohta, pp. 191–226. Tokyo: Iwanami.

Hirahara, Haruyoshi. 1975b. "Reorganization of Educational Administration" (Kyoiku gyosei no saihensei). In *Postwar History of Japanese Education* (Sengo Nihon Kyoiku Shi), ed. Kaoru Ohta, pp. 250–268. Tokyo: Iwanami.

Horio, Teruhisa. 1988. *Educational Thought and Ideology in Modern Japan: State Authority and Intellectual Freedom.* Tokyo: University of Tokyo Press.

Japan Pedagogical Association, The Study Commission on Teacher Education. 1982. *A Study Concerning Practical Strategies to Improve Teacher Education* (Kyoshi kyoiku no kaizen ni kansuru jissenteki shohosaku ni tsuite). Vol. 4.

Japan Teachers Union Second Council on Educational Reform. 1983. *Education Reform in Modern Japan*. Tokyo: Japan Teachers Union.

Japan Teachers Union Education Reform Committee. 1986. "Our Proposal to Reform Education—How to Change Japanese Education." In *The National Council on Educational Reform and Educational Reform*, Vol. 3, ed. Gyosei. Tokyo: Gyosei.

Japan Teachers Union. 1989. *The Forty-Year History of the Japan Teachers Union* (Nikkyoso Yonjunen Shi). Tokyo: Rodo Kyoiku Senta.

Kaigo, Tokiomi. (ed.). 1975. *Education Reforms: Postwar Japanese Education Reforms I* (Kyoiku no Kaikaku: Sengo Nihon no Kyoiku Kaikaku I). Tokyo: University of Tokyo Press.

Keizai Doyukai. 1984, July. *In Pursuit of Creativity, Diversity, and Internationalization* (Sozosei, tayosei, kokusaisei o motomeru). Tokyo: Keizai Doyukai.

Kinoshita, S. 1983. "The Postwar Curriculum" (Sengo no kyoiku katei). In *The Encyclopedia of Curriculum* (Kyoiku katei jiten), ed. Morihiko Okazu, pp. 25–36. Tokyo: Shogakukan.

Kiyose, Ichiro 1956. "Rationale for Proposing Legislation for the Organization and Conduct of Local Educational Administration" (Chiho kyoiku gyosei no soshiki oyobi unei ni kansuru horitsu teian riyu). In *Education of Japan: Historical Materials* (Nihon no Kyoiku: Shiryo), ed. Osamu Kanda and Masami Yamazumi (1985), pp. 297–299. Tokyo: Gakuyoshobo.

Kyoto Seminar to Consider Global Issues. 1983. "Seven-point Recommendations to Vitalize School Education" (Gakko kyoiku kasseika no tameno nanatsuno teigen). In *Education of Japan: Historical Materials* (Nihon no Kyoiku: Shiryo), ed. Osamu Kanda and Masami Yamazumi (1985), pp. 364–365. Tokyo: Gakuyoshobo.

Liberal Democratic Party Education Research Council (1972) "Fundamental Reform on Teacher Education and Re-education as well as Teacher Status and Compensation" (Kyoin no yosei saikyoiku narabini mibun taigu no kihonteki kaizen ni tsuite). In *Education of Japan: Historical Materials* (Nihon no Kyoiku: Shiryo), ed. Osamu Kanda and Masami Yamazumi (1985), pp. 162–164. Tokyo: Gakuyoshobo.

Maki, Masami. 1993. *Development of Effective Internship Programs (Kokateki na Shoninsha Kenshu Puroguramu no Kenkyu Kaihatsu)*. Tokyo: Kokuritsu Kenkyusho.

Migishima, Yosuke and Makoto Shirai. 1984. "Policy on Teacher Education and its Critique" (Kyoin yosei seisaku to sono hihan). In *Teacher Education: Problems and Perspectives* (Kyoshi kyoiku: kadai to tenbo), ed. Yosuke Migishima and Shinichi Suzuki, pp. 53–112. Tokyo: Keiso Shobo.

Ministry of Education. (Japan). 1980. *Japan's Modern Educational System: A History of the First One Hundred Years.* Tokyo: Mombusho.

Ministry of Education (Japan). 1989. *Education in Japan.* Tokyo: Mombusho.

Ministry of Education (Japan). 1992. *The Basic Survey Report on Schools: Institutions of Higher Education* (Gakko Kihon Chosa Hokokusho: Koto Kyoiku Kikan). Tokyo: Mombusho.

Ministry of International Trade and Industry, Council on Industrial Structure. 1980, July. *Industrial and trade policy for the 1980s* (1980-nendai no tsusho sangyo seisaku). Tokyo: Tsusansho.

Miwa, Sadanobu. 1988. "The Problematic Internship Program." *Educational Law* 75: 11–16.

Miyatani, Ken. 1979. "Inservice Education: (Genshoku kyoiku). In *History of Schools: History of Teacher Education* (Gakko no Rekishi: Kyoin Yosei no Rekishi), ed. Tsutomu Shinoda and Takehiko Tezuka, pp. 242–252. Tokyo: Daiichi Hoki.

Mukoyama, Yoichi. 1985. *The Law to Improve Teaching* (Jugyo no Ude o Ageru Hosoku). Tokyo: Meiji Tosho.

Nakasone, Yasuhiro. 1984.) "Seven-Point Proposal for Education Reform," as quoted in Leonard Schoppa (1991), *Education Reform in Japan,* pp. 214–215. London: Routledge.

National Council on Educational Reform (NCER). 1986. "The Outline of the Deliberation Process." In *The National Council on Educational Reform and Educational Reforms* (Rinkyoshin to Kyoikukaikaku), ed. Gyosei, pp. 231– 376. Vol.3. Tokyo: Gyosei.

National Council on Educational Reform (NCER). 1988. *Recommendations for Education Reforms* (Kyoiku Kaikaku ni Kansuru Toshin). Tokyo: Okurasho Insatsukyoku.

Nishizawa, Kiyoshi. 1992. Interview with Nishizawa, Vice Chairman of the Japan Teachers Union, July 25.

Ohta, Kaoru. 1985. "Criticize the Reforms by the National Council on Educational Reform, An Interview." In *All About the National Council on Educational Reform* (Rinkyoshin no Subete), ed. Aideru, pp. 36–47. Tokyo: Aideru Publications.

Otsuki, Takeshi. 1982. T*he History of Postwar Voluntary Education Movement (Sengo Minkan Kyoiku Undoshi).* Tokyo: Ayumi Shuppan.

Rohlen, Thomas P. 1983. *Japan's High Schools.* Stanford: Stanford University Press.

Sato, Hideo. 1974. "Normal School Order and the Establishment of Teacher Training Policy" (Kyoin seisaku no tenkan to kyoin yosei seido). In *Japanese Modern Education: A History of the First Hundred Years* (Nippon kindai kyoiku hyakunen shi), ed. Kokuritsu Kyoiku Kenkyusho *(pp. 1281–1295),* Vol. 3. Tokyo: Kokuritsu Kyoiku Kenkyusho.

Sato, Manabu. 1991, July. "Case Method in Japanese Teacher Education: Traditions and Our Experiments." A paper presented at the 4th annual meeting of Japan/US Teacher Education Consortium, Stanford University, Stanford, CA.

Sato, Manabu. 1992. "Japan." In *Issues and Problems in Teacher Education: An International Handbook*, ed. Howard B. Leavitt. Westport, CT: Greenwood Press.

Schoppa, Leonard. 1991. *Education Reform in Japan: A Case of Immobilist Politics.* London: Routledge.

Shimahara, Nobuo. 1979. *Adaptation and Education in Japan.* New York: Praeger.

Shimahara, Nobuo. 1986. "Japanese Education Reforms in the 1980s." *Issues in Education,* 4(2), 85–100.

Shimahara, Nobuo. 1991. "Teacher Education in Japan." In *Windows on Japanese Education,* ed. Edward Beauchamp, pp. 259–280. Westport, CT: Greenwood Press.

Shimahara, Nobuo. 1992a. Overview of Japanese Education: Policy, Structure, and Current issues." In *Japanese Educational Productivity,* ed. Robert Leestma and Herbert J. Walberg, pp. 7–33. Ann Arbor: Center for Japanese Studies, the University of Michigan.

Shimahara, Nobuo and Akira Sakai, 1992b. "Teacher Internship and the Culture of Teaching in Japan." *British Journal of Sociology of Education* 12(2): 147–162.

Shinoda, Hiroshi. 1979a. "Training of Elementary School Teachers" (Shoto kyoin no yosei). In *History of Schools* (Gakko no rekishi), ed. Hiroshi Shinoda and Takehiko Tezuka, pp. 13–98. Tokyo: Daiichi Hoki.

Shinoda, Hiroshi. 1979b. "Teacher Certification Law and Teacher Education" (Kyoiku shokuin menkyoho to kyoin yosei). In *History of Schools* (Gakko no rekishi), ed. Hiroshi Shinoda and Takehiko Tezuka, pp. 193–202. Tokyo: Daiichi Hoki.

Teacher Education Council. 1983. "Recommendations to Improve Teacher Education and the Certification System" (Kyoin no yosei oyobi menkyoseido no kaizen ni tsuite). In *Education of Japan: Historical Materials* (Nihon no Kyoiku: Shiryo), ed. Osamu Kanda and Masaki Sumiyama, pp. 372–375. Tokyo: Gakuyoshobo.

Teacher Education Council. 1987. "Policy for Improving Teacher Quality and Competence" (Kyoin no shishitsu noryoku no kojo hosaku nitsuite), No. 1 and 2. In *Motonori Tsuchiya* (1988), "How Do Teacher Certification and In-service Education Change" (Kyoshi no Menkyo to Kenshu ha Dou Kawaru), pp. 58– 109 and 130–145. Tokyo: Rodojunposha.

Tsuchiya, Motonori. 1984. *Postwar Education and Teacher Training* (Sengo kyoiku to kyoin yosei). Shin Nippon Shinsho.

United States Mission on Education to Japan. 1946. "Report of the United States Education Mission to Japan." In *Society and Education in Japan*, ed. Herbert Passin (1965), pp. 278–284. New York: Teachers College Press.

Yamada, Noboru. 1979. "Universities and Faculties for Teacher Education" (Kyoin yosei no daigaku/gakubu). In *History of Schools: History of Teacher Education* (Gakko no Rekishi: Kyoin Yosei no Rekishi), ed. Hiromu Shinoda and Takehiko Tezuka, pp. 203–241. Tokyo: Daiichi Hoki.

Yamaguchi, H. 1980. "Modern Problems of the Curriculum" (Kyoiku katei no gendaiteki kadai). In (*School and Curriculum* (Gakko to Kyoiku Katei, ed. S. Sato and H. Inadapp, pp. 46–52. Tokyo: Daiichi Hoki.

Yokohama National University Institute for Modern Education. 1983. *Central Council of Education and Educational Reform* (Chukyoshin to Kyoiku Kaikaku). Tokyo: Sanichi Shobo.

JAPAN'S *JUKEN* INDUSTRY

 Tuvia Blumenthal

"No single event, with the possible exception of marriage, determines the course of a young [person's] life as much as entrance examinations, and nothing, including marriage, requires as many years of planning and hard work."[1] Although written more than a quarter of a century ago, this quote seems to be even more relevant for present-day Japan. While acceptance to a university is an important event in the life of any individual in every country and is very much the concern of candidates and their close relatives, in Japan it is of wide social interest. Pictures of successful students, overcome with joy, appear on the front pages of newspapers and weeklies; correct answers to tests are published and eagerly read; and high schools are ranked according to the number of graduates they manage to send to top universities. Because large companies recruit their new workers from these prestigious universities and their policy, in turn, is to accept students through entrance examinations, Japan's formal school system has become insufficient—and the *juken*—examination preparation—industry has emerged. While cram schools exist in other countries, they do not have the same magnitude and importance as they do in Japanese society, where they affect the great majority of households. The role of the industry in the Japanese educational system, its major characteristics of development during recent years, and its affect on the well-being of Japanese families are some of the questions tackled in this article.

Scope and Development

The *juken* industry in Japan comprises three elements: *juku*, *yobiko*, and private teachers. The term *juku* was used during the Edo period to denote small schools founded by individual scholars or educators specifically for

————————— Tuvia Blumenthal is Professor of Economics, Monaster Center, Ben-Gurion University, Beer-Sheva, Israel.

1. Ezra F. Vogel, *Japan's New Middle Class* (Berkeley, Calif.: University of California Press, 1963).

teaching martial arts, special skills, or the doctrines of particular philosophical schools. Since the early Meiji period, after the implementation of universal elementary education, *juku* came to mean privately run tutoring establishments, often specializing in a particular subject such as English, the abacus, or piano, as opposed to ordinary public or private schools. *Juku* are divided into two types: *keikogoto*—those teaching subjects outside the school curriculum—and *gakushujuku*—those used for cramming subjects taught in school, mainly the Japanese language, mathematics, English, and natural and social sciences. In this study we are concerned only with the latter type, namely, cram schools that repeat or extend material learned in regular schools.

Juku can be divided into several categories: (1) *shingaku juku*, which help children to pass entrance examinations for higher levels of schooling; (2) *hoshu juku*, which help children to improve their achievements in school; and (3) *sogo juku*, which offer classes for both types of children.

Yobiko are preparatory schools for university entrance examinations. Most of their students are "ronin," those who failed in their attempt to enter into their preferred university and are preparing for next year's exams. Some of these students are senior-level high school pupils. In general, the children in *juku* are elementary and junior high school students, while those in *yobiko* are high school pupils or *ronin*. In practice, the distinction is not so clear: some *yobiko* have classes for junior high school pupils, while some *juku* also cater to senior high school students. The distinction is also not always reflected in the name of the institution: one of the largest chain *yobiko* in Japan is called *Kawaii Juku* (darling or cute *juku*).

Another distinction between *juku* and *yobiko* is in their legal status. *Yobiko* are considered to be schools (*gakko hojin*) and are under the supervision of municipal boards of education. This supervision is mainly concerned with physical conditions but not curricula or teachers' salaries. *Juku*, on the other hand, are not considered to be schools by the Ministry of Education and are privately owned or incorporated. There is no need to get a license either to open or teach in a *juku*.

One source of data on *juku* development over time can be found in two surveys conducted by the Ministry of Education in 1976 and 1985. A comparison of the results of the two surveys shows how this industry, starting from a limited number of *juku* in large cities, is growing, becoming more organized, and penetrating into remote areas of rural Japan. At the same time, as the number of students increases, the financial power of the industry also grows, and it is becoming a multibillion yen industry. In 1976 the total number of children going to *juku* was 3.1 million, i.e., 20.2% of elementary and junior high school pupils (see Table 1). In 1985

TABLE 1 *Juku Attendance by School Level and Sex, 1976 and 1985* (in percent)

		(Total)	Elementary School							Junior High School			
				Grade Level							Grade Level		
			(Total)	1	2	3	4	5	6	(Total)	1	2	3
	1976	(20.2)	(12.0)	3.3	4.8	7.5	11.9	19.4	26.6	(38.0)	37.9	38.7	37.4
	1985	(26.3)	(16.5)	6.2	10.1	12.9	15.4	21.1	29.6	(44.5)	41.8	44.5	47.3
boys	1976	(21.8)	(13.3)	4.4	5.2	7.8	13.3	21.4	28.8	(40.6)	40.2	42.2	39.4
	1985	(27.6)	(17.7)	7.4	11.5	14.3	16.8	22.6	30.6	(45.9)	44.2	45.3	48.1
girls	1976	(18.4)	(10.8)	2.1	4.4	7.2	10.6	17.2	24.3	(35.2)	35.5	34.9	35.3
	1985	(24.9)	(15.1)	5.0	8.7	11.5	13.9	19.6	28.6	(43.0)	39.1	43.6	46.4

SOURCE: Ministry of Education, *Jido Seito no Gakkogai Gakushu Katsudo ni Kansuru Jittai Chosa* (Survey of out-of-school activities of children), 1985, p. 6.

the number went up to 4.5 million children, 26.3% of the elementary and junior high school population. In both years the number of boys was somewhat greater than that of girls. For example, in 1985, 27.6% of the boys and 24.9% of the girls went to *juku*. *Juku* attendance goes up with grade level. In 1985 only 6.2% of first-grade pupils went to *juku*, but the share went up to 29.6% in sixth grade and 47.3% in the third year of junior high. Altogether 16.5% of elementary school pupils and 44.5% of junior high pupils went to *juku*.

Juku attendance also goes up with the increase in city size (see Table 2): the percentage for 1985 was 12.3 for villages of less than 8,000 people but 29.9% for towns of more than 100,000 people. Between 1976 and 1985 there was an increase in attendance in all town and village sizes, but the increase was especially dramatic in the small-size population centers. For example, while the percentage of *juku* attendance went up from 44.5% to 48.6% for third-year junior high school pupils in towns of more than 100,000, it went up from 11.8% to 22.8% for pupils of the same school in villages of less than 8,000. The average number of children per *juku* was 136.7 and 125.3 in 1976 and 1985, respectively. Dividing the number of children attending *juku* in these two years by these numbers, we get an estimated total number of *juku*, namely, 22,900 and 35,900 for 1976 and 1985, respectively.

Turning to the composition of *juku* teachers, we find that there has been a large reduction in the number of those with previous teaching experience, and in 1985 almost half of *juku* teachers had no previous experience

TABLE 2 *Juku Attendance by City Size and School Level, 1976 and 1985*
(in percent)

City Size	Total		Elementary School		Junior High School	
	1976	1985	1976	1985	1976	1985
Total	20.2	26.3	12.0	16.5	38.0	44.5
Over 100,000	23.4	29.9	14.4	19.5	44.5	48.6
30,000 to 100,000	19.7	25.7	11.3	14.9	38.1	46.0
8,000 to 30,000	15.1	18.3	8.0	10.6	28.6	33.3
less than 8,000	6.4	12.3	3.2	6.8	11.8	22.8

SOURCE: Same as Table 1.

in teaching. There was a reduction in the share of students (including graduate students) from 32.9% to 29.2%, a sharp reduction in regular school teachers from 17.2% to 4.7% and of other teachers with previous teaching (from 27.3% to 18.2%). Other teachers without teaching experience grew from 22.5% to 47.9%. This shows that a separate occupation of *juku* teaching is emerging.

The Effect of Tuition Fees on Family Budgets

When looking at the effect of *juku* expenditure on the family budget, we have to distinguish between the average expenditure of all families, including families who have children going to *juku* and those who do not; the expenditure per child going to *juku*; the expenditure on *juku* per family who has *juku*-going children (one or more); and the accumulated expenditure on *juku* per family over the years. Average monthly expenditure on tutorial fees (including *juku*, *yobiko*, and private teachers) is provided in a survey published in 1988, showing that during the period 1975–88, tutorial fees increased more rapidly than total living expenditures and expenditures on education.[2] Tutorial fees rise with the family's income (see Table 3), with families in the highest quintile of income spending almost ten times as much as families in the lowest. The heaviest burden of tutorial fees falls on families with the family head of ages 40–49 where children are of school age (see Table 4). As to the effect of the household head's occupation (see Table 5), heavy spenders on tuition fees consist of corporate administra-

2. Management and Coordination Agency, *Annual Report on the Family Income and Expenditure Survey*, 1988, p. 107.

TABLE 3 *Yearly Average of Monthly Expenditure per Household on Tutorial Fees by Yearly Income Quintile Groups* (all households–1988)

	Average	Yearly Income Quintile Group				
		I	II	III	IV	V
Annual Income (¥ 10,000)	595	256	399	525	684	1,110
Tutorial fees (¥)	2,855	557	1,550	2,710	4,039	5,416

SOURCE: Management and Coordination Agency, *Annual Report on the Family Income and Expenditure Survey*, 1988, p. 107.

TABLE 4 *Yearly Average of Monthly Expenditures on Tutorial Fees by Age Groups of Household Head* (all households–1988, in yen)

Average	Age Groups				
	~29	30–39	40–49	50–59	60~
2,855	67	1,775	6,770	1,961	380

SOURCE: Same as Table 4, p. 199.

TABLE 5 *Yearly Average of Monthly Expenditure of Tuition Fees per Household by Occupation of Household Head* (all households–1988, in yen)

Average	Non-Office Workers	Office Workers	Individual Proprietors	Corporate Administrator	Professional Services	No Occupation
2,855	1,959	4,025	2,334	4,822	4,493	301

SOURCE: Same as Table 4, p. 206.

tors, those providing professional services, and office workers, namely, occupations where higher education is necessary.

It should be remembered that these data refer to all families, including those without children and those where the children are above school age and therefore, do not reflect the real burden on families. However, the change over time can indicate the increase in this burden (see Table 6). It is interesting to note that the real cost of tuition increased more than

TABLE 6 *Real Yearly Expenditures on Tutorial Fees 1958–1988* (all
households-1985, in yen)

	1968	1973	1978	1983	1988
Tutorial fees	4,433	8,091	15,650	24,173	33,786
Index	100.0	182.5	353.0	545.3	762.1

SOURCE: Same as Table 4, pp. 301, 438.

seven-fold between 1968 and 1988. A better indication of the effect of the
so-called "second school system" on family budget is the expenditure per
pupil (see Table 7), provided by the Survey of Education Expenditures by
Parents. The heaviest expenditure is for junior high school pupils, followed by senior high students of private schools. Here again, we have to
remember that the numbers are averages for all pupils, including those
who do not have additional education. They do not reflect the actual burden of families of two or more children who go at the same time to *juku* or
yobiko.

According to the survey of the Ministry of Education, the average
monthly payment for a child going to *juku* went up from 5,200 yen in 1976
to 9,200 yen in 1985. The increase was larger for junior high pupils—from
5,200 to 10,200 yen—while for elementary school children it was from
5,200 to 7,800 yen. Utilizing the total number of pupils, we can estimate
the total annual income of the *juku* industry from monthly tuition fees that
amounted to 249.6 billion yen in 1976 and 499.0 billion yen in 1985. It has
been estimated that in 1989 total revenue of the industry surpassed ¥1
trillion.[3]

In a survey carried out in Tokyo between April 1988 and March 1989,
of 385 families with children in elementary or junior high school attending
juku, the following expenditures on *juku* were recorded: the average annual expenditure per child amounted to 283,571 yen, the average number
of children going to *juku* per family was 1.3 children, and the average
expenditure per family reached 377,849 yen.[4]

Organizational Structure

Juku range from a small classroom in an owner's home to chain *juku* with
tens of thousands of pupils and from private *juku* owned by one individual

3. Daiwa Shoken, "Gakushujuku Gyokai no Gensho to Shorai Tembo (Present condition
and future prospect of the *gakushujuku*), *Daiwa Toshi Shiryo*, September 1989.

4. *Sankei Shimbun*, November 11, 1989.

TABLE 7 *Average Annual Expenditure per Pupil on Juku (Including Private Teachers), 1977–1987* (in yen)

	1977	1978	1979	1980	1981	1982	1983	1984	1985	1986	1987
Kindergarten											
(public)					831	920	1,005	1,621	1,723	1,771	1,863
Index					100	110.7	120.9	195.1	207.3	213.1	224.2
Kindergarten											
(private)					1,857	2,296	3,060	3,621	3,849	3,957	4,078
Index					100	123.6	164.8	195.0	207.3	213.1	219.6
Elementary school											
(public)	4,012	4,695	5,328	6,151	6,145	6,264	7,161	8,135	8,648	8,890	9,434
Index					100	101.9	116.5	132.4	140.7	144.7	153.5
Junior high											
(public)	12,849	15,226	17,392	20,004	26,416	28,703	30,063	30,957	32,907	33,828	35,716
Index					100	108.6	113.8	117.2	124.6	128.1	135.2
Senior high											
(public)	6,756	6,797	7,867	9,113	10,886	10,802	10,277	12,376	13,156	13,524	14,312
Index					100	99.2	94.4	113.7	120.9	124.2	131.5
Senior high											
(private)					18,181	17,664	18,696	19,955	20,737	21,318	22,704
Index					100	97.2	102.8	109.8	114.1	117.3	124.9

SOURCE: Ministry of Education, *Hogosha ga Shishutsu shita Kyoikuhi Chosa* (Survey of educational expenditures by parents), 1989, pp. 40–48.

to incorporated ones. According to data collected by Nikkei Business, in 1988 there were 63 *juku* whose declared income was above ¥40 million.[5] *Juku* chains have branches all over Japan and benefit from scale economies through a central supply of teaching materials and a central collection of data. Every pupil is ranked within the national scale, which includes all the pupils within the chain. Branches are often administered on a franchise system in which every *juku* principal pays the center a certain fee for the right to carry the chain's name and for teaching material and computer analysis, but they are administratively and financially independent.

Pupils study according to a centrally planned program without taking into account specific materials taught at local schools. Students may thus be subject to different material and their school grades may actually suffer, causing dissatisfaction among parents. The small independent *juku* are more perceptive to the specific needs of their pupils, since they utilize

5. Zenkoko Shijuku Hodo Center, *'89 nenban zenkoku gakushujuku shotoku ranking* (1989 publication of income ranking of *gakushu juku* in Japan).

teaching material prepared by local teachers as well as mock exams prepared by nationwide companies. This can also reduce costs since the *juku* do not have to transfer a part of its income to the center. We have here an example of product differentiation: in general, children who are ambitious and eager to be admitted to high-ranking schools or universities prefer a chain school that offers special courses aimed at high-ranking universities, while those satisfied with a low-ranking neighborhood school prefer the local *juku*. This product differentiation explains the coexistence of both types of *juku*, which is not dissimilar to the coexistence of supermarkets and local family-owned stores.

Between 1976 and 1985, there has been an interesting change in the structure of the *juku* industry. In 1976, 88.3% of *juku* were privately owned while 11.7% were incorporated. In 1985 the distribution was 74.5% and 25.5%, respectively. There has also been a substantial increase in chain *juku* between the two years, from 5.9% in 1976 to 27.0% in 1985. It is also interesting to note that 70.1% of the *juku* existing in 1985 were established after 1976. A new development in recent years has been the organization of *juku* as joint stock companies. At present there are four companies of this kind.

It is often said that the Japanese labor market is characterized by the lifetime commitment of a worker to a company and by job security. Labor relations in Japanese schools conform closely to this model. Teachers are recruited after finishing a university and passing exams and are not fired unless they break the law, irrespective of their teaching ability or devotion to the job. However, labor relations in *juku* are the direct opposite. The teaching staff in a *juku* and *yobiko* is generally composed of a small core of full-time and a large body of part-time teachers—retired teachers, teachers who are employed in schools (public school teachers are not allowed to work in *juku* but sometimes do so nonetheless), students, and others. Teacher contracts are usually for one year (sometimes for one semester), and there is a close monitoring of work. In the large *yobiko* this is sometimes done by a television camera mounted on the ceiling of a classroom, reflecting whatever is happening in class, and a questionnaire is given to students to evaluate the relative merits of a teacher. Each teacher's contract is personal and includes the number of teaching hours as well as salary.

Technological changes have been introduced in some *juku*. Facsimile machines are being used in some as a substitute for frontal teaching. Students sit at home and transmit their answers to exercises and receive corrected ones in return without ever having to move away from their rooms. If they have questions, they can send them and get the answers right away. The advantage lies in saving the time and cost of commuting to *juku* and in not having to stay out late at night. Another device introduced into the *juku* is the personal computer with special software programs. One of the largest *yobiko* is using a satellite to broadcast lectures of famous teachers to their branches all over Japan. Japanese chain *juku* have also opened schools abroad in Korea, Brazil, Australia, and the United States. With growth, the industry has received recognition from MITI as a service industry, and in 1988 a nationwide association of *gakushu juku* was established. One purpose of the association is to enable *juku* to receive assistance, such as development loans and tax reductions for investment in equipment.

Why Did the *Juken* Industry Develop in Japan?

In order to understand why the *juken* industry has developed in Japan and reached its present dimensions, we have to describe some of the characteristics of the Japanese educational system. Japan is known as a *gakureki shakai*, a society where great importance is attached to a person's educational history. The university where students finish their studies is more important than their actual achievements during the study period. Large companies often recruit their workers from a few top universities before they graduate, which means that enrollment in a prestigious university secures employment in a large company. Japanese universities are ranked in a pyramid structure, with a few national universities and fewer private universities at the top. Acceptance to universities is through entrance examinations that test mainly the candidate's detailed knowledge of facts and speed of answering questions. Exam questions are often multiple choice or require only writing down a missing word, number, or name. A considerable amount of memorizing and training is needed in order to pass this examination. The higher the university's rank, the more difficult the entrance examinations.

Senior high schools are also ranked, the criterion being the number of students from each school who are able to get into high-ranking universities. In order to be admitted to high-ranking senior high schools, entrance examinations based on the same principles as the universities', must be taken. This requires additional studies and endless repetition of the material, which is undertaken at the *juku* or *yobiko*.

Another characteristic of the Japanese school system lies in its considerable uniformity, with very little choice of subjects and almost no variation in teaching material as prescribed by the Ministry of Education to all schools. This makes for uniformity in subject matter and means that *juku* have to provide only a limited number of subjects, which are taken by pupils of different schools. Changes over time in the course of studies are

272

few and infrequent. The school is based on egalitarian principles whereby all pupils learn almost the same material at the same level of difficulty. The teaching method is almost invariably the frontal method with very little discussion or debate.

These characteristics have facilitated the emergence of *juku* and *yobiko* for cramming facts and data as well as teaching exam-passing techniques such as speedy answering. Uniformity in the course of studies makes it possible to put children from different schools in the same *juku* without worrying too much about differences among schools. However, the greatest driving force behind the industry is the desire of children and their parents to reach the high-ranking universities and, toward this purpose, high-ranking senior high schools. It should also be mentioned that when we consider private schools, the competition already starts at the junior high or even elementary level, and farsighted parents, whose children go to public schools, enroll the children in *juku* at an early age.

To understand the degree of competition in the race to enter universities, we should consider the following data: in 1989 the population of 18 years old was 1,930,000 of whom 1,701,000 graduated from high school (88%); 823,000 applied for universities (48.4%) to which 277,000 *ronin* should be added, totaling 1,100,000 applicants. The number accepted was 702,000 (63.8%)—477,000 (67.9%) in four-year and 225,000 (32.1%) in two-year universities. These numbers show that approximately one out of three applicants is not accepted at any university at all. The number of children not accepted to universities of their choice is, of course, much greater. Since the number of applicants to universities is much larger than the number of students who are accepted, a screening process has to be devised in order to decide who will be accepted and who will be rejected.

In Japan the widely used screening device is the entrance examination, and it exists at the university and high school level as well as for private junior high and elementary schools or kindergartens. University entrance examinations are taken in two stages: the first is a nationwide test in five subjects (Japanese, English, mathematics, social sciences, and natural sciences). Then there is a second examination prepared by each university or faculty. Eligibility for acceptance is determined by a weighted average of the scores of both tests, the weights differing by university and faculty. Thus, at the University of Tokyo, nationwide exams account for 20% while the specific exam weighs 80%. Each examination is taken in one day, lasting six or more hours. It therefore tests not only knowledge of specific fields but also speed in answering questions, willpower, and endurance.

The *juku* and *yobiko* fulfill two functions related to entrance examinations: one is the teaching, drilling, and cramming of material for the examinations and the second is the selection of students. Concerning the first function, school teachers are often unable to cover in class the amount of teaching material prescribed by the Ministry of Education, and even the prescribed material is not sufficient for success in entrance examinations to prestigious schools and universities. The *juku* are based on the (reasonable) assumption that the ability to pass examinations is only partially dependent on natural intelligence and memory and is to a large degree a matter of mastering exam-passing techniques. For this purpose *juku* must know the general types of questions that are expected to appear on the tests, which they gain by the close inspection and research of past exams.

The service provided by *juku* and *yobiko*, however, is not only in teaching but also in providing information about the candidate's probability of passing the entrance examinations of different schools. Since there are only two terms in which entrance examinations for national universities can be taken, a candidate can make two types of errors: attempting a school entry beyond one's ability and failing or taking an examination for an "easy" school and forgoing the chance of acceptance at a more prestigious one. Thus, the level at which one should apply becomes a most important question for candidates, and information about this is readily supplied by the *juken* institution. The large *yobiko* or the special companies compile and then supply this information to the smaller *juku*. The magic word in this connection is *hensachi*—the value of standard deviation. All universities (as well as senior high schools and private junior highs) are ranked according to the difficulty of passing their entrance exams. Students, on the other hand, are ranked according to their ability to succeed in passing entrance examinations, done by the use of mock exams (*mogi shiken*) where results are collected for a large number of students and placement in that distribution is determined. A student whose rank is y can apply to all schools of rank x for which $y > x$ and has a good chance of success.

How can the large increase in *juku* attendance in recent years be explained? The following are some of the reasons:

1. A second baby boom has intensified the competition for entry to universities. Between 1960 and 1985 the number of elementary school children increased by 15% and junior high school by 27%.[6]
2. An increase in household income has caused an increase in the demand for educational services, including informal teaching.

---

6. New Business Kyogikai, *Showa 61 nendo sabisu sangyo kozo ni okeru kyoso yoin ni kansuru chosa* (FY 1986 survey of competition factors in the structure of service industries), 1987.

3. The introduction in 1979 of the first-level unified examination for all national universities (and recently some private universities) made it necessary for all candidates to study for the same exam.

4. Several built-in mechanisms caused an increase in *juku* attendance: one is the case known in Game Theory as the "prisoner's dilemma." The story is told about two gangsters, Yamada and Tanaka, who were apprehended by the police and put in prison in two separate cells for interrogation. If both keep quiet they would be released, because the police did not have enough incriminating evidence against them. If Yamada opens his mouth while Tanaka keeps quiet, Tanaka would be prosecuted and go to prison for 10 years, while Yamada would receive only one year. The same in reverse would happen if Yamada kept quiet while Tanaka opens his mouth. Now, if both of them speak to the police, both will get a reduced sentence of three years in prison. It is quite clear that the best solution for both is to keep quiet and go home. However, if they do not trust each other, both will talk and end up with a prison term.

Here, we are in a similar situation. Consider an applicant to Tokyo University whose probability of passing the entrance examinations is 50% if no applicant goes to a *juku*. If he or she is the only applicant going to *juku*, the chances go up to 80%. However, if everybody prepares themself through a *juku*, chances are again down to 50%, and income is reduced by the amount paid to *juku* as tuition fees. Since every mother is afraid that the other children will go to the *juku*, she has no choice but to send her child as well. However, this is not the end of the story. Since everybody gets additional studies in order to pass entrance examinations and the number of students accepted by a particular university is constant, the university has to ask more difficult questions in order to distinguish among the applicants. This calls for a self-perpetuating cycle of additional preparation and so on. It explains why today's examinations of first-rate universities are more difficult than those of a few years ago.

A second mechanism that has increased *juku* attendance is related to the formal school system. When more children in a class go to a *juku*, the school teacher can delegate some of the work to the *juku*. This then makes it necessary for children who do not attend *juku* to start doing so. Often it is the children themselves who demand to be sent to *juku* since their friends do so.

Summary

The *juken* industry, consisting of *juku* and *yobiko*, has become an integral part of the Japanese educational system, which has as its focus the passing of entrance examinations. This industry has both negative and positive effects on Japanese society. On the negative side we can mention the reduction of free time available to children for more pleasant and mind-broadening activities and the hardship on parents who must devote a substantial share of their income for these additional studies. These expenditures may well be one reason for the reduction in the desire to have children, seen in Japan in recent years. Additionally, while memorization, paying attention to details, and cramming of facts were desirable qualities when Japan was borrowing foreign technology, they may not be adequate for the future when Japan is called upon to take a leading role in technological innovations.

One positive effect of the *juku* concerns the reduction of free time for young children, which may be one explanation for the low rate of juvenile delinquency in Japan. It may also have contributed to the high level of primary and secondary education in Japan, as reflected in the high scores Japanese children attain in international comparisons of scholastic achievements.

Several developments will have an impact on the future of the *juken* industry. Japan has already passed the peak of *juku*-aged children as a result of the second baby boom. The number of children in these age groups is estimated to decline by 28.9% between 1985 and 2000.[7] This will cause fierce competition among *juku* and *yobiko* and probably reduce their number. On the other hand, it can be expected that a larger share of high school graduates will continue on to higher education, thus mitigating this contrary effect.

Any changes in the employment practices of companies, such as less emphasis on school history and an increase in the importance of individual merit, would also reduce the desire for entry into prestigious universities and consequently the need to prepare for them. Likewise, the introduction of a differential system in schools under which the more capable students would get advanced teaching may also reduce the demand for out-of-school additional training. Also, a change in university entrance examinations, directed to selecting students by their future potential rather than their past acquisition of facts and details, may also reduce the need for *juku* and *yobiko*. These changes may be initiated by the Ministry of Education or come as a result of public pressure, but such changes will probably take a long time. While criticism of the *juken* industry is prevalent, it seems that most Japanese still accept it as a necessary evil.

---

7. Daiwa Shoken, "Gakushujuku Gyokai," p. 16.

The Role of the Education Mama

By Tony Dickensheets

Tony Dickensheets teaches at the college level and in city elementary schools in Charlottesville, Virginia. As a postgraduate student in East Asian studies, he traveled and studied in Japan and China, spending six months as a student at Nara University of Education.

Among the many factors that helped make Japan the economic giant it became in the second half of this century, one of the most frequently cited is the work ethic of the stereotypical salaryman. These dark-suited legions are the legendary engines powering one of modern history's greatest economic successes. But behind every great man—or salaryman—is a great woman. And in Japan, women in general, and the *kyōiku mama* in particular, have been the pillars supporting the salarymen. By extension, they helped drive the nation's tremendous postwar development. The work and influence of Japanese women can be seen in the nation's education system and in its social stability, both crucial to a nation's economic success.

While I lived in Japan, I stayed with three Japanese families who would probably qualify as typical. The fathers were salaried workers. The mothers were responsible for seeing to the education of their children. I was most impressed by the fact that the mothers seemed willing to devote their lives to ensuring that their children would be able to enter good schools.

Like most Westerners, I had believed that the tremendous growth of Japan's economy since the 1960s was the result of government policies under the Ministry of International Trade and Industry, through a work force willing to put in 16-hour days. Within several months, however, I became convinced that a key element in the economic miracle had been overlooked, or at least vastly understated. That is the role that Japanese women have held and continue to hold in maintaining the social and educational foundation that has been so vital in the nation's half-century of economic achievement.

There is always a strong relationship between the quality of a nation's education and its economic growth, since education promotes development of a better work force, increases the stock of scientific and technical knowledge, opens people's minds to new opportunities and enables a society to meet the demands for better-educated members as the economy expands. Education also fosters economic growth by promoting social stability.

Fully aware of the importance of education, the Japanese started to encourage its systematic application in the Tokugawa Period (1603–1868). The most significant and enduring innovations in the education system were made during the Meiji Era, from 1868, when intellectuals decided that the role of women in Japan's modernization would be to educate the next generation of leaders and citizens. The feeling of most women then, as now, is summed up in the 1874 lament of scholar Mori Arinori (1847–1889), who said, "Ah, the duties of women are so difficult and their responsibilities so heavy!" (Edwin Reingold, *Chrysanthemums and the Thorns: The Untold Story of Modern Japan* [New York: St. Martin's Press, 1992], 114).

Hence, the policy of *ryôsai kenbo* (good wife and wise mother) was promulgated, defining the position of women as the managers of household affairs and nurturers of the nation's children. In the past century, this philosophy has become part of the Japanese mindset and has been key to the education of several generations.

After World War II, national educational policy underwent several modifications to accommodate the requirements of economic revitalization and development. This reinforced the 1872 Code of Education, which had given women equal access to elementary education for the first time in the nation's history. Education policy during and after the Occupation further enhanced the ability of women to act as partners in the education process. In addition, moral education and Japanese characteristics were re-emphasized in the educational system to accompany a Japanese style of economic growth and competitiveness. The Fundamental Law of Education in 1947 extended coeducation to all levels of schooling. And in 1958, after the Occupation had ended, morals and ethics were again part of the curriculum. Universal education was mandated to provide Japanese children with a diversified set of skills and knowledge, which would prepare them for the crucial needs of technological innovation and internationalization in Japanese industries. All these demanded the successful collaboration between schools and families in the education process, and illustrated the importance of an education policy in which women were fully included.

Japan, perhaps more than any other nation, seems to have both the educational system and the culture to fully utilize women in the role of child-rearing. Unlike many Asian nations, Japan regards the education of girls as being of nearly equal importance to the education of boys. After graduating from high school, most Japanese women go on to higher education at colleges or universities. In the West, it is assumed that a woman with a college degree who stays at home to raise her children is wasting her talents. In Japan, however, it is believed that a mother must be well-educated and knowledgeable to be fit for her obligation to help educate her children.

Shaping the Next Generation

Japanese women in the second half of the 20th century are not simply housewives in the Western sense, but are known as kyôiku mama, or "education mamas," whose duties involve raising and helping educate Japan's next generation of leaders, workers and citizens. They judge themselves, and are judged by society, on the basis of the success of their children. Although many other mothers in other nations help their children with their homework, Japanese mothers are devote so much of their time, interest and energy to the education of their children that they make the kyôiku mama a purely Japanese phenomenon.

In homes where I stayed, the television set was on much less of the time than in most American households. The mother, whose son was studying for his college entrance exams, told me, "My job is to be at home to cook food for my son when he is hungry, and to help him when he has questions." While I lived there, I seldom even saw the son. Between his classes and *juku* cram courses, he normally studied about 16 hours a day. Even at mealtime, it was not at all uncommon for his mother to take dinner to his room on a tray.

The degree to which Japanese women immerse themselves in their children's lives is rare even among other women in Asia. Indeed, many Japanese women

> The mother, whose son was studying for his college entrance exams, told me, "My job is to be at home to cook food for my son when he is hungry, and to help him when he has questions."

seem to regard their children as their *ikigai*, or their essential reason for living, because they sacrifice any hope of a possible career to devote all their talents and energies and the best part of their lives to the tasks of ensuring that their children become productive members of society.

Japanese women contribute to economic progress in two ways: They help their children through the academic process and through the socialization process. Although some mothers can be so zealous in the effort that their sons never really cut the apron strings, their efforts overall are positive. Mothers are, in effect, partners with teachers in guaranteeing continuation of the level of education that has been the competitive advantage for Japan in its modern social and economic development. Although the Japanese government indeed sets the goals of the education system, success of that system is in the hands of the teachers—most of whom, at least in the elementary grades, are women—and the mothers of Japan. They, more than any other group, will shape Japan's future.

Integrating Fundamental Values

School in Japan is an all-encompassing part of a child's life from around the age of three, from before kindergarten. Mothers teach their children how to recognize *kana* and *kanji* characters at home, and preschool teachers concentrate on fundamental preacademic skills such as perseverance, concentration and the ability to function as part of a group. When children start attending school, their mothers usually work part-time at most, to be at home when the children return. Besides providing hot meals and clean clothing, they help children with homework and take an interest in what they do in school. This is where the higher education level of Japanese women comes into play: Mothers ensure that their children complete and master their homework, and help them with whatever learning difficulties they may encounter. Even after children begin attending juku, mothers still serve as very useful tutors and shoulders to lean on. They instill in their children the importance of a good education, and they are the major motivators in the lives of their children, ensuring that they always strive for the best.

In part because the fathers are seldom home for family activities, mothers support the school-based socialization process as well, providing emotional support for their children and teaching them traditional values of discipline, hard work and the importance of contributing to the group.

Students in Japan, even from an early age, spend much more time with school activities than do their counterparts in the United States. One study showed the average school year for Japanese children is 243 days, compared with 178 days in the United States. And a recent study found that, while 76 percent of U.S. high school seniors spend less than five hours a week on homework, just 35 percent of their Japanese counterparts expend such little effort.

Besides spending about two more months of the year in school, they devote a substantial amount of their school vacation with classmates and teachers, either working on school projects, going on class trips, or taking part in school athletic events. I was surprised to find that children in Japan have homework to complete during their summer vacations. At the elementary school in Virginia where I teach part-time, the children hardly have homework during the regular—much shorter—school year.

One Sunday morning in October, I visited a middle school with a Japanese friend who was studying to be a teacher. The whole school—students, parents,

One study showed the average school year for Japanese children is 243 days, compared with 178 days in the United States. And a recent study found that, while 76 percent of U.S. high school seniors spend less than five hours a week on homework, just 35 percent of their Japanese counterparts expend such little effort.

K

teachers, and even the principal—had turned out for Sports Day, a national holi-
day marked by an event that is all but unheard of in the United States. Japanese
schoolchildren are, in a sense, salarymen in training. And just as the salaryman
dedicates his life to the company, so do children devote themselves to the school.
The goal of school is to prepare for the life of work. Children learn how to devote
themselves to their schools and organizations, and how to get along with people
whom they see more often than members of their own families. To the Japanese,
the socialization aspect of education is as important as the academic aspect
because it imbues children with the values that continue to produce the kind of
behavioral conformity that ensures social stability. The Japanese see this as key to
sustaining success in the next century, and it is one part of the traditional Japanese
culture that will not—nor should it—change.

Women are at the heart of it. As wives, they usually manage the family finances,
do most of the household chores and are the primary child-raisers, so their husbands, the salarymen, can be free to devote themselves to their companies. As
mothers, these women give their children all the spiritual and material support
they can muster, to help them concentrate on their studies and participate in

76 The Role of the Education Mama • Tony Dickensheets

school activities. If it were not for the substantial amount of work undertaken by Japanese mothers at home, it would be much more difficult for the schools to deal with their part in the socialization process. With the Kyôiku mama providing a stable family life, schools need not concentrate too much on disciplinary problems. Instead, teachers can concentrate upon teaching their charges about modesty, cooperation, sacrifice, forbearance and all the other attributes of a Japanese group. And this is done with full support from the mothers.

The link between salaryman and student extends to attire. As the salarymen tend to wear dark, conservative suits and starched white shirts and sober ties, students wear their school uniforms. And, apart from differences in style, recently departing somewhat from the traditional Prussian-influenced, high-collar tunics, or distinctions in the color or school badge, they are much alike. The uniformity is not so much a matter of school pride, although that is certainly part of it, as it is about pressing children to conform to societal expectations and norms, and representing the school or organization with honor. Japanese mothers are very diligent about making sure that their children are properly dressed, sometimes running from their houses to bus stops after discovering that a child has forgotten a hat. Strict dress codes will prepare schoolchildren for their future employment, when they will be dressed in uniforms of a different sort.

Not All Women Fit the Role

Until the late 1980s, the conventional wisdom that women were the nurturers of society went largely unchallenged in Japan. Since then, however, a growing but not very vocal movement has emerged from the changed expectations of younger women. Unlike the women's liberation movement in the United States in the 1960s, the present counterpart in Japan seems to be more individually oriented.

In the most personal aspects of a woman's life, especially marriage and bearing children, young Japanese women are clearly much more independent-minded than the women of their mothers' generation. A 1990 survey by the Women's Studies Society of Japan found that 96.7 percent of the women who responded who were then working intended to keep working after marriage. Of those not working, 82.5 percent wanted to find work. This still-silent movement among a segment of young Japanese women no longer willing to accept the stereotypical role of housewife and mother has concerned the central government. The 1988 National Family Survey conducted by the Prime Minister's Office showed that young women are postponing marriage, to the point that the average age of marriage for Japanese women is 27; only Sweden's is higher. And one-third of the women do not marry before the age of 30 (*Chrysanthemums and the Thorns: The Untold Story of Modern Japan*, 119).

According to the Ministry of Health and Welfare, the total fertility rate, a measure of the birth rate for women of childbearing age, had fallen to a low of 1.46 in 1993—well below the level needed to sustain the population level. Obviously, a trend of population decline is not good for Japan either culturally or economically. Economically, with fewer workers, the economy will be strained to support programs to care for an increasing proportion of elderly people in the population. Socially, the family structure will change radically.

In 1990, when Hashimoto Ryûtarô, now prime minister, was minister of finance, he remarked in a Cabinet meeting that the falling fertility rate was a direct result of the higher education level of Japanese women, who were being distracted from

In 1990, when Hashimoto Ryûtarô, now prime minister, was minister of finance, he remarked in a Cabinet meeting that the falling fertility rate was a direct result of the higher education level of Japanese women, who were being distracted from their duties in the home.

their duties in the home. What Hashimoto was saying in 1990 clearly sums up the way of thinking of the majority of Japanese society about the role of women in 1996: They should be at home, raising the children.

The Kyôiku mama clearly has proved her value. To encourage the process to continue, however, will require the combined support of government and business. Tax incentives should be provided to companies to encourage them to establish day-care centers for women who work but who have children too young to attend school. For working women with children in school, work schedules should be flexible, to match the school schedules. Certainly, Japan would not want to take on the social anguishes associated with the "latchkey kid" syndrome in the United States. When children come home to a mother who does not have the time or energy to be with her children, the children are deprived of valuable encouragement and supervision to further academic achievement, and they have no one to turn to with their school or personal problems. The effects show up in lower secondary school achievement scores, higher dropout rates, higher crime rates among juveniles and higher rates of teenage pregnancy.

Government and private-sector incentives and policies must be established that will make it feasible for Japanese women to continue to support the education of the nation's children even if they work. Although there will be financial burdens for companies, one need only study current history to realize that it would be well worth the cost in terms of the long-term economic and social benefits of maintaining the institution of the kyôiku mamas, who have become such an integral part of the nation's economic and social success.

Among Friends: The Seductive Power of Bullying

By Nishiyama Akira

Nishiyama Akira is a reporter for Kyodo, the Japanese news service, where he specializes in family issues. He is the author of several books on the subject, including Sanagi no Ie *(Sheltering Cocoon), in 1994, and* Adaruto Chirudoren *(Adult Children), in 1996.*

An eighth grader in Nishio, Aichi Prefecture, Ôkôchi Kiyoteru, hanged himself on November 27, 1994. It was later found that he had been a victim of persistent bullying. His tormentors had been his classmates, whose methods of torture included repeated demands for large sums of money. A day before Ôkôchi killed himself, he had received yet another impossible demand, this time for ¥120,000.

The long note he left, however, was curiously lacking in spiteful recriminations against the bullies. Instead, there were relentless phrases of self-blame and a painful sense of guilt for everything he had ever done. He wrote, "If I had just refused to pay the money, nothing like this would have ever happened. I am really sorry. Please do not blame the people who took the money. I should be blamed because I was the one who gave the money so willingly." He also told his parents, "I am really sorry that I have always been the cause of worry for you. I was such a selfish child. It must have been really difficult to have me as your son."

Bullying is a dangerously addictive power game. Once the participants—the victim and the bullies—become caught up in the game, they can rarely escape from its psychological grasp. Watching on the sidelines are the silent spectators, who in their hurry not to be the victims themselves lend their passive support to the bullies, further closing any avenues of escape. Ôkôchi fell into this game as the victim, and the only way out he could find was to die, apologizing that he had ever lived.

Ôkôchi is only one of the five schoolchildren who took their own lives in 1994 because of bullying. Bullying itself is nothing new; it has always been an unspoken fact of life in school. But the increasing number of bullying victims who have killed themselves in recent years has nudged this pervasive problem to the axis of media attention.

No Other Way Out

Probably the first time that *ijime*, bullying in school, received extensive media coverage was in April 1969, when the mutilated and beheaded body of a high school boy was reported by another student as having been found in the foothills of Kawasaki, Kanagawa Prefecture. Two days later, the student who claimed to have "discovered" the body confessed to the killing. He said, "I have been bullied ever since I was in junior high school. I thought killing him was the only way to escape this hell." The boy stabbed his tormentor more than 40 times with a heavy mountaineering knife, driven by fear that he might still revive.

In the boy's desperate mind, the brutal murder was perhaps the only way to crawl out of his hellish trap. The story is no less tragic than the suicide of Ôkôchi.

but there is a difference: The victim of the bullying in this case at least tried to fight back, albeit in a misguided manner.

Bullying in school would recur even after this scandalous murder. But the psychology in the bullying game was to undergo subtle but significant changes. From the latter half of 1985 and peaking in 1986, 17 years after the murder in Kawasaki, the number of suicides by bullying victims showed an alarming increase. The numbers indicated that the victims no longer lashed out violently against the bullies in their own defense; they were more likely to let themselves be bullied into resigned submission and even self-destruction.

Shikagawa Hirofumi, an eighth grader in Nakano Ward, Tokyo, who killed himself in 1986, was just such a victim. He left a note that described in detail the sort of torture he had received. He was ridiculed, humiliated and beaten. He was forced to run constant errands for his belittling tormentors. The bullies doodled mustaches on his face with felt markers, forced him to climb up a tree to sing a song with his classmates witnessing his humiliation, and even staged his mock funeral, watching his discomfort with glee.

His note was his final cry against the injustice he had suffered. He wrote, "I don't want to die yet, but this is living hell. I am going to kill myself, but I don't want somebody else to become the victim after I die or the whole thing would be meaningless. Please stop this stupidity; that is my dying wish." The pencil with which he had obviously written the note was found in his pocket. Its end had been crudely bitten off to expose the lead so that he could continue to write his last protest. He could not fight back while alive; his only weapon against his tormentors was his own death.

"He was really good at intuiting people's feelings, and he would always try to lift our moods by making witty remarks and doing funny things," his father recalled after Shikagawa's suicide. Said his mother, visibly trying to contain her feelings: "He was such a friendly, funny boy, who never caused any problems. He talked so much at dinner that he was always the last to finish his meal. When he was away, the house felt as if a light had been turned off." His parents remembered Shikagawa as a good son, who had always acted cheerful and was deeply caring. But that cheerfulness may have been a desperate attempt to restore warmth in a family where none existed. His parents fought constantly, and he apparently blamed himself for his parents' marital problems. He was the glue that was holding together a seriously troubled home.

Compensating for Sadness

Shikagawa showed very few outward signs that he was really a sad, lonely child, especially in front of his father. He appeared grown-up, a child who was more concerned about his parents than himself. When his mother left home for a time, he tried to be a "surrogate spouse" to his father. He would leave thoughtful notes for his father, who was often home late from work: "I'm sorry I could not brew coffee for you." "Sorry I couldn't wait up for you." "Don't forget to take a bath."

The "good" boy was drawn into a band of school hooligans in June during his second year in junior high school. One of his classmates said, "In the beginning, he looked rather pleased to run errands for others and to be shoved around. After he was bullied, he would even entertain the bullies and make them laugh." Accustomed to always being the one to sacrifice his needs and please others, he seemingly could not say "no." If he needed the company of others and their

attention to alleviate his sense of isolation, his bullies also needed him. The inter-dependent "power" relationship can be addictive, and in many cases of ijime the bullies' demands of total submission from their victim never stop escalating. Shikagawa's uncle said of his nephew after his death: "If you are clever enough to cruise by the rules, you'll be OK. But there are some people who simply can-not do that. Those people care too much about people around them, and their sensitivity forces them to play the role of the clown. My nephew was too kind-hearted. And he got lost in his desperation to forget his loneliness."

Soon after Shikagawa's suicide, a teen idol singer, Okada Yukiko, jumped to her death from the top of a building. A huge media story, it made death a much more familiar concept for the young: more than a hundred youths, all in their teens, killed themselves in the month that followed. The line that separated life and death appeared to have blurred, as children seemed to be increasingly indif-ferent toward their own lives.

Seven years after Shikagawa's death, I wrote a series of articles entitled "Bullying as a Power Game" on the death of a ninth-grade pupil in Osaka in April 1993.

The boy was killed after more than three and one-half hours of violence and humiliation. The two killers, both of them classmates of the victim, had even forced him to masturbate in front of them before they beat him to death. The victim showed no resistance, and with apparent resignation gave himself up to the whims of his tormentors. He just sobbed throughout the long ordeal that resulted in his death.

Troubled Homes a Common Factor

My investigations into the lives of the three boys all revealed troubled homes. The father of Tarô (all three names are pseudonyms to protect the identities of the families), the leader of the two killers, was an alcoholic who had amassed debts of ¥10 million to pay for his drinking habits. His father and mother fought violently, but for the outside world they kept up a facade of being a happy family. The house was neatly kept, while husband and wife played gentle father and obedient mother before others as if none of the fights had ever occurred. Tarô was caught between his warring parents and forced to assume the role of the family clown, who had to hide his own unhappiness in order to try to please his parents and patch up what was left of the family.

Tarô, the good boy, was in many ways typical of children of an alcoholic parent. Another characteristic he shared with other children of alcoholics was his fascination with power. Raised in the shadow of an alcoholic father, who turned into a violent tyrant who demanded absolute submission when drunk, Tarô had trouble relating to his peers as friends; he was more comfortable in power situations in which he was either their master or slave. The makings of a bully were all there, and so were the makings of a bullying victim.

The father of Jirô, the other killer, was a compulsive gambler who was rarely home. After finishing junior high school, he migrated to Osaka to find work. He never achieved economic or social success, amassing considerable debt over the years. His only solace, and his obsession, was gambling. When he won at gambling, he said that he felt as if he had beaten God, who had given him short shrift in real life. Gambling gave him his only power.

Jirô's father was totally indifferent to his wife, and did not even notice her absence for some time when she had run away with another man. Jirô, left to his own devices, lived for a while on instant noodles, while developing a persistent sense of guilt. He felt, he later said, that it was all his fault that his mother had abandoned him; it was because he was worthless and did not deserve to be loved. Children ridden with the feeling of worthlessness are often quite adept at adjusting to changing situations, and Jirô was no exception. He had been a victim of bullying himself, but after transferring to a new school and meeting Tarô, he quickly changed sides to become one of the bullies.

Saburô, the murdered boy, was raised in a family dominated by an authoritarian father who had often been beaten as a child by an alcoholic father. The son of an alcoholic and an experienced player in a power game, the father demanded that his son be strong. Saburô, however, learned early on never to try to compete with his strong father, but instead settled himself into the submissive role of an obedient son. He yielded to his father completely, offered his devotion and avoided doing anything that might disrupt family relations. When the situation got to be too much, he sought lone refuge in the fantasy world of computer games, or the otherworldliness of psychic phenomena.

When Tarô and Jirô met Saburô, they knew they had found the perfect victim. Tarô had just been taken off the school track team; he had failed to follow the team's strict training regimen. Deprived of a chance to win races and prove his worth, he needed some other outlet for his pent-up aggression. Jirô had just moved to the school and quickly allied himself with Tarô, eager this time not to be the one to be bullied. With all the participants for the power game of bullying present, the game could begin.

While I was researching the background of the three boys, I relied on Saitô Satoru, a psychiatrist and former chief researcher at the Department of Sociopathology at the Tokyo Institute of Psychiatry, for psychological insights. Of all the details I reported to him, he showed a particular interest in one piece of information about Tarô: His mother insisted on taking a bath with him. Tarô recounted, "My mother would just come into the bathroom. I really hated that. But even when I said 'Stop it,' she wouldn't listen. I couldn't have told her I hated it, because it would've hurt her. So I tried my best to cover my body with a towel. I hate to be touched by other people, and I hated it when my mother stroked my cheek as if I were still a small child. But she was somebody I had to protect, so I could not say, 'I hate it.' And I hated myself for not saying it."

Tarô tried to tolerate his mother's intrusion as much as he could, but he could not fight his discomfort. He started to wear T-shirts and shorts in the bath; he also wore a baseball cap and sunglasses to insulate himself further from his mother, who would not accept the fact that her son did not want her any more in the bath.

Saitô explained that Tarô's mother wanted to keep her growing son forever as her baby, who needed her constant care. By touching her son in the bath, she was telling him that she would never allow him to grow up. "She was an 'invading mother.' Tarô thus felt compelled to grow up quickly and become a 'real man.' That was his only way to defend himself. He was seeking a situation where he could be strong and dominating like a 'real man.' He found the other two boys, and the rest just happened."

Saitô called the relationships between the three boys a triangular encounter between Tarô, who was desperate to establish his male identity; Jirô, who wanted to be a bully in order not to be bullied; and Saburô, who was eager to please and needed the attention. Far from unusual, this relationship is typically observed in many of the bullying cases in school, at work and in society at large. And the seemingly fragile triangle is supported firmly by a shared sense of isolation and loneliness. Both Saburô and Shikagawa, perfect victims, were drawn into a triangular relationship and trapped there.

This raises another question, though: Why did the participants in bullying let the violence escalate until it resulted in death? Some possible answers to this question suggested themselves when I was doing reports on spousal abuse. The similarities I saw were significant.

The use of physical violence gives the offender a heady ride on an emotional roller coaster. First, tension gradually mounts as the offender stores up his anger. Next comes the moment of release, then there is deep regret. The husband, racked with guilt after beating his wife, begs for her forgiveness and promises never to repeat his behavior. The feeling of remorse, however, starts to build up tension again, which has to be released. The stronger the sense of guilt, the stronger the tension becomes, which makes the release even more gratifying. As

He started to wear T-shirts and shorts in the bath; he also wore a baseball cap and sunglasses to insulate himself further from his mother, who would not accept the fact that her son did not want her any more in the bath.

the three-stage cycle is repeated, it gains speed and escalates in its degrees of violence. It is an addiction. And so is bullying.

The Ministry of Education, Science, Sports and Culture released a report on bullying in May this year, based on a nationwide survey it conducted in 1994. In the survey, a total of 20,000 respondents, including students from elementary school to high school, their parents and teachers, were questioned. The results show that bullying, just like wife-beating, is habitual, and is not something that easily passes. Those who answered they were bullied indicated how frequently they suffered: the most frequent answer was "every day." More than half the bullying victims said bullying took place at least two or three times a week.

Just as a husband takes out his aggression on somebody closest to him, bullies choose to torment those who are close to them. The Education Ministry survey revealed that about half the bullying cases were among friends. Emotional attachments and the inability to deal with them were clearly at the bottom of bullying, making the whole issue more complex.

Familiar Patterns of Behavior

The emotions involved also mirror those in wife-beating. About 30 percent to 40 percent of the bullies in the survey answered that they felt "sorry" for their victims and felt "remorse" after bullying them. Only 15 percent of them said that they "had fun." Those who were bullied naturally wanted the bullying to stop. They wanted to be allowed to transfer out of the class at school to escape the bullies, and some even wanted to "take revenge" if an opportunity presented itself. The offenders regret their act, and the victims want the offending act to end. But once they are trapped, those feelings have very little, if any, effect.

As I continued to look closely into many bullying cases, their complex and often murky background issues often crystallized into one phrase: "Adult Children," which is short for "Adult Children of Alcoholics." It is also used for "Adult Children of Dysfunctional Families," which is a broader term referring to those whose homes were dysfunctional for various reasons: alcoholic parents, drug abuse, workaholic parents, gambling problems or estranged family relationships. The terms were first born in the United States during the 1970s in an attempt to label elusive but real problems that haunt the children from troubled homes.

Adult Children, who are raised in broken homes, take it upon themselves to hold their families together. They feel an enormous sense of responsibility and are often obsessed with being in control. They want more than anything else to take away the pain and lessen the tensions which plague their families. They even feel guilty when they do not sacrifice their own needs for their families' sake. On the outside, they are the devoted sons and daughters desperate to please, but there is hidden hatred inside them. Also buried deep inside them is the nagging feeling that they should not have been born. Many of the bullies and their victims whom I looked at, including Shikagawa, Tarô, Jirô and Saburô, fit this description of Adult Children.

The victims of bullying, and probably the bullies themselves, live in a hell from which very few can escape unscathed. Often the only way out, they think, is death. The real tragedy of these bullying stories, however, is the fact that for the increasing number of children who have a profound doubt about their own self-worth, this "hell" is the only place where they feel they truly belong.

56 Among Friends • Nishiyama Akira

Perhaps real adults, who also operate in a society where a sense of security is often provided by the power relations of controllers and subordinates, should take heed of the message these boys and girls are sending us. To become mature adults, it seems, we must learn how to face solitude.

Tile-capped Thatched Roof by Tanaka Ryōhei

The Role of the Japan-U.S. Relationship in Asia: The Case for Cultural Exchange

Kenichiro Hirano

S ince the cold war wound down in 1989 Japan and the surrounding region—East Asia or, more broadly, the Asia-Pacific
region—have been in a kind of holding pattern. The collapse of
the cold-war setup meant that the world had to seek a new order,
but such a paradigm has been slow to emerge. Although other
regions find themselves in similar circumstances, the task of
designing a new stable, peaceful post–cold war order in Asia and
the Pacific has been regarded as especially difficult, since the
events that put an end to the cold war did not occur in this
region—a region where, in fact, vestiges of the cold-war order
persist today.

In the circumstances, what kinds of new relationships Japan
will build with the United States and Asian neighbors is an
important concern not only for the people of Japan but also for
those of other Asia-Pacific countries. But due in part to the continuing disarray in domestic politics and an anemic press and
public debate, the Japanese have not addressed the issue in a
focused, lucid manner. The question of these new relationships
is one of security, broadly defined. The end of the cold war made
it possible for Japan and the Japanese to build new relationships
and design a new security system. But no national debate indicating an adequate grasp of this fact was seen. Vigorous debate

KENICHIRO HIRANO is a professor of international relations at the University of Tokyo.

JAPAN REVIEW OF INTERNATIONAL AFFAIRS   Fall 1994

over national security had occurred when the 1951 Japan-U.S. Security Treaty was revised in 1960, and again when the revised treaty was extended in 1970; but from 1989 onward Japan was becalmed, in a state of suspended judgment on security.

This stasis came to an abrupt end on April 17, 1996, when Japanese Prime Minister Ryutaro Hashimoto and U.S. President Bill Clinton announced the Japan-U.S. Joint Declaration on Security: Alliance for the Twenty-first Century. Clinton pronounced that the joint declaration put teeth in the Japan-U.S. "alliance," but the Japanese public was simply bewildered. Japan's security had been underwritten by America since 1952, when the security treaty took effect. The joint declaration did serve to redefine and reconfirm the bilateral security setup, as the Japanese government maintains. But was redefinition and reinforcement of the Japan-U.S. arrangements the only way in which Japan could address its security and the building of stable relations with the other countries of Asia and the Pacific in the post–cold war era? Having drifted along from 1989 to 1996, engaging in hardly any substantive debate at all, the Japanese were jolted out of their inertia by the sudden exercise of one particular option.

What kind of debate should have taken place during those years? Actually, there had been a nebulous sort of debate. In Japan, because of the need to update the 1976 National Defense Program Outline, an advisory body called the Advisory Group on Defense Issues was set up in February 1994. It issued its report (called the Higuchi report after the group's chair, Hirotaro Higuchi) in August that year. In the United States, the Department of Defense launched a review of the bilateral security arrangements in the latter half of 1994 and issued a policy document titled *United States Security Strategy for the East Asia–Pacific Region* in February 1995 (called the Nye report after one of its key architects, Joseph Nye). Factors behind these developments included suspicions over North Korea's nuclear ambitions, the spreading perception of a "Chinese threat," and heightened tension between China and Taiwan. In November 1995 Japan adopted a new National Defense Program Outline; the joint declaration followed five months later.

These circumstances are immediately relevant to Japan-U.S. security and the concept of a new Asia-Pacific order, but elucidating them is not my object here. Leaving aside the question of whether the choice represented by the joint declaration was a wise one, I would like to approach my main theme by examining what options its adoption in effect excluded. In doing so, I will bear in mind various concepts of a post–cold war Asia-Pacific order, including those touched on in the Higuchi report.

We can posit three pairs of apparently mutually exclusive options for the region. The first is whether to attempt to guarantee Asia-Pacific security and bring about a new regional order by means of a bilateral security framework or by means of a multilateral regional security framework. The second is whether Japan, in choosing its security framework and its major partners in a new regional order, will tilt toward the United States or Asia. And the third is whether to define security and a regional order in political and military terms or in more comprehensive terms, including economic and cultural aspects.[1] In the case of all three pairs, the joint declaration represents selection of the former option and, at least for the time being, rejection of the latter. Although a number of Asian initiatives for multilateral regional frameworks, an Asian orientation, and comprehensive security have emerged since the cold war, beginning with Malaysian Prime Minister Mahathir bin Mohamad's East Asian Economic Caucus (first advanced as the East Asian Economic Group in 1990), the Japanese government appears to have come down on the side of a bilateral security framework.

I have presented the above sets of options as dichotomous pairs, but this need not be the case. A political choice can be made to include both of the options in a pair. In regard to bilateral versus multilateral frameworks, for example, as the late Masataka Kosaka has observed, even in the post–cold war world

1. For a recent lucid study of the major features of the security debate in postwar Japan, see Akihiko Tanaka, "21 seiki ni mukete no anzen hosho" (A model for Japanese security in the twenty-first century), *Kokusai Mondai*, no. 436 (July 1996), pp. 2–15. According to Tanaka, one characteristic of this debate is that the concept of security has been perceived in comprehensive rather than narrowly military terms. This, he asserts, is an advantage when considering post–cold war global security. [A translation appears in this issue of *Japan Review of International Affairs*, p. 276-290—Ed.]

both unilateral and multilateral initiatives may be considered necessary, and in such cases should be undertaken simultaneously.[2]

What means are available to create a regional order for Asia and the Pacific that combines the latter options in the three pairs above so that this order complements rather than opposes one premised on the Japan-U.S. security setup? One means, I think, is establishment of a multilateral framework for cultural exchange in Asia and the Pacific, with Asian nations as the core members. Below I will examine, primarily from the standpoint of Japan and the Japanese, ways in which cultural exchange in the broadest sense can contribute to security and the formation of a new regional order. I will also consider the significance and potential of the kind of Asia-Pacific cultural exchange that includes Japan-U.S. cooperation, as opposed to cultural exchange that, in tilting too strongly toward Asia, excludes America.

International Exchange in a Changing Asia

In thinking about the kind of cultural exchange that can contribute to Asia-Pacific security and to a new regional order, naturally enough it is necessary first to understand Asia's present situation. Most East and Southeast Asian countries were enjoying dramatic economic growth before the end of the cold war, and the pace has not slowed since 1989. Almost all the region's countries have achieved economic takeoff, and their governments and people alike have become increasingly confident of continued growth.

In regard to the formation of regional frameworks, the Association of Southeast Asian Nations has become one of the world's major regional organizations, and the Asia-Pacific Economic Cooperation forum and the ASEAN Regional Forum, created with ASEAN as the nucleus, now encompass the entire region. Political as well as economic interdependence has deepened, and there are lively international flows of people, goods, money, and information. In addition to the traditional percep-

2. "21 seiki no kokusai seiji to anzen hosho no kihon mondai" (Diplomacy and security in the twenty-first century), *Gaiko Forum*, special issue (June 1996), pp. 4-23. [A translation appears in *Japan Echo*, vol. 23, no. 4 (Winter 1996), pp. 60-69.—Ed.]

tion of Asian diversity, a perception of Asian commonality is
growing.

Asia's recent fluidity—flows of people, goods, money, and information:
In Tokyo today, it is commonplace for the Japanese to rub shoulders with people from other Asian countries in trains, subways,
and other forms of public transport. The outsiders may not look
different from the Japanese, but as soon as they start talking with
one another it is obvious that they come from some other Asian
country. Nor is this a phenomenon restricted to big cities like
Tokyo; it is seen in provincial cities and even rural communities.

Figure 1 charts the trends in Japan's international exchanges
from 1968 to 1988 (admittedly the data are somewhat old, predat-

FIGURE 1
Trends in Japan's International Exchange, 1968–1988

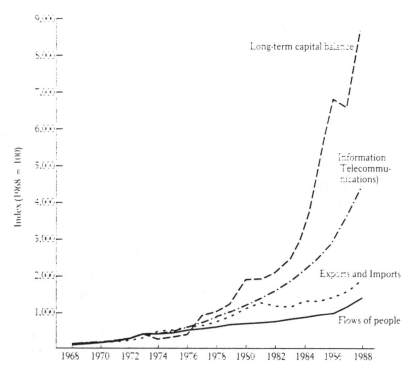

Source: Based on Ministry of Posts and Telecommunications. *Tsushin hakusho: Heisei 2 nen ban*
(White paper on telecommunications for 1990) (Tokyo: Ministry of Finance Printing Bureau, 1990),
p. 174.

FIGURE 2
Trends in Outflows of Japanese and Inflows of Foreigners, 1952–1988

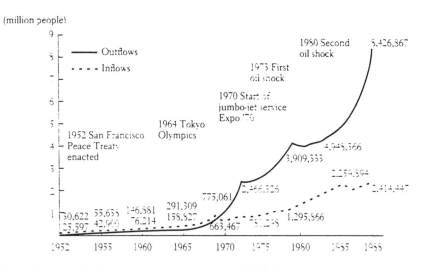

(million people)

Source: Based on Study Group on Immigration Statistics, *Wagakuni o meguru kokusai jinryu no hensen: Shutsunyukoku, zairyu tokei ni miru kokusaika no genjo* (Changes in international flows of people involving Japan: Internationalization as seen in immigration and residence statistics Tokyo: Ministry of Finance Printing Bureau, 1990), p. 6.

ing the end of the cold war, but upward trends are clear). Over these 20 years the annual flow of money, measured using the long-term capital balance, into and out of Japan rose form a base of 100 to nearly 9,000. Likewise, the annual flow of telecommunications messages jumped from 100 to 4,500. The annual flow of goods expressed by values of exports and imports increased almost 20-fold, and the annual total number of people going abroad from Japan and coming to Japan increased 14-fold. Figure 2 provides more details on flows of people. During this period outgoing Japanese increased about 20-fold and incoming foreigners about 5-fold. In the 1990s the number of Japanese traveling abroad annually has risen to over 17 million. Even though most are tourists, this is still indicative of what has been called the age of global migration.[3]

The greatest manifestation of this global migration is the international flow of Asian workers, a flow that includes several

3. See Stephen Castles and Mark J. Miller, *The Age of Migration: International Population Movements in the Modern World* (London: Macmillan, 1993).

currents. One is the migration of Southeast Asian and Indian workers to the Middle East. According to statistics, international labor migration from Asia took off in the 1976–78 period. The gulf crisis of 1990–91 put an end to this, but at its peak about 3.5 million Asians a year were going to the Middle East. Another current is the migration of Asians, including refugees, to North America. According to U.S. Department of Commerce statistics, in the 1970s and early 1980s Asians were the largest group of immigrants into the United States.[4] A third current is international flows within Asia. Especially noticeable have been the influx of people from Afghanistan, Bangladesh, Pakistan, the Philippines, South Korea, and Thailand into Japan and movements of people among ASEAN countries. The latter deserves special mention as a new development.[5] The table shows a small part of the labor migration among ASEAN countries, estimated to total 500,000 people[6]—a phenomenon symbolic of the region's increased fluidity in recent years. Japan has its own distinctive pattern of inflows. In the latter half of the 1980s large numbers of people entered Japan from Brazil, China, the Philippines, South Korea, Taiwan, and Thailand. The numbers from Bangladesh, Iran, Malaysia, and Pakistan also rose, but there was no dramatic increase in people from the United States.

The South Korean government removed the last restrictions on travel abroad in 1989 (the Japanese government had done this in 1964, the year of the Tokyo Olympics). In Southeast Asia people are used to border-hopping by airplane for shopping, and there is a long tradition of international flows of people, goods, money, and information through cross-border trade. Even so, the present scale of international flows is the result of rapid and massive change during the last 10 years. Asia's recent fluidity, seen in the swift rise of international mobility, is truly amazing. This is not the kind of fluidity that signifies international political insta-

4. See Kiriro Morita, ed., *Kokusai rodoryoku ido* (International labor migration) (Tokyo: University of Tokyo Press, 1987), appendix, pp. 8–9.

5. For an overview of international labor migration in Asia, see Yasuo Kuwahara, "Untied Knots: Migration and Development in Asia," in *International Labour Migration in East Asia*, Japan-ASEAN Forum 2 (Tokyo: United Nations University, 1993), pp. 47–69.

6. Manolo I. Abella, "Manpower Movements in the Asian Region," in *International Labour Migration in East Asia*, Japan-ASEAN Forum 2 (Tokyo: United Nations University, 1993), p. 14.

Migrant Labor in ASEAN   (1,000 people)

		Country of employment			
		Malaysia			
	Brunei	Peninsula	Sarawak	Sabah	Singapore
Country of origin					
All countries	40.0	26.7	11.3	50.1	— (150)
All ASEAN	— (32.5)	15.4 (240)	11.3 (10)	49.0 (395)	— (96)
Indonesia	— (3)	1.6 (200)	2.0 (10)	43.6 (145)	— (20)
Malaysia	— (12)	—	—	—	— (30)
Philippines	— (9)	7.5	1.3	5.4 (250)	— (30)
Singapore	— (0.5)	—	0.1	—	—
Thailand	— (8)	6.0 (40)	2.0	—	— (16)

Note: Figures in parentheses are estimates.

Source: Based on Manolo I. Abella. "Manpower Movements in the Asian Region." in *International Labour Migration in East Asia*, Japan-ASEAN Forum 2 (Tokyo: United Nations University, 1993). p. 13.

bility, however. Rather, I think it is an indication that historic changes are underway in Asian, especially Southeast Asian, societies, thanks to the relatively stable regional politics and good economic performance that prevailed even before the end of the cold war.

Asian diversity and commonality: With a few exceptions, the countries of Asia and the Pacific now sanction the movement of people, goods, money, and information within the region. This tolerance is the result of governments' economic-growth policies. Ten years ago government officials and intellectuals in all Southeast Asian countries voiced apprehension concerning and opposition to the prospect of "transnationalization" as a result of the influx of Western and Japanese companies and of multinationals.

Today no one expresses such sentiments. What happened is that, on the assumption that borders would remain stable, Southeast Asians themselves began crossing those borders with relative freedom.

How has this increased mobility changed Asians' perception of Asia? Governments and the public alike used to chant the mantra of "Asian diversity." ASEAN was formed and operated as a loose regional organization in order to respect the diversity of Southeast Asian countries, and this is seen as the secret of its success. Kishore Mahbubani, permanent secretary of Singapore's Ministry of Foreign Affairs, has stated categorically, "The Asia-Pacific region is used to diversity; Europe is not." International mobility has increased because of the stabilizing effect of regional organizations, chiefly ASEAN, and governments' de facto approval.

Has the concomitant growth of international contacts diminished the traditional emphasis on Asian diversity and encouraged a perception of Asian commonality? According to Yoichi Funabashi, for the first time in history "the region . . . is being Asianized."[8] And Akira Iriye has observed that "there is diversity [in Asia], but in the long historical perspective, Asia is beginning to show a cohesion never before seen."[9] Whether Asia as a whole is being Asianized, as Funabashi claims, is arguable, but I do agree with his assertion that "Asia's 'Asianization' is paradoxically the result of the globalization of its economy and media."[10]

Given the rise in international contacts in the Asia-Pacific region—over 90% of the people moving around in the region, as discussed earlier, belong to the region—might there be a growing sense of Asian commonality? Could this lead to the emergence of an Asian exclusionism, as feared by Samuel Huntington and other proponents of the "clash of civilizations" school of thought? I do not believe so. I will endeavor to show why, using Huntington's own reasoning. In "The Clash of Civilizations?" he

7. "The Pacific Way," *Foreign Affairs*, vol. 74, no. 1 (January/February 1995), p. 105.

8. "The Asianization of Asia," *Foreign Affairs*, vol. 72, no. 5 (November/December 1993), p. 77.

9. "Anpo o tou: Zoku 'saiteigi' o do miru ka, 4" (Looking at security: How to view the "redefinition" of security, series 2, part 4), *Asahi Shimbun*, June 21, 1996.

10. Funabashi, "The Asianization of Asia," p. 79.

states, "Villages, regions, ethnic groups, nationalities, religious groups, all have distinct cultures at different levels of cultural heterogeneity. The culture of a village in southern Italy may be different from that of a village in northern Italy, but both will share in a common Italian culture that distinguishes them from German villages. European communities, in turn, will share cultural features that distinguish them from Arab or Chinese communities."[11] Several lines later, he writes, "People have levels of identity: a resident of Rome may define himself . . . as a Roman, an Italian, a Catholic, a Christian, a European, a Westerner."[12] I take issue with almost all of Huntington's thesis, but I do agree with him on these two points. This is because in the first passage he notes the multilayered structure of culture, in the second multiple identities.

Understanding the perceptions of Asia and of themselves held by people engaged in international mobility in Asia and the Pacific in terms of these two concepts, we see that precisely because individuals move across borders, they become aware of their village culture, regional culture, ethnic culture, and national culture as discrete entities that exist simultaneously. And as individuals who belong partially and simultaneously to a number of cultural groupings, they perceive themselves as having multiple identities.

In the past, when international mobility was restricted and the few Asians who went abroad did so only as representatives of their countries, there was little or no consciousness of the multilayered structure of culture. An individual who traveled from country A to country B in the region noticed the differences between the two only on the level of national culture. This led perforce to the conclusion that Asia was marked by cultural diversity. Today, however, migrant workers, relying on the bonds of their ethnic group, can easily find a niche in an ethnic enclave when they reach their destination. It is easy for them to retain their ethnic ties while moving globally, and they also keep their

11. *Foreign Affairs*, vol. 72, no. 3 (summer 1993), pp. 23–24. For my critique of Huntington's thesis, see "Bunmei no shototsu ka bunka no masatsu ka? Hanchinton ronbun hihan" (The clash of civilizations or conflicts of cultures? A critique of Samuel Huntington's thesis), *Hikaku Bunmei*, vol. 10 (November 1994), pp. 21–37.

12. Huntington, "Clash of Civilizations?" p. 24.

sense of national identity because they have to carry state-issued passports. Because it is easier to move across national borders, it is also easier to retain ethnic and other identities. When international travel is frequent and the multilayered structure of culture and the multiplicity of identity become evident, individuals going from country A to country B in Asia become aware of commonalities of culture and identity on some levels while perceiving differences on other levels. This should lead to the conclusion that Asian culture possesses both diverse and shared elements.

In fact, Asians in this age of international mobility, while affirming the uniqueness of their own cultures, are discovering how much they share with one another in terms of the past; the present, including the advantages and disadvantages of economic development; an "Asian culture" that is part of individual Asian countries' cultures; and shared behavior and values, along with the sense of affinity this generates. Recently I attended an international symposium in Kuala Lumpur, "Dialogue Among Asian Cultures," sponsored by the Malaysian Strategic Research Centre. Coincidentally, the three papers presented by Malaysians pointed out the striking correspondences between the role played by Islamic, Indian, and Chinese culture in Malaysian culture and in the cultures of other Asian countries. The most interesting commonality now being discovered by Asians is that all their countries include numerous ethnic groups and that all are shrewdly promoting ethnic coexistence. The revival of ethnicity, and with it the discovery of the multilayered structure of each country's culture, is among the elements Asian countries share today.

As long as the awareness of Asian commonality focuses in this way on parts of culture, it is highly unlikely to lead to the creation of a monolithic "Asian civilization," no matter how much commonality is stressed. And although awareness of Asia-Pacific commonality on the regional level may grow in future—and I certainly hope that it does—such efforts will probably not be limited to that level. Between the two passages quoted above, Huntington writes, "Arabs, Chinese and Westerners . . . are not part of any broader cultural entity. They constitute civilizations,"[13] which in his view are the basic fault lines dividing peoples. Elsewhere he quotes Donald Horowitz as observing, "An Ibo may be . . . an Owerri Ibo or an Onitsha Ibo in what was the Eastern region of Nigeria. In Lagos, he is simply an Ibo. In London, he is a Nigerian. In New York, he is an African."[14] Are we to suppose that when in New York this African ceases being an Owerri Ibo or an Onitsha Ibo, an Ibo, and a Nigerian, and that he is now only an African belonging to the African civilization? On the contrary, he is all these things simultaneously. He achieves these multiple identities precisely because he has moved vertically from one level to another by having moved intranationally and transnationally. International mobility enables this African in New York to develop what may be called global identity as an individual living together with other peoples on this planet. Similarly, it is becoming both possible and necessary for people of Asia and the Pacific to go beyond their identity as Asians and develop a global identity. I believe that this kind of awareness is behind the Southeast Asian advocacy of "open regionalism."

Asian confidence and its pitfalls: Today Asians, especially political leaders, are becoming increasingly confident of economic development and of the regional integration epitomized by ASEAN. Talk of the "Asian way" and the "Pacific way" indicate that this confidence extends to the domain of culture. Although most Asian countries are regarded as still in the process of building modern nation-states, Asians appear to accept with equanimity the notion that the world has entered the post–nation-state period in the sense that, in the global context, nation-states and national cultures are now perceived in relative terms. This too is a sign of Asians' cultural confidence.

It is important, however, to be aware of the pitfalls accompanying overconfidence. Might preoccupation with economic growth lead to overlooking the danger of environmental destruction? Are Asian countries' cultures giving people what they really want? It is good to hope for changes and development as well as

13. Ibid.
14. Ibid., p. 26.

preservation of tradition, but is there appropriate debate on the
question of which aspects of culture to change and which to
leave intact? Overemphasis on Asian values and culture tends to
encourage exclusion of non-Asian values and cultures, which is
counterproductive for Asian cultural development itself. Aside
from anything else, it is contradictory for those who extol the
diversity and potential for change of Asian culture and contrast
it with Western culture to perceive the latter as monolithic.

Asia and Japan

Let us look now at Japanese attitudes toward the above-men-
tioned changes in Asia and toward Asian culture. There has been
little worry that the development of erstwhile newly industrializ-
ing economies might lead to their catching up with and overtak-
ing Japan; generally speaking, the Japanese have viewed Asian
development amicably, partly because of the widespread theory
that the Japanese economy has had a positive effect on the
region's economic development, and have watched their neighbors' growth benignly, reminded of Japan's own rapid-growth period. Whatever the case in the economic sphere, in the broader
cultural sphere there is undeniably something of an "Asia boom"
in Japan today. On a superficial level, a mounting interest in
Asian culture extending from movies and music to ethnic cuisine
has been observed. On a deeper level, it is possible to see a psychological tilt toward Asia accompanying a deepening skepticism
over modern Western values.[15]

The Asia boom: Young people are in the forefront of the rising
interest in Asian culture. Their interest in and knowledge of

15. See Takako Kishima, "Kindai no chokoku' saiko: Nihon shakai no kozoteki hen-
kakuki ni okeru han Seiyo, han Ajiashugi no taito to sono imi" (Rethinking the "conquest
of modernity": The emergence and meaning of anti-Westernism and pan-Asianism in
a time of structural change in Japanese society), in Ajia ni taisuru Nihon (Japan vis-à-vis
Asia), vol. 2 of 20 seiki Ajia no kokusai kankei (Twentieth-century Asia's international
relations), ed. Committee for Compilation of Papers Commemorating Professor
Shinkichi Eto's Seventieth Birthday (Tokyo: Hara Shobo, 1995), pp. 145–90. Kishima
maintains that arguments advocating "the conquest of modernity" and Asianism have
emerged in three periods of structural change in Japanese society: the 1930s and early
1940s, the late 1960s and early 1970s, and the period from the late 1980s onward.

other Asian countries' movies, music, fine arts, performing arts, and other aspects of culture are much stronger and richer than their elders can imagine. In recent years there has been a considerable and consistent increase in the proportion of university students studying Chinese and other Asian languages, a trend due less to calculation that such language skills will be an advantage in the job market than to a healthy curiosity about the unknown. Meanwhile, such factors as geographical proximity, the development of transportation and telecommunications, low air fares, and a sense of cultural affinity have made it easier for students to visit other Asian countries. The most popular destination for the millions of Japanese traveling overseas annually remains the United States, the figure rising from 1.85 million in 1986 to 3.68 in 1990. Following America are South Korea, Hong Kong, Taiwan, and Singapore, in that order (1990 statistics); in the same five-year period the number of people bound for those four destinations increased from 1.88 million to 3.85 million.[16]

The knowledge accumulated by Japanese company employees and their families stationed in other Asian countries has also trickled down to the general populace. For many years intellectuals, the media, and Asian-oriented activities have been introducing various aspects of Asia to the public as well, and these efforts are now paying off, generating an Asia boom symbolized by the proliferation of restaurants specializing in Asian cuisines.

Older Japanese harbor mixed feelings toward Asia rooted in the events preceding and during World War II. As a result, they have a keen interest in postwar Asia and have consistently taken the attitude that it is correct to emphasize Asia. This emphasis, however, unlike young people's interest, is bound up with complex emotions that sometimes hamper healthy exchange and

---

16. Ministry of Justice, Immigration Bureau, *Heisei 4 nen ban shutsunyukoku kanri: Kokusaika jidai e no arata na taio* (Immigration control, 1992 edition: New responses to an era of internationalization) (Tokyo: Ministry of Finance Printing Bureau, 1993), p. 175. According to a 1994 survey by the Association of International Education, Japan, a total of 2,578 people from Japan were studying in the six ASEAN countries (Brunei, Indonesia, Malaysia, the Philippines, Singapore, and Thailand), while a total of 4,956 people from ASEAN countries were studying in Japan. Cited in Sylvano D. Mahiwo, "Japan-ASEAN Relations: Agenda for Cultural Cooperation in the 21st Century," in *Regional Cooperation and Culture in Asia-Pacific*, ed. Khien Theeravit and Grant G. Stillman, Japan-ASEAN Forum 5 (Tokyo: United Nations University, 1995), p. 183.

mutual understanding. As is often pointed out, ever since the beginning of the Meiji era (1868–1912) modern Japan's foreign policy has basically oscillated between preoccupation with Asia and cooperation with the West. There is a risk, albeit small, that the general public's present emphasis on Asia is colored by this diplomatic legacy and thus may invite an either-or preoccupation with Asia that precludes cooperation with the West. This is the obverse of the risk of an exaggerated stance of cooperation with the West—which is to say America—whose corollary is exclusion of Asia. It is wise, I think, to be prepared for the possibility that a heightened impression that Japan is being jerked around by the West could trigger an exaggerated psychological tilt toward Asia in reaction.

Exchange with Asia: In my observation, Japanese exchange with the rest of Asia is extremely lively today.[17] In addition to the Asia boom, we are enjoying an "NGO boom," and the two overlap in some ways, since Asia is the focus of most Japanese nongovernmental organizations' international activities. The majority of Japanese active in international exchange concentrate on Asia. There are two reasons for this. One is the Japanese psychological preoccupation with the region, based both on the Japanese mentality and on remorse for the past—a trait especially highly developed in the type of person attracted to NGO international-exchange activities.

The second reason has to do with the fact that international flows of people involving Japan overwhelmingly center on Asia. Most of the foreign workers who come to Japan (and often remain illegally) are from other Asian countries, and the number of women from other Asian countries who are brought to Japan as brides to alleviate the shortage of Japanese women willing to marry into farming families has risen. The help of international-exchange activists is both desirable and necessary if Asian residents are to settle into the community. As Tadashi Yamamoto

17. For the past 10 years or so I have taken part in the Hakone Conference, a nation-wide network of Japanese public- and private-sector international-exchange activists. This has allowed me to observe the status of activities in Japan and the thinking of the people involved.

has written, "The weight of grass-roots programs has increased significantly, and the core of international exchange has come to include helping foreign residents in the community, aiding refugees from Asia, and conducting educational and other activities designed to promote in-depth understanding of and respect for other cultures and values, especially those of people from other parts of Asia to whom local Japanese residents are exposed on a day-to-day basis."[18]

Yamamoto has noted that one distinguishing feature of Japanese international-exchange activities resulting from these circumstances is "a notable shift of emphasis from the West to Asia."[19] That these conditions have wrought a change in the philosophy and methodology of Japanese international-exchange activities is also important. Today, Japanese international exchange is overwhelmingly "internal," which is why grass-roots activities have come to be regarded as its core. Local governments, too, have had to engage in "internal international exchange," while their interaction with local governments in other countries has become more active. All of Japan's 47 prefectural governments now have departments charged with international exchange. A new relationship of cooperation between the public and private sectors has also emerged.

The fact that the greatest demand for "internal international exchange" is emanating from Asia is strengthening interaction with other Asian countries. Governments and individuals alike have both expectations of and a sense of affinity with Japan, as seen in the Malaysian government's "Look East" policy, which advocates the Japanese model of development. There is no denying that responding to these expectations and this sense of affinity through international exchange makes the Japanese feel good. Without exception, Japanese involved in international exchange vis-à-vis other Asians either at home or abroad appear to develop a stronger sense of affinity and commonality with them. This also leads to a keener appreciation of the cultural differences of various Asian countries and ethnic groups.

18. "Grass-Roots Exchange in a New Era," *Japan Review of International Affairs*, vol. 10, no. 2 (spring 1996), p. 137.
19. Ibid.

Through international exchange with other Asians, today's Japanese are reaping the greatest benefit of international cultural exchange—an immediate awareness of the multilayered structure of culture and the multiplicity of identity. Moreover, first-hand contact with other Asians is making it possible to respond appropriately to the changes underway in Asia. Through recognition of cultural diversity and commonality and of cultural change, the philosophy of *kyosei*, or "living together"—cooperation grounded in the spirit of tolerance, which enables people to cooperate to achieve common objectives while maintaining respect for one another's cultural differences—is taking root in Japan. In fact, unless this philosophy does take root, the Japanese will be unable to resolve the dilemma of an either-or emphasis on cooperation with Asia or the West, and will be unable to establish a stable position in the Asia-Pacific community.

The Role of the Japan-U.S. Relationship in Asia

In view of the changes taking place in Asia, what role can Japan and the United States, and their peoples, play to ensure that international cultural exchange is utilized to promote the stability and growth of Asia and the Pacific? The region will not be able to achieve stability and growth unless the rest of Asia, Japan, and the United States enjoy a relationship in which all three parties cooperate on an equal basis rather than a relationship in which one party wedges itself between the other two. I will address this issue on the assumption that the changes in Asia and Japan's exchange with Asia are as I have described. The first step must be to examine some of the differences in the philosophy and methodology of international exchange that are thought to exist between Japan and the United States.

Differences in Japanese and American exchange with Asia: US-Japan Dialogue for International Exchange Organizations, a private-sector forum, has met once a year in Japan since 1994. Attending the first two meetings, I observed some interesting differences in Japanese and American approaches to private-sector international exchange. Local international-exchange NGOs in America are represented in Washington by the Alliance for International Educational and Cultural Exchange Organizations. In my understanding, this is a kind of pressure group whose activities include lobbying. Wanting to do something to shrink the gap in the numbers of exchange students traveling between Japan and the United States (more than 10 students go from Japan to America for every student traveling the other way), the Alliance sought a Japanese counterpart with which to discuss the problem. Since there was no equivalent organization in Japan, a group of like-minded people hastily put together a group to talk with the Alliance. Actually, it had never occurred to the Japanese to think about bilateral student exchange in such "pragmatic" terms as numerical balance. America is known as the most highly developed country in the area of private-sector international exchange, but my overall impression is that Japan has come from behind to take the lead, at least in this regard.

The Alliance and local groups are having a hard time because of federal and state cuts to international-exchange budgets. At the 1995 US-Japan Dialogue meeting an Alliance representative acknowledged that American NGOs needed to rethink the notion that international-exchange activities depend on public funding. Whereas international-exchange NGOs in the United States rely on the government, in Japan such activities have been moving steadily toward decentralization and private-sector initiatives. In societal structure, too, the two countries present a marked contrast. The United States has a structure of local communities, states, and the federal government. It seems to me that Americans' sense of being part of a multilayered culture extends no further than the national level. Japanese society has been perceived by both its own people and outsiders as having a homogeneous structure, but recent so-called internationalization has brought with it a growing awareness of being part of multiple layers of culture both inside and outside Japan.

The two countries also differ in their approach to people of other cultures. The only way the United States, a nation of immigrants, seems to know how to handle people from other cultures is to assimilate them, turning them into American citizens. Traditionally, Japan has been regarded as strongly assimilationist, but recently it has accepted people from diverse cultures (internal internationalization), and the Japanese are now trying to respect cultural differences rather than smooth them out.

Another contrast is seen in the extent to which Americans and Japanese are accustomed to acculturation, the process of adapting to different cultures. Historically, Japan is highly acculturated, a quality it shares with other Asian countries.[20] As a result, Asians have more sensitivity and equanimity in the face of the universalities and particularities of culture than do Americans. We can look to Asia with hope in regard to tolerance of cultural differences and the ability to respect them while cooperating for the sake of shared goals—in short, *kyosei*, the basic attitude that is the key to future coexistence.[21]

Japan-U.S. cooperation: Nevertheless, the United States undeniably has the world's richest historical experience of cultural contact, acculturation, multiculturalism, and private-sector international exchange. There is much that Asia, Japan included, can learn from America. For example, Asia prides itself on having consensus building as one of its cultural skills, but if tolerance and *kyosei* are to be emphasized still more in future, Asia could fall into the trap of ambiguity. There must be debate over acculturation, the selection of elements from other cultures, and the question of whether a particular cultural element is universal or particular. But Asians are not known for skill in debate. For the sake of the further development of culture in Asia and the Pacific, it might be desirable to let Americans take the lead in cultural debate.

Above all, there can be no denying that in the modern period

20. Fred Halliday of the London School of Economics, discussing the development of individual societies from the viewpoint of international relations, has written that "what may previously have been seen as discrete, isolated, national histories, now appear much more clearly as the result of international processes, of imitation, competition, defensive modernization and influence." *Rethinking International Relations* (London: Macmillan. 1994), p. 120. See also Mahbubani, "The Pacific Way," p. 107.

21. Although pessimism regarding the feasibility of multiculturalism is mounting in the United States, there is greater optimism in Asia, including Japan. See my "Multiculturalism and the New International Order" and other papers in the proceedings of the sixth Symposium on American Studies in the Asia-Pacific Region, *Multiculturalism in the United States and the Asia-Pacific Region* (Tokyo: International House of Japan, 1996).

America has been Asia's cultural model. Through this learning process Asian countries have built fairly close-knit networks of exchange with America, including personal exchange. These networks should be utilized to expand further the Asia-Pacific region's international and cultural exchange. Meanwhile, if we confine ourselves to recent times, we must grant the Japanese a slight advantage in expanding exchange networks with Asians while managing (albeit barely) to cope with the rapid changes sweeping through Asian society.

The first step toward equal cooperation among Asia, Japan, and the United States is for Japan and the United States to draw up a blueprint and present it to Asia for consideration. For example, a plan could be proposed for modifying the EAEC, which in its present form stresses exclusion of America, into a more open regional forum. An effective way of doing this, it seems to me, would be to develop it into an East Asian Cultural Community, or EACC. But it can hardly be said that the Japanese government and people have undertaken the policy debate and measures needed to promote such a change. And although the United States first expressed the wish for active involvement in the Asia-Pacific region with Clinton's proposal of a "new Pacific community" in a speech at Tokyo's Waseda University in July 1993, it has clung to the aspiration for economic and trade hegemony over APEC. Nevertheless, we can see some movement toward inclusiveness, if we look at the situation in terms of greater recognition of the multilayered structure of culture.

In Conclusion: Toward the Formation
of Cultural-Exchange Networks

A mix of large and small regional organizations fulfilling diverse functions is the most effective way of promoting regional stability. European integration was made possible by a history of varied regional organizations, as well as the existence of a sense of shared culture generated by a long tradition of international, including cultural, exchange. Flows of people across the East-West divide played, in the end, the decisive role.

International mobility in the Asia-Pacific region will probably

309

continue to increase. If there is one thing that Asia, Japan, and the United States should consciously and actively undertake at this historical juncture, it is the creation of regional networks of cultural exchange, networks that will promote understanding of both the diversity and the commonality of the region's cultures, large and small. Sylvano Mahiwo of the University of the Philippines has suggested that "universities, educational and cultural institutions, academic organizations, and other entities performing similar functions with regional standing . . . be invited and strengthened for the cultural cooperation and development network. The envisioned cultural cooperation institution or center will link various designated institutions and organizations in the region in equidistant coordination relationships."[22] I myself have proposed, as one new transnational network in the region, "an APUN (an Asia Pacific University Network) or UNINAP (a University Network in Asia Pacific). The APUN or UNINAP would not just be a program of sporadic student exchanges or faculty exchanges between two universities. It should be a more tightly knit multinational university consortium covering all the Asia Pacific countries."[23] International cultural-exchange networks of many other kinds—of theaters and troupes, of concert halls and musical ensembles, and of museums, to mention just a few— should also be created.

In this article I have discussed the potential of cultural exchange in Asia and the Pacific as one approach to a regional order characterized by multilateral regional organizations, an Asian orientation, and comprehensive security, as opposed to an order dominated by the Japan-U.S. security setup. My conclusion is that the creation of regional cultural-exchange networks that include the United States would open the way for the creation of a new framework for regional security. I am sure that my readers, too, will be aware that the main players in international relations in this debate have shifted from nations and governments to private-sector organizations and individuals.

22. "Japan-ASEAN Relations," p. 188.
23. "Japan's Cultural Exchange Approaches in Asia Pacific," in *Peace Building in the Asia Pacific Region: Perspectives from Japan and Australia*, ed. Peter King and Yoichi Kibata (St. Leonards, Australia: Allen & Unwin, 1996), pp. 95–96.

Acknowledgments

Beauchamp, Edward R. "Reforming Education in Postwar Japan: American Planning for a Democratic Japan, 1943–1946." *Journal of Curriculum and Supervision* 11 (1995): 67–86. Reprinted with the permission of the Association for Supervision and Curriculum Development.

Thakur, Yoko H. "History Textbook Reform in Allied Occupied Japan, 1945–1952." *History of Education Quarterly* 35 (1995): 261–78.

Caiger, John. "Ienaga Saburo and the First Postwar Japanese History Textbook." *Modern Asian Studies* 3 (1969): 1–16. Reprinted with the permission of Cambridge University Press.

Dore, R.P. "Textbook Censorship in Japan: The Ienaga Case." *Pacific Affairs* 43 (1970–71): 548–56. Reprinted with the permission of the University of British Columbia.

Yoshimasa Irie. "The History of the Textbook Controversy." *Japan Echo* 24 (1997): 34–38. Reprinted by permission of the publisher.

Gottlieb, Nanette. "Language and Politics: The Reversal of Postwar Script Reform Policy in Japan." *Journal of Asian Studies* 54 (1994): 1175–98. Reprinted with the permission of the Association for Asian Studies Inc.

Gerbert, Elaine. "Lessons from the *Kokugo* (National Language) Readers." *Comparative Education Review* 37 (1993): 152–80. Reprinted with the permission of the University of Chicago Press.

Beauchamp, Edward R. "Education." In *Democracy in Japan*, edited by Takeshi Ishida and Ellis S. Krauss (Pittsburgh: University of Pittsburgh Press, 1989): 225–51. Reprinted with the permission of the University of Pittsburgh Press.

Amano, Ikuo. "Postwar Japanese Education: A History of Reform and Counterreform." *Japan Review of International Affairs* 11 (1997): 70–84. Reprinted with the permission of the Japan Institute of International Affairs.

Lewis, Catherine C. "What Is a Successful School?" In *Educating Hearts and Minds: Reflections on Japanese Preschool and Elementary School Education* (New York: Cambridge University Press, 1995): 178–202, 226–27. Reprinted with the permission of Cambridge University Press.

Hayes, Louis D. "Higher Education in Japan." *Social Science Journal* 34 (1997): 297–310. Reprinted with the permission of JAI Press, Inc.

Pharr, Susan J. "Burakumin Protest: The Incident at Yōka High School." In *Losing Face: Status Politics in Japan* (Berkeley: University of California Press, 1990): 75–89. Reprinted with the permission of the University of California Press.

Rhodes, Larry, and Morimitsu Nakamura. "From School to Work in Japan." *Compare: A Journal of Comparative Education* 26 (1996): 261–68. Reprinted with the permission of Carfax Publishing Company, Inc.

Maher, John. "Linguistic Minorities and Education in Japan." *Educational Review* 49 (1997): 115–27. Reprinted with the permission of Carfax Publishing Company, Inc.

Shimahara, Nobuo K. "Teacher Education Reform in Japan: Ideological and Control Issues." In *Teacher Education in Industrial Nations: Issues in Changing Social Contexts,* edited by Nobuo K. Shimahara and Ivan Z. Holowinsky (New York: Garland Publishing, 1995): 155–93. Reprinted with the permission of Garland Publishing, Inc.

Blumenthal, Tuvia. "Japan's *Juken* Industry." *Asian Survey* 32 (1992): 448–60. Reprinted with the permission of the University of California Press.

Dickensheets, Tony. "The Role of the Education Mama." *Japan Quarterly* 43 (1996): 73–78. Reprinted with the permission of the Asahi Shinbun Publishing Company.

Akira, Nishiyama. "Among Friends: The Seductive Power of Bullying." *Japan Quarterly* 43 (1996): 51–57. Reprinted with the permission of the Asahi Shinbun Publishing Company.

Hirano, Kenichiro. "The Role of the Japan-U.S. Relationship in Asia: The Case for Cultural Exchange." *Japan Review of International Affairs* 10 (1996): 314–34. Reprinted with the permission of the Japan Institute of International Affairs.